THE ABUSE
OF POWER

THE ABUSE OF POWER

**A true story of sex and scandal
at the heart of London's elite**

ANTHONY DALY

MIRROR BOOKS

First published as *Playland* by Mirror Books in 2018

This edition published in 2019

Mirror Books is part of Reach plc
10 Lower Thames Street
London EC3R 6EN
England

www.mirrorbooks.co.uk

ISBN 978-1-912624-29-4

In memory of John (Jackie) Duddy and
Bishop Edward Daly, two souls fused together
for eternity in a moment of violence.

And for Damie

Feeling caged in: the author
photographed near his home in
Creggan Estate, Derry in February 1975,
before he left for London.

AUTHOR'S NOTE

In her memoir, *Old Bloomsbury*, Virginia Woolf lamented her failure to capture the conversations of the early Bloomsbury Group: "Talk, even talk of this interest and importance is as elusive as smoke. It flies up the chimney and is gone." What I wanted to do in this memoir was to recapture some of the conversational smoke from my past; in the encounters I had, the discussions I listened to and the events I witnessed in 1975.

The fact is, storytelling is storytelling and both fictional and non-fictional storytelling use the same sorts of narrative devices: scene, description, exposition, reflection and voice. All literature is shaped by the writers' imagination and consciousness. Although I have created and approximated dialogue that I can't recall word for word, I have tried to capture the emotional truth and the essence of my interactions with people as I remember them; to reveal the honest heart of the story. Writing dialogue served another purpose for me; I wanted to raise the dead, I wanted to hear their voices again.

Introduction

According to the Nobel Laureate Elie Wiesel, it's a mark of being human to want to forget. The Ancients saw it as a divine gift. Without forgetting, we would live in permanent paralysing fear of death. We are reminded of that fear at the extremes of human experience, particularly in the shadow of violence. This is why I'd worked to forget, to keep my memories locked away. After all, how can we continue in our daily lives carrying the burden of the past at every step?

I'd made sure that the person who went to London in 1975 no longer existed. Or so I thought.

Whether we're conscious of it or not, the past lives on in us, and sooner or later we're going to have to confront it. It's impossible to stop it catching up with us. It starts as a trickle seeping through the cracks and quickly becomes a torrent… It hit me with full force in July 2014.

It was a bright Sunday morning in Derry and white clouds scudded overhead. Light was dappled by the trees as I walked the dog to get my morning paper. For many years now stories had seemed to appear almost weekly in the papers about people in authority sexually abusing children.

The floodgates were opened in Ireland in the early 1990s when Father Brendan Smyth pleaded guilty to the sexual assault of more than 140 children over a 40-year period. The Taoiseach Albert Reynolds subsequently resigned when it appeared the authorities had been protecting a child abuser in the church. Cases began to emerge of sexual and physical abuse in parishes across Ireland. It was impossible to avoid the television and newspaper coverage: it felt as if a collective exorcism was being performed on generations who had suffered in silence. My own demons were already becoming restless when further revelations emerged in 2010 about a church cover-up.[1] I was prompted at that point to write a long letter to a retired bookseller in England, in the hope that I might get some answers about what had happened to me in the context of a much greater cover up, also from 1975. I did not receive an answer to my letter and let the matter sink again to the depths of my consciousness.

There was more to come, however, as the world of pop music and light entertainment had its own Father Brendan Smyth, whose name was Jimmy Savile. The revelations about this intelligent but profoundly maladjusted eccentric and serial abuser were followed by claims about other celebrities. The incredible courage of their survivors saw these abusers appear in the dock, at last. The situation became yet more unsettling for me. News reports started naming politicians, including some in their graves. But none of this had prepared me for the newspaper headline that confronted me as I entered the shop that summer morning.

The story on the front page of the Sunday Mirror named politicians who were allegedly involved in having sex with underage rent boys around the early to mid 1980s. My hands were shaking as I read the story. I could not know the truth of

---

1   Cardinal Sean Brady admitted that in 1975 he had witnessed two teenage boys sign oaths of silence after they gave evidence to a church inquiry that they had been sexually abused by Father Brendan Smyth.

those claims, but I did know that some of the politicians named in the story were having sex with underage boys and young men several years earlier, in the mid 1970s. I knew because I was one of those young men.

Later that afternoon I read the article again. My mind was in turmoil and I felt physically sick with worry. I was in a state of shock. Everything that I'd successfully buried for 40 years was in front of me, as if the abusive hands of the past had now reached into the present. I was having difficulty breathing. I went into the bathroom and splashed water on my face; the person staring back at me in the mirror was ashen.

I came back into the room and handed the paper to my wife. "Read that," I said.

She looked at me quizzically and glanced down at the article.

"Why did you want me to read this?" she said distastefully a few minutes later.

I couldn't answer because I was crying, silently and uncontrollably. She looked over and at first thought I was putting it on. Joking. Then she saw the grief and she came to me. I stood up and she took me in her arms.

"What's wrong, what is it?" I was still unable to speak.

I cried painfully for a long time. Finally, I told her I had been raped in London when I was 20 years old.

I pointed to the newspaper. "I was involved in that," was all I could manage. I could tell her no more for now. I had to drip feed some of the horror over the next few weeks. She said no matter what had happened she'd support me and would be there for me. She said the last time she'd seen me cry like that was when our baby girl had died.

Over the next few days I started to have flashbacks and began to feel emotions I'd not felt in years. Raw visceral fear. Intense shame. Burning anger. I had to tell someone: I could no longer keep this to myself. Strangely enough, the first person I could think of was a priest. I had enormous respect for Bishop Edward Daly and so did most of Derry. He'll be forever remembered in the iconic film footage of him waving a white handkerchief at advancing paratroopers, appealing for a truce as he tried to save the life of a mortally wounded friend of mine on Bloody Sunday. Bishop Daly was someone I felt I could confide in about my experiences in London in 1975, and I wanted his advice. So I met him and told my story while he listened patiently.

"Why didn't you come forward earlier about this?" he asked.

"Who'd have believed me?"

His silence was enough to let me know he agreed with me. After a pause, he told me he'd have to share what I'd told him with the police. "The days of priests not reporting cases of sexual abuse are over," he said.

I nodded. In the circumstances, I knew I was going to have to speak to the police but I was unsure of who to approach, given that my abuse had happened in London so many years before.

Bishop Daly said he knew a detective from Liverpool who was now employed by the Police Service of Northern Ireland (PSNI) to assist with the new investigation into the Bloody Sunday killings.

"He's a good man. I'll get him to phone you." The Bishop leaned forward and said almost in a whisper, "You have carried this burden long enough, Tony. You have to tell your story."

In the weeks ahead the flashbacks and panic attacks began to get worse and I went to my doctor and was prescribed medication for depression.

I spoke to the Bloody Sunday detective and arrangements were then made for me to fly to London to be interviewed by the Metropolitan Police. It felt strange being back in London again and I made my way to Holborn Police Station with a sense of dread. This was not going to be easy. And so it proved. For two days I was questioned about everything that had happened to me. I broke down and cried often throughout the interview, but I truly unburdened myself for the first time in 40 years. At the end of it I wept tears of exhaustion.

I subsequently underwent counselling. It was a painful process but slowly I began to confront my demons and come to terms with my past. Like having a dimmer switch in a dark room turned up ever so slowly, I began to see outlines, parts of things that had long lurked in the shadows. Eventually, with a terrible brightness, the past was revealed, uncovering the full horror of things I had not wanted to see. I spent many hours locked away in isolation, meditating on the past.

I wondered if I should have taken the advice of Valerius Maximus, a writer who urged Roman citizens to "leave ugly shadows alone where they lurk in the abyss of shame". However, I realised that not only was I the guardian of an important footnote to history, but also that forgetting some things, some people, was wrong. What had happened to Damie? To the other Dilly boys I had met? What became of the children? To those who didn't escape? I'd spent my whole adult life trying to forget people I'd shared awful experiences with, but forgetting about them was a kind of mental murder. I pledged to remember them properly, and to honour them: it wasn't enough to unburden myself to Bishop Daly and the police.

I looked at the books on the shelf and pulled out Night by Elie Wiesel. One passage in particular caught my eye – "For the survivor who chooses to testify, it is clear: his duty is to bear witness for the dead and the living. He has no right to deprive future generations of a past that belongs to our collective memory." I was only too aware that hundreds if not thousands of teenagers had had their lives ruined, their futures torn from them. A generation of youngsters had been treated as sordid playthings by the rich and powerful. Their stories had never been told. It was as if they didn't matter. I knew what I had to do. There was no time to waste. I had a duty to tell the story.

Prologue

On Monday 22 September 1975, six men were convicted at the Old Bailey of numerous sexual offences against boys. Charles Nicholas Hornby, 36, was fined £1,000 and jailed for 30 months; of the others, Basil Andrew-Cohen, 39, and Malcolm Raywood, 43, were both jailed for six years; Andrew Novac, 29, for six and a half years; and David Archer, 28, for five and a half years. There is no mention of any sentence being handed down to the sixth man. His name did not appear in newspaper reports at the time and has been redacted from documents held at the National Archives at Kew. The case became known as the Playland trial because the men had been involved in an organised rent boy racket run from the Playland amusement arcade just off Piccadilly Circus.

Charles Hornby, the man given the shortest sentence, was an Old Etonian and an underwriter at Lloyd's. Once an officer in the 9th Lancers, he owned a country estate in Gloucestershire and had been shooting with Prince Charles. Because of his position and background, the press predictably singled him out, and it was he who featured prominently in the headlines. The other defendants were described as "nobodies," but they were in fact part of the underworld gang that managed the rent boy operation, whereas Charles Hornby was a Playland client. As an Establishment figure, he served as sacrificial lamb, and his very public fall from grace deflected attention from reports that many other VIPs were also clients of an extremely sordid and exploitative business.

The police investigation that led to the trial was deeply flawed. Its surveillance operation was limited to the activities of men roaming around the Playland arcade, and the arcade owners were never questioned. Neither were any of the senior underworld figures that police would have known were linked to Playland. The investigation remained superficial because figures involved in the rent boy trade were part of a Soho crime syndicate that had been paying a fortune to corrupt police officers all the way up to the top. The trial judge accepted that many other people should have been in the dock.

The Playland trial was sandwiched between two much bigger trials being held at the same time, the Guildford Four and Birmingham Six bombing trials. It was an era of IRA atrocities and of public revulsion and hostility towards the Irish community in Britain. This provides an important context for my involvement in the Playland racket, which began when I accepted an offer of help from Charles Hornby and another man called Keith Hunter. I climbed into a taxi with them in Piccadilly Circus and plunged into a world of sexual abuse and exploitation. As a young, naive Irishman, I was easily trapped. My abusers offered a choice between a world of parties, expensive hotels and restaurants, or prison, with its obvious terrors. I could either do as they said, with their wealthy clients, or be taken to a police cell to have a terrorist confession kicked out of me.

I embarked on a journey into a very dark realm: a world of drink and drugs, of gangsters and rent boys, of businessmen, politicians, pimps and paedophiles. Because of what happened to me and the fact that I kept a diary at the time, I am in a unique position to tell the real story of Playland.

PART 1

A Sold Life

O thou, my lovely boy, who in thy power
Dost hold time's fickle glass, his sickle, hour…
Sonnet 126 William Shakespeare

In order to rise from its own ashes,
a Phoenix first must burn.
Octavia E. Butler

CHAPTER 1

Capture

I'm being watched.

In my peripheral vision I can see them. Young lads, teenagers, some wearing black eyeliner. One even wearing lipstick, one with painted fingernails. They're nodding in my direction to alert others. Someone is whistling to get my attention but I'm trying to avoid direct eye contact.

The arcade was full of them. It was like a vat of teenage hormonal soup in here. Lads venting their rage at the pinball machines, firing steel balls with the flippers and clocking up vast scores. I too poured more money into the slot and watched the tumblers spin, knowing their eyes were glued to my back. A group of them had stopped playing the machines to look over at me and were talking excitedly. I tried to make out what they were saying but it was lost in the cacophony of unrelenting laser blasts, beeps and metallic thumping.

The fruit machines had all but fleeced me, but I fed my last few coins into the slot, pulled the lever and watched the tumblers settle on another losing configuration.

"No luck," I heard a voice say over my shoulder.

I held my hands up and shrugged. "It's been that kind of day," I said, turning around to see a middle-aged man smiling at me.

For a fraction of a second a more serious look crossed his face and he stood there expectantly, as though waiting for me to say something. I was about to oblige, but suddenly felt self-conscious and a little vulnerable. Why was I attracting so much attention? I sensed danger. I nodded goodbye as I pushed past him and headed for the door. What was this place anyway? Had I stumbled on some teenage gang patch? I hurried outside, glancing up at the neon lettered Playland sign that glowed over the arcade entrance. The vertical spine of the letter Y extended below the rest of the name, with an arrow at the bottom pointing to the doorway like a devil's tail. A bitterly cold breeze brushed my cheeks and I pulled up my collar and buried my hands in my pockets.

Coventry Street links two of the busiest places in London, Leicester Square and Piccadilly Circus. I walked back to Piccadilly Circus and stood outside Boots the Chemist.[2] I looked across, transfixed by the neon displays. The enormity of the billboards was something else. Coca-Cola, Cinzano, Fuji Film, Skol Lager. I suddenly felt a long way from home. I ran between the traffic and crossed the road to take a closer look at Eros, who was gracefully poised and taking aim above the fountain. I hoped that before long, like him, I would be able to spread my wings in London.

I'd spent the last hour trying to forget the desperate spot I was in. Now a cold blast of reality brought everything home. I had no money in my pocket to pay rent and I wasn't going to get paid until the following Friday. On top of that I was really tired and desperately needed something to eat. Placing my hands wide apart on the railings, I leaned forward, taking the weight off my tired legs while I tried to think what to do. I could feel an almost imperceptible vibration running through the railings. It might have been caused by the endless traffic or the subterranean

---

2   In 1975 Boots the Chemist was located on the southern side of Piccadilly Circus, opposite from where it is today.

rumbling of the Tube trains deep below; but it was as though the city was convulsing and the tingles I felt in my fingertips made the hair stand on my arms and the back of my neck. I shivered and braced myself.

I'd been in London a week now and already my dreams of a better life across the water were unravelling. I'd felt on top of the world when I woke this morning. London in 1975 was everything Derry wasn't. Huge, confident and teeming with vibrancy. Buildings that dwarfed anything I'd seen before dominated the skyline, crowds of people bustled in every direction and music and fashions I'd only read about in magazines surrounded me wherever I went. Crazy floral-patterned shirts, high waisted trousers, the widest denim bell bottoms I'd ever seen, platform shoes. Early disco, glam rock and ethnic beats I'd never heard before. I'd been drinking it all in like a man lost in the desert. After years of feeling essentially imprisoned and living in fear in Derry, I felt like a free man. I felt like I could breathe again, as though I had control over my destiny for the first time in my life.

But with this newfound freedom came choices, and I was soon to discover that a few bad decisions would quickly put an end to my brief London honeymoon period.

I'd finished my first week in the rare and antiquarian book department of Foyles Bookshop in Charing Cross Road and, having been given the Saturday off, had gone for a walk down Oxford Street. A wide-eyed Irish innocent abroad, I marvelled at the scale of it all. Having walked the mile and a half down to Marble Arch I was coming back up on the other side of the street when, passing Oxford Circus again, I came across a group of about 15 people who were looking at something. The people at the back were straining to see what was going on. The main crowds flowed past, uninterested, but this little group were suspended there like flotsam trapped in the bend of a stream. I had to have a look.

I could see a man standing behind a little fold-up trestle table, placing a dice between three plastic cups on the surface. He covered the dice with the middle cup and then deftly shuffled the cups around in rapid but graceful sweeping movements. I inched closer, as some people became uninterested and moved on, until I was standing in front of the table. People who had placed down bets in front of the correct cup – fivers, tenners, even twenties – were being handed winnings of £20, £40, £60. I watched the rounds of bets over and over, men shouting and slapping down notes on the table with exaggerated gestures, before whooping as they lifted their winnings. Every time, I was able to correctly identify the cup that covered the dice. As I watched, the tension in me grew. In my pocket was a £20 note.[3] I'd worked a lying week and wouldn't get paid until the following Friday. That £20 was all I had to pay the coming week's rent and to live on. I stood there conflicted, knowing I could treble my money in an instant. All my natural fail-safe instincts were holding me back. I'd never gambled before and now here I was contemplating doing something completely reckless. Temptation suddenly got the better of me and I leaned forward to place my £20 note in front of a stationary cup. The cup was lifted away… and the dice wasn't there. I'd followed its every move under *that* cup as he weaved it around but it had simply vanished in front of my eyes. I was crushed. I stood there trying to work out what had happened, hating myself. I desperately pleaded with the man that I needed the money to pay my rent. One of the men by my side suddenly shouted "copper", and the dice magician, four of the men around me, the folding table and my £20 vanished into the crowd.[4] Then it started raining.

---

3   £20 is worth £154 in today's money.

4   In April 2016 police warned tourists of this same scam taking place on Westminster Bridge. This particular scam has been used to rip off newcomers to London since Victorian times.

In a daze I carried on walking up Oxford Street, trying to contain the sense of panic slowly consuming me. I found myself at the corner of Charing Cross Road again. I considered going into Foyles and asking a member of staff for help, advice or money, but I just couldn't bring myself to do it. I didn't really know anybody well enough to beg for a loan of £20. I'd walked three miles and was feeling tired and exasperated. I couldn't bear the thought of returning to my hostel and sitting alone in my room torturing myself for what I'd done. So I walked down Oxford Street again. I needed time to think, to calm myself and consider my options. Arriving at Oxford Circus the majestic curve and symmetrical edifice of Regent Street presented an appealing diversion. As the light faded and darkness fell the street guided me irresistibly into Piccadilly Circus.

Piccadilly Circus revealed itself in an overwhelming rush of people, traffic, fumes, noise and light. I struggled to drink in this heady cocktail of toxic urbanity. This was surely what Disraeli meant when he called London a modern Babylon.

Allowing myself to be carried along by the crowds of people, I thought about what I could do. Phone home. We had no telephone. Phone my aunt Doreen, she has a phone. How long would it take to send money to me? Two days? Christ. Tell a priest at the hostel? Offer to pay off the arrears in instalments? But I'd only been there a week and in arrears already. Would Foyles give me a loan? Unlikely. I ticked off more implausible options one by one. The thought of having to contact home and beg for money was humiliating. One week in London and I was crying for help. I could hear them all now. "We warned you not to go," they'd say self-righteously. "You're too young. Pack it in and come home. We'll pay for the flight at this end."

I carried on walking until Playland Amusements suddenly loomed into view. In my pockets was some change and the last pennies I possessed. Surely at some point I had to get lucky…

But luck was having nothing to do with me, and I'd lost all my coins in those machines. Now, standing in a pool of animated rainbow-coloured neon, I was cold, my pockets empty. I figured perhaps it was time to call it a day. I was resigned to going to sleep hungry and dejected.

Pushing off from the railings, I wondered if it was considered acceptable to thumb a lift in the centre of London. Suddenly a double-decker bus belched a cloud of blue smoke in my face. I coughed and instinctively turned away, and it was then that I saw him in sharp focus as the blue haze cleared. About 30, short and stocky, he was walking towards me with a sense of purpose. For a moment I thought I knew him, or that he knew me. It seemed as if he'd followed me out of Playland. He stopped directly in front of me. He looked across the piazza.

"Cold, isn't it?" he said, blowing into his hands.

"Yeah, it's getting very cold now," I replied.

He did a double take and looked into my face. "Well you're not a local lad anyway," he laughed. "Australia?"

Now I laughed. "No."

He laughed again. "Scotland?"

"No, I'm from Derry. It's in the North of Ireland."

"Northern Ireland! Shit! You're far from home; but then I can't blame you. It's insane over there, mate."

I smiled. Things were definitely crazy back home.

"So, what are you looking for?" he asked.

I offered a puzzled smile at the strange question and then stated the obvious.

"Food."

His brow furrowed and his expression asked a question. I quickly summarised my story; how I came to be standing in Piccadilly Circus without a penny to my name.

"You've been royally ripped off mate. That scam is one of the oldest in the book. Tourists and some people who've had a little too much to drink are easy prey." He made a gentle punching movement at my chin and smiled. "And the odd Irish lad falls for it as well."

We chatted for another couple of minutes by the railings, but he seemed keen to be moving on. He offered a hand and we exchanged names. His was Keith Hunter. He said he was going to meet a mate in a pub and that they'd be going for a meal. I was welcome to join them if I wanted. Instinctively, I held back.

"I don't know. I really don't have a penny to pay you."

He shrugged his shoulders. "Not a problem, mate, it'll be on us. Jesus, I'd hate to see you go hungry. My mother was Irish."

He laughed and barked out a smoker's cough. "Come on." He winked at me, pulled his coat tighter, then turned and started to walk away. "Take it or leave it, mate, up to you."

Most of the caution circuitry in my brain had already been blown that day and my hunger was now overriding any natural reticence to walking off with a total stranger and joining another for a meal. One half of my self-preservation instinct was telling me not to go, but the other half, the hungry half, was telling me the first law of self-preservation is to eat. The offer of food and friendship might not happen like this anywhere else, but this was London and it seemed the kind of magical place where random fortunate occurrences like this went on all the time.

I was now ravenous and decided to throw caution to the wind. You had to take risks.

"Hold on," I shouted and ran after the man disappearing into the crowd. I caught up with Keith and he laughed and threw an arm over my shoulder.

"Good lad!" he exclaimed, pulling me towards him, and then stuffed his hands into the pockets of his black overcoat and quickened his pace.

"I'm late," he said.

"Sorry," I replied as I willed my aching legs to keep up with him. I then headed up Shaftesbury Avenue with the Artful Dodger.

A short time later we entered a smoky pub called the Golden Lion in Dean Street. The place was jammed with people, probably on the first leg of their Saturday night revelries. I made my way behind Keith as he cleared a path to the middle of the floor. The hazy amber light that filtered through the smoke confirmed to me what I'd suspected about Keith's appearance. In Piccadilly Circus, his face seemed to have a semi-permanent frown, halfway between a laugh and a scowl, but I hadn't been sure if this was an effect of the flickering neon. It wasn't. He scanned the tables with the same steady frown until a flicker of recognition turned up the volume of the smile. He led me over to one of the tables in the corner, where two men were seated. The older of the men rose immediately and said goodbye to his companion.

"See you tomorrow then, Charlie," he said.

"Okay, chat soon," a smooth cultivated voice replied.

At that, I was introduced.

"Charlie, this is Anthony."

I reached over and shook the large, warm, firm hand.

"Charles," he corrected.

"Tony," I said. "Pleased to meet you." I was offered the warm seat beside Charles. Keith offered drinks but I insisted on a Coca-Cola. I was not really a drinker and was certainly not going to drink on an empty stomach. Charles held his hand over his glass so Keith went to the bar and returned with a pint of beer for himself and a Coke for me.

The Artful Dodger gave a brief account of my day's misfortune and the gentleman beside me gave the impression of listening courteously, but he was paying more attention to scanning the bar and glancing over to the door from time to time, as if expecting another companion to arrive. The men made a little small talk and I started to feel awkward, as if I were intruding and preventing them discussing more important matters.

Charles had the appearance of a dark-haired Clint Eastwood combined with the British sophistication of Edward Fox . The Eastwood element showed in the forehead, the high-fronted, combed-back hair, and in the eyes. The Fox aspect was notable in the cheeks and chin. The slightly prominent upper teeth and the full lower lip provided their own unique signature. Charles Hornby's accent oozed pure upper class. The words flowed clearly and precisely, and his voice carried an air of confident authority.

I figured Charles must come from a very distinguished family, as he had success written all over him. I glanced across at Keith and couldn't help thinking they made an unlikely pair. Charles, smooth, sophisticated, charming, and Keith rough and ready and heavily reliant on industrial language to get his views across. There was obviously a close if peculiar class-defying bond of friendship between them. Keith drew me into their conversation with an invitation to tell them a little about myself. They both nodded encouragingly as I told my recent history and they exchanged little smiles of acknowledgement and understanding as I recounted something I considered to be of particular interest.

When we finished our drinks, Charles slapped his hands on his thighs and said, "Shall we eat?"

I was thankful for a pause in the conversation and never as much in need of a meal in all my life. Charles stood up. At six foot four, he towered over everyone.

When I stood I felt light-headed. I assumed it was the sugar rush of the Coke in my empty stomach sending skyrockets of energy up to my brain. We put on our coats and left. In the circumstances, I was pleased I'd given a good account of myself and was happy they hadn't judged me harshly. On the contrary, they'd seemed friendly and genuinely interested in me.

A short walk later, back across Piccadilly Circus again. We were seated in Gardner's Steak House, a smart-looking restaurant off the Haymarket; menus in hand and a bottle of red wine in front of us. It was onion soup for starters and then sirloin steaks all round. Never had a steak been so succulent in all its medium rare pink exquisiteness nor so greatly appreciated.

After a few blissful bites, Charles said, "Listen, Anthony, don't worry about the meal, it's on me, ok?" He gave a little wink. "And we can arrange a few quid for you, a little loan or something."

"That'll be great, thank you so much. I'll pay you back as quickly as I can." I couldn't believe my luck.

As the meal progressed there was much good-humoured banter interlaced with friendly but probing questions. I was subjected to a civil and refined interrogation. I found the reassuring warmth in Charles's voice disarming. He enquired about my background, where I worked, where I was staying in London, my interests, the situation in Northern Ireland; everything. I'd not actually had a proper conversation with anyone for seven days and felt pleased just to be able to chat like this. By the time the second bottle had arrived I was in full flow, enthusing about books and bookselling, history, cinema, music and my analysis of the Troubles back home.

By the time we'd finished desserts, I'd finally been able to extract some information about my benevolent dinner guests. Charles was married with three young children, two boys and a girl. He told me he had the most boring job imaginable in the insurance industry; owned a flat in London where he lived during the working week, but that his main family home was in Gloucestershire. On weekends he enjoyed playing the country squire and loved hunting. He chatted a little about his children with all the pride of a loving father. His wife was a full-time housewife, who used to spend quite a lot of time in London, but now preferred the tranquillity of country life.

Although Keith was the one who actually did most of the talking, he actually revealed very little. The only things I learned were that he was in an on/off "relationship", was self-employed and had a number of business interests including procurement and property management. He also revealed that he did some work for the government and was involved in security work. Coming from Northern Ireland I stopped in mid-bite and looked quizzically at him.

"Security?" In Northern Ireland the terms *security situation* and *the Government* had ambiguous overtones, which offered a licence to introduce drastic measures to deal with *the Troubles*. He smiled, sensing my unease.

"I provide security men for warehouses – that kind of security; and I do some procurement work for civil servants."

We passed a couple of pleasant hours and I felt completely at ease. I had food and wine in my belly and was in the company of two successful businessmen who were treating me as an equal. Perhaps luck hadn't given up on me after all. When it was clear the time had come for us to part company, I diplomatically waited, hands expectantly in pockets, ready to reach out at the appropriate signal to take the money that had been promised. I wanted to know what the arrangements would be for paying the money back.

Charles turned to me after paying the bill. He looked concerned. "I'm really sorry but that took up most of the cash I had. I wasn't expecting three for dinner, sorry. I've just enough money for a taxi home. I actually thought I had more money in my wallet."

Keith then reached in his pockets and retrieved a few coins.

Charles's expression changed from concern to embarrassment. "Oh goodness. This is awful. Look, we're going to my flat for a nightcap. I have cash there. Why don't you join us for a drink, Anthony?" Charles towered over me and looked down. "One for the road, and I'll pay for a taxi home for you." He placed a reassuring hand on my shoulder. "*Really* sorry about this, old boy. We can't abandon you now." He laughed and looked at Keith.

Keith nodded towards the door. "Come on, mate, I feel like shit about this. Let's have one for the road at his place and you'll get sorted out. Look, why don't we meet up again next week again for a drink. I'd love to know how you're getting on in your new job, but we need to be hitting the road now."

I felt totally deflated. I just wanted to get home, but I didn't have a penny. Now that nagging doubt and turmoil was rising in me again. I really needed that loan so there was no choice. I'd have to go. How could I possibly insult them and throw Charles's offer of money back in his face? I'd been throwing caution to the wind all day, why stop now.

"All right," I said, with a forced broad smile on my face. "One for the road it is then."

We walked back to Piccadilly Circus, reasoning there would be better chance of getting a taxi more quickly around there. The wine I'd drunk and the fact it was now very dark heightened the impact of the Dilly. It looked as if someone had cranked up the brightness control of the neon displays. For a second the surreal craziness of the whole day hit me. Losing my money at that stupid dice game, finding myself in Piccadilly Circus for the first time, Playland with its youthful clientele, the random encounter and offer of help from Keith, the pub and the sophisticated businessman, the wonderful meal and now this taxi journey to what?

One dominant colour saturated the Dilly, shining down from on high and reflected back up off the wet ground. It was the blood-soaked red of the Coca-Cola sign. The colour of danger. Strange, but for a second the combination of traffic fumes, the smell of ozone from the underground and the odour of something burning on a food stand made me think of the gasworks in the Bogside or a faint whiff of CS gas. The smell of fear. A shiver rippled through me. I never knew fear could feel so exhilarating.

I followed Keith into the taxi, feeling nervous but also excited. There was an otherworldliness to it all. It was like climbing into a black coach floating on a sea of colour. Was I drunk?

Charles closed the door. "Ennismore Gardens," he instructed.

We moved off and the neon light faded away like the sunset of an alien planet. I was sitting between Charles and Keith, who rested his arm across the back of the seat and over my shoulder. As we sped across London, I tucked in my elbows and rested my hands, prayer-like, on my legs. In spite of all my reservations and doubts, I had willingly got into the taxi with Charles and Keith. Deep down, and if I was being completely truthful with myself, I did actually want to spend more time with them. I was completely alone in London and this was a perfect opportunity to make new friends. Influential friends who, I reckoned selfishly and naively, might be able to help me out – like now – if I ever needed it. I rested my head back against the seat and allowed myself to relax. Keith moved his arm down from the seat so that it was resting on the top of my head, his hand brushing my shoulder. I was driven to Knightsbridge, like an unsuspecting lamb to the slaughter.

CHAPTER 2

Derry

As the sun broke through a patch of low grey clouds and reflected off the puddles, Martin kicked an empty can high into the air down Broadway on the Creggan Estate, Derry.

"Charlie Cooke's charging through the Leeds players," he shouted breathlessly, chasing manically after the can. "He looks up, swings the ball into the box and Osgood's there with a diving header. He scores!" He flung himself forward and landed awkwardly on someone's front lawn, skidding on his chest and hands, as we collapsed in fits of laughter.

It was May 1971. Martin was still wallowing in the glory of Chelsea's FA Cup Final victory against Leeds the previous year and I was heading back to school with three friends after bunking off for lunch break.

"Are you going to ask her out or not?" Kevin turned to me, a teasing smile spreading across his face. "Because if you don't, I will."

I grinned and dodged his playful dig in the ribs, but before I could respond I caught sight of a British army foot patrol suddenly turning a corner ahead of us.

"Oh shit," said Eugene, as we stared straight ahead, feeling a now familiar sense of dread.

We'd barely had time to acknowledge the usual flak jackets and guns heading down Broadway, when suddenly the soldiers came under attack from a gang of older youths running from some backyards. Stones and bottles rained down and we suddenly found ourselves in the line of fire, directly between the soldiers and rioters. It all happened so fast. And we froze in panic.

A Land Rover appeared out of nowhere and screeched to a halt, just beyond the reach of the stones. A volley of CS gas was fired, four or five canisters, which fell short of their target and bounced and hissed around me and my friends.

We were completely enveloped in a thick cloud of white burning gas. I couldn't see beyond the smoke. I didn't even know what direction I was facing. Falling to my hands and knees, it was as though I were inhaling fire. My eyes, nose and throat were burning, nasal secretions and saliva, streaming down my chin. I finally crawled away from the toxic vapours and lay down on the grass verge, choking and rubbing my eyes. Even the skin of my face felt painful. Martin, Eugene and Kevin staggered and fell beside me, breathless and speechless. When I was able to focus through the tears I could see that the Land Rover, the foot patrol and the ambushers had vanished as quickly as they'd appeared.

We stood up and brushed down our school uniforms and made our way back for afternoon classes in St Joseph's. At the school gates Ted Armstrong was blowing his whistle to rally the stragglers back from lunch break. He threw us a questioning glance, but we said nothing and walked past him, heads bowed, our damp bloodshot eyes fixed on the ground. We didn't want to be given detention for being involved in a riot. We were fifth years after all. The teachers never stopped telling us we were supposed to be role models to the other pupils.

This was the Derry I grew up in. A riot could break out anywhere, like an unexpected tornado touching down without warning and flattening all before it. As a 16-year-old, I was already developing a weary sense of resignation about such incidents.

Sitting in the classroom that day, dabbing my sore eyes with a wet tissue and feeling my heart pounding like a kettledrum, I had the same reaction to violence I've always had. I've never ever got used to it. Even when it became a regular part of my life. As a child, the fear of violence was always there. I was living in a city where even death, however shocking, was becoming routine. Beyond the school gates, society was falling apart.

My mum was only too aware of the violent conflict raging on the streets outside and she'd made me promise never to get involved. I kept that promise religiously. When others I knew would head off for a bit of recreational rioting after school, I'd head home alone. I've never thrown a stone at a soldier, a policeman or anyone else in my life.

We lived in Creggan, a large housing estate on the outskirts of Derry. Up on a hill, we were the first to get snow in winter and the last to see ice melt away from the roadside. During the snowfall of 1963 we couldn't get out of the house for three days. Many a morning I'd scrape happily away at the frost on our bedroom windows to see out. Despite the harsh winters, there was genuine warmth in the house, thanks to my mother, Eileen, who raised six children on a pittance. She was the gentlest of souls, a kind-hearted woman with a quiet disposition, who put her faith and trust in God. But if my mother came to embody love, light and security, my father represented coldness, darkness and danger. In size, temperament, religious belief and in every other conceivable way, they were a totally mismatched couple. The only thing they had in common was their raven black hair. As I got older the delicate balance between them seemed to shift, and my father's anger began to dominate the house.

With each passing year the problems I was having with my father got bigger. His personality had now manifested itself in all its selfish, violent, misplaced anger. His reactions to the slightest childhood misdemeanours were out of all proportion to the perceived offences. On one occasion he went into a drunken rage and pounded his fists into a door, actually splintering the wood with each blow, before slamming the front door shut and vanishing into the night. I lay awake in bed for a long time, wondering if when he came back he would really hurt us. If, as it seemed, he hated us so much, would he come back and set the house on fire to get rid of all of us? He'd accidently set the house on fire before.

I had slowly moved from merely disliking my father to positively hating him. When his temper exploded in an uncontrollable stream of oaths, he terrified me, regardless of whether his abuse was directed at me, my siblings or my mother. As a child, I wasn't able to comprehend my father's nature. I did not have a frame of reference for understanding the fact that he was a violent alcoholic. He was also as strong as a bull with the stamina of a heavyweight boxer. He could fish and he could hunt. He was a marksman with a rifle. In the circles he moved in, the docks and the bars, he had a reputation. Men feared him.

I have a very clear memory of him on the one and only occasion when he was both drunk and in good form. He sat me on his knee and rubbed his cheek against mine. The stubble was rough and unpleasant. The smell of alcohol was overpowering. I'd never been this physically close to him before and couldn't bring myself to look into his eyes. He told me about how strong and brave he was and that he could feel no pain. To prove this point, he reached for a broad knitting needle, held it to his cheek and in a twisting motion drove it through the cheek, into his mouth and out through the other side of his face. He opened his mouth to give me a close-up of the impressive feat, then retracted the needle: to my amazement the holes did not bleed. This was the closest thing to affection I ever received from my father.

So, I'd learned to live with the fear of violence at home from a young age. Like an odour that clings to your skin and clothing, it's hard to ever shake off. If I close my eyes now I can still touch the large stinging red welts forming on my thighs after my dad had taken a belt to me and my brothers. I yearned to free my mother from him, too. Sometimes when I'd hear him shouting downstairs, I'd lie on the bed, clamp my hands over my ears and sing *Downtown* aloud. As a troubled nine-year-old I loved that Petula Clark song. It transported me away from Derry and far away into the heart of a bright, noisy, vibrant city.

Thoughts of how I could go about killing my father began to occupy my thinking more and more. I couldn't do it, of course, but my wishes almost came true one day when the Provos commandeered his car, put a bomb in the boot and abandoned it across the bottom of Fahan Street, while my father was in the pub. The bomb disposal unit carried out a controlled explosion. However, my father had just collected a barrel of tripe to feed his greyhounds with, so when the army blew up the car, fleshy debris was scattered over a wide area. Times being what they were, the army reasonably concluded this was the eviscerated remains of a human body that had been placed in the boot.

They soon found out who'd been driving the car, and the police contacted the local priest to inform my mother of my father's untimely demise. By a strange coincidence, my dad, assuming his car had simply been stolen, had asked a friend to give him a lift home. Both Father Carolan and my dad landed on our doorstep at the same time. When I learned of his apparent death and untimely resurrection, I rolled my eyes and cursed my luck. But despite the oppressive living conditions and constant threat of death and violence, we learned to make the most of things.

Not all encounters with the army were bad. One evening I was walking home with a couple of guys that I didn't know particularly well. They were more like friends of my friends. I should explain that in Derry parents will, if the surname permits, name a child after someone famous. For example, the Kennedy family who lived not far from where I lived in Circular Road, named their children John Fitzgerald, Robert and Jacqueline. On the night in question, I was stopped by an army foot patrol. I was with Michael Rooney, a brother of Hugh, who was a very good friend of mine, and another boy whose surname was Tracy. The soldier asked for our names.

"Mickey Rooney," was the first response.

He turned to the second boy. "And you?" he enquired.

"I'm Spencer Tracy," came the reply.

The soldier put away his little notebook and looked at me. "Don't tell me," he said, "you must be Humphrey fucking Bogart." He laughed and told us to get on our way.

If humour offered a release from the unrelenting oppression we faced, another big escape presented itself through books and music. My literary tastes had become very eclectic: I was dipping into Shakespeare and Blake and many other authors, but I was really devouring the works of Arthur Conan Doyle and the doorstep thick novels of Irving Wallace. While my two older brothers and all my mates were listening to rock and pop, I was listening to Rossini and Mendelssohn. I was buying a series of LPs called *The World of Your Hundred Best Tunes*, which, true to the title, opened up the world of classical music for me. My only concession to pop/rock was the Moody Blues, whose music I was drawn to because of their powerful melodies, choral elements and lush orchestrations: it was a kind of symphonic rock, often with a sense of yearning. But I'd also discovered a much bigger feast to gorge on in the music of Ennio Morricone. Ever since I'd seen *The Good, the Bad and the Ugly* I was entranced by the unique soundscapes of his music. I'd lose myself completely in his scores

– at times quirky and at times haunting – and for a few fleeting moments it felt like Derry with all its troubles no longer existed.

It helped that a classmate, Jackie Duddy, shared the same love of Morricone. Whilst Jackie would not have been in my close circle of friends, when we did chat it was always about the Maestro. We unexpectedly encountered Morricone again one day in the assembly hall at school, as the class were treated to a screening of *Once Upon a Time in the West*. By the end of the film Jackie and I were the only two left in the hall long after everyone else had left. Jackie was, at least on the surface, a tough, streetwise kid. But as we began to talk about the film we'd just seen and how the music had affected us, I realised that Jackie, who was the Long Tower boxing champion of the year, had a sensitive side as well. I had never imagined I could open up to a kindred soul and talk about being moved to tears by music. I began building up a collection of film soundtracks: John Barry, Jerry Goldsmith, Elmer Bernstein and, of course, Morricone. And I started lending Jackie a few of my treasured spaghetti western LPs. We'd snatch a few moments in school talking about different composers and new film scores we'd each come across.

At the same time as my inner world was expanding rapidly, the world outside was being reduced to a permanent monochrome brutality. While I was getting lost in a world of music and books, confrontations between the army and the people of Derry had risen to a new level. Petrol was being bottled again. By now the rioting around the edges of the Bogside and the city centre was a daily occurrence. Incendiary devices were being placed in city centre stores, causing a lot of damage.

Then the killing started. Lance Corporal William Jolliffe of the Military Police was killed when the Land Rover he was travelling in was attacked with a barrage of petrol bombs, causing it to crash. Two unarmed men, Seamus Cusack from Creggan and Desmond Beattie from Rosemount, were shot dead by soldiers during a riot. A nine-year-old boy, Damian Harkin, was crushed to death when a speeding army lorry skidded, mounted the pavement and crushed him against a wall. The army fled from the scene, leaving the boy and the horrified onlookers. A 22-year-old, Bombardier Paul Challenor of the Royal Horse Artillery, married with a one-month-old child, was shot dead by a sniper whilst on duty in an observation post. One bloody tragedy followed another, creating an index of death that reaped hatred and a thirst for revenge. Seventeen people would be killed in Derry that year: soldiers, IRA Volunteers and civilians.

It suddenly seemed as if nowhere was safe. In November 1971, the Provos started a concerted bombing campaign against business and economic targets that saw the city centre suffer considerable destruction. In the run-up to Christmas, graffiti appeared urging shoppers to "buy now while shops last".

At that time, I was just taking up my first job in the APCK Bookshop. The Association for the Promotion of Christian Knowledge was Derry's only bookshop, located near the top of Shipquay Street, which swept down through the ancient city gate and into the Guildhall Square. Religious books formed only a small part of the shop's offering. It also included quite a good section on Irish literature and history. I got to meet visiting authors, including Seamus Heaney and Brian Friel. As well as serving on the shop floor, it was my job to unpack and shelve the new books that arrived up in the first-floor storeroom. This gave me the opportunity to spend hours reading. I managed to get through dozens of Pelican books with their famous blue spines (the non-fiction imprint of Penguin). I read history, art, psychology, politics and science. I was in my own university, following my own curriculum.

One evening shortly after closing time, the assistant manager and I were doing a sweep of the shop to look for any suspicious objects. As I was walking past the Irish section, a fireball exploded from a shelf at eye level. I jumped back, hair and eyebrows singed, as some chemical concoction sizzled and spat at me. Flames began to climb the shelves, incinerating books, and soon spread across the ceiling. We grabbed a couple of fire extinguishers and fought back. When the fire brigade arrived the battle was already over.

Until that night I'd never imagined the Republican movement would target a bookshop or a library. There was something in Irish blood that went all the way back to the Book of Kells: the written word was special. Love of learning and literature was encoded into our DNA. Nonetheless, I went home stinking of smoke, burnt hair and burnt paper.

Soon after I witnessed another incident that deeply disturbed me, when I happened to come across a group of men and women tying a girl to a lamppost. She looked about 18. Her hands were already tied behind her back and they were binding her with rope around her chest, waist and thighs. Her bowed head had been roughly shaven, and tufts of hair stood out between patches of bristle. I watched in disbelief as they poured lukewarm tar over her head and then tipped a bag of feathers over her. I felt her shame, humiliation and helplessness. I thought about the scene in her home when they had come for her. The anguish and despair of her family. The talk among the crowd was that girls in the Bogside and Creggan were socialising with soldiers and carelessly giving information about men on the army's wanted list. They were now being targeted and taught a lesson. But this girl wasn't an informer; she was a fiancée. She'd fallen in love with a young British soldier. I walked away, sickened.

This was a world I didn't want to live in, so I shut it out and focused on my work. The bookshop became not only my place of employment, it became my sanctuary. In the evenings at home,

I was able to escape into different novels, different worlds. Far away from guns, bombs, petrol and tar.

New Year's Eve was quiet. Only two explosions and the usual widespread rioting. Things couldn't get much worse, I thought. How wrong I was.

CHAPTER 3

Death

In January 1972 my brother Fred asked if I wanted to attend an anti-internment rally. It had been billed as the biggest yet, to proclaim to the world the injustice of internment without trial. A real carnival of a parade. It was a nice bright Sunday, but I couldn't really be bothered.

"Who's speaking at it?" I asked.

"Fenner Brockway."

"Who's he?"

"He's a member of the House of Lords."

I shook my head emphatically. "I'm not walking all over the city to listen to some boring old fart from Parliament."

Fred tried again. "The Rev Terence McGaughey will also be speaking. Imagine: a Presbyterian Minister addressing thousands of Catholics."

"I'm definitely not going now," I said.

"Bernadette Devlin will be there too, she's speaking as well."

"Bernadette?" I asked, suddenly becoming interested. Now she would be worth seeing. Bernadette was an MP whose fight for civil rights had seen her spend time in prison. I'd been captivated by Bernadette since the three-day-long Battle of the Bogside in 1969. Her heroic fight for justice and freedom was fast becoming mythical.

"Hold on, I'll get my coat. I'm coming."

We made our way to the Bishop's Field, where thousands had gathered in the bright January sunshine. Perfect blue sky, crisp air, smiling faces everywhere. Attempts were made to get the masses into some kind of order so that the march for liberty could get underway. A large banner bearing the legend CIVIL RIGHTS ASSOCIATION was hoisted on top of a flatbed lorry.

I turned to Fred, "Jesus, we're going to be here all bloody day."

Finally, we set off, down Southway, through the Brandywell and Bogside. Then the march turned up Westland Street, heading in the direction of Creggan again.

"What the hell are they doing?" I complained. "Why not walk straight through the Bog to the bottom of William Street? Could they have taken a longer bloody route?"

"They want to walk down the length of William Street and through to the Guildhall."

"My legs are tired."

When we reached Aggro Corner (the junction of William Street and Rossville Street), the march was directed over Rossville Street towards the Free Derry corner.

"What happened to the Guildhall?" I turned to Fred, but Fred had vanished. I looked everywhere, weaving in and out of the crowd. No Fred. This was impossible. I was never going to find him. I stood up on a low wall and looked out over the multitude. A familiar face caught my eye. It was Jackie Duddy. He was smiling and waving at me. He beckoned me over, but rather than fight my way through the crowd, I shrugged my shoulders and pointed towards the Free Derry wall. He gave me a thumbs-up sign before disappearing among the ocean of bobbing heads.

When we reached the wall, the stewards fanned out and made room for the lorry to position itself alongside the Free Derry wall, as a speaker's platform. A few youngsters started to sing and clap. And then she appeared. Bernadette! Finally, I got to see her. A living symbol of the struggle for civil rights. Loudspeaker in hand, she looked exactly as I had seen her on TV and in newspapers, dressed casually in her trademark jeans and sweater. Her first few words were garbled and distorted by the loudspeaker. People were cheering, jeering and shouting. The noise gradually subsided and I listened intently, all thoughts of where Fred might be long gone.

And then I heard the sound of a gun being fired...

There is a very loud crack. Not the kind of gunshot you might hear in a movie. This is short and sharp, and immediately triggers the survival instinct. Everyone doubles over. Bernadette tries to keep everybody calm to prevent a stampede.

"Stand your ground," she shouts defiantly. "We outnumber them 15 to one. They can't put us all in jail."

Then there is a rapid burst of gunfire. The crowd surges forward and scatters in complete panic. Women and children scream in terror and the faces of the men turn ashen in disbelief.

The Bogside is a natural amphitheatre submerged below the city walls and enclosed by high- and low-rise flats. The place is a theatre of acoustic illusions. It's impossible to tell where the gunfire is coming from.

I'm pushed forward and no longer in control of my own direction. People are pushing from behind. A woman falls in front of me and her hysterical daughter tries desperately to pull her to her feet. I stop for a second to try and help but I'm being pushed to the ground myself. I have to keep moving to stay upright and to survive. I manage to break from the mob and run towards the Brandywell. I don't stop running until I am home.

A moment earlier and a few hundred yards behind me, in the car park of the Rossville Flats, Jackie Duddy is running from an armoured personnel carrier. The vehicle pulls to a stop. "Private R" jumps out. Between 60 and a hundred people are trapped as they try to filter through the narrow exits between the blocks of flats. Jackie and a few others are separated from and behind the main group of people. A local priest, Father Edward Daly, is also running away from the Paras and begins to overtake Jackie. Jackie turns slightly and smiles as he sees the priest running past him. Private R assumes a kneeling position and takes aim.

Private R squeezes the trigger of his SLR rifle. A 7.62m. round travelling at 2,600 feet per second enters the outer part of Jackie's right shoulder. Before the smile fades from his face, the bullet will pass behind the upper part of the arm bone and the right shoulder blade before bursting through the inner right rib and the second thoracic vertebra. On striking the spine, the bullet will be deflected slightly upwards and will fracture the left collarbone and adjacent parts of the first and second ribs before exiting the body through the upper part of the chest, leaving a ragged exit wound. In the millisecond it takes the bullet to pass through the upper chest, the top of each lung will be damaged; the windpipe, the gullet and the left common carotid and subclavian arteries will be severed. Bleeding from the damaged blood vessels and lungs will cause rapid death.

Father Daly turns and sees Jackie fall forward onto his face. A couple of men try to drag Jackie to safety, lacerating his face and hands. He is too heavy. They turn him over onto his back. Blood is pouring out over his shirt. Father Daly takes a white handkerchief from his pocket and waves it in the air as he crouches beside Jackie. He is joined by a volunteer from the Knights of Malta, who tries to staunch the flow of blood with a pad. Bullets whizz past their heads; a couple strike the ground near them. The volunteer starts to weep.

"Father, are we going to be killed?"

Father Daly also breaks down and weeps as he administers the Last Rites to Jackie.

Jackie's dream was to box for Ireland in the Olympics in a couple of years' time. That dream was buried with him on the hilltop cemetery overlooking Derry City. He was 17 years old.

Five other Paras opened fire in the car park that day, some shooting over people's heads, some at the flats, some directly into the crowd. Between them they fired 32 shots. Four other people were hit. At least 10 army photographers took between them over 1,000 photographs, and the event was also being filmed from a helicopter taking cine film. Not one of these pictures was ever produced as evidence in support of the army's claim that they had come under heavy and sustained attack. In subsequent inquiries the soldiers claimed that between them they shot three nail bombers, one petrol bomber, one man with a pistol and three men with rifles, hitting eight targets in total. Private R stated that he shot Jackie because he was about to throw a bomb. But there was no such device, no explosive, no glass or petrol around Jackie, just blood. Private R continues to insist to this day he shot a bomber. The Bloody Sunday Inquiry concluded otherwise. Justice has yet to be served.

In the six months following Bloody Sunday, 256 people died: more than during the previous three years. The bombs got bigger and deafeningly louder. We were frequently evacuated from the bookshop when a car or van bomb made its way into the city centre, which was gradually being devastated, street by street. Even when you're standing in a crowd waiting for a bomb to explode, the noise of the blast shocks you to the very core. Your entire body goes rigid as you duck instinctively. To this day, any unexpected noise makes me jump.

* * * * *

In the early hours of 31 July 1972, I was awakened by a soldier kneeling over my bed with an SLR rifle pointed at my face. He motioned for me to get out of bed. Several houses in Circular Road, including mine, were taken over by the army. The operation was the largest movement of troops in Europe since the Hungarian rising, the biggest British military operation since the Suez Crisis in 1956 and the biggest in

Ireland since the Irish War of Independence. There were now 30,300 soldiers across Northern Ireland, including two armoured battalions. Twelve thousand soldiers would be directly involved in Operation Motorman that day.

The goal was to retake various 'no-go' areas in Northern Irish towns. The nationalist area known as Free Derry was enclosed by 29 barricades, 16 of which were considered impassable, even to the army's one-ton armoured vehicles. So HMS *Fearless* steamed up the Foyle and delivered converted Centurion tanks, which simply drove over the barricades, flattening everything before them. Twenty-six companies surrounded Free Derry, and the army erected barbed wire barricades to prevent anyone leaving or entering. The city was virtually cut off from the outside world. One-thousand three-hundred soldiers and 300 armoured vehicles flooded into Free Derry, unopposed. The IRA had already simply faded away across the border, knowing there was no way they could offer resistance against those troop numbers and that hardware.

Once our house had been secured we were allowed to move between rooms. Fred and I ran to a bedroom window to get a view of what was happening outside. Coming down Watery Lane was a Centurion tank, still in its desert yellow ochre colours since deployment in the Middle East. The tank was the same width as the lane. It drove over a booby-trap device. We saw a bright yellow and orange flash appear from under the tank followed by a loud bang, which shook the window. The tank slowed down for a brief moment, then moved on again. It was unstoppable.

On the other side of the Lane, in Creggan Heights, a 15-year-old boy called Daniel Hegarty came out to see the tank with his two cousins as it trundled onto the road, but they were warned to go back by a neighbour. As they crossed the road to walk back home, a soldier fired a burst of four shots at the boys from his machine gun, at point-blank range. Daniel was hit twice in the head and died instantly; another boy was injured. The soldiers claimed the three boys had been armed and were running towards them. They pulled away without checking the dead or wounded and never thought to arrest the third boy. As usual, the soldier was never charged or convicted of murder.[5]

In our house the officer in charge was very polite and civilised about the whole inconvenience of having to take over our home. So, my mum responded in kind and made the soldiers a cup of tea. I took a cup out to a soldier who was lying on the ground outside. He sat up against the wall and laid the rifle across his knees as I handed him the tea and biscuits. His hands were shaking, whether through cold or fear I didn't know, but I couldn't help wondering if they'd been briefed to prepare for an all-out war with the IRA.

For the first time I started to think of escaping Derry and leaving this madness behind. By now I'd seen too much. Jackie's senseless and tragic death had planted the seed of a thought in me and as time wore on I watched it take root. When I saw residents cowering, mothers holding their kids close as gun battles raged between the Provos and the army, it grew. One ordinary day, a bomb warning sent me running from the bookshop with staff and customers, alarm bells ringing in our ears. We watched an explosion blow the bookshop apart. My place of work, my precious literary refuge, had been destroyed. The expression "soul destroying" had never really meant anything to me until I walked through the remains of the shop, water dripping from the fractured ceiling as I studied the dynamics of what Semtex

---

5   The 1973 inquest into Daniel's killing recorded an open verdict, but a second inquest was ordered by the Attorney General in 2009, following examination by the Historical Enquiries Team. The British government apologised to the Hegarty family for having described Daniel as a terrorist. After a further seven years of inaction, in 2016 the DPP confirmed that a decision had been taken not to prosecute the soldier concerned. That decision was the subject of a judicial review and in April 2019 the DPP reported that the soldier was to be prosecuted for murder..

could do to a bookshop. Then one night, bored soldiers fired from a sandbagged watchtower at me and my friends as we made our way home past an empty factory. As we fell to the ground and lay in terror, whilst tracer bullets ripped through the darkness and tore up chunks of sod from the ground behind us, I decided: I had to get out of Ulster.

A couple of other things happened to reinforce my decision. Firstly, I was arrested by the army, taken off a bus on my way to work. In Piggery Ridge, an army camp at the top of Creggan, I was photographed like a common criminal and interrogated. It didn't take them long to establish that I was a bookseller, not a bomber. I was released without charge. Secondly, and much more pleasantly, I fell in love.

As Christmas approached and 1974 drew to a close, I was introduced to Agnes McHugh. Agnes was a friend of my brother Fred's girlfriend and was home from studying art at a college in Lowestoft. We hit it off instantly and spent nearly every night of the week telling each other the story of our lives in the Gweedore Bar. Agnes looked like a young Suzi Quatro, whose hit single *The Wild One* had been in the charts for weeks. She immediately stole my heart and I was transformed from a shy bookish type into a much more outward-looking, less introverted young man. I'd never been able to feel this comfortable with another person. I became carefree, contented, radiant – jubilant, even. So this was what being in love was like. The odes, the sonnets and the song lyrics suddenly acquired a deeper level of meaning and significance. There was life beyond this monochrome brutality after all.

When the holidays ended and she returned to England in January 1975, I was heartbroken. I had never felt so lonely in all my life. I couldn't even concentrate on reading a book. I wrote to Agnes every week. It was unbearable. I had to find a way to see her. One night I pulled one of my favourite Morricone records from its sleeve, dropped the needle onto the vinyl and lay back to listen. As the ghostly harpsichord and plaintive melody gave way to Edda Dell'Orso's melancholy soprano, tears began to roll down my cheeks. I closed my eyes and could still see Jackie Duddy waving at me. He would have known why this music was telling me to leave.

The solution came in the form of a job advertisement in the *Bookseller* magazine. Foyles bookshop in London was looking for a sales assistant for their antiquarian book department. It would all fall into place, I just knew it. I was going to get that job. I would escape from Northern Ireland and would only be a train journey away from Agnes. Our Christmas romance, our love story was going to continue.

CHAPTER 4

London

I was lead into her modest office and without looking up she gestured for me to take a seat. On the desk in front of her was my hand-written job application and she was giving it her full attention. She slowly turned the page and continued reading, the biro in her hand followed her progress down the margin of the page. When she finished reading she fixed her blue-green eyes on me.

"Will it be Anthony or Tony," she asked.

"Tony," I replied. She reached across the desk and with a warm smile and a friendly handshake she introduced herself.

"Christina Foyle."

No introduction on her part was necessary. I already knew about her. The great Christina Foyle. She looked and dressed like royalty and in the world of bookselling she *was* royalty. She was 64 years old and her small mischievous eyes sparkled from a face that didn't have a wrinkle on it. She was wearing a tweed skirt, cream blouse and powder-blue cashmere cardigan. The scent of lily of the valley hung over her like a veil. I couldn't believe she was actually taking the time to interview me personally. She was the owner of the biggest and best bookshop in the world: Foyles of Charing Cross Road, London.

I was aware that I had three years and four months' experience in bookselling whereas she'd been selling books for 47 years.

Yet I didn't feel nervous. I was confident about my knowledge of literature and passionate about selling books. For some years now I'd been dabbling in buying and selling some old volumes as a hobby, which is why I'd applied for the position of assistant in the Rare and Antiquarian Book Department.

The interview turned out to be more of a pleasant conversation between two book lovers. She was particularly interested to hear about the trials of running a bookshop in what she called the 'war zone' of Northern Ireland. My stories triggered memories she had of working in Foyles during the Second World War.

"Over nine million books were destroyed in London during the Blitz," she said wistfully, "that's the entire stock of this building." She went on reminiscing for a few moments then returned to my application form.

"So why do you want to work in Foyles?"

I eloquently delivered my well-rehearsed answer, pleased to see her nodding her head in acknowledgement of my dreams and aspirations.

"And who do you like reading?"

"Conan Doyle, H.G. Wells, and I've read a little Kipling, George Bernard Shaw, Somerset Maugham, John Galsworthy and J.B. Priestley." Hoping to appeal to her sense of espionage, intrigue and glamour, I added Ian Fleming and Frederick Forsyth to my list.

Christina gave a hint of a smile. "That's a splendid list. I've met them all," she nodded.

"Conan Doyle and Wells?" I asked, open-mouthed.

"Well, I was young at the time. I was in my teens when I met Conan Doyle."

She closed her eyes for a second. "Wells died in 1946; I was in my 30s when I met him. It doesn't seem *that* long ago, you know. I can remember my father asking Conan Doyle, who was something of a spiritualist, if he'd been in contact with any famous literary figures. He replied that he'd been in contact with Oscar Wilde, who declared that, 'Being dead is the most boring experience in the world.'"

She gave a little high-pitched laugh and sat back in her seat. She then enjoyed telling me about some other famous encounters.

Assuming a more serious tone, she said, "The most important thing you should know about Foyles is that we strive to have the highest possible reputation for genuine courtesy, such courtesy as really well-bred people would show to visitors to their own homes."

"I understand that," I said.

"Well then, welcome to Foyles. When can you start?"

"The week after next," I replied instantly.

"Fine," she smiled, "we shall see you then."

When I was out on the pavement in Charing Cross Road, I looked into the window of the classics department and saw my distorted ghost of a reflection staring back at me . I replayed the unconventional interview over and over again in my head. I then realised we'd not even discussed wages. Not to worry, I thought, minor detail. I've just been offered a job in Foyles! I couldn't wait to get back to Derry and tell everyone.

I wasn't the only one with a new job. Margaret Thatcher had been elected leader of the Conservative Party that same day. My birthday.

* * * * *

My mum immediately started to talk me out of going. But I was having none of it. I'd never been as focused and determined as I was now. I'd briefly tasted the London elixir of life beyond Derry and was intoxicated at the possibilities it offered.

35

I felt that securing this job in Foyles, the cathedral of literature, had been the greatest achievement of my life. I even started entertaining the notion of opening my own bookshop, once I'd gained the necessary expertise. I reassured mum that I was only a short flight away: Belfast to London took an hour. It wasn't like I was emigrating to America or Australia. She was making a fuss over nothing.

I worked a week's notice in APCK Bookshop and on Sunday 23 February 1975 I left home with a small suitcase and was driven by Fred to Aldergrove Airport.[6] We left early in the morning while everyone was still in bed. My mum always rose early on Sunday to go to eight o'clock Mass, but this morning she couldn't bring herself to say goodbye so she stayed in bed. She would go to a later Mass in St Mary's Church.

A few hours later I was standing in the foyer of Hope House in Quex Road, just off Kilburn High Road. Once my mum had reluctantly accepted the fact I was going to London, she set about finding suitable accommodation. She asked Father Joe Carolan to use the network within the Catholic Church: if I was going to live in London, then she wanted me safe under the watchful eyes of religious orders. Word soon came back that a suitable establishment for a young Catholic was Hope House, a hostel for men, managed by another Father Carolan and run by the Sisters of Hope.

I didn't have any objections to Hope House. I saw this as a temporary place to stay until I was settled. I was to share a dormitory with two other guys until a single room became available. The room was quite spacious with two wardrobes, a dressing table and bedside lockers (with no locks), and it looked clean. Communal showers and toilets were at the end of the hall.

---

6   Now Belfast International.

I pushed my suitcase under the bed and went straight out to walk around and explore the area. Kilburn Park Tube station was only a 10-minute walk away, so getting to work would be handy enough – change to the Northern Line at Euston and get off at Tottenham Court Road, then dander a few yards down Charing Cross Road to Foyles.

I went to bed early so I'd be fully refreshed for my first day at work. However, I couldn't get to sleep because it was freezing. I pulled back the sheet to discover another thick rubber sheet underneath, which felt like ice to the touch. It looked as though the hostel also housed alcoholics on a regular basis. I finally went to sleep only to be awakened by my two room-mates returning from a social gathering somewhere. Thankfully, they went quietly to bed.

When I awoke the next morning they'd already gone. In the busy dining room, I joined the queue for a cooked breakfast and went to an empty table. The other residents were older than me and it was clear they weren't white-collar workers. These men were navvy stock from the Republic of Ireland. The finest, meanest, toughest labourers, joiners and bricklayers you could hope to employ. Broad-shouldered, thick-necked, red-faced, unshaven, hard-drinking Irish muscle. They could spread roads as easily as they could spread butter on toast.

Mine was the only shirt and tie in the room and I looked like a puny schoolboy sitting in the high security wing of a prison where all the inmates happened to be Irish. My presence didn't go unnoticed and before long a sausage bounced off the back of my head. I didn't look behind me to see where the laughter was coming from and I made a point of not leaving quickly. I wasn't going to send any signals of weakness to my fellow diners. When I finished my tea I slowly walked to the door and was relieved no other items of breakfast followed me.

* * * * *

At Foyles, I was directed by an assistant to the second floor. A quick walk around provided visual evidence of why it was named in *The Guinness Book of Records* as housing more books than any other bookshop in the world. Within a week I learned that it also had a reputation for the virtual impossibility of finding the book you were looking for. The shop was crammed with volumes. There were ceiling-high bookcases around the walls, and others that stood at right angles to the walls. Tall four-sided pillars of books sprung up everywhere; there were also waist-high bookcases with selected volumes displayed on top. There were books on every conceivable subject jammed in every conceivable place. It was this unrivalled selection that attracted customers from all over the world, but the stock was vast. Individual departments could be large and sprawling with no easily deciphered method of arranging books by subject. And if it was hard to locate a specific book, it was more exhausting still to purchase it, as the shop operated a system requiring customers to queue three times: you had first to collect a sales docket, then to find a cash booth and pay for the item, and finally to return to the counter and collect the book.

That first morning, adjusting to Foyles' idiosyncrasies, I weaved between the bookshelves until I spotted the illuminated sign suspended from the ceiling that said, in bright orange lettering, ANTIQUARIAN AND BOOK COLLECTING. A black arrow pointed left and I walked into my new department and into my dream.

The rare book department looked rather like the beautiful drawing room of a mansion or the private library of a stately home. It was a large, square room and a great glittering crystal chandelier hung from the high ceiling and bathed the room in a bright but soothing yellowish light. There were no windows, and therefore no natural daylight, nor any outside views to distract from the gorgeous rows of books: leather-bound volumes in reds, greens, blues, browns and blacks, their tooled gold titles and authors' names gleaming from the spines, their raised bands forming symmetrical lines across the collections. I breathed it all in and smelled that exquisite fragrance that only comes from antiquarian books: a leathery, liquorice, musky, indefinable smell that encapsulates the essence of aged literature; the product of bygone generations. The furnishings, the carpets and the absence of windows gave the room a hushed, almost reverential ambiance, as if the combined thoughts of the assembled authors demanded silence and respect.

A gentleman suddenly appeared like the Wizard of Oz from behind a curtain, where there was a small storage area full of boxes of books, old ledgers and bundles of papers. He waved a hand around the room as if introducing me to the authors on display, and then took a few moments to explain the torturous payment process and give me a set of keys to the bookcases and cabinets.

"I seldom have the time to be here," he said, "so God knows when I'll see you again. I'm working in Beeleigh Abbey today," he added, as if I should know what or where that was. Then, cream-coloured raincoat over his arm and a small box in his hands, he was gone. My induction to Foyles in general and my department in particular had lasted less than five minutes. I spent the rest of the day getting to know the works and authors who surrounded me.

That afternoon I came across a set of bound copies of the *Strand Magazine*, which was published monthly between 1891 and 1950. I settled at my desk and reintroduced myself to *A*

Scandal in Bohemia, the first Sherlock Holmes short story, which had appeared in the July issue, 1891, illustrated by Sidney Paget. When I finished the story I looked around the room in rapturous delight, smiling at the treasures on the shelves. Each volume held the promise of knowledge, wisdom, adventure, escape. It occurred to me that I might possibly have landed the best job in the world, little realising that I would soon be embroiled in a scandal of my own.

* * * * *

As the week progressed I realised I was being left entirely to my own devices. I'd familiarised myself with every set of books, every title and every author in the department. Relatively speaking, the rare book department was very small, with fewer than a thousand books. Occasionally a customer would drift in, usually because they were lost, but sometimes intrigued by the otherworldliness of the windowless dead end, a respite from the busy confusion of other departments. Very occasionally that rare customer, one who was actually interested in antiquarian books, would step in and request to have some of the bookcases unlocked so that he or she could lovingly inspect the contents. Rarest of all was the customer who would actually buy something. I knew from experience who to approach and who to leave alone.

In terms of customer sales, I wasn't exactly rushed off my feet. So, I decided to go on quick forays around the floor I was based on and got chatting to some of the assistants manning the other sections. The more I learned about Foyles the more worried I became. Everyone I spoke to told me they'd worked in Foyles for less than six months. They revealed that all staff were employed on weekly contracts and let go just before they'd attained six months' employment, the reason being that employees would gain limited job protection rights after six months. This didn't seem to bother a lot of staff, many of whom were foreigners. Indeed, the backbone of the workforce appeared to be a floating population of youngsters who were learning English from book titles on the job.

Sooner or later, I was told, I'd receive the dreaded "white paper" in the weekly pay packet. "Don't get sick," one employee warned me: Foyles didn't pay sick leave, "and some sick people get sacked". It was also a well-known fact that Christina paid the worst wages outside of the catering industry. I still didn't know how much I'd be paid. I was starting to feel rather nervous.

On Wednesday, I was informed that a single room had become available at Hope House. I was delighted. The room was quite small but warm and cosy and I soon stored away my scant possessions.

"Have you heard the news?" the nun asked sombrely as she handed me the room key.

"No," I answered, feeling a little anxious.

"A policeman has been shot dead by the IRA."[7]

Neither of us said anything more, but a familiar feeling of fear began to gnaw away at me for the first time since I'd arrived in London.

By Friday, I'd reflected at length on some of the negative things I'd heard about Miss Foyle and the way she treated staff. Taking everything into account, I felt confident and relaxed about my position. I reasoned that whilst many members of staff might easily be replaced, I was a specialist in possibly the most

---

7   Liam Quinn, a US citizen and IRA volunteer, had been stopped in Central London by the police, who thought he was acting suspiciously. Quinn ran away, but at that moment, 21-year-old PC Stephen Tibble, who was off-duty, happened to be passing on a motorbike. He headed Quinn off, dismounted and tried to block his path. Quinn pulled out a .38 Long Colt revolver and shot Tibble twice in the chest at point-blank range.

specialist department of the shop. These books were unique high-value items. Any fool off the street could sell general fiction or non-fiction, but I was something of a connoisseur with a passion for the field.

I was self-taught on the subject of antiquarian books. As soon as I'd left school I saved up and bought and sold old and rare books as a hobby. With the profits I made I bought more expensive books and made ever greater profits. Buying and selling a few books had taught me about supply and demand, how inflation works and how market forces determined prices. I knew about book printing, production and the different materials used in binding: buckram, morocco, calf and boards. I knew the correct terminology for book sizes. I was also a good salesman: I could engage a customer by drawing his or her attention to the beauty of a book's tooled gold titles, gilt edges, luxurious moiré silk endpapers, and the smooth soft leather bindings, worthy of the contents they enclosed. I could assess and grade the condition of books and I could value a book by reference to the edition, the impression, the imprint, provenance and associations with previous owners. I also suspected that I had something many of the other assistants did not have – *enthusiasm*. I was in my element.

It's difficult to categorise book collectors, but the majority of my customers were very wealthy. Indicative of my clientele was a gentleman who I knew only as John. He was well-dressed, with a smooth, ruddy pink complexion and friendly disposition. One afternoon, after browsing for about 20 minutes, he hurriedly selected three collections of books, about 30 volumes in total. He quickly went off to pay, saying that his young daughter was waiting in the car. I boxed up the books and followed him down to his maroon Rolls-Royce, parked right outside the front door on Charing Cross Road. A pretty, smiling young girl of about 13 or 14 was sitting in the front passenger seat. He shook my hand and gave me a generous tip. John was in fact Viscount Althorp, soon to become the eighth Earl Spencer. Six years later I watched him on television as he led that daughter, Diana, up the aisle of St Paul's Cathedral.

After what seemed a long tiring week, I was glad to see closing time on Friday. I called into a cafe in Kilburn on the way home and had a fish supper. The news on the TV was terrible. A Northern Line Tube train had failed to stop at Moorgate Station and crashed into a bricked-up tunnel, killing 43 passengers and injuring many more. My first working week in London was proving to be a shocking one for the capital. I couldn't seem to get away from tragedy and, as I read the newspapers, I quickly realised I hadn't left the Troubles of Northern Ireland behind me.

The story of how the young married police officer, Stephen Tibble, had been shot dead on the streets of London by the IRA particularly chilled me. Surely that couldn't happen here, could it? I had rarely watched the news back in Derry because I could see death and destruction all around me. Now I was beginning to realise there was plenty of terrorist activity in London too. And it didn't take long before it dawned on me that anyone Irish was under suspicion.

* * * * *

Irish Republicans killed nine others during 1975 and were responsible for multiple bombings. Many commuters avoided the London Underground, fearing it might be the next target. People were reluctant to go shopping in the West End. At times it seemed London was a city under siege.

In August 1973 James Lees-Milne, an expert on English stately homes, wrote in his diary: "The IRA activities now spreading alarmingly to London must I fear make most

Englishmen detest the Irish with deadly loathing. Why the hell do we not send every Irish citizen back to Eire, impose passports and ban suspects from entering this country?" The following month he suggested that all IRA activists be shot and a form of martial law introduced. This was even before the Guildford and Birmingham pub bombings. Lord Arran, a Conservative whip in the House of Lords, thundered similarly: "I loathe and detest the miserable bastards... savage thugs... may the Irish, all of them, rot in hell."

It wasn't just the Irish who were under suspicion. There was a growing fear of "subversive and extremist elements" within Britain. Sections of the right-wing Establishment were becoming fearful of the Labour Party falling under commu-nist control, via its Trade Unionist paymasters.[8] A mood of intolerance was starting to harden, and (in part because of the power the army had been able to wield in Northern Ireland) rumours had begun circulating about an armed coup impos-ing a right-wing junta.[9]

Against this backdrop, Londoners were trying to get on with their lives. But the living was not easy as the country was in economic turmoil. In 1975 the average annual London house-hold income was between £2,000 and £3,000, real earnings having fallen by 18 per cent. (When I opened my first ever little brown pay packet, I calculated that my annual salary with Foyles was to be £910 per annum (around £7,000 today); £17.50 per

8   Those of a more paranoid disposition within MI5 even thought Prime Minister Harold Wilson was working for the Soviets.

9   In January 1975 a rather sinister army recruitment advertisement appeared in The Times, warning that a country "can lose its freedom little by little, without being overrun", and asking, "Are you prepared to fight?" The implication was that new recruits should be prepared, as was already happening in Northern Ireland, to direct their guns against fellow citizens.

week (£134 today) after 25 per cent tax was deducted.) Taxation provoked heated debate and resentment, if not rage.[10]

Homelessness was a major problem. Many post-war housing estates and entire districts had fallen into disrepair and decay. Public slum clearance schemes were being used to make space for brutal-looking high-rise towers, but money for reconstruction had run out due to the economic crisis. Even parts of central London were boarded up and blighted. By 1975 there were an estimated 100,000 houses lying empty in the capital and 30,000 people had resorted to squatting.

Communes were established in derelict properties by radical groups, hippies, feminists, gays, musicians and anarchists. Fashion and music were fusing together to kick-start the punk revolution, with a bondage and sado-masochistic motif evident in Vivienne Westwood's King's Road shop, SEX. Later in the year, a new band called the Sex Pistols would perform their first gig two doors down from Foyles bookshop.[11]

Sexual boundaries and taboos were being pushed aside in literature and film with daring advances that were constantly challenged in the courts. Although judges prompted juries to find particular works "obscene", the juries kept returning verdicts of not guilty. When in 1971 the publishers of a book called *The Mouth and Oral Sex* by Paul Ableman were found not guilty of distributing material that was obscene and could deprave and corrupt, it was a milestone. The authorities gave up and accepted that any writing on sex, fiction or non-fiction, no matter how extreme, if published by

10   In 1955, the year I was born, the average earner with a wife and two kids paid less than 4 per cent in income tax and National Insurance. By 1975 the top rate of tax payable was 83 per cent.

11   The venue was the Saint Martin's College of Art and the band were kicked off stage after 20 minutes by the shocked organisers. In 2014 Foyles bookshop moved their flagship store to this building.

a mainstream publisher, was beyond prosecution. They would therefore in future only target the small-fry underground press. The columnist George Gale complained that, "It is almost certainly impossible now to write a book which would attract prosecution for obscenity."

By the mid-Seventies three out of four people agreed that "adults should be allowed to buy whatever indecent or erotic books and magazines they like", as long as "no one is hurt and the experience brings pleasure".[12]

If novels can reflect the times we live in, then a book called *Last Bus to Woodstock*, by Colin Dexter and published in January 1975, is a case in point. The book was selling quite well in Foyles. It introduced a new fictional detective called Inspector Morse, who was a frequent visitor to strip clubs and something of a connoisseur when it came to both classical music and pornographic magazines.

Novels aside, there was plenty of political intrigue, sex and murder going on in real life. In November 1974, just three months before I arrived in London, Labour MP John Stonehouse had tried to fake his own death in order to avoid charges of fraud, theft and forgery. That same month, the Anglo-Irish peer Lord Lucan also disappeared after apparently bludgeoning his nanny to death and attacking his estranged wife. Meanwhile, a public scandal was brewing involving Liberal MP Jeremy Thorpe and his lover Norman Scott.

A group called the Paedophile Information Exchange held their first AGM in March 1975. PIE campaigned openly and lobbied for the age of consent to be abolished. They proclaimed the sexual rights and liberation of children and considered inter-generational relationships to be beneficial and developmental for

---

12   Sandbrook, Dominic, *Seasons in the Sun: The Battle for Brittan 1974-1979* (London: Allen Lane, 2012)

the younger partner. At the same time, across the country, and in circumstances which suggested a sexual motive, young boys were being found murdered.[13]

Into this cauldron of political, social and sexual turmoil, I arrived to forge a new life and develop my career in the rarefied world of antiquarian bookselling. I'd unwittingly moved from troubled Derry to troubled London. In spite of everything, however, at that time I still considered London to be the lesser of two evils. But the balance of evil tipped somewhat in London's favour when I drove away from Piccadilly Circus with Charles Hornby and Keith Hunter.

---

13   Garnett, Mark, *From Anger to Apathy: The British Experience since 1975* (London: Jonathan Cape, 2007)

CHAPTER 5

Halter Breaking

Huddled in the taxi between two men I'd only known for a couple of hours, I sat silently looking out at the black, wet shiny night before I felt my eyes closing and sleep start to creep up on me. I could hear the occasional muffled conversation between Charles and Keith. Then the taxi came to a halt and I was gently tapped on the cheek.

"We're here," I heard one of them say. I rubbed me eyes, stepped out of the taxi and gave an involuntary shiver as the cold air filled my lungs.

Ennismore Gardens has an Irish ring to it; it could be a street in the Creggan area of Derry. The address seemed familiar, almost reassuring. Number eight Ennismore Gardens is one of the nine houses located on the imposing northern side and it was this address that Charles and Keith led me into. I was taken into a wide hall, up the stairs and into an enormous drawing room. Although large, the room had a warm cosy feel to it. A few tall gold-columned lamp stands with dark shades were strategically placed on tables around the room. The light reflecting off the yellow-coloured walls was comforting and the walls featured paintings and old framed prints of flowers and shrubs.

My coat was taken and I was invited to sit on a settee upholstered in cream material. Almost immediately a bottle of red wine was produced. Charles poured and despite my protests the glass was filled to the top. He sat beside me, raised his glass and said, "One for the road." I was tired and any notion of drinking more had left me. The effort of even having to make conversation seemed too much and I was starting to regret that I'd come back with them. I just wanted to borrow the money and get a taxi home.

"Cheers." Glasses were raised.

Keith became very animated and started to engage in playful banter with Charles, trying to provoke a response to his criticisms about football teams, fellow business associates, the state of the economy and political parties. It became clear that Keith was a Labour supporter, whilst not surprisingly Charles was a Conservative. The debates had more volume than substance, as if the intention was to keep me awake rather than score any points over a particular argument. When I had drunk half of the glass, Charles was there with the bottle topping it up again. I pleaded with him not to give me any more.

"Nonsense," he replied. "I wish to belatedly toast your birthday and success in your new job. Every success and good fortune, Mr Daly." Glasses were raised again and more wine was consumed. Charles loosened his tie and opened the top couple of buttons on his waistcoat. He sat his glass on a table and threw himself back and deep into the settee.

"So, Anthony, tell me what your plans are for the future. What do you hope to achieve in this great city of ours?" He was starting to sound drunk.

I told him of my plans to learn as much as I could about the antiquarian book trade in Foyles and of my dream, one day, of opening my own little bookshop here in London.

"I have to tell you," Charles said, "that I am very good friends with a man who works in bookselling. I must introduce you, although he just sells the usual predictable rubbish, best sellers, magazines, newspapers and the like."

"Does he own a shop?" I asked, now becoming more alert and feeling less tired by the prospect of making another valuable contact in the book trade.

"Not really. He's involved in running a chain of bookshops. He's in charge of all the buying."

Keith stood up and drained his glass. "All right, enough of this poncey bookselling business. The only books I'm interested in are books that involve betting, gambling, the horses and the dogs."

Charles also stood up. "Nature calls." He gracefully bowed out of the room with an exaggerated wave of his arm.

Keith started asking me about my family again, what my parents did, how many brothers and sisters I had, covering much of the ground we'd already discussed at the restaurant. I wondered if he was so drunk he couldn't remember what I'd already told him. Charles soon came back with small glasses of port on a silver tray.

"You really must try this, Anthony."

"No thanks, really, Charles. I've had enough. It's time I was going."

I drank down the last of my wine, shuffled to the edge of the seat and sat my glass on the table with an air of finality. I looked around to see where my coat had been left. Keith had taken a glass of port from Charles.

"Fuck, this is good stuff, Charles. Very nice."

"Nothing but the best," Charles laughed, and insisted I try the port.

"Okay," I said, "then I really need to go."

"Absolutely, old boy." Charles eased himself down beside me. "Well, what do you think?"

"It's very strong but nice," I said taking little sips. I'd never tasted port before. I sat back in the settee again, resigned to the fact that I'd need to stay a little longer. All I wanted was to get the money, sort out how I'd repay it and leave, but I couldn't be pushy about it. I was at his mercy.

I noticed a few large books sitting on a table between the windows. I walked over and started looking through them. If I could move around a little maybe they'd get the message that I really wanted to go. The books were large pictorial volumes about gardening.

"Do you do much gardening, Charles?" I asked.

He shook his head and laughed. "As little as possible."

Keith joined in the laughter. "When he's in the country, Charles just wants to ride things and shoot things. Come to think of it, that's all he wants to do in London, too."

They both laughed loudly and fell back in their seats.

I sat on the edge of the table and leafed through the books, pretending to be interested. I wanted to keep my glass as far away from Charles as possible. The conversation turned to horse racing before finally tapering off into a moment's silence. Keith resumed but this time the frivolity had gone.

"That was some fucking mess at Moorgate yesterday. Poor bastards. How the fuck can you drive a train straight into a brick wall? Jesus Christ."

Charles regained his air of superiority, all humour and signs of drunkenness having evaporated from his demeanour.

"The Underground is falling apart just like the rest of the country. The sooner we get a proper government the better."

They then mentioned the killing of the young police officer and discussed the impact the activities of the IRA were having in London. I felt rather uncomfortable. I was mentally and physically exhausted and Northern Ireland was just too heavy a subject to try and discuss at this hour.

I closed the book and had a little trouble adjusting my vision from the dust jacket to the rest of the room. I started to feel a little light-headed.

"Are you feeling OK?" Charles asked.

I sat down in the chair next to Keith. "I'm wrecked," I said. "I really need to be going now. Thanks for helping me out like this. What about the repayment, Charles, what way do you want to work this?"

At that moment I was overcome with a wave of nausea. "I'm sorry, I drank too much. I'm not feeling very well."

Keith leaned over towards me. "You actually don't look too well."

He stood up. "I'll get you a drink of water," he called back, leaving the room.

I looked at Charles. "I really need to be getting home, Charles, thanks again for everything."

Charles reached for me as I rose unsteadily to my feet. "Look, why don't you stay here for the night? We have no shortage of bedrooms. I'll drive you home first thing in the morning."

I shook my head. "No thanks, I want to go now."

Keith appeared with a glass of water. I drank it down in a couple of gulps. My face felt hot and flushed. I was embarrassed to have gotten into this state but now I needed to get out. I spotted my coat over a chair by the door and walked over unsteadily. Charles took the coat from me and held it out for me to put it on.

"Hang on, I'll phone for a taxi," Keith said and disappeared again.

I looked directly up into Charles's face. "I'm so sorry about this, I never drink this much."

"Don't be silly," he replied and put a hand on my shoulder to steady me. "We had a great evening and I really enjoyed your company."

Charles steered me out of the drawing room and along the hall.

"Let's get you down to the front door for a breath of air, you'll feel much better. The taxi won't be long. Oh, and I have the money you need here."

Just as we passed an open door, Charles suddenly turned me at a right angle and pushed me into a dark room. His hands were now gripping my shoulders. Another figure emerged from the darkness and pulled me forward. I was violently flung face down onto a bed. Charles and Keith flipped me over onto my back. I was slapped hard on the face. I was shocked, stunned, and disorientated, my vision blurred and my head spinning. My shoes, trousers and underpants were pulled off. I tried to kick out with my legs but I seemed to have lost control of them. I reached out with my arms to try and grab something, someone. Keith slapped me in the face again and I was tossed over onto my belly. I tried to push myself up but Keith threw himself across my back and pinned me down with his arm and elbow pressing down on my neck.

I felt his breath at my ear. "Fucking move and I'll break your fucking neck, you Irish cunt."

Charles pulled my legs apart and I felt a cold wet stabbing pain as a finger entered me.

"That's it," Charles said, "just getting us greased up. Just relax."

I tried to move but realised it was impossible. In one way I'd sobered up, but in another way I felt as if I was detached from reality and was observing and experiencing this from somewhere else. I started to wonder if this was really happening, or if it was a dream, a nightmare. Charles then slowly entered me. I had experienced pain before. Pain from falls, pain from cuts and bruises, pain from being strapped in school, pain from my childhood beatings. But this pain presented itself in extremes of both physical and mental torture. This was the pain of both the body being violated and the pain of total humiliation that comes with the abject loss of dignity. An assault on the very soul.

Charles's movements became faster and faster as he pummelled into me. I couldn't move, couldn't believe pain like this, and could barely breathe with the weight of Keith lying across my back. All I could do was endure and wonder how much longer, how much longer.

Keith started licking my neck, my cheek and the inside of my ear. I smelt his aftershave: a concoction of green plants, cedar and moss, but also with a clinical, antiseptic scent that made me feel as if I were being subjected to a medical procedure. I smelt the alcohol from his breath, felt the stubble on his chin, felt his saliva running down my cheek and over my lips. Charles was vigorously grunting and groaning. He panted breathlessly.

"How are we doing there, Keith? He's very quiet, is he still breathing?"

Keith eased his weight off me a little and positioned his face directly in front of mine, our noses touching. I opened my eyes. They were now the only weapon I had and I willed my eyes to speak for me. I showed him pain and despair, but above all hatred. My visual resistance displeased him. He moved above me again.

"He's fine, in fact the little bastard's enjoying it." Keith then sank his teeth into the back of my shoulder. I screamed. That was the breaking point. The last vestiges of anger and the will to fight left me. My body and my spirit collapsed. They had won. I was theirs. I didn't care anymore. The pain of the violence was now matched by the feeling of not caring. From this point nothing mattered, they could do whatever they wanted; they could take all night with me, or they could kill me now. I cried tears of acceptance and submission.

Finally, Charles groaned loudly and I felt his full weight push against me, then tense and finally rest on me.

"Oh Jesus," he whispered.

Keith's face was in front of me again. He pushed his tongue deep into my mouth. I tasted nicotine, but it didn't matter. Charles collapsed on top of me and now, with the weight of both men on me, I was suffocating, but it didn't matter. It would all soon be over. At least unlike some of the other pupils in my class in secondary school, the Troubles had not taken me. I'd survived shootings and bombings; I'd survived Bloody Sunday and lived to see 20. A pity I was now going to die after a week in London. I wondered if all of this was retaliation for the murder of the policeman. Had all this been planned? I had a brief flicker of an image of my mother being told news of my death and that was the thing that hurt the most. The realisation that I was about to die made me do something unusual. I instinctively reached out and held Charles's hand. Took the hand of my murderer and squeezed it. I needed to hold someone's hand at the moment of death. Straining my neck, I moved my head and looked at him. He had a puzzled look on his face. It was then that I passed out.

I regained consciousness and opened my eyes for a second and saw darkness. Then the outlines of bedroom furniture became visible. I closed my eyes again. I was lying on my side in a foetal position. I was completely naked and was not alone. Charles was lying beside me. He was aware I was awake and positioned himself behind me, putting his hand through my hair. He moved his hand under my arm and across my chest. I felt his breath, then kisses on my neck and down to where Keith had bitten me.

"It's going to be all right," he whispered. Then he entered me again. I thought nothing, felt nothing. He raped me again, more gently this time but it was no less a rape than the first vicious assault.

I awoke again in early morning daylight, naked, bedclothes removed, the pain from the shoulder bite stinging. I was lying on my back, staring at the ceiling, aching all over. I felt movement at my feet. Charles, also naked, was kneeling at the foot of the bed. He'd been performing oral sex on me. He held my penis in his hands. He smiled at me and continued. I could barely raise my shoulders from the bed. My head fell back onto the pillow. The light was hurting my eyes so I let my arm rest over my brow. I was in his bed, tired, weak and in pain. I was broken, my humiliation was complete. He was in complete control of my body.

As if reading my mind, Charles paused and said quietly, "I own you, Anthony, you're mine."

At that moment in time, he was right. I was helpless and penniless and he was taking ownership of my body in the most intimate way possible. I gripped the headboard behind me and bit my lip. Charles had won. There was nothing more he could take from me – apart from my life.

I shuffled to the shower and washed as best I could. The movement of my arms was restricted by pain and my legs felt as if I had run a marathon. It was as if I'd been in a fight, which of course I had. I put my clothes back on and felt as unclean as before. When I could afford to, I'd burn these clothes.

Charles matter-of-factly called me into the kitchen, where he'd prepared scrambled eggs, tea and toast. I joined him at the table but could barely look at him. I felt ashamed, vulnerable, nervous and angry. There was no sign of Keith. He talked as if nothing had happened. Small talk about the weather. Sunday papers had been delivered and he glanced down at the headlines. Moorgate, the Tibble murder and the forthcoming referendum on whether Britain should remain in the EEC (it had joined in 1973).

I ate in silence, refusing to comment on anything he said.

He turned to a back page and chuckled. "Aston Villa won the Football League Cup yesterday."

I could keep silent no longer. "Are you serious?" I asked angrily.

He looked a little puzzled.

"How can you talk like that as if nothing happened? Why did you do that to me?" My eyes welled up.

Charles sat his cup down. "For Christ's sake, Anthony, don't try and be so bloody parochial this morning. You knew exactly what you were coming here for last night."

I was incredulous.

"Jesus Christ," I said on the verge of tears. "I needed help, you said you would help me."

Charles rolled his eyes as if suffering the tantrums of an ungrateful child.

"You didn't say you needed help, you said you wanted money. There's a big difference. Especially when you're in the Dilly"

"Yes, a loan. I wanted a loan"

"I'll give you the bloody money. You've earned it – no loan, no repayments, it's all yours."

He walked out of the kitchen and returned with some notes. He counted out £30 and placed it in front of me.

"There you are, now for Christ's sake cheer up. You peddle your arse around the Dilly, you allow yourself to be picked up. You score a fine meal from a couple of punters. Don't act the naive innocent. You knew exactly what you were doing. You get into a car with two strangers, take all the drink you're offered and then think you can just pretend it's all a polite social gathering, that you can just get up and leave. Not bloody likely."

He dabbed his mouth with a napkin and rested his elbows on the table, hands joined under his chin.

I couldn't believe he was saying those things. Suggesting that I had been out looking for sex. He was completely wrong. How could he think that? I'd been in London six days. I knew nothing about Piccadilly Circus. But I *had* followed Keith and I *did* get into that taxi. Was this *really* all my fault? I hadn't been thinking straight last night. I remembered feeling nervous but also strangely elated. I wiped a tear from the corner of my eye.

"Look, I knew you were a little edgy and uptight, I knew you were over from Ireland, assumed you were a first timer. New to the game." Something that looked like guilt flashed across Charles's face for a second. "That's why I added a little spike to your drinks to lighten you up, relax you."

I couldn't believe what I was hearing. "You drugged me?"

"Yes," he replied.

"With what?"

"Mandrax, starting with your Coca-Cola in the bar." He studied the blank look on my face.

"I'm reliably informed it's a methaqualone-based, sedative-hypnotic drug," he explained enthusiastically. "Very popular and very cheap. Easier to get than Smarties and when mixed with alcohol," he smiled, "who knows what can happen?" He frowned a little. "I fear I may have administered something of an overdose last night. It's not like I use the stuff myself. Sorry about that. I'm also informed by those who use them that they can increase sexual arousal. They call them randy mandies." He smiled and winked at me. "Seemed to work this morning."

I shook my head in disbelief. I couldn't understand how he could simply have a cup of tea, read the papers and explain the effects of a drug he had administered before raping me.

"Well, you didn't exactly push me out of bed this morning," he added defensively.

What world did this man inhabit? I needed to get out of this place now. I collected my coat from the floor of the bedroom and made for the front door.

"Hold on," Charles called out as he appeared from the kitchen. "I phoned for a car while you were having a shower, it'll be here in a minute. Please sit down for just one minute. I want to say something and I want you to listen very carefully."

We went to the drawing room and he sat opposite me.

"Anthony, I really enjoyed your company last night. False modesty and gullibility aside, you're handsome and smart and funny, and obviously very open and honest. Very trusting. Those are nice qualities. I like that. I know some people who would love to meet you. Important people."

He spoke in a smooth, rich, confident tone. I refused to respond to his oily compliments.

"There's something different about you, something rather special." He studied me intently. "Was I your first last night? Was it your first time? I was your first, wasn't I?"

I ignored the questions.

"Look, I know a lot about horses, and I've worked with a few stubborn mules in my day. But I break them, train them, breed them. They do what I want them to do in the end. Jump over a fence, trot this way or that way, lie down, get up." His voice took on a more forceful tone. "I ride them and I make them winners. I turn them into valuable commodities. You, Anthony, are like a young Irish horse. You have great potential. I can tell you're not a one-trick pony."

He rose and joined me on the settee.

"I broke you in last night. But you *were* asking for it, whether you know it or not. It may not have been entirely pleasant, but it was necessary. The first hurdle of the race."

I shook my head.

"Not pleasant? Jesus Christ," I snarled at him. "Were we in the same room, on the same bed? And that other animal bit me, he fucking bit me."

I took a deep breath and exhaled, trying to regain my composure. He placed his hand on my knee.

"You could make a lot of my friends very happy and you would be very well rewarded. You could make more in a night than you make in a week in that bookshop. The best-paid apprenticeship you'll ever be offered. And like a prize horse, you will be well groomed and looked after. You will be protected. No one else will ever take advantage of you. You will be in my stable. Safe."

I lifted his hand from my knee and dropped it.

"You're wrong about me. I'm not that kind of person, and I'm not an animal to be trained. You have completely got the wrong impression of me and if I've done anything to give that impression, I am sorry."

A car horn sounded from below. We both stood up. Charles walked around in front of me, blocking the doorway.

"I'm sorry you feel that way, Anthony. I work in the insurance industry. When bad things happen I have to pay out a lot of money. Some of my colleagues will not have slept this weekend thinking about what Moorgate will cost them. So, part of my job is about preventing bad things from happening in the first place."

I wasn't quite sure what he was getting at. Was this some kind of a threat? Was he trying to convey a warning? From my perspective the bad things had already happened – to me.

"Look, Charles, just let me go. I won't tell anyone about this. I don't want anyone knowing about this, ever."

"Well that's just the thing you see," Charles leaned his tall frame against the door.

"Some people, people who are very close to you, might find out about this."

"What are you talking about?" I demanded.

Charles stood aside and waved me through to the hall.

"Let me see you down to the car."

We descended the stairs.

"Last night when you were well and truly out of it, I took some very revealing, not to say, creative photographs of you. I have to say, you are particularly photogenic. The close-ups of Keith's cock in your mouth will be quite breathtaking, as the experience seemed to be for you at the time. Keith is getting an amateur photographer friend of his to develop the pictures this morning."

I stopped in mid-step, suddenly feeling sick to the stomach. "Please don't do this to me, Charles, I promise I won't tell a soul about it. I just want to forget it ever happened. I've been through worse during the Troubles and I've always just got on with it. Same with this, I'll forget all about it. I was stupid and drunk. It was just a misunderstanding, it was my own fault and you've taught me a lesson."

Outside, a silver Ford Granada was waiting. Charles opened the back door for me to get in.

"Please, Charles," I pleaded.

"It would just be awful," he said, "a devout Catholic like your mother. Imagine that poor woman getting an envelope addressed to her, opening it, seeing her son doing this. God help her, it would break her heart. She'd never get over something like this. Anyway, just think about my offer, and my photographic insurance policy."

He looked at the driver.

"Basil, this young man is going to Kilburn."

He gave a broad smile.

"I'll be in touch. Take care now." He closed the car door and we drove off.

I looked out the back window to see Charles, his arm raised, waving goodbye with the fingers of his hand.

I spent the rest of that Sunday in bed, curled up in a ball, restless, tossing and turning. As much as I tried to put everything to the back of my mind, the events of the previous night replayed themselves over and over again. I felt sick with apprehension, sick from the nervous cramps that gripped my stomach. I'd never felt as miserable or as alone in all my life.

CHAPTER 6

The Abbey

I was back in Foyles early on Monday morning, having eaten the largest fry-up I'd ever consumed. I'd not had any food since Sunday morning and was ravenous. I busied myself, systematically removing books from the shelves, then dusting them and wiping the shelves clean before replacing them. A thought suddenly came into my head. I left the department and found the reference section. I looked up an *Oxford English Dictionary* and found the word "parochial". One of the definitions was "narrow-minded, having a narrow outlook; small town; conservative". I assumed this was the definition Charles Hornby had in mind when he threw the accusation at me. Of course, I was bloody parochial. I was from Northern Ireland. Small town, Catholic, conservative, backward, shy and retiring. I was born in a state of sin and baptised with the waters of guilt. As a child I'd been told that every time I committed a sin, it was as if I was driving the nails further into the hands and feet of Christ. Every impure thought, word or deed was another step down into the fires of hell and eternal damnation. Charles was suggesting that in order to be true to my new urban and cosmopolitan self, to cast off this cloak of feigned prudishness and religious suppression, I was to engage in same-sex assignations with strangers, prostitute myself to his "very important people" and rejoice in having shed my parochialism. Charles had also said I had been peddling my arse, looking for it. How could he have thought that? I was starting to doubt myself. Had I unconsciously been giving out these signals? *No*, I told myself. All I had wanted was food, the loan of some money. But from total strangers? I'd been naive, foolish and stupid, and I hated myself for that.

Around mid-morning an elderly gentleman entered the department. He was smartly dressed in a broad pinstriped dark blue suit and well-groomed with neatly cut grey hair. He glanced over in my direction and nodded briefly. I nodded and smiled back. He walked to the far corner of the room, hands in his trouser pockets and started looking at the rows of books. He would then walk across to another wall, study a few shelves there, before crossing again to the shelves he had just been looking at. I waited at my desk for about 10 minutes before deciding to approach him. I had an instinct for when customers wanted to be approached.

"Good morning, sir. Are you looking for anything in particular?"

The gentleman had a broad face with pleasant features. His thin lips looked tightly pressed together, as if he were trying to suppress a smile. He looked directly at me with eyes that seemed to be the same colour as Christina Foyle's, a light blue that had faded to grey.

"Yes," he said in a crisp clear voice. "You."

"Excuse me?" I said, completely mystified.

"I'm looking for you."

I wanted to ask why but was afraid what the answer might be. I'm sure I blushed. I simply did not know how to respond. I took a couple of self-protective steps backwards. He obviously saw the confusion and alarm on my face.

"Perhaps there has been some mistake," he said. He smiled at me, said goodbye and walked out of the room.

I retreated behind the desk and dropped into the chair. The encounter had completely unsettled me. I forced myself to calm down. Was it all a misunderstanding? After all, the man did say he thought there'd been a mistake. Perhaps I was being paranoid, understandable after what had happened to me at the weekend. I convinced myself it was indeed a mistake of some kind on the man's part. This encounter was just too soon after what had happened with Charles and Keith to be linked in any way. The incident did however make me think about the statement Charles had made about meeting some of his important friends.

I hoped I had made it perfectly clear that I wanted nothing to do with him or his friends. What about the photographs, his warning? How did I know for a fact they had even taken pictures? He could have lied to frighten me, and he had succeeded. If in any other circumstances a man came in and said he was looking for me and then thought he'd made a mistake, I would have thought nothing more about it. I was reading too much into it, on the heels of that weekend. *I'm going to get over this*, I told myself, *I'm fine now*. I was mentally trying to play down my own rape. I'd been shot at, caught up in explosions, had been arrested and interrogated by the army in Derry, and all for no reason. I'd felt helpless during those times in Ulster, just as I'd felt helpless with Charles and Keith. But I lived through it all. I had survived before and I'd survive this.

That same day, a member of the Chinese community, Fookie Lang, had been shot dead outside his own restaurant in a gangland killing. He was suspected of being a police informer. It seemed that London had more in common with Derry than I'd ever imagined. London and Derry seemed to be violently joined at the hip. I tried not to think about this killing, but it really unsettled me.

The following morning, I was startled when the phone in my department rang for the first time. I had been engrossed in volume three of *The Tyburn Chronicle: Or Villainy Display'd in All Its Branches*, published in 1769. The loud clanging ring startled me. I was asked to go to the apartment on the top floor immediately. Mr Batty wished to see me. Mr Ronald Batty was number two in Foyles, by virtue of being the husband of Christina Foyle. He'd actually been a predecessor of mine, as he was an expert in antiquarian books and had managed the rare book department. He was what I aspired to become, so it was with some excitement and a little nervousness that I took the lift to the top floor. I'd assumed I'd misheard the lady who phoned me: it had to be *de*partment, not *a*partment – but I'd actually been right. I was ushered into an enormous apartment, situated on the top floor of Foyles.

This was the London home of the Foyles and it was truly beautiful. The sitting room walls were lined with dark wooden panels, but the room itself was anything but dark. The light flooded through the windows from Charing Cross Road, directly hitting a large fireplace. Bright floral patterns sprang from the curtains and a large three-piece suite. Single pieces of Louis XVI furniture such as formal chairs and an ornate table featured around the walls of the apartment.

Mr Ronald Batty was sitting on the big floral settee, delicately holding a cup of tea and a saucer. A man with his back to me was sitting in an armchair facing his host. Ronald gestured for me to come forward and I walked quietly across the plush carpet, feeling as if I were approaching royalty. He pointed to the other armchair.

"Anthony, I believe," he said.

Ronald was rather portly and he looked small in stature, but that may have been due to the size of the chair. He was bald on top, but what thin hair he had on the back and sides was still largely black and slicked shiny with hair oil. He wore a dark three-piece suit and looked impeccable.

I looked at his guest for the first time. It was the gentleman who had been in my department the day before. He too had a cup of tea and a saucer on his lap. Being in such gentlemanly company, I was expecting to be offered a cup, but no offer was forthcoming. I sat back in the chair and crossed my legs, trying to look at ease but probably failing. I was surprised to see this man again and I waited anxiously for the introduction.

"This is Mr Charles Irving MP, a friend and a valued customer of Foyles."

I reached across and shook his hand.

"Pleased to meet you… again," I said.

He smiled, bowed his head slightly and said, "Hello."

Ronald looked at me earnestly.

"I want you to accompany Mr Irving to Beeleigh Abbey later this afternoon. He wishes to have a look at some books. See that Mr Irving gets everything he needs. I think you'll find the abbey very interesting."

"Where is it?" I asked.

"It's near Maldon in Essex, and it houses one of the most valuable book collections in the world." Ronald nodded to the door, promptly indicating my very brief meeting was over.

"You will be called when the car is here later today. Goodbye."

The meeting had been short and sour. Mr Batty didn't present himself as the jolly person he appeared to be; he was direct and to the point. After his wife Christina's charm, it came as something of a shock. But then again, they say opposites attract.

I still didn't know what to make of Mr Irving, but I was even more inclined to believe he'd thought I was someone else when he was in the shop the previous day. Maybe he'd been expecting the man I'd met in the department the first day I started. No matter, I would be going to Beeleigh Abbey that very afternoon. I couldn't wait. I was eventually summoned and made my way out by the side door of the building on Manette Street, where the bookshop ran the entire length of the street. Mr Irving was sitting in the back seat of what I was later told by Norman the driver was a Mark II Jaguar.

Of course, I'd never been driven anywhere by a uniformed chauffeur before. On the journey out of London I learned more about the unexpected visitor to the shop. He'd been elected an MP just over four months ago and was the Member for Cheltenham. Three years before that he'd been Mayor of Cheltenham and he'd been involved in local politics for years. I neglected to ask what political party he belonged to. Like cars, British politics was something else I wasn't remotely interested in. I'd endured enough politics in Northern Ireland to last me a lifetime.

He told me he was interested in championing the needs and rights of victims of crime. I was on the verge of telling him about the other Charles I'd met at the weekend and reporting *that* crime, and the needs of *this* victim. But I changed my mind when he went on to explain that in the same way there were two sides to a coin, there were also two sides to a crime. He was also passionate about the rehabilitation of offenders. I suggested that he move to Northern Ireland, where he could devote the rest of his life to working with victims and offenders. Over there we had both in spades.

Charles was very wealthy. His family business consisted of a chain of hotels, the first of which, the Irving Hotel, had been opened by his father. He'd been chairman of the group for many years. I was relieved he wasn't asking me any questions, so I kept questioning him.

"What kind of books do you like?"

"I love a good thriller," he replied, "detective stories and such like."

I then spent a good 15 minutes grilling him about authors and particular titles. I followed this up with more questions about antiquarian books.

Mr Irving was not particularly interested in old books himself, but had a few friends who loved rare books with beautiful bindings. He was on the hunt for a volume or two on travel, specifically the grand tours of 18th- and 19th-century aristocrats such as James Boswell and Lord Byron, who used to embark on journeys across the Alps and through Europe. As our journey progressed, I found Mr Irving to be very pleasant and easy to get on with. Finally, I ran out of questions to ask him. After a few minutes, he asked me what part of Northern Ireland I was from.

"You have a lovely accent," he said.

Unlike at the weekend, this time I did not volunteer the story of my life. I kept my answers short and said as little as possible.

We finally arrived at a grand estate beside the River Chelmer. I was impressed.[14] The abbey was set in three acres of beautiful woodland and gardens. Charles and I were led hurriedly through the house by a member of the domestic staff, who gave the appearance of having better or more important things to do. I rushed along, taking in stone walls, arches, wooden beams and furniture so dark it appeared to have been painted black.

We then reached the library and it took my breath away. The room looked like a church but with the pews removed and bookshelves fitted around the walls and between the windows, which ran along one side of the room. High above, row upon row of thick black wooden beams curved across an arched ceiling,

---

14   William Foyle had purchased Beeleigh Abbey in 1943 and had lived there until his death in 1963. It was now the country home of his daughter, Christina, and her husband, Ronald Batty.

from which hung circular metal chandeliers emitting soft electric light. Cosy settees and solid formal chairs were placed around a few working tables. Parts of the stone floor were covered in carpets, which gave the large spaces a homely feel. It was the most beautiful sight I'd ever seen, a veritable Aladdin's cave shelved and stocked with some of the rarest and most expensive books in existence. I felt I was walking on hallowed ground. In a far corner was the Wizard of Oz, who had given me my five-minute induction in the Charing Cross Road shop. He was on his knees, taking books out of boxes and checking the contents against delivery notes. He looked across at us and I detected a look of genuine surprise when he recognised me, a look that said, "What on earth are *you* doing *here*?" Charles approached him and they spoke quietly for a moment. The Mighty Oz, the keeper of this magical book kingdom, came over to me.

"Have a look around. I'll be showing Mr Irving some books over at that table."

I scanned the shelves, mesmerised. The books on these shelves made the stock in my department look like tacky second-hand cast-offs. William Foyle had spent his entire life building up this private collection. This was the Foyle private library. These books were not for sale. However, the books that Oz was sorting out were for sale. Beeleigh was rather like a warehouse for the stock that would make its way to the rare book department in London. The books might be bought at auctions, or Foyles might be invited to view collections at the homes of wealthy families who were disposing of them following the death of an owner, or who wished to raise cash in hard times. The stock was delivered here, sorted and priced before being transported to Charing Cross Road.

One by one I lifted down the hefty volumes and sat at a circular table. I could not have been sitting in a more appropriate environment as I carefully turned the pages of some of the first books ever produced by the human hand. There were hand-written and illuminated vellum manuscripts produced by monks; there were medieval manuscripts and books of hours; there were examples of the first books ever printed. Finally, I sat on the edge of my seat, practically kneeling at the literary Ark of the Covenant – the First Folio of the works of William Shakespeare. The collection also contained second, third and fourth folio Shakespeares. I was transported back through the centuries and exposed to the genius of man expressed in literature. I'd never felt as privileged or as moved to have been given the opportunity to spend an afternoon in one of the greatest English private libraries of the 20th century.[15]

* * * * *

I had been allowed to see, to smell and to touch these works of art. My senses had been fired up, but this visit had been an act of bibliographic seduction. Whilst I may not have had to pay an admission fee to see Beeleigh Abbey and enjoy the literary bliss of that afternoon, I did have to pay with my body that night.

When we left Beeleigh Abbey, I found myself travelling not back to London but further into darkest Essex. Charles had emerged from the Beeleigh library with a copy of William Beckford's *Italy, with Sketches of Spain and Portugal* in two volumes, published by Richard Bentley in 1834. Charles told me that a dear friend of his, an "armchair traveller", would enjoy these books. Charles also reasoned that Foyles would be closed by the time we got back to London, so he suggested I join him for dinner at a

---

15   A year after Christina Foyle's death, the Beeleigh Abbey book collection was sold for £12.6 million in July 2000. It was the most valuable collection of books ever sold in Britain or Europe.

house he had at his disposal, an hour or so drive away, and then return back to London. He also added, as a further incentive, that this house also had a fine library, although nowhere in the same league as Beeleigh Abbey.

As we drove on I was still in a state of elation and I enthused endlessly about the books I'd seen and touched, smelt and read. It was clear that Charles did not fully appreciate the importance or historical significance of the library at Beeleigh. When I'd finally quietened down, I realised that I was none the wiser as to Mr Irving's intentions, beyond buying books that afternoon. I turned the matter over and over in my head. There could not possibly be a link between Messrs Hornby and Hunter, and Irving and Batty. It was ridiculous to consider it. The more I thought about it the more I convinced myself that my visit to Beeleigh Abbey could be nothing other than work related. I'd had an incredible afternoon and I actually felt rather important to be in the company of a Member of Parliament. I turned and looked at Charles, he gave me a little smile and I smiled back. I felt happy and relaxed, and as usual, hungry.

It was very dark when we arrived at our destination, a large house set among gardens, which looked dead and lifeless. The chauffeur went in first and turned on some lights. It was very cold inside and had a distinct smell like a mixture of damp and mould, and the sooty odour of a draft that blows down a chimney. Charles led me into a large dining room and flicked a light switch, which illuminated a chandelier suspended over a 12-place solid oak dining table. The room had a large white marble fireplace and a gold framed oil painting of a hunting scene hung above the mantelpiece. Charles suggested I light the fire and I asked where I would get coal and sticks. He took a moment to think, and then said, "I'll get Norman to sort it."

Norman the chauffeur had gone directly to the kitchen when we arrived, and judging from the clanging of pots and pans in the otherwise empty house, it seemed as if Norman could cook as well as drive. Charles went off to the kitchen and a moment later Norman, wearing an apron, dropped a coal shuttle, sticks, newspapers and matches at the doorway. I set about lighting the fire, and then went in search of the library, which turned out to be a large but disappointing bookcase in a sitting room with a bay window.

The books here included works by Dickens, Thackeray, the Brontës, Trollope and Eliot. I was about to return to the fire when I came across T. E. Lawrence's *Seven Pillars of Wisdom*, 1926. This was one of the legends Christina Foyle told me she had met. I took a seat, opened the volume and read the beautiful poetic dedication at the beginning of the book. I flicked through the pages and admired the stunning full colour portraits of some Arab leaders. I then came across a passage where Lawrence was describing his capture at Deraa in Syria. Considering what had happened to me at the weekend, I could not believe what I was reading. Lawrence described his brutal rape and torture at the hands of Turkish soldiers. The shocking event was recalled in horrific, almost pornographic detail. I could scarcely believe Lawrence could write so openly and frankly about this. As I closed the book, trying to absorb his powerful confession I was suddenly startled by Charles calling from the doorway.

"Dinner's ready," he smiled.

Back in the dining room, a couple of lampshades cast a sympathetic light over the room. The fire was now blazing and a single tall candle burned on the table. Places had been laid out facing each other at one end of the table. A simple meal of chicken, chips and vegetables awaited, with two glasses of white wine.

"Where's Norman?" I asked.

"Oh, he just made himself a sandwich before he left."

"He's gone?" I asked, feeling my stomach knot and a ripple of nervousness spread through me.

"He'll be back early in the morning to take us into London," Charles explained reassuringly. "I hope that's all right with you."

In the circumstances I felt there was only one thing I could say. "Yes."

There was no point in asking about the sleeping arrangements. The warm fire, the cosy dining arrangement and the romantic candlelight told me everything I needed to know. I had been treated to a perfect afternoon's outing and was now being wined and dined. What more could a boy ask for? I wondered if this was what Ronald Batty had meant when he requested that I saw Mr Irving got everything he needed. Charles smiled broadly and raised his glass.

"Cheers," he said.

From that moment on I had only one objective in mind – to get as drunk as I possibly could. Before long I had had three glasses of wine to Charles's one. I asked him to get another bottle, which he did. We passed a civilised enough hour chatting in the big, silent, empty house. I talked about the books I had seen at Beeleigh Abbey and he talked about the beautiful building itself and the surrounding grounds. The conversation then turned to politics. He became very animated and talked passionately about the things he wanted to change for the better. He was particularly vocal about Britain's place in Europe, as he'd been one of those campaigning vigorously for a vote on getting out of the EEC.

When we had finished eating, Charles produced a humidor containing large cigars and offered me one.

"Cuban," he said.

"Of course," I replied, pretentiously.

I tried to read the cigar band but I couldn't focus on the small print because I was drunk. The air above turned a smoky blue as we exhaled with satisfaction. Then I started showing off, as I do regrettably when I've had too much to drink.

"Did you know that in the entire works of Shakespeare, tobacco is not mentioned once?"

He laughed and said, "No, that's something I didn't know."

I blew a large jet of smoke directly into his face.

"Smart arse," he said, and retaliated with a puff of smoke in my direction.

I started drooling about the Folio Shakespeares I'd handled at Beeleigh and continued to ramble on about bookselling. Then, out of the blue, Charles made a startling admission, although it was not one that surprised me given the situation. He told me he was gay, and explained how difficult it was for a person in his position to find love.

Now it was his turn to start drinking more quickly. I could think of nothing to say, no words of empathy or acknowledgement. He talked about his commitment to public life, to the business his father had established, the burdens of responsibility placed on one as an MP. Finally, he stopped.

"Forgive me," he said, "I've been doing what politicians do best – talking."

I wasn't sure if I'd been listening to a sermon or a confession. Either way, his mood lifted and he smiled again. He then stood up, blew out the candle and walked to the door. I followed and we went upstairs into a surprisingly warm bedroom. There was a red glow from an old fashioned three-bar electric heater. Someone had considerately turned down the bed sheets. Everything looked nice, tidy and ready. On top of a bedside locker stood a jug of iced water, two glasses and a tube of lubricant.

We sat on opposite sides of the bed and undressed. He appeared to be as awkward and as embarrassed as I was. I slipped under the sheets shivering in spite of the warmth in the room. He climbed in and lay beside me. We'd not spoken a word since leaving the dining room. He turned on his side and put an arm around me.

"You're shivering," he said, and moved closer.

I said nothing and looked straight up at the ceiling, where the light from the heater created abstract patterns in tones of red and black. Charles raised himself on his elbow and moved over to kiss me on the mouth. I turned my head away and he started gently kissing my cheek and neck. He them positioned himself on top of me, his elbows taking most but not all of the weight. I was sober enough to know what was going to happen but drunk enough not to care. He moved down, kissing my neck, my nipples and my belly. He pushed the bedclothes off with his feet and slid down until his head was between my legs. I stared at the glowing bars of the electric fire for a long moment then shut my eyes tightly. I felt him take me in his mouth. A distorted image of the burning bars formed in the darkness behind my eyes and started spinning around in my head like a blazing comet trapped in the orbit of my skull. I felt dizzy and instinctively moved my hands down and held his head as if to steady myself. The light became a white supernova and exploded inside my brain.

After a few wordless moments he rose and turned me over on my belly and I felt his weight on top of me.

"Relax," he whispered, and I felt the stab of entry for a moment, then nothing more than a mild discomfort registered in the sedated connections of my nervous system. He didn't last long but he lay on top of me for a while before shifting onto his side.

I had just turned 20. Mr Charles Irving, MP for Cheltenham, was 51 years old. I was asleep in moments. I dreamt about Lawrence of Arabia.

> *"The little things creep out to patch themselves hovels*
> *in the marred shadow*
> *Of your gift."*

* * * * *

I was awoken by a voice that seemed distant and muffled. My eyes blinked to adjust to the light and I had no idea where I was. The room had an orange glow and I could see through a gap in the curtains that it was dark outside. I couldn't understand why I was naked. My eyes focused on the glowing bars of the electric fire and I remembered. The bedclothes had been pulled down and Charles, fully dressed, was standing by the bed looking down at me. He had a troubled look of concentration on his face, as if trying to solve a crossword puzzle. I reached down and drew a sheet protectively around me.

"Norman will be here to collect us in about 45 minutes. Are you all right, Anthony?"

"What time is it?"

"Six-thirty."

I turned on my side facing away from him. He sat on the edge of the bed and ran his fingers through my hair. I shivered involuntarily and moved away from him.

"I'm afraid we have no hot water. Just get dressed and I'll see if there's anything we can have for breakfast."

He left the room and I heard him descend the stairs.

I got out of bed and draped the sheet around me. I felt unclean. My head was thumping and my mouth felt furred and dry. I drank a glass of lukewarm water and padded across the landing, shivering and carrying my clothes in a bundle, as I looked for the bathroom. The shock of an ice-cold shower brought me to my senses and I washed and dressed quickly.

Heading downstairs, I found Charles in the dining room with a bowl of cornflakes awaiting me. The house was freezing and my shaking hands struggled to get the spoon past my chattering teeth.

Charles stood behind me and repeatedly rubbed the tops of my arms and combed back my damp hair with his fingers.

"You'll catch your death."

He reached for his overcoat and placed it over my shoulders, my arms and the back of the chair.

The drive back to London couldn't come soon enough. I sat in the back seat as far as possible from Charles, almost pressed against the door, my head resting on the window. The journey was long and silent. Charles reached over a couple of times and put his hand on my knee and asked if I was all right. I nodded and said quietly that I was fine. After another long period of silence, he hesitantly posed an unexpected question.

"Would you like to go to a party this weekend?"

I said nothing, assuming he would interpret my silence as a rebuff. Norman cocked his head back, and with his eyes still firmly fixed on the road ahead, asked breezily, "What's the excuse this time?"

"Thatcher," Charles replied. "The election of our glorious new leader is a cause for celebration. Also, some of my colleagues will be celebrating their first anniversaries as MPs. Plus, the usual grandees and their hangers-on will grant us the pleasure of their company. All food and drink free, courtesy of the Monday Club."

"Can I come?" Norman pleaded in mock sincerity.

"Fat chance," Charles laughed. "Attendance by strict invitation only."

"What's the Monday Club?" I had to ask, still trying to appear uninterested by looking out the window.

"The Monday Club," Charles explained, happy at last to have engaged me in conversation, "is what you might call a pressure group, a very powerful one, made up of like-minded individuals who are positioned somewhat on the right of the party. They see themselves as the custodians of the traditional Tory values and principles. I'm not a member myself. I've only been in the House a few months, but I did get an invitation. Please say you'll come, Anthony. You'll meet some wonderful people and make new friends. It's a great opportunity for you to be presented."

"Presented?" I asked.

"Sorry, well, what I mean of course is – introduced."

I shook my head. "I won't be there, Charles," I said rather forcefully so he would be left in no doubt about my intentions.

He shifted a little nearer. "I love hearing you say my name. That accent melts me."

I rolled my eyes, turned back to the window and said nothing more.

Eventually we made our way into central London, the West End and Charing Cross Road. As we pulled up outside Foyles, Charles said he'd also be going to his place of work, the House of Commons.[16] As I reached to open the door he suddenly slid over beside me and clutched my arm so tightly it hurt.

"You were wonderful, Anthony," he said, and quickly kissed me on the cheek.

Back in my department, surrounded by my beautiful books, I sat behind my desk and buried my face in my hands. I breathed in deeply and exhaled slowly, savouring the aromatic consolations of antiquarian books.

---

16   Later that day Mr Irving asked a question in the House about local authorities' obligations for making empty houses habitable.

There is an organic polymer found in trees called lignin. It is chemically similar to vanillin, the primary extract of the vanilla bean. When trees are made into books, over the course of time the lignin in the paper breaks down and starts to smell like vanilla. This is why collections of antiquarian books smell so wonderful. I had noticed that many of my customers smelled the books before they even opened them.

I soon settled into the rhythms of the day and the routine of the job. Every now and then during a particularly quiet spell, I would set off on a brief reconnaissance around my neighbouring departments, trying to chat to anyone who would take the time to speak to me. Everyone seemed too busy, or maybe they resented the fact that I had what they considered to be a cushy number, while they at times were rushed off their feet. I felt like an outsider, a one-man department in search of a companion.

Later that afternoon I found some comfort in the fact that the day had passed without any incident. By closing time, I felt an overwhelming sense of relief. Perhaps now it was over and I could begin to heal myself, to get over it; get back on track and get on with my life. When it was time to go home I pulled on my coat and put my hand in my pocket. I pulled out three £10 notes. A gift from Charles Irving along with a little handwritten note of appreciation. A payment for services rendered. It was 30 pounds: nearly two weeks' pay. The money made me feel as though I had betrayed myself. Thirty pieces of silver earned in my own little garden of Gethsemane.

CHAPTER 7

Parliamentary Privilege

The next day was cold enough to see sleet fall and vanish on the wet ground during rush hour. Every morning there were barrows by the roadside outside Foyles selling fruit and flowers, and one stall with a blazing brier of coke, roasting chestnuts as it spat sparks into the chilly air. I was greeted with a broad smile by a lady wearing a padded leather hat pulled down over her ears. I saw her every day and her kind motherly face always cheered me.

Around mid-morning as I was sitting at the desk checking off stock that had been delivered from Beeleigh Abbey, Charles Hornby and Keith Hunter walked into the rare book department. My stomach gripped with apprehension. My face burned in humiliation.

Inside the doorway, Charles turned right and Keith turned left. Without looking at me they slowly made their way along the walls in a pincer movement, tracing their fingers along the glass cabinets as if looking for a particular title. They approached my desk from either side and I raised myself out of the chair, looking at one, then the other. Their faces deadpan, they stared straight at me. Then Charles's face lit up in a maniacal smile.

"Congratulations!" he shouted.

I looked to see if any heads had appeared at the doorway. This room was always hushed and people often whispered, as if in a church. Charles reached out and grabbed me by the shoulders.

"Well done, Anthony, the old man was delighted. I just knew you were a natural, a real find, and I understand you were very handsomely rewarded. Everyone walked away happy."

His cultured authoritative accent made every word he spoke sound like a universal truth. As frightened as I was, there was an anger welling within me: having violated me, they'd now violated my place of work. I had to make a stand. This was going to stop. Before I could find the words I wanted, Charles continued.

"I understand you have received an invitation to a party this weekend. You will of course be accepting. Arrangements will be made."

I found my voice but it was trembling.

"Arrangements won't be made," I said quietly and urgently. "I won't be going to any fucking party. This is over. Now leave me alone or I'll go to the police."

Charles and Keith looked at each other. Now Keith was smiling.

"Well, well, the boy has balls."

Charles looked at me earnestly. "Mmm, let's see. The police… yes, the police. A young Irish lad arrives in London. He starts work last week. Two days later a young policeman is murdered in broad daylight."

"I was in here last Wednesday," I said swallowing hard.

Keith leaned forward a little. "Nobody said you pulled the fucking trigger, but you came over here to support the gang. You are part of an IRA cell. They send over a little sleeper to get a nice job in a bookshop in the West End. Who would suspect? You walk around, you watch, you listen, you gather intelligence. You live in a Paddy hostel with your fucking thick mick mates. A den of fucking terrorists. All I have to do is click my fingers and you're made. You're nicked." He clicked his fingers in front of my face. "You are so fucking frameable, you should be an oil painting."

He laughed in my face.

Charles looked down at the books I'd been sorting on the table.

"Now, now, Keith, let's be civilised here. Anthony, I have been informed by Mr Irving that you two got on like a house on fire." Charles picked up a book from the desk. "What have we here?" he said with mock interest. He turned to the title page. *Novels and Poetical Works by Sir Walter Scott;* Cadell & Co, Edinburgh 1829. He studied the engraved frontispiece. Charles was holding volume one of a 60 volume set: the first collected edition of the works of Scott. It was a superb set of books in exquisite condition.

"Lovely," he commented. "I've been told by a close friend who works in the bookselling business that a book is practically worthless without the title page. What do you think, Keith?"

He handed the book to Keith, who took the book, held it in one hand and with the other hand carefully tore off the title page. I lunged forward to grab the book but was violently pushed back by both of them. Keith picked up volume two. Charles stretched out his arms, his palms facing upwards.

"Let's be reasonable here, Anthony. How about I give you some time to think it over. I'll come back at lunchtime, I'll take you out for a bite to eat and we can discuss the matter further."

"No," I said firmly, "I'm not doing it."

Keith tore the title page from the second book and threw the book over his shoulder. It landed on the floor with a dull thud. He immediately lifted volume three and repeated the movement. The title page was torn off with a flourish, a rasping tear followed by the thud of the book hitting the floor behind him. I could take it no longer. I couldn't just stand there and watch the books being destroyed before my eyes.

"All right," I said, as volume four was about to lose its title page. "I'll meet you at lunchtime." I reasoned that by agreeing to meet Charles for lunch, it would get them out of the shop, stop the wanton destruction of the books and give me some time to think.

"Splendid," Charles smiled. "See you outside at one o'clock." He turned and walked to the exit.

Keith leaned forward until he was inches from my nose. "Mr Irving said you followed him to bed like an obedient little puppy." He smiled, winked at me, blew me a kiss and silently withdrew from the room.

My mind was in turmoil again. Should I report this to the police? Should I go upstairs and tell Ronald Batty what was going on? I didn't know who I could trust. Because of my experiences in Northern Ireland I was deeply suspicious of the police. Even as a child living in Creggan, long before the Troubles had started, I'd felt frightened by the occasional policeman walking his beat with an Alsatian, a handgun and a baton hanging from his belt. What would happen if I walked into a police station and said people had threatened to implicate me in the murder of one of their colleagues?

I was born in Ireland, but my maternal grandfather was English. Frederick George Burder had been born in Kingston upon Thames in 1897, but his mother, for some reason, brought her young son to live in Derry. He went on to serve in the Royal Inniskilling Fusiliers. I was therefore biologically Anglo-Irish, but now I was suddenly feeling very Irish and very vulnerable in my grandfather's homeland.

I felt I had no choice but to meet Charles. Things had spiralled out of control that weekend. We'd all been drunk. Maybe I had been partly to blame by being overly friendly and they'd got the wrong message. Charles was clearly a wealthy and well-educated gentleman. Surely, if I honestly explained my situation to him and could convince him that I would never tell anyone about what had happened, he would just let the matter end there. I would have to find a way to appeal to his basic sense of British decency.

* * * * *

At lunchtime I met Charles outside the shop. We took a short walk and he led me into La Capannina restaurant in Romilly Street. As soon as we sat down I started to plead with him, but he was having none of it. He silenced me with a raised arm.

"Hush. The menu. What do you fancy, old boy?"

I wasn't sure I could eat anything. I gave the menu a cursory glance.

"Just soup," I said. "I don't really have the time to eat much. I need to get back to the shop as soon as possible."

"How impolite," Charles said. "I have gone to some inconvenience to be here. I offer you lunch, you might have the good grace to say nothing of gratitude, to accept my hospitality. For goodness' sake, put yourself at ease, relax and have a decent lunch. We have a busy afternoon ahead of us."

I froze, gripped with fear. "What do you mean?"

"I shall be spending some money on you, young man; or to be more accurate, investing in you. A fine young animal needs to be groomed, conditioned." He put a little piece of bread in his mouth and licked his finger. "Made presentable."

I leaned forward a little, aware of the other diners around us.

"Charles, I really need to get back to work. Please stop playing this game with me."

"Firstly," he said, "I can assure you this is no game. Secondly, it's all been arranged. You have the afternoon off. Wonderful, isn't it?" He beamed.

I had visions of receiving a note from Christina Foyle in my next pay packet. I was becoming more distressed and confused.

"How?" I asked.

"You are out assisting a client, in an indirect sort of way. There is one thing you need to know about your chosen career here in this great city. The bookselling fraternity are close-knit. By a lucky coincidence, a very close friend of mine just happens to be one of the most important, most influential men in bookselling. Not just here in London, but in the country. I will of course arrange an introduction, and if you play your cards right your career could take off in ways you can't imagine. You have no idea how fortunate you are, the opportunity you are being given."

My situation was becoming more surreal than ever. Here I was having lunch with the man who'd raped me, the man who was blackmailing me and who had threatened me, and he was telling me how fortunate I was. During the rest of the lunch, I continued to try to reason with him but to no avail. Finally, I said, "What do I have to do to get out of this and make it stop?"

"That's just the thing, you see. As with some bad insurance policies, you don't have a get-out clause."

I had never felt so trapped, so cornered, so helpless or desperate. I decided to try one last drastic offer to solve the problem.

"Look, Charles," I said in utter desperation, "let's go to your place for the rest of the afternoon, just me and you. I'll do anything you want. Anything. We'll call it quits. I promise I will never mention this to anyone. Ever. Let's do it, let's go now." I put my hand on top of his.

He delicately moved his hand away, glancing around to see if anyone had noticed.

"Well, well," he said, "that's quite an offer. The best I've had this week without having to pay for it." He sat back in his chair and dabbed the corner of his mouth with a napkin.

"To be brutally honest, Anthony, you're not even my type. You're about five years too old for me. My tastes run to the younger boy. Don't get me wrong, you are a very handsome young man. They will be fighting over you."

"Who are they?" I asked.

He brushed back his hair with his hand.

"Friends, clients, associates: men of means. This weekend you are going to be elevated in society. You will have the privilege of associating with your elders and betters."

"Why did you even pick me up, why did you do that?"

Charles's expression completely changed, as if a mask had slipped.

"Last week was a difficult week for me, I had received some bad news. I was drowning my sorrows when you were offered to me in a pub, like a dodgy watch or a stolen coat. So, I decided to have you. You were… a distraction. But also, because you were different. Most of them come from Scotland or the North of England. They run around London like rats: hungry, homeless and horny. They'll do anything for money. The little bastards are sewer bred and gutter educated, but this is exactly what makes them so attractive to some of my friends, who have a taste for rough trade."

I was taken aback by his honesty and his contempt, and I felt worthless and even more used than before for having offered myself to him.

"But I'm not rough trade. OK, I come from a working-class background, but even worse for your friends, I'm Irish. I'm not homeless, I work in a bookshop. I'm not desperate for money."

Charles smiled sarcastically. "You looked pretty desperate last Saturday night."

I ignored this. "Your associates will want nothing to do with me," I argued, feeling as if I was clinging to the edge of a cliff.

"Don't kid yourself," he replied. "You're just rough trade with a few O levels. But you have a soft centre and a nice back story. The troubled youth from the Emerald Isle. You will provide a nice contrast." He lit up a cigarette. "Tell me, did you enjoy your little visit to the abbey?"

"Yes."

"We thought you'd appreciate that. Your Irish monks were illuminating manuscripts when we were still scrabbling in the mud. You have your saints and scholars, but we have our empire builders, our entrepreneurs and our politicians. That's how we conquered the world."

He sat back, then brought his finger and thumb close together and focused on the small gap between the digits. "There is a very small and exclusive niche market for a handsome and intelligent young man like you. You have a beguiling innocence and sweetness. That's why you will be welcomed into the fold. You are going to make a lot of money. You have youth, looks, you are well read, you can hold a conversation, you have a point of view. Some people I know would like to spend time with a young man like yourself – someone intelligent and discreet who won't embarrass them at the dinner table or in polite company."

Charles reached over and gripped my wrist. "But you need to know something: you are not going to walk away from this, do you understand? This weekend you will be in one of two places. You will be at that party, making new friends, having drinks, and having a good time; or you will find yourself in a police cell having a confession kicked out of you. The choice is yours, but I promise it will be one or the other. Do you understand?"

I looked directly into his eyes and I knew he could see defeat.

"Yes," I said. "I understand."

"Beeleigh Abbey was just a little taster. Behave yourself and we will take you to wonderful places and show you amazing things. That's how it works. You make their dreams come true and in return, they'll make your dreams come true."

He sprang out of his chair so quickly he startled me. For someone so tall he could move athletically.

"Wonderful," he sang. "Now, speaking of dreams, we have some shopping to do."

As we stepped into the street he looked at my hair, which was quite long and covered my ears. "Much too scruffy," he said distastefully. "You are in need of some Italian grooming."

We walked a short distance to Tony & Dino's in Dean Street. I sat in a traditional chrome-finished chair, upholstered in red leather. The barber draped a gown around me and positioned himself behind me. "What are we doing today?" he enquired.

"Short," said Charles authoritatively, "Make him look a little younger, a little more boyish."

The barber went to work and I was soon presented for inspection.

"Wonderful," he said, "just wonderful. And now we need some clothes."

As we walked towards Piccadilly, Charles delivered a lecture on men's fashion and male grooming. He was considered one of the smartest dressers in London. In 1965 he'd even been featured in *Gentleman's Quarterly* magazine. (His celebrity status assured by that *GQ* appearance, the following year he wedded the glamorous debutante Amanda Fitzwilliam Hyde.)

We stopped at Saxone, an upmarket men's shoe shop next door to Playland, where he quickly picked out a pair of heavy Oxford brogues.

"Next, the shirt," he announced. "It's my belief that a suit is an accessory to the shirt, not the other way around. In a room full of suits, it's the shirt which sets you apart, from the type of collar to the finish of the cuffs. You'll soon see."

He took me to a shop called Turnbull & Asser on Jermyn Street. Within seconds I was being fawned over by an impeccably dressed assistant, then subjected to a 10-minute discussion about my jaw line, my complexion and the colour of my hair and eyes. Finally, Charles approved two shirts. I surprised myself by thanking him. He smiled.

"Next, the suit, for those special occasions." He smiled again. "And there will be many."

We entered Blades of Burlington Gardens. I was introduced to Charles's friend and ex-business partner, the aristocratic Mr Rupert Lycett Green, a tall rake of a man with chiselled features and eyes as fixed and staring as those of a tailor's dummy. After exchanging brief pleasantries about wives and children (Rupert was married to Candida, daughter of John Betjeman), Rupert showed Charles some suits on display. They discussed the cloth, the cuts and the geometry of tailoring. A few lengths of fabric were draped over my shoulder.

Once a fabric had been decided, Rupert and Charles discussed pockets and button details and other little touches. It was to be a classic three-piece, single-breasted suit; dark blue with a very faint pin stripe. I was measured, and it was arranged that I would call in for a fitting the following Saturday morning. Then we were off again.

In Simpsons of Piccadilly, a very large department store, I acquired a light grey suit with a faint panel window check, a pair of black trousers, a pair of cream trousers and three ties.[17] Finally, in Swan & Edgar, I was furnished with socks and underwear. When I had the temerity to ask Charles if a pair of jeans was out of the question, he offered a withering look.

---

17   The former Simpsons department store building is now home to Waterstones Piccadilly, Europe's largest bookshop.

As Charles led the way to the subterranean car park in Brewer Street, I contemplated the prospect of having to attend the party that weekend. Apprehension gnawed at my insides, sickening me.

We weaved between rows of parked cars until we stood beside a red Austin Mini. Surprisingly, and evidently with much practised agility, Charles folded his great height in behind the wheel. There were red checked blankets lying in the back seat that smelled of wet dog. We took off with some speed.

"Are you taking me home?" I asked hopefully.

"No, we're going to my place. I want to see what your new clothes look like. You can put on your own little fashion parade. And I have one more little gift for you."

I felt physically sick at the thought of having to go back to Ennismore Gardens, where I'd been attacked. I took a deep breath and tried to control my nerves. My hands began trembling. But instead of Knightsbridge, we went to Marylebone: 38 Montagu Square. Charles saw the fear and confusion in my face.

"Home," he said, "and for God's sake relax. Stop being so serious and gloomy."

Once inside a shiny black front door reminiscent of 10 Downing Street, he showed me a front bedroom to get changed in and took up position in an armchair in the living room. He told me what outfits to wear and I walked repeatedly in and out, showing off his purchases. He uttered encouraging little remarks and comments, interspersed with nods of approval.

"Now try that with the red tie," he would instruct, or "Keep on the shirt, but with the cream trousers."

He sat back deep into the chair with an air of satisfaction and crossed his legs.

"Now," he said, "I want to see you in a pair of those Y-fronts." I gave him a frown and swallowed dryly.

"Just the Y-fronts," he said.

I hesitated and he silently waved me out of the room with the back of his hand.

I then appeared before him feeling embarrassed, belittled and vulnerable.

"Turn around," he instructed.

I turned slowly and faced him again, feeling like Christ before Pilate. He unfolded his legs, knowing that I would see he was aroused. He rested his cheek on his fist. I tried to stare him down but realised that this could come across as being provocative, a kind of come-on. I submissively dropped my eyes to the floor and joined my hands protectively in front of me.

"Mmmm, tempting," he said.

He left the chair, walked over and stood behind me. I was aware once again of how tall he was and how vulnerable I was. I heard him tear open a cellophane wrapper, followed by the sound of cardboard being unfolded. I closed my eyes. Suddenly, a few drops of cold liquid fell on one side of my neck, then the other. A faintly oriental, woody fragrance met my nose. It reminded me of the smell of my rape, being similar to the aftershave I had smelled then. Charles put his nose on my neck and inhaled slowly. I shivered all over.

"Galbanum, neroli, petitgrain, bergamot," Charles whispered as if invoking ancient gods. "After a while the sensual undertones will emerge, making you smell clean and fresh. Exquisite," he sighed.

He stood in front of me and held out a little bottle. "Grey Flannel by Geoffrey Beene of New York," he revealed. "It hasn't even been commercially released here yet. No one else in our little confection of street sweets will look like you and no one else will smell like you. What do you think?"

"It smells like polish," I replied.

Charles stroked my chin.

"Philistine," he smiled. "You have so much to learn."

My humiliation complete, he stood behind me and rested his hands heavily on my shoulder. He massaged the wound on my shoulder left by Keith's bite. It hurt.

"Anthony," he warned, breathing in my ear, "I have now invested a lot of time, money and affection on you. This weekend I start making a return on that investment." He released me from his grip.

"Now," he said finally, "I have other business to attend to." He patted my backside. "Get dressed. I'll take you home."

I almost ran to the bedroom and changed.

He dropped me off at Hope House. I collected my shopping bags and the shoe box and retreated to the sanctuary of my little room. I laid out all the clothes on the bed. I thought about where I might be when I was wearing them and what I would have to do when I took them off. I walked down the corridor to the bathroom and knelt down. I said an Our Father and three Hail Marys, then vomited into the toilet.

* * * * *

That weekend I was "presented". The surroundings were plush and within earshot of Big Ben. If women had been here earlier, they had been banished. Among the men in suits and formal evening wear, there was a whole other group of guests. It seemed as if the event had been gatecrashed by a small group of teenage boys from another party. They looked to be from about 16 up to my age, and they presented themselves in varying degrees of casual, tacky or glamorous flamboyance. Denim and bright colours, silk shirts, platform shoes. They ranged in appearance from ordinary boy next door to guys pushing gender boundaries with their rouge and eyeliner. I could not understand why I had been asked to wear a suit. I was one of the young people but dressed like the older men. There was no sign of Charles Irving. I felt a pang of disappointment at the absence of any familiar face. Someone who might help me, tell me what I was supposed to do.

I was approached by a bald, bespectacled gentleman in his mid-30s who introduced himself as Stephen, no surname. He smiled.

"I must say, Anthony, you are looking very smart this evening."

"Thanks," I said nervously.

Stephen told me that some of the attendees were celebrating their first anniversaries as Members of Parliament. He leaned in close, as if imparting sensitive information. "There was a bit of a bash going on this evening, but our friends in the Monday Club have piggybacked on the occasion. And, of course, we're toasting the Head Mistress's leadership victory." Stephen talked about Westminster as if it was a large college, referring to those in the House as teachers, prefects and pupils.

I was cordially introduced to a few "First Years", one of whom was Mr Peter Morrison, MP for Chester. He looked inconvenienced by my introduction. Stephen proudly informed me that Mr Morrison was one of the first courageous backbench MPs to encourage Mrs Thatcher to stand for the Party leadership.

Stephen then politely abandoned me. I'd never felt so out of place in all my life. I didn't fit in with the suited older men and I didn't fit in with the younger denim-clad boys. I finished my vodka and ladled a large glass of punch from the bowl. I gulped it down, and then quickly chased it with a second glass. The distinctive deep bass chimes of Big Ben told me I had been here for just 45 minutes. It seemed longer.

One man, with a comment about "Irish eyes", made room on the two-seater settee that he shared with another man, and patted the space between them. I filled my glass with punch again and squeezed in.

"I'm Keith," he slurred.

We shook hands awkwardly in the confined space. "Keith who?" I asked bluntly, the drink now washing away my reticence.

"*Sir* Keith," he emphasised. "Joseph." He sounded indignant, as if I should have known who he was. Sir Keith looked a little shabby, a little schoolteacher-ish. His wiry hair was plastered down with an oily substance, and a moist film of perspiration glowed above his troubled eyes.

The predictable questioning began, followed by the drunken compliments. When I told Sir Keith that I had turned 20 on 11 February, he remarked that he had stood down as Shadow Home Secretary on that very day, the same day that Margaret won the leadership of the Party. At this, the gentleman on the other side of me launched into a tirade of friendly abuse at Sir Keith for not having had the balls to stand for election himself.

"You could have been Party leader, you bloody fool."

There was light applause from a few gentlemen standing close by, one of whom declared that he had not fought in the war to see a bloody woman lead the Party.

"Well, she was the leader of last resort," his companion offered. "None of the other possible contenders would stand against Heath, silly buggers."

I had no idea what anyone was talking about, but I made a half-hearted attempt to engage Sir Keith in a conversation on a personal level.

"What do you do now?" I asked.

"I am Shadow Minister with Responsibility for Policy Information and Research," he declared.

"Shadow Minister for Bollocks," someone shouted.

"What do *you* do, young man?" Sir Keith asked.

One of the three men who had now moved to behind the settee butted in: "Can't see him having the energy to do a day job as well."

I excused myself, saying I needed another drink, and prised myself out of the settee. I filled my glass with more punch. Another boy arrived at the drinks table and gave me a white tablet to take. He then lined up several glasses, grabbed a bottle of champagne from an ice bucket and carelessly poured the drink across the glasses, which fizzed and overflowed, much to his delight. After a short while I felt stunned, as if I had been hit on the back of the head with a cosmic baseball bat. I then felt mellow ripples undulate through my body, in a stream of intoxicated blood. I turned and defiantly faced the room, as if I were about to give a speech at a wedding reception.

A fresh wave of cigar lighting had commenced, seeming to bond the three or four small groups in the room closer together, creating a strange kind of compacted intimacy. I was summoned to the settee again by Sir Keith and squeezed in once more. The other gentleman was now unconscious.

The other boys had by now settled down, some sitting on gentlemen's knees, some sitting on the floor by the chairs. I was taken aback when the boys starting kissing some of the men, in full view of the others. The drunken rowdiness was now becoming sexually charged as inhibitions faded and the men and boys became more intimate. The kissing became more passionate and the boys started to undress, or to be undressed by the men. One man knelt in front of one of the boys, undid the boy's jeans and pulled them down, followed by his underpants, and started performing oral sex on the boy. The men who were standing moved closer for a better view. They were shouting obscenities and instructions to the active participants. As drunk as I was, I could not believe what I was witnessing.

Then the party games started. Four of the boys in various states of undress knelt in a row. Men would fill their own mouths with different drinks and then let it flow into the open mouths of the boys. One man approached the boys with a bottle of champagne and filled their mouths to overflowing. Men took turns approaching the boys for oral sex. The boys were then directed to perform various sex acts on each other, while some of those observing masturbated.

Sir Keith was clearly becoming aroused as he watched these activities. He started kissing my cheek and licking my ear.

"You smell wonderful," he whispered.

The three men standing behind our settee started to jeer and offer encouragement. Sir Keith put his hand between my legs and started feeling me.

"I'm sorry I missed your birthday," he slurred. "Perhaps I could blow out your birthday candle."

One of the observers behind slapped him on the back. The others egged him on whilst applauding wildly. I closed my eyes in drunken abject humiliation as Sir Keith fumbled with my zip. When I opened my eyes I saw that some of the men with the boys were now also in various states of undress and a tableau of sexual frenzy was unfolding in front of my eyes. Every time I shut my eyes tightly, the noise in the room seemed to amplify to the point of being painful, and my stomach turned in response to the whirling nausea in my head.

I opened my eyes again and suddenly the noise became a muffled drone, as if my head had just been submerged under-water. I looked into the distance and my eyes fixed on a man. He stood silent and motionless behind the wild animated antics of the others. He was staring straight at me, seemingly oblivious to all around him. The expression on his face was intense but ambivalent. He could have been looking at me sympathetically, reading my anguish; alternatively, he could have been gazing with envy, wishing that it was he who was sitting beside me.[18]

Sir Keith looked into my face with drooping tired eyes. But if I thought I was about to get some respite from this madness I was mistaken. Two of the men suddenly came from behind the settee and took me by the arms, lifting me out of the seat. One of them roughly pulled off my jacket, while the other removed my tie. They forced me into a kneeling position, and one of the men undid his zipper. I closed my eyes. I was actually worried my new clothes would get stained or torn. Suddenly, a scuffle broke out and the man was pushed violently to one side. Mr Peter Morrison, the 'first year' I'd met earlier, stood before me. I was hoisted to my feet and directed towards a door, to protestations from Sir Keith and some of the others.

"Fuck off," Mr Morrison advised them. "He's booked. This one's mine."

He led me out into cold darkness and then into a bedroom. The door was closed and Mr Morrison laid me on the bed. I felt the rest of my clothes being removed and then his head was between my legs. After some time, when Mr Morrison had exhausted himself on me, the door opened.

"Three?" someone asked.

"Of course," replied Mr Morrison, with the satisfaction of one who slides his leftovers to a subordinate.

I awoke some time later. The room was in darkness. I was freezing, shivering uncontrollably and entangled in arms. Easing myself up a little, I carefully lifted the limbs from around me and

---

18   Two weeks later I would be introduced to this 52-year-old man. Like Sir Keith, he was a knight of the realm and his name was Sir Michael Havers, MP for Wimbledon. He had been appointed Shadow Attorney General on 18 February.

reached down and felt a blanket. I pulled it up and cocooned myself it in. After a few moments, listening to the breathing on either side of me, I fell asleep.

CHAPTER 8

Playland

Charles Hornby had arranged for me to meet my third client, a member of the House of Lords no less. I was picked up outside Westminster, where I had given him a blow job in the back seat of a chauffeur-driven car. Lord Back-Seat offered a polite handshake and a warm smile, before running his fingers through his hair as he offered instruction and encouragement. I was then dropped off in Coventry Street.[19] Keith greeted me by the railings outside the entrance of Playland.

"Follow me, mate," he said, "I want to show you something."

He led me through the crowd, along one of the aisles between the maniacal machines to the back of the building. He gestured to a concealed spiral staircase in the corner of the building.

"After you," he offered.

I anxiously made the long climb, up through five storeys. Keith said how ironic it was that Playland was built on consecrated ground.

---

19 Apart from being a yellow property on the Monopoly board, Coventry Street has form. In the late 1800s, Charles Hirsch, a French bookseller, sold expensive pornography from under the counter. Oscar Wilde was a customer. In 1925 *John Bull* magazine professed to being outraged by "a well-known tea shop and public house in Coventry Street where painted and scented boys congregate every day without molestation of any kind… sitting with their vanity bags and their high-heeled shoes, calling themselves by endearing names and looking out for patrons.""London," the magazine trumpeted, has become "a Modern Gomorrah" filled with "rouged rogues."

In fact, he told me, Playland was built inside the remaining shell of a partially demolished St. Peter's church. New false-panelled walls covered the original old stone walls. Finally, we reached a small door. I hesitated for a moment and was pushed out onto the roof. I braced myself against a cold breeze as we clambered over various obstacles to the edge. Keith placed a hand on my shoulder. The view was amazing. We looked across pools of light radiating out into the night, the domes and spires and chimneys of the city. The twinkling lights of the capital peppered the base of a charcoal sky.

"What do you see, my son?"

"The Dilly."

"Nah, beyond that."

"The city. The sky."

"Getting close. What you're looking at is opportunity. Possibilities. The sky's the limit."

He stood behind me and grabbed my arms and stepped with me onto a ledge.

"Jesus, Keith. What are you doing?" I felt panic grip me.

He manoeuvred himself close beside me. Leaned into me. I smelt that aftershave again.

"Work with us," he said firmly but quietly.

I turned my head and looked directly into his eyes. He looked dangerous.

"Cooperate. Do what we tell you."

I thought about the bite mark he had left on my shoulder.

"I'll show you the ropes. I'll show you things you won't fucking believe. I'll teach you things."

He put an arm across my shoulder and forced me to lean forward, looking directly down onto the street.

"Look at them," he sneered, nodding at the hordes of people milling about the street. "Fucking rats."

He suddenly jumped back and I followed him onto the roof.
I realised I'd been holding my breath and as I stepped forward I
tripped, gasped and fell. Keith grabbed the lapels of my coat and
effortlessly lifted me onto my feet. Keith Hunter may not have
been tall but he was as strong as an ox.

"Charlie Hornby's fucked," Keith said, turning to look over
the city.

I was taken aback.

"What?"

He ignored me.

"Let's go back down," he said. "There are some people I'd
like you to meet."

There was a travel agency on the first floor above the arcade.
On the same floor, in a couple of rooms at the back of the
building, seemed to be the arcade's administration, finance and
"personnel" functions. One room was for "entertaining private
guests" and other undisclosed purposes. My first impression was
that if the arcade was not owned or leased by elements of the
London underworld, they certainly had a stake in the place.

Keith directed me into one of these rooms. I was made to
stand to attention by a wall at the back of the office. Keith took
a seat beside a drinks cabinet and I was joined at the wall by a
man known as the Fruit Machine, an 18-stone minder with dark
shoulder-length hair. He was called the Fruit Machine because
he was mechanical in his movements, was unquestioning and
functioned with an automated efficiency and ruthlessness when
dealing with "personnel" problems. The Fruit Machine was
also gay and worked in the arcade, so it really was an inspired
choice of name.

I learned a lot about Fruit in the following weeks. He looked
about 35, but I later learned that he was much younger. He'd
been associated with the Richardson gang in 1964 when he

was 17 and became the boyfriend of one of the gang members. Eddie Richardson ran a fruit machine business as a front for other endeavours, so perhaps the name was given then. When the Richardson gang, also known as the Torture Gang, was arrested in 1966, Fruit went to work for the Krays. He became one of Ronnie's select stable of rent boys, who were offered to politicians and celebrities as "entertainment". He'd progressed to doing some freelance work in "security", finally ending up in Playland. One of the perks of the job was that he had the pick of any of the arcade's boys he fancied.

A few gentlemen seated in front of a large desk were having a discussion about one of their former associates, Jimmy Humphreys. Jimmy had been extradited from Amsterdam and given an eight-year sentence in April the previous year for a number of offences, some involving violence. His first anniversary inside was six weeks away. Whilst in prison, Jimmy was apparently singing like a canary. However, most of those being implicated in his statements were police officers. A number had been arrested and charged. When Jimmy's flat in Dean Street had been raided in 1973, the police had found literally tons of pornographic material and a number of his personal diaries. The men in the room were speculating as to what financial transactions might be recorded and who might be named in the diaries: politicians, businessmen, people of position. The man behind the desk, Mr Fisher, or the Fish as I subsequently heard him called, cautioned that the men's smiles might soon be "on the other side of your fucking faces", given the business they'd conducted with Jimmy in the past.

I was summoned forward to the desk. I swallowed apprehensively, my throat dry. On a table by a window were a couple of knives, batons, knuckledusters, a pair of handcuffs, a selection of pornographic magazines and a couple of large, realistically shaped dildos. I felt afraid, vulnerable, sick. I was aware the Fruit Machine was directly behind me.

I was welcomed into the Firm and into our mutually beneficial business arrangement. Keith had assured Mr Fisher that I was potentially a valuable asset, but that I had a lot to learn about the business. One of the men seated by the desk eyed me from head to toe. "He's a bit long in the tooth, if you ask me."

"Yeah," another added. "He couldn't compete with the teenagers."

"Charlie and I are just breaking him in," said Keith. "We are considering our options. Charlie's been preparing him to work upmarket. He doesn't want him working the arcade. What we have here, lads, is a little bit of class, a little bit of culture. Charlie is making plans, or so he thinks."

"I just wanna clarify a couple of things," the boss said, sounding more Sid James than Vito Corleone. He looked between me and Keith while speaking. "I don't know what sorta crap Charlie Hornby is putting into your heads, but just to be clear, you and our young friend here work for me, not him. I'll decide who works the arcade. If he wants us to sublet our merchandise, that's fine – we can come to an arrangement or something. We can discuss the matter – but, to be frank, I think Charlie has enough fucking things to be concerned about."

Keith nodded in silent obedience.

"Charlie's just a fucking punter, a client. It's not like he's a business partner." I suddenly recognised the man who was now speaking. He'd been sitting with Charles Hornby in the Golden Lion pub the night I was introduced to him. A man in his early 40s, his name was Malcolm Raywood, aka Tony The Butcher. I would get to see quite a lot of Malcolm. He just loved that the Playland boys called him The Butcher. He thought, in a Chicago gangster kind of way, that the name conferred a degree of menace on him and gave him more credibility in the presence of the Fruit Machine. In reality, Malcolm was a simple thug who was only called The Butcher because he lived in a flat above Eatmore butchers (or, as one Playland wit called it, Eatme butchers) in Garratt Lane, Earlsfield, a predominantly Asian area of South London.

Malcolm stood up and leaned against the wall by the table. He picked up one of the dildos and slapped it menacingly into the palm of his hand a few times, as if playing with a truncheon.

"It was us what found you," he said, looking directly at me.

"Actually, it was me who recruited him," corrected Keith.

"Yeah, but it was Charlie who fucked him," Malcolm laughed.

The boss waved his hand.

"I don't care who found or fucked him, it don't matter. He's in this office now and he works for me. Clear?"

Everyone nodded. The boss looked over my shoulder and gestured to the Fruit Machine. I was pulled violently backwards, dragged over to one of the walls and pinned against it with an elbow across my throat. I winced as Fruit suddenly made a gripping movement towards my crotch, but stopped short, then gently started feeling me up.

Malcolm walked over with the dildo and slowly slid the head into my mouth.

"Are we clear about how things work around here?" Mr Fisher asked. I nodded my head as best I could.

"That's good, Pretty Boy," Malcolm said, silkily.

Fruit pouted his lips and blew me a little kiss, then released me. My eyes were brimming with tears, partly from being choked, partly from fear.

"Off you go, Pretty Boy." Malcolm squeezed my arse.

As I left the room I looked over at Keith, thinking what a bastard he was. This was all his fault. He winked at me. Across the hall, a door was ajar and I could see a couple of ladies sitting at a table sorting out piles of money.

* * * * *

I walked into the dark chill air and gripped the railings outside the arcade to stop myself shaking. I spat the taste of rubber from my mouth. Someone had followed me out and I sensed him standing behind me. He asked me if I was looking for business. "Go fuck yourself," I shouted at him.

Someone else behind me laughed loudly. It was a boy in his late teens. I walked away, and saw the youth follow me. I actually recognised him. He was one of the boys I'd noticed looking at me the first time I went into Playland.

"Want to go for a bite to eat?" he asked.

"OK."

At an American hamburger restaurant in nearby Panton Street he introduced himself as Damian McKenna. Damie was from Glasgow, 17 years old and was nearly as tall as me, but skinny as a rake. He had a mop of poker-straight fair hair with blond highlights, which swept down over his forehead and covered an eye. He continually and gracefully ran his fingers through the blond streaks, brushing the hair back, but within seconds it was down over the eye again. A small gold earring pierced his left ear. Damie had toned down the hard-core glam look of some of the other boys and created a softer androgynous look. He was pioneering and prefiguring what would become the New Romantic look as adopted by Visage, Spandau Ballet and Duran Duran. Damie was confident, flamboyant, good looking and streetwise beyond his years.

Leaving behind two older brothers, an older sister, an alcoholic father and a dead mother in Glasgow in late 1973, Damie arrived at Euston station, 15 years old, homeless and penniless. He couldn't believe his luck when he was offered a bed for the night within minutes of his arrival. The kindly gentleman who picked him up was called Roger Gleaves. Roger ran a network of hostels for homeless boys in the capital. He had established a number of charitable organisations and had given them names with either religious or paramilitary connotations, such as *The Old Catholic Church Community Services Department* and *The Voluntary Services Corps.*

That first night Damie was taken to a hostel on Branksome Road in Brixton, where he spent the night in bed with the 41-year-old Roger. Damie was gay and this was not the first time he'd used his body to get what he wanted. He had been selling himself to men for sex in Glasgow since he was 13, but he knew it was time to leave Scotland when his drunken father suggested Damie replace his mother in the marital bed.

It didn't take Damie long to find out that he was one of dozens of boys and young men that Roger was abusing. Roger's appetite was prolific and insatiable: he was having sex with up to four boys a day. Homeless, hungry and penniless, they were doing what Roger wanted either through desperation, blackmail or the threat of violence. When anyone stepped out of line, lied about anything or held back money, the violence was immediate and explosive. Many of the wardens who managed his hostels in places like Lambeth, Hackney and Islington were also interested in boys, of which there was an unlimited supply.

I told Damie about my troubles and about *the* Troubles. An hour or so passed quickly as I recounted everything that'd happened to me in London. Damie couldn't offer any solutions but he warned me to do as I was told until we could figure out what my options were. He couldn't believe some of the stories I told him about Derry.

"Shit," he said, "you were dodging bullets in Derry, while I was dodging sperm in Glasgow."

I laughed loudly and genuinely for the first time since I'd arrived in London. We were having a great craic, but then Damie announced rather suddenly it was time for him to go to work. He said if he wanted to eat the next day, he had to work tonight. This surprised me because he'd told me earlier about the sort of money he was making, so I asked him what on earth he spent it on.

"I blow it as soon as I get it – on drugs, clothes, LPs, drinking, clubbing." He pointed his finger in the direction of the Dilly. "And I throw away a fortune in Playland."

It seemed that the money reminded him of how he'd earned it and he couldn't wait to get rid of it. I knew the feeling.

"Look, I have money, let's go for a drink," I offered. "Take a night off."

So, we headed into Soho and got drunk in the Lion. Damie then suggested we go to a place called The Regency Club in Great Newport Street. It was actually a pub, but they now charged £1 for life membership and a 25p admission charge (50p at weekends). The drink was also expensive: 40p for a bottle of beer and 25p for a Coke. Damie had neglected to tell me that the Club was exclusively gay. I may have blended in well enough with the other customers, but I didn't feel entirely comfortable, either because of what I was wearing or because of what I was thinking.

* * * * *

And so began my career in queer. During the evenings when I had to report to Playland, I felt like a schoolboy who had to do seven or eight hours of obscene detention every night. In the beginning I felt so angry, so frustrated and yet utterly helpless. I cursed the Firm under my breath, I hated the hold they had over me. I despised every one of the bastards for putting me through this. The wolves would circle in the arcade, before one would approach me and ask the inevitable question. I'd then have to get a member of the Firm to sanction the transaction and they'd take the introductory fee, before I would leave with the punter to go… God knows where. I was literally driven to drink and to drugs – provided by a punter on arrival at their home or a hotel where they might be staying. The alcohol and the psychoactive substances helped me make it through each torturous fucking night. It's been said that you can get used to anything. Speaking from experience, I'd say this is true. In Derry it was constant riots, army checkpoints, barricades, bombs, bullets and death. Survival depends on acceptance of a situation and playing down how bad things really are. It's the same with sexual abuse. Repetition and acceptance of abuse normalises it and renderers it tolerable. Adapt, endure and survive. It's not so much about evolution, it's a kind of devolution; you become something a little less human. My inverse transfiguration took me from anger to acceptance, to apathy, to numbness.

I was now spending so many evenings in Playland that I assumed that the plans for me to work exclusively upmarket had been shelved. The place was even starting to feel like a home. Maybe they had decided I wasn't so sophisticated after all. When I asked Keith what had happened to Charles's ambitious plans for me, he told me not to worry about Charlie, that he was busy with other matters. He told me to be patient, that I was serving my apprenticeship. "This is on-the-job training," he shouted over the noise. He even suggested that I should try recruiting some new boys myself, as someone my age would probably do better than the Firm's old hands.

Like most of the arcades in central London, Playland was staffed mainly by Asians who made a half-hearted attempt to supervise the more boisterous teenagers, mopped up the odd spill and swept up fag butts. They wanted nothing to do with me. Instead, I'd nod at familiar faces among the pinball junkies, a couple of sequined glam rockers and the denim-clad juvenile rent.

Meanwhile, the Firm's men would continually scan the arcade, eyeing up the prospects for new rent, nodding in the direction of this boy or that. They would fill their pockets with 2p and 1p coins from the cash desk or the automatic coin dispensers, then give the coins to the youngsters to play the machines. They'd stand behind them, cheering them on, patting their backs, putting an arm around a shoulder or a waist, praising their skills and dexterity on the nudger buttons and levers. After a few free goes on the machines, a bit of friendly banter, the men would offer them a drink across the street in the Coffee House, and there suss them out. Had they a place to stay, would they like to go for a meal? If they struck it lucky and a boy went off with them, sex would be inevitable, whether consensual or not. The boy would be offered a chance to earn a lot of money, and would be passed around Firm members who were interested, before being offered to punters at large.

Playland's illuminations were accompanied by a cacophony of sounds: rattles, bleeps, booms and constant shouting. The newest machines had introduced digital scoring and a novel invention – the video game – complete with electronic sounds. As well as the pinball tables and the one-armed bandits, there were Air Hockey tables, Pong, the table tennis video game, the

Periscope machine and, just inside the Coventry Street entrance, a racing car with state-of-the-art graphics on the TV screen above the steering wheel. Playland even had a couple of rifle ranges. The noise was overwhelming. In the melee, it was easy for punters who knew what they were doing to enter alone and leave accompanied.

Some punters preferred to wait at the bottom of the steps in Great Windmill Street rather than go into Playland. A member of the Firm would approach them, go back into the arcade and bring out a boy. A price would be agreed and the punter would hail a taxi and depart.

CHAPTER 9

The Dilly

On Sunday afternoons, I went to the only part of London that I felt I knew: Piccadilly Circus. What I liked about the Dilly was that it seemed to have so many escape routes, in all directions, above and below ground. Escape was an illusion, but the plaza and its environs was a good place to indulge the fantasy of freedom. I soon got to know every inch of the area, every doorway, every glittering sign – the arches, the little alleyways, steps that descended into dodgy-looking basements, like the bar beneath Snow's Public House. It was a kind of hunting ground and boys like me were the prey, we were trapped.

There were all sorts of characters at Piccadilly Circus. Hungry desperadoes, leather-clad dreamers, homeless runaways, chain-smoking chancers. Anyone with a secret or story to tell could be found there. And we were all united by the desire to escape our past.

That sense of escapism ran deep and Damie told me that more often than not rent boys used nicknames. These names were usually selected to create a new identity or project a glamorous persona, which was often wildly at odds with the sad, desperate reality of their lives. Damie's Dilly name was Tiger. Two outrageous 20-something Dilly queens called Ruby Tuesday and Lady Penelope were in fact Frank and Miles, who lived in a squat in Hackney. Frank had been an alcoholic plumber from Manchester and Miles was a farmer's son from South Yorkshire. Both gay, they found each other in London and discovered Piccadilly Circus as a place where they could ply an illicit trade and forget their past.

Some were christened by other boys on the streets or by a regular punter or a pimp. The boys could create an appealing back-story for themselves that might make them more marketable; it would usually feed into a punter's fantasy. Individual histories could change from week to week. Boys could become whoever they wanted to be in the Dilly.

It was a strange kind of alchemy. The boys had to turn punters' dreams into reality. For punters, it was the perfect place to lose yourself. The downside for the boys was that the lies, the duplicity and the constant danger could become too much. For some, the possibility of violence, the health risks, the permanent threat of arrest and the constant paranoia eventually meant that they ended up trusting no one, including themselves. Many became hopelessly addicted to drugs.

Where Coventry Street met Shaftesbury Avenue was the London Pavilion, a cinema, but once a popular music hall and sadly now dressed up like a whore, its beautiful features hidden behind hoardings, while gigantic neon letters glowed across the façade. The sleaze started with La Pigalle Striptease Revue Bar, with its garish light bulbs that flickered off and on. Two darkened doorways along was a sex shop, and next door to that… Playland.

Playland Amusements was not a particularly conspicuous place. It was practically invisible in daytime and in the evenings it was outgunned by the much brighter and brasher establishments on Coventry Street. The rainbow coloured sign above the Coventry Street entrance staked its claim in electrified glass tubes of bright rarefied neon gas, and beneath this the word amusements in cursive, white hot script. The entrance resembled a small shopfront, but once inside the L-shaped building turned left and the premises opened up and spread out all the way back to Great Windmill Street, where the main entrance to the arcade was actually located. When you ascended the steps and entered Playland from Great Windmill Street, you were immediately hit by the full impact of the place: the light, the noise and the crowds. It was the biggest and the best amusement arcade in the country.

Further down Coventry Street, past neighbouring twin restaurants the Aberdeen Steak House and the Texas Pancake House, in pride of place at the junction with Rupert Street, was another amusement arcade. Fun City was smaller but much more visible than Playland. It looked bright, clean and well fitted-out. That arcade soaked up a lot of trade as people made their way from Leicester Square, and many people would have considered it to be the better arcade, but as far as punters were concerned the low-key, less visible aspects of Playland were virtues, not disadvantages. It was possible to pick up rent in Fun City, but those in the know went to Fun City to play with the machines, Playland to play with the boys.

* * * * *

The Firm had taken control of me. Before long, my life had been split in half. I'd been split in half. By day I was selling books and by night I was selling my body. I was determined to make sure I remained in control of at least one half of my existence. No matter how late I got back to Hope House, I brushed my teeth and set the alarm so that I rose in time to be at work for 8:45am. No matter how I felt, no matter how dog sick or tired or hung-over I was, I made it into work.

Fortunately, by their very nature and rarity, antiquarian books are not bestsellers. I never had to deal with the big promotions for new books that went on sale in the other departments. I had my own self-contained haven of tranquillity in the busiest book shop in London. The fiction department on the ground floor was something else. Whenever I read in *The Bookseller* about the next big publishing event, such as the much-anticipated *Salem's Lot*, my heart went out to the poor sales assistants and cashiers down below.

I was therefore able to rest all day, deal with the occasional customer, take little naps and write my diary. I had started to keep a diary when I left school, just a pocket diary to record key events, activities and appointments. Now I began updating the diary two or three times a week with events I'd never thought I'd be committing to paper. Names, initials, locations – and I introduced a rather obvious code to denote the specifics of sexual activity. This was a journal that would never be published. The contents of my emerging work were pornographic and painful: dispatches from the edge of Hell, recording a descent into self-destruction. I mostly recorded events after they'd happened, but occasionally I would enter an appointment in advance. If Keith or Charles needed to contact me, they would simply phone 01-437 5660 and ask to be put through to antiquarian books. One such telephone booking for the third week in March read: *"To meet Tony Hetherington – Law? Civil Servant? Flat – Notting Hill."* A follow-up entry for this encounter records: *"2 Schoolboys with a man! St. Pauls?"*

My "handlers" asked me to leave Foyles. Keith wanted to know why I continued working there for a pittance, when I could earn more in 15 "fucking" minutes at night than I'd earn in a week.

"You'll burn yourself out," he complained. "You can't work late nights and hold down a day job. It's not possible. Plus, you're no good to anybody if you are tired all day *and* exhausted at night. Punters won't be impressed if you fall asleep on the job."

There was no way I was going to leave Foyles. I was not going to abandon my dreams and my career. The days were the longest days, confined in that large room in Foyles, but at least I was getting rest. The nights were the longest nights. Apart from 30 minutes at lunchtime, I wasn't seeing any daylight. I had the darkness of the underground and the dull dark slate sky of morning walking down Charing Cross Road to work. When I finished at the end of the day, it was dark again outside.

My routine involved being controlled and abused by night, then bookselling by day; day in, day out. I knew that if I could adapt to the routine in Derry of working amid the explosions and the killings, then I could adapt in London to the routine of working amid the sex, drink and drugs. But it was a question of how long I could survive.

* * * * *

Keith, it seemed, had listened to my comment about working upmarket. On some occasions, I was now being delivered to VIPs, or as I unfairly labelled them, Vacuous Inbred Pricks. That's when it became clear to me that not only Charles Hornby but the Firm itself numbered politicians and other people of prominence among their clientele. One evening I was told to wear a suit, shirt and tie. I was informed I'd be meeting some big-shot Parliamentarian. I'd be taken to Whitehall later that night. But before that, I was escorted to Piccadilly Circus by the Fruit Machine and pushed into a car that had pulled up to the kerb. This was unusual because the risk of being spotted by the police was great. It was safer for rent on foot, under the arches. It also gave rent more time to look into a punter's eyes and assess their psychological disposition.

I never did ascertain why the lecturer from the London School of Economics chose to drive into the pulsating heart of

Piccadilly Circus, but as we drove off to Harrow, the effects of the vodka and bennies (street name for the stimulant Benzedrine) that I'd consumed earlier had kicked in, so I couldn't care less. When we arrived at his home, I was surprised when his wife opened the front door. This will be a first, I thought, but she quietly retreated to the kitchen.

"Where?" I said matter-of-factly.

He pointed to the top of the stairs and I waited for him to lead the way.

"Oh, it's not for me, it's my son. He's in his room. First door on the right at the top."

It turned out that the lecturer and his one-time lesbian, social worker wife were a very liberal couple who'd been part of a hippy commune in 1968. Now they were "unconventional" professionals who took a very enlightened view on all things sexual. Their 18-year-old son had confided to his parents that he was sexually confused. The supportive parents, eager to help their son work through his problems, had already secured the services of a female prostitute to relieve their son of the burden of virginity and let him explore the mysteries of the female form. I was now being called upon to educate their child in the intricate chemistry and physiology of the male-on-male enterprise.

I descended from my high very quickly and felt completely inadequate and embarrassed at being party to this experiment.

"I'm really not the best person to be doing this," I said apologetically.

The situation painfully brought home to me the realisation that I was still a virgin, in the heterosexual sense of the word. Their son could very possibly be much more experienced than me, in both gender areas.

"I think he needs someone more experienced in…"

"No, you were specifically recommended for this..." His words trailed off. "He's a sensitive, intelligent boy. He likes his books and his music."

Then the last thing your son needs is another sensitive, intelligent boy, who likes his books and his music, I thought. Put another way, the last thing he needed lying in bed beside him was a tortured mirror of himself. *Who the hell recommended me for this gig?*

I tapped gently on the bedroom door and a polite muffled voice said, "Come in."

He was sitting up against the headboard of the bed, his legs folded up in front of him, reading a copy of the New Musical Express. His pale face was framed by a halo of tight curly Leo Sayer hair. Massive bell-bottom jeans spread out like the sails of a small boat, waiting to be folded. Steve Harley and Cockney Rebel were playing on the radio singing *Make Me Smile (Come Up and See Me)*. The song had entered the charts two days ahead of my birthday and I'd been hearing it playing every day, on the way to work, in a shop or cafe at lunchtime, on the way home from work. The song would become my reluctant theme song, a song that not only spoke to me, teased me and mocked me, but came to haunt me. I even heard it in my sleep. It held the number-one slot for nine weeks. With every passing day, with each new experience, each new degradation, a line of the song would take on a new significance. It was to become a musical albatross around my neck.

"Hi," I said, "I'm Tony."

"Hi," he managed. "Trevor."

Maybe you'll tarry for a while, Steve suggested.

Trevor looked puzzled at the fact that I was wearing a suit so I told him I was going to a party later. The only chair in the room was covered in clothes, so I took off my jacket and draped it over the heap of unwashed garments. I sat at the bottom of the bed. There was a silent pause. I scratched my head awkwardly.

"So, how was she?" I grinned, not knowing what else to say.
His face lit up in a broad smile.

"The hooker?"

"Yes."

"Don't know. We didn't do anything. We just talked."

The ice broke and we chatted more comfortably. Trevor
wasn't confused. He was just shy, quiet and musically talented
(violin) and gay.

I jumped from the bed and started looking through his record
collection. I lifted out a few Moody Blues LPs.

"I have all these," I said excitedly.

Trevor rolled a joint and we played different tracks from a
few Moody LPs.

We talked music, books and movies. Being here, like this, was
so normal, so ordinary. I thought about the many nights I passed
like this with my friends in Derry.

It was soon obvious that the problem in this household was
not Trevor, but his parents and the upbringing he'd been subjected to. His dad considered Trevor to be a failure in all the things
he considered important, including academia (Trevor attended
one of the "lesser" colleges in London) and sport (at which he
was useless). In short, Trevor had been a disappointment. We
talked and talked and laughed.

Later, I forced myself to look at my watch. The music and
the chat had accelerated time. I'd been here for an hour and a
half. Shit. I wished I could stay another few hours and then go
home to my bed like a normal person, but I had a "gathering"
to attend, somewhere near the Houses of Parliament, and I
would be late. Tough.

"One for the road," I said, placing *Seventh Sojourn* on the turntable, resting the needle at the last track on side one. The slow duet
of the flute and the harmonium opened *Isn't Life Strange*, one of the

group's longest songs. We sat at each end of the bed and listened to the melancholy reflections of Justin Hayward and John Lodge.

"I suppose we should let my parents listen to what they've paid for," Trevor smiled.

He started moaning in simulated ecstasy and I vigorously joined in, bouncing on the bed a little for good measure. We turned up the aural passion groaning and moaning loudly, throwing in the occasional OH GOD! for good measure, whilst doubled over in restrained laughter. Then we came, musically, loudly and enthusiastically.

We jumped off the bed and I grabbed my coat.

"If you really want to have sex with a boy, let me know," I offered. "I have a friend called Damie and he could use the money. But it would be a lot better if you just get out and meet a real boyfriend."

"I will," he promised.

He hugged me and said thanks.

Downstairs, dad was waiting impatiently by the front door, car keys in hand. He had a look of concern on his face and he fidgeted nervously with the car keys.

"Well?" He enquired anxiously.

I shook my head as if delivering news of a terminal illness.

"Gay as Tunisian ceramic," I said authoritatively.

I drifted past him, my head still high in the cumulus of marijuana. As he drove me back to Playland, he started feeling my leg and asked if I wanted to go for a drink with him. I told him I had a prior engagement and he'd have to make an appointment.

"Who recommended me?" I asked.

Dad shrugged his shoulders, eyes fixed on the road ahead.

"Just friends in low places."

From Playland, having downed another couple of pills with a Coke, I was transported to my next appointment, humming *Isn't Life Strange*.

* * * * *

I was late for the little get-together in Whitehall and was greeted with disapproving looks from some of those present. The host put a drink in my hand and I was introduced. The last person I was presented to was sitting in an oxblood leather Monks Chesterfield club chair. It was the man I had seen staring at me at the awful Monday Club party. I was pointedly and rather awkwardly left standing beside him. His name was Sir Michael Havers MP, QC, Shadow Attorney General. It was clear I was to be his assigned companion for the evening. He patted the broad rounded arm of the chair and motioned for me to sit down. Sir Michael threw me a hint of a smile. He rested back into the chair, smoking a large cigar and nursing a large whiskey.

The atmosphere was convivial and friendly, very civilised compared to the last occasion when the Honourable Mr Havers had watched silently from the shadows whilst I was being sexually abused a few weeks earlier. I had learned so much about London in the meantime and had lost so much of myself.

From their reminiscences, it was clear most of the men had been in the armed forces at one time or another, men like Major John Gouriet. I was told the others present included a couple of businessmen, politicians and television celebrities, although there was just one face I recognised from TV. Also present were a couple of Playland's finest and most experienced pinball players, boys in their late teens or early 20s. I was surprised to see that, like me, they were smartly dressed. They exuded a confident charm and indifference, which at times almost bordered on contempt for their clients, as they played with them and insulted them in smutty good humour. I was just about beginning to feel that I could pass myself off confidently when I was with one client; but not in these circumstances, not in a group. I felt nervous and inadequate, especially in the company of these masters of the Dilly. The rent made a point of conspicuously scanning me from the feet up and pouting their lips and fluttering their eyelashes at me. Little giggles had followed me to my seat.

I was not the only one who looked and felt uncomfortable. One of the men, an MP called David Mitchell, was clearly uneasy about the presence of the Dilly boys. He threw them disapproving looks, and in return he was singled out for some particularly bitchy vitriol that only streetwise rent could dispense with such ease and devastating effect. David came across as a very warm and genuine man and I thought I detected a note of sympathy towards me for the company I was keeping, though whether that meant the men or the rent boys or both, I didn't know. David said he'd seen me at the first party I'd attended, but that he'd left early. He held my hand for a beat longer than was necessary, and looking me straight in the eyes he said, "Sorry." All I could do was nod my head a little in acceptance. It's easy to detect little sparks of decency in dark places. David seemed like a decent man.

A particularly hot topic of conversation during the evening was the forthcoming referendum to let the British public decide if the country should remain within the EEC. Another matter which provoked some debate was the death the previous Thursday, of a Labour MP. There was talk of a by-election and speculation as to the chances of a Tory taking the seat.[20]

A door in a far wall opened and a silver-haired elderly man entered the room. His hair was tousled, his shirt was wrinkled and his eyes looked tired and bleary.

20　The Labour MP William Hamling died on 20 March 1975. Peter Bottomley, a Conservative candidate, was subsequently elected MP for Woolwich West at the by-election in June that year. That same month, the country voted by a large majority (67.2%) to remain in the EEC.

"I dozed off," he laughed, tucking his shirt into his trousers and pulling up his zipper.

Another man passed out of the room through the same door, drink in hand. He left the door ajar and after a short while Sir Michael tapped my back.

"Shall we?" he said. He stood up and I followed him out. As we passed an open door I glanced in. The other man was sitting in a chair, eyes closed, drink in hand. His trousers and underpants were around his ankles and he was being masturbated by a boy who was kneeling in front of him. The boy turned around. He had a black eye and a cut on his lip. It was Damie. He looked surprised but his face lit up like a Christmas tree. He gave me a wide-eyed grin followed by a thumbs-up sign, then continued with the task in hand. Sir Michael had also seen what I'd seen.

Inside the office at the end of the corridor, Sir Michael stood me against a wall and knelt down in front of me. Without saying a word, he undid my belt and zip and proceeded to give me a blow job. I closed my eyes. This was starting to become a familiar situation. But there were some things I was never ever going to get used to.

* * * * *

I wasn't always expected to get straight down to business with clients. One man in particular was clearly looking for something more complex from me. On a few occasions the Firm would permit Charles to arrange for me to meet one of his associates. He'd made it sound as though this client would be somebody a little different. I was assured we'd get on well, that we'd have so much in common: same interests, so much to talk about. But potential areas of commonality were not immediately apparent the first time I saw him. For a start, Simon was 22 years older than me, a lot taller, heavier and, as I was to learn later, wealthier – much wealthier. I may have looked passably smart in the clothes I'd been told to wear, but Simon looked a lot smarter in his gray, double-breasted suit, silk handkerchief flowering from the pocket, gold cuff-links adorning his crisp shirt.

I had got changed after work and been picked up outside Biddy Mulligan's pub on the Kilburn High Road, while the afternoon light was still dull and hazy, filtering through angry ebony clouds. It was dark by the time I was dropped off outside a red brick block of flats in Notting Hill. Basil, the driver, told me he'd collect me in about an hour's time.

Simon smiled enthusiastically and shook my hand firmly. I felt the nervous energy of a job interview flutter in the stomach. Simon patted my shoulder reassuringly as I sat down on the settee. He poured drinks and I made sure he didn't see me swallow the dexies, which I washed down with the vodka. A moment later I handed him the empty glass and he was taken aback by my insult to the social etiquette of a first meeting.

"My, my," were his only words as he refilled my glass.

As he told me his story, I realised they had been right. We did have a lot in common, at least as far as books were concerned. Simon was the Director of Retail for WH Smith. He had been appointed to the board the previous year. When I told him my story, he was clearly interested, intrigued even. By the time I'd told him I was now working for Foyles, he'd become quite animated by my back-story. As if to empathise with where I currently was in my lowly career, he told me he had to work his way up the ranks with WH Smith. It had taken him 17 years to get to where he was now; starting off as a trainee manager; buying stationery and based in a dreary warehouse in Sheffield. He compared working in the North of England to being like Stanley in Africa and the hardships of being so far away from civilisation. As much as he tried, it was difficult for him to draw parallels between our experiences. Me: St Joseph's Boys' School in Creggan, APCK Bookshop in the city centre and now Foyles. Him: Eton, New College Oxford, national service with the Grenadier Guards, followed by a trainee management position.

We chatted about books and bookselling for ages, which suited me just fine, as the drugs and vodka made me more talkative and lowered my inhibitions. After some time, Simon moved a little closer to me on the settee.

"I'm so glad we met, Anthony," he said. "They told me that I *simply* must meet the book boy. And here you are." The smile melted and he looked serious. "May I kiss you?" he asked politely.

"If you have to," I replied. "I mean, if you want to, that is."

I remembered the warnings I'd been given in the upstairs office in Playland: "One step out of line, pretty boy, and you won't be pretty no more. Remember your manners. Be polite, do whatever you're asked to do. Keep everybody happy. It's not a lot to ask... is it, Pretty Boy?" I had nodded my head in agreement. It seemed I had acquired a new name.

Simon kissed me on the cheek, then the lips. I removed myself mentally from the situation, becoming an observer rather than a participant as Pretty Boy and Simon got more intimately acquainted. They went quietly to the bedroom and undressed. They both lay on the bed. More kissing. The younger man's head was directed downwards. Thank God for vodka and dextroamphetamine. They take you so high when you have to sink so low.

* * * * *

Soon I began meeting Simon two or three times a week. Sometimes all he wanted to do was talk; an activity I was more than happy to accommodate. Usually, I'd be delivered by Basil or another Firm member, but sometimes I'd be told to make my own way to whatever rendezvous location had been selected for us, often a discreet, anonymous-looking flat. He appeared to have taken something of a shine to me. I had the distinct impression he was trying to sweep me off my feet and dazzle me by telling me about some of his famous friends. He told me that Richard Burton and Elizabeth Taylor were very good friends of his. I didn't believe him until one evening in Ennismore Gardens he showed me the photographs of himself and his wife on board the *Kalizma*, Burton's yacht. Sure enough, there was Simon, all smiles, standing between Burton and Taylor, arms around the couple's waists; Simon sitting at a table with Burton, more smiles, glasses raised; Simon and his wife at Taylor's 40th birthday party in Budapest. Then he showed me more photos of himself with other guests at the party: Princess Grace, Ringo Starr, David Niven, Susannah York, Michael Caine and Stephen Spender. Jesus Christ! I was impressed. This big birthday party had been just three years ago.

Simon admitted that the friendship with the Burtons came about through his wife, Sheran. Sheran Cazalet and Elizabeth Taylor had been friends since they were little girls. The Cazalets had other, more regal connections. Sheran's father, Peter, was the Queen Mother's horse trainer. Out came old wedding photos – though not that old: Simon told me he'd only been married for seven years. The bride seemed to be struggling to smile and the groom looked more uncomfortable than any man I'd ever seen with a new bride on his arm. The couple radiated restrained dread, like a pair of reluctant impostors making their way to the gallows.

There was the Queen Mother and her daughter, Princess Margaret, at the wedding. And there was Richard Burton again, sporting a top hat, and Taylor with her 33.19 carat diamond ring. Burton had told Simon he presented the ring to Elizabeth on the *Kalizma* when it was moored on the River Thames in May, just a month before Simon's wedding in 1968. Noel Coward and John Betjeman were among other notables in the wedding photos. I pointed to another face that looked familiar in the wedding party.

"I think I know him," I said nervously.

The man looked fresh-faced and skinny to the point of being unhealthy. His frame looked artificially elongated, as if it had been distorted by some photographic mishap. It was Charles Hornby.

I waited for Simon to say something, but no comment was forthcoming. As I looked back and forth between Charles and Simon in the photograph, I was struck by a powerful resemblance between them – and tried to suppress the shock that came with the sudden realisation that Simon must be Charles Hornby's brother. The man with whom I felt most at ease, the client I could have ordinary conversations with, was the brother of the man who had viciously raped me. I convinced myself that Simon couldn't possibly behave like Charles. I paused and took a deep breath, careful not to show any emotion, determined not to think about possible answers to the questions that were racing through my mind. I had to stay calm.

Simon showed me a few more photos taken on board the *Kalizma*.

"This is us a few months after our wedding." He handed me the album. "We joined the Burtons in St Jean Cap Ferrat."

"Cap what?" I asked.

Simon gave me a surprised look.

"My ignorance of geography, dear boy, is matched only by my ignorance of sport," I giggled in an upper-class English accent.

"St Jean Cap Ferrat is in the South of France, *dear boy*. It's a favourite holiday destination for the aristocracy, movie stars, authors and other wealthy sorts," he explained. "You really must go there some time."[21]

"Oh yes," I smiled, "I really must."

"I'm being serious," he replied, running his finger along the top of my leg. "If you play your cards right, who knows?"

21   Simon told me he had once visited Somerset Maugham at the author's home; Villa Mauresque in Cap Ferrat. Later, Simon introduced me to Maugham's nephew Viscount Robin Maugham (whose father had been the Lord Chancellor of England). I was told that Robin was also a distinguished, celebrated and bestselling author (embarrassingly for a bookseller, I had never heard of him). Robin was visiting London on business to do with the publication of his latest book – a memoir. I fawned over Robin at dinner and told him he was the most famous author I had ever met. Later, in bed, it was his turn to do the fawning. Five years later and just five months before his death, I received an unexpected package. It was a copy of one of his novels, The Wrong People, and he had signed it: For Tony, with all best wishes, from Robin.

CHAPTER 10

Soho

A couple of weeks earlier I'd arranged to meet Damie at the Piccadilly Cafe in Denman Street. It was St Patrick's Day. As a special treat, Damie said he'd introduce me to his world. If Piccadilly Circus was the brightest star in the West End galaxy, then Soho was the most interesting planet. We'd agreed to dress down for the occasion, so I wore jeans, a maroon T-shirt and a black leather jacket. Damie's idea of dressing down was somewhat different from mine. He was wearing a pair of navy Perma-press double knit slacks in houndstooth check, smoothly styled with slant front pockets, big wide belt loops and hemmed cuffless bottoms. He had a small leather bag slung over his shoulder. His white silk blouse was hidden by the latest in western denim, a hip length button-front jacket with a large white fur collar.

"I thought I'd try out a new look," he said. "New casual attire."

"It doesn't work."

That was as tactful as I could manage. I thought he looked ridiculous.

For the evenings he assured me that he *really* dressed up. Had Damie dressed like this in Derry he'd have been stoned to death. I tried to play it cool but I was affronted to be seen walking beside him. After numerous backward glances from passers-by,

I promised Damie that if he ever dressed like that again in my company, I'd kill him.

Over tea and jam doughnuts, Damie told me more about his landlord, the strange Mr Gleaves. The night he was picked up from Euston Station, Damie knew exactly what the deal would be. A roof over his head in return for sex. On arrival at Branksome Road, he was given a cup of soapy tea from a vending machine and a round of stale toasted bread. He was led through a wreck of a house, barely illuminated by dim 40w light bulbs, to a room occupied by another youth. He took the vacant creaking metal-framed bed opposite his roommate.

During the night he was awakened by Roger, taken to the landlord's room and violently fucked as a down payment for his accommodation.

It was only next morning that Damie saw what a shit-hole the property actually was. Back in his own room, he asked his roommate where the bathroom was. The boy laughed and opened a wardrobe door. He pointed to a bucket, placed there by previous residents because the toilet was a squalid red brick outhouse, the door of which was hanging off the hinges, with rain leaking through the asbestos-sheeted roof. A cold-water shower had been rigged up in the adjoining shed. The two houses that formed the hostel catered for up to 20 boys and young men.

Roger took Damie through the administrative details after a breakfast of fried eggs and beans. As Damie had no employment card, Roger gave him someone else's who'd been the same age. Damie could now sign on at the Labour Exchange with his new identity. The unemployment money would of course be given to Roger, who would also receive £9 from the government for Damie's board and keep.

Roger had refashioned an RAF jacket and sown on badges and braid to give the quasi-official appearance of someone working for a benevolent youth support organisation offering shelter and salvation. Nine years earlier Roger had founded his own branch of an obscure religious sect and called it the Old Catholic Church in Great Britain. He consecrated himself Vicar General of the Order and ordained himself Bishop of Medway. He even bought bishop garments complete with mitre and staff.

His HQ in Brixton had a printing machine and he ran off headed notepaper for his various social enterprises. The London Borough authorities loved him as he enabled them to demonstrate they were addressing chronic homelessness problems on their patches. The police were glad to see him do his nightly rounds of the train stations with his mobile soup kitchens to rescue young desperadoes arriving in the capital. What the police didn't know was that Roger was running his own little criminal empire and taking a percentage of everything his residents earned, be it through theft, prostitution or legitimate work.

I told Damie more about my associates at Playland. When I mentioned Keith, he said that Roger and Keith did some work together. Roger ran his own informal employment agency and got some of his boys jobs working for various dodgy security firms across London. Keith was a customer and he employed some of Roger's workforce occasionally. Damie told me that Roger also surrounded himself with "heavies" to help with enforcement issues.

Roger had occasionally been seen on the prowl in Playland, but all the rent boys knew he was a weirdo. They'd heard stories of rape and violence at his hostels so they knew to avoid him.

"Why don't you try and find somewhere else to stay if he's that bad," I suggested.

"It's OK. I'm managing just fine. Anyway the fucker's been in jail since last year."

"What?" I said, surprised. "Roger? Why? What happened?"

"I can't really say much. Roger still has his hostel wardens and a few of his mates looking after his interests. We've been warned to keep our mouths shut."

It was the first time I'd seen the streetwise hustler look a little nervous.

"No problem," I said, "but be careful. Look after yourself."

"Always."

He gave me a mischievous wink. We finished our tea and set off on an alcohol-soaked tour of Soho.

Soho was a disreputable, squalid, smelly enclave, boxed in by Oxford Street, Charing Cross Road, Shaftesbury Avenue and Piccadilly. The buildings were rancid, rundown affairs with leaking drain-pipes and flaking paint. Old fly-posters were peeling off walls, rubbish fell from overcrowded dustbins and blew along the gutters. The streets were saturated with signs that jutted out from every shopfront, advertising adult books and magazines, strip shows, bars, cafes, and newsagents. Narrow alleyways stank of urine. The area was little more than a slum, albeit a very bohemian, risqué slum in which urban decay was the backdrop against which artists, poets, writers, gangsters and pornocrats applied their skills.

We entered Meard Street and there in all its bleakness was a dive called Macabre, which opened at 11:45am. Damie warned me we weren't going there for the pleasant surroundings, but because he got the drink at discounted prices (Damie provided discounted services to management as part of a reciprocal arrangement). After a couple of bevvies, I had to get out of the place. It was making me depressed just being there, so Damie suggested a more colourful oriental alternative. He introduced me to Chinatown and we entered the Pink Elephant in Newport Place.

In the course of our pilgrimage I was introduced to some lovely, warm, genuine, friendly habitués of the village, all real characters for whom Soho was home. Around mid-afternoon we were feeling peckish so we entered the rather bohemian Patisserie Valerie on Old Compton Street and gorged ourselves on cream cakes and chocolate éclairs, before continuing on our quest. I happened to hear somewhere on a radio news report that a group of Irish people, now being called the Guildford Four, had attended a committal hearing.

We chatted about music. Damie's current favourite was a Scottish band called Pilot. The group had had a big hit in late 1974 with a song called *Magic*, and it was still getting loads of airplay. Every so often in the weeks that followed, Damie would burst into *Ho ho ho it's magic.* I asked Damie what he thought of the Bay City Rollers, who were enjoying their first number one with *Bye Bye Baby*. His comprehensive musical assessment was that they were shite. Somewhat surprisingly, he also called them "queer bastards"! He didn't do tartan.

By late afternoon as the daylight faded, the Soho shopfronts began to glimmer in saturated reds, greens, blues and pinks, as the neon strip lights and signs transformed the monochrome tacky dreariness of daytime Soho into a wonderland of temptation and intrigue. Doors that had been closed during the day now opened for trade, their entrances modestly concealed by curtains of beads and brightly coloured ribbons. As the shadows and darkness descended on the place, the colours grew brighter. The human sleaze oozed from some of the doorways onto the streets and alleys. Every time we left one pub to go to another, the narrow streets had got busier. They were thronging with tourists, businessmen, curious elderly married couples, touts and pimps, con artists, Danny La Rue-inspired queens and solitary young men posted at various corners, scanning the rabble for passing trade.

Soho was Disneyland for grown-ups. Curious, free-spirited young people, having dispensed with their school uniforms and added a few years to their appearance with a little make-up and some faux chic, gathered from second-hand clothes shops, could easily blend in with the avant-garde milieu of the quarter.

One of Damie's regular punters managed a sex shop, and Damie touted for business for the man by handing out leaflets. In fact Damie admitted that he had been in something of a relationship with the man. It was, Damie said, "A father and son thing." If this meant what I thought it meant, I was rather shocked, as it was a "father and son thing" that Damie had fled Glasgow to escape. Through his association with the man, Damie had picked up a lot of information about the workings of the Soho porn dealers.

There were at least 60 hard-core pornography retailers in Soho, and each of the outlets had two rooms. The front room displayed the soft-core girlie magazines and the back room housed the hard-core material: books, magazines and 8mm films, including imported child pornography. The proprietors would pay off police officers to be allowed to display some of the hard-core stuff in the front rooms and to stay open later. In fact, unlike other retail outlets in London, the porn shops opened for 12 hours a day or more, seven days a week.

They were certainly in the right market-place. Soho had 39 small sex-cinemas, 16 strip clubs, 11 more sex-oriented clubs, and a dozen licensed massage parlours, as well as peep shows, clip joints, gambling dens, numerous ordinary pubs and a few good restaurants. Soho had also been home to the film industry for over 60 years and all the big film companies had offices there. One of Damie's punters worked for Paramount Pictures and had offered Damie a job as a message boy. Damie asked the man if the job would bring him into contact with movie stars. When the man laughed, Damie told him to stuff his job.

"So how hard is the hard-core?" I asked naively.

"Extreme and explicit. We're talking full colour and full detail. Group sex, straight sex, gay sex, bi sex, kiddie sex, animal sex; all the usual positions, many unusual positions; various sexual perversions involving bodily waste products; and sexual violence involving just about any object you can imagine." Damie laughed. "Kenny, my Soho daddy, taught me that pitch."

He moved towards one of the open doorways. "Here, I'll introduce you to him, I'll show you what I mean."

"No, it's OK, thanks all the same, I'm hungry."

We ended up in Pizza Express back in Dean Street. This was also the home of Dean Street Records, the specialist movie soundtrack outlet I'd ordered all my Ennio Morricone Italian import records from, when I lived in Derry. In the restaurant there was a pretty young blonde girl in her late 20s eating alone at a table opposite us. As soon as the pizzas were brought to our table, she invited herself over to join us.

Apart from the blonde hair, Marjorie was a Sandy Shaw lookalike. She was also an "actress". I naively asked her what she'd appeared in, and discovered that since the summer of 1970 Marjorie had been appearing in *Pyjama Tops*, a Paul Raymond production that was running in the Whitehall Theatre near Trafalgar Square. She had a non-speaking part as a swimmer. The "play" was set around a transparent-sided swimming pool into which nude actresses periodically plunged. I knew who Paul Raymond was. APCK bookshop in Derry ordered in a copy of one of his publications, *Men Only*, for a customer. The magazine was securely stored under the counter for him, between the pages of his *Irish Times*. Such a magazine would *never* have appeared on the shelves in Derry.

Unsurprisingly, the conversation turned to Soho, porn and gangsters. I told them about my visit to the upstairs office in Playland and the name of the man Mr Fisher had been so concerned about, Jimmy Humphreys. Marjorie raised her eyebrows.

"Jimmy? I know Jimmy. I've met Jimmy. He is… was… a good friend of Paul Raymond's."

Marjorie explained that Jimmy was one of the biggest porn barons in Soho. He owned a number of strip-clubs and bookshops. Jimmy she said, also fancied himself as a "movie" producer, for whom the age of the "actors" was not too important.

Marjorie smiled as fond memories came to her.

"Jimmy: good-looking Bermondsey boy, quiet voice, smart dresser. He wanted to be like Paul, be successful."

A little laugh broke through her smile.

"Jimmy opened his first two strip clubs on Old Compton Street about 10 years ago. The competition tried to burn him out because he refused to pay for protection, but Jimmy had a better idea. He paid the police for protection. He built a little empire and the more money he made the more of the Met he bought. You name it, he had them all in his pocket – the Flying Squad, the Serious Crime Squad, the Dirty Squad."

"So why is he inside?" I asked

"GBH. He stepped over the line and his connections couldn't help him. Plus, the Met got this new Commissioner who was determined to clean up police corruption." She frowned and shook her head. "Jimmy had a terrible temper. He got a few of his mates to carve up a guy called "Pooky" Garfath. Garfath was an old ex of Jimmy's wife Rusty, and he'd been sniffing around again. Gave him a bad slashing. Jimmy fled to Amsterdam. So, his Missus contacted A10, they're the cops that investigate cops, and she told them all about the police officers that Jimmy had been paying. Jimmy was extradited back and got sent down for eight fucking years."

Finally, she paused, offered us cigarettes, lit them up, and blew smoke at the ceiling.

"Now he's biting back and the shit's hitting the fan. Jimmy has named 38 fucking detectives," she laughed. "The word on the street is that Jimmy has paid his associates to track down Pooky and cut his two hands off."

Damie rose and went to look for a toilet. It was time for him to introduce some white powder to his nasal cavities. He had offered me some earlier but I said there was no way I was going to get into that shit. I'd stick with BMD, bennies, mandies and dexies.

Marjorie winked at me. "That's a nice boyfriend you have there, Derry."

"He's not my boyfriend," I said earnestly.

"That's what they all say, sweetheart."

Damie returned, blinking his watery eyes. He said, "I have a story about Roger Gleaves."

I threw Damie a look of caution. "Are you sure about this?" I said, conscious of his earlier reluctance to speak about the hostel boss.

"Fuck it," he said in his broad Glaswegian accent. The drink and coke had chased away his earlier inhibitions. We huddled conspiratorially around the table.

"Tell us all, Glasgow," Marjorie whispered, checking no one near was listening.

The previous year Damie had met and befriended another Scot working the Dilly, a 19-year-old called Billy McPhee, from Bannockburn. Billy, who'd left a girlfriend in Scotland, quickly learned the rules of the Dilly. Having sussed out the younger competition, he cleverly came up with the idea of dyeing a blond streak down the front of his naturally dark hair to make himself stand out to potential punters. He was immediately nicknamed Billy Two-Tone by the other boys.

Billy had thumbed down a car near Carlisle. He was given a lift to London by another Scot called Jim Hyland, a well-built man in his late 20s who worked as the warden for Roger's hostel in Hackney. Working the Dilly, Billy had started out by sleeping rough on the nights he couldn't get a bed, but he quickly became disillusioned with that and went to Hackney to find Hyland.

Hyland welcomed the fellow Scot with open arms. They spent hours together at the hostel with Billy running errands, helping out, answering the phone. They became close, then lovers. At the same time Hyland was also seeing a girl from Croydon, who also helped out in the hostel. Hyland had never got on with Roger, they had one argument after another. He was also incensed by the fact that Roger was abusing younger boys. On one occasion, Hyland stormed into the Brixton HQ and dragged a 13-year-old boy from Roger's bed. Eventually, Hyland and Roger were threatening to kill each other. One day Hyland decided he'd had enough, it wasn't worth the grief. He cashed in £60 of DHSS hostel cheques and made arrangements to go to Brighton to hide out. He pleaded for Billy to go with him, but Billy had gotten the London bug and wasn't going to leave. Hyland vanished. He found work in Butlin's and phoned Billy to tell him that he'd changed his name to Tony Scott.

Roger went berserk and ordered his heavies to find out Hyland's whereabouts from Billy. But Billy refused to speak: he would not betray his lover. Roger sent three men around to beat the information out of Billy. They failed. When people saw Billy's battered and bruised face, he told them he'd been in a car crash. Damie was becoming quite emotional as he told the story of Billy's loyalty and love for Hyland.

Roger then sent another crew round to extract the information.

"They took him away in a mini and punched him, smashed up his face with a metal jack, burned him with cigarettes. Billy never said a fucking word. Never even made a sound. They drove him to Roger's Osterley hostel, led him into a little office and tied him to a chair. They beat him mercilessly with a lump of wood. Broke his arm. Played Russian roulette with a .38 revolver in his mouth."

Damie took a long drag on his cigarette.

"Billy still refused to tell them where Hyland went. Finally, they drove him down the A28, stabbed him 20 times and threw his body in a ditch. Billy Two-Tone was braver than all those bastards put together."

We sat back in our chairs. Shocked.

"Jesus Christ," I said. "I thought Belfast was bad."

Marjorie was speechless and had turned quite pale.

"Then what happened?" I asked.

"The story about what happened to Billy spread around the other hostels and onto the streets, everyone in Playland was talking about it. Billy was one of their own. Do you know the first thing the fucking doctor said when the police brought him to the scene of the crime? He said Billy looked like a junkie or a homo."

Damie's voice cracked with emotion. "That could have been anybody, it could have been me."

We waited in silence for Damie to continue, as he wiped a tear from the corner of his eye.

"They soon found out who the murderers were and arrested them. Of course, the trail led to Roger. And when the police burst into Brixton HQ, surprise, surprise, Roger was in bed with a boy. That was last August. They've all been banged up since. The trial's supposed to be starting in a few weeks' time. One of the murderers, a guy called Woodland, is supposed to have told the cops that Roger had an acid bath lined up for Hyland in Branksome Road."

Marjorie had heard enough. She was content to retreat from the harsh realities of the world by splashing around in her West End fish bowl. We kissed her goodbye, promising that we'd meet up again. The three of us walked out into the cold, busy Soho night and breathed in the sweet and toxic aroma of exotic food and petrol fumes. Marjorie walked away purposefully, holding her fur coat at the throat.

I called after her. "Did anyone ever say you looked like Sandy Shaw?"

She turned her head and laughed, then pointed to her face and started singing *There's always something there to remind me*.

Damie and I ended up back in Macabre. This time the place was heaving. The smoke was suffocating, the noise deafening. A man walked over to Damie and started to chat into his ear. Damie nodded his head and then motioned for me to stay where I was, indicating he'd be back soon. I slowly mouthed the words "fuck sake" for him to lip read. He shrugged his shoulders and walked to the stairs with the man.

I was approached by two young men, who invited me to a party somewhere in South London. Suddenly, I felt nauseous and light-headed. I made for the stairs, pressed my way through the crowd and hurried outside, by now feeling violently ill. I ran behind a stack of beer barrels and boxes filled with rubbish. As I put my hands against the wall to steady myself, I had a vivid image of Billy Two-Tone being brought to his knees with multiple stab wounds, the blood pumping from his body. I thought about the terror he would have felt in his last moments; his parents in Scotland sitting by the fireside, wondering. Then the contents of my guts painfully spewed against the wall. A few yards away Damie was bent over a dustbin, trousers around his ankles, being enthusiastically fucked by the man who'd picked him up in the bar. I closed my eyes, feeling sick again.

When they had finished and the punter went on his way, I walked over to Damie as he was tucking in his blouse and doing up his zipper.

"Could you not leave it for one night?"

"Normally, I could," he replied, "but the offer was just too good to turn down."

He picked up his bag.

"How much?" I asked

He held up a wad of notes. "Fifty fucking pounds," he smiled triumphantly, before bursting into, *Ho ho ho it's magic!* "Mr Big Time works in the City. He's 45 and married with three kids. We've done business before."

"Did you know he'd be here tonight?"

Damie paused for a second, eyes raised to the stars in a little lost boy expression. "Mmmmmaybe."

I shook my head in disbelief, cleared my throat and spat on the ground.

Damie walked back to the bin and picked something up from a windowsill. He returned and held it out in front of my face.

"KY Jelly," he announced. "Now on special offer at Boots, Piccadilly Circus."

CHAPTER 11

The Grenadiers

In the second week of March it suddenly occurred to me that I'd forgotten about Mother's Day, the previous Sunday. I felt ashamed at not remembering it, as I'd always bought my mum a card and little gift. This was the first Mother's Day I'd been away from home and it troubled me that she'd think I'd forgotten about her. I thought about her all the time. Some nights and early mornings after I got home from the parties or the solo assignments, I'd fall across the bed and cry like a child, thinking about my mother, my father, my family back home in Derry. As my body filtered the pollution out of my system and the high faded away, the depression would crawl over me like black mist. I stank of other men's sweat, stale aftershave and sex. If my family ever found out about this, I'd kill myself. I made myself that promise. I'd destroy this fucking body. Better that than have to live with the shame.

* * * * *

Keith made another unexpected appearance in Foyles. He said he had some very good news for me. I'd no longer have to work Saturdays in the bookshop. It had all been sorted. I didn't bother asking how or by whom.

"Well, show some fucking thanks," he barked.

I ignored him.

"We have an important job for you this evening."

"Who is she?

"Don't get fucking funny with me Pretty Boy or I'll put your fucking face through that."

He pointed to the glass counter in front of me. He looked over at some shelves. "Have you any good title pages I could take with me?"

"I'm sorry, Keith. I'm tired. Who is he?"

"Like I said before, pack in this shit useless boring job. How much have you earned with us?"

"I don't know."

"Well, I'll tell you. Last week you were paid £230 quid. We keep records of these things," he smiled.

At that moment I decided I'd also keep a record of payments I received. I'd chronicle the wages of sin on the accounts page at the back of my diary.

"Anyway," Keith went on, "he's an important military man."

"Military man?" I felt the now familiar nervous dread take hold of me.

"Yes," he confirmed. "Army. You should feel right at home, like you're back in Derry."

The feeling of dread turned to a feeling of despair.

"Please, Keith," I pleaded, "please don't do this to me. I can't be associated with the military over here, it's too dangerous. I can't get into this kinda trouble."

"Calm down, Pretty Boy, there won't be any trouble. We look after you now. You're safe. He's just another punter who happens to be military. You'll be fine."

"I can't do this. Please, Keith, I'll do anything else."

Keith moved closer. "You'll fucking do whatever and whoever I tell you to."

I could feel his breath on me. "If we can kill 13 people on the streets of Derry and get away with it, we can easily see that a little accident happens to a member of the Daly family."

That was all it took. He owned me again. And at that moment I knew there was no escape. I decided I'd become whoever they wanted me to become. Like any good actor, I'd lose myself in the role. I'd give them a drug-induced performance worthy of the West End stage.

Keith turned to leave. "Another bit of good news: you don't even have to dress up. Wear casual clothes."

He walked towards the exit, his arm raised a little, waving goodbye.

* * * * *

My client picked me up outside Prunier, a fancy French restaurant,[22] and led me down St James's Street. When I saw the tall red-brick tower, I immediately assumed it was a military barracks and I felt contractions in my chest as the muscles went into spasm. Anything could happen to me in there. I could be gang-raped or murdered. For a split second I considered my options as adrenalin and cortisol pumped up my muscles for fight or flight. I pretended to cough and brought two mandies to my mouth. I needed to relax.

We walked along a dark passageway and through a solid jet-black door into a dark hallway. Upstairs, past a maze of rooms, he led me into a small, sparsely furnished, monastic-looking bedroom.

---

22   In 1975 the Prunier Restaurant was located at the corner of St James's Street and Little James's Street.

"Make yourself comfortable," he said quietly but authoritatively.

I sat on the edge of the bed, and he poured me a large measure of gin with a drop of tonic. My first taste of gin. I hated it, but didn't care as long as it produced the desired effect.

"Cheers," he said, raising his glass confidently. "So, you're from the Bogside?"

I didn't quite know how to read the tone of his voice.

"Is that a question or an accusation?"

I surprised myself with the directness of my answer. My instinct was to be defensive.

He smiled. "You must be from the Bog: you're putting up the barricades already. Relax. I know you're new to this. It'll be OK. You're on a learning curve."

I held out my glass for a refill and tried to change the subject. The last thing I wanted to do with a soldier was talk about Derry. I lifted an old book that was sitting on top of his bedside locker. *The Grenadier Guards 1939-45* Volume One by Lt. P. Forbes, published 1949.

"So, you're in the Grenadier Guards, then?" I asked, taking a deep slug of the gin. "Give me your name, rank and number."

"I think in the circumstances it's you who are the prisoner of war," he laughed. "I'll give you my name, it's Chris. He stood up and filled the glasses again.

"Take off your clothes."

I felt unsteady on my feet and my head was spinning. He helped me with a couple of buttons. Then, falling back onto the bed, I indulged him.

Later, when we were lying side by side, he stunned me by telling me he'd served in Derry in 1969.

"Talk about a fiasco," he said. "We had to buy maps from the Automobile Association to locate the Irish towns."

"Actually, they're British towns," I corrected. "That's why the problems are there in the first place."

"We were made to feel very welcome. The factory girls gave us tea and sandwiches. We were just dropped in there, totally ignorant of the history and background to all the disturbances. We had no intelligence, no police presence – they had been withdrawn. Thankfully, there was no sign of the IRA."

"You missed all the action by two months," I chided. "The Grenadiers and the Bogsiders: that would have been a good fight."

"Believe me," he said, "I've seen all the action I want to see in Derry. I've been on a few tours."

I started giggling uncontrollably.

"You're drunk," he said, and he was right. I was seriously intoxicated.

"I just pictured a rock band called the Grenadiers doing tours in Ulster."

"Right", Chris said finally, "I need to get you out of here, and for Christ's sake keep quiet."[23]

* * * * *

My second encounter with the military was just two days later. It was a Friday night. I'd been told to dress casually again, so I assumed I'd be going to a pub, at least to begin with, before being taken somewhere else. However, we went straight to a gigantic complex of red-brick, high-rise buildings. I was led to a flat and introduced to a small group of men. As usual I was drugged up, yet still sick with worry. Each and every one of these encounters was a journey into the unknown and my overriding emotion was fear. Thankfully, there was a Dilly boy there, Andrew, who was

23   In August 2014 I retraced my footsteps down St James's Street with a Detective Constable from the Met and showed him the side entrance I had been taken through in 1975. We returned to the main entrance and the DC showed his badge to a police officer who was manning a barrier. He asked what the building was. We were informed this was St James's Palace, one of the royal residences.

about my age, so I was relieved that at least I wouldn't be the sole source of entertainment for the group.

The chat and the drink started to flow. During sentimental reflections on the good old days, the men's backgrounds started to emerge through the smoke, drink and drugs.

Another visitor was soon delivered.

"Ah, Richard," one man cooed.

"Another pretty boy," someone exclaimed.

Richard was instructed to sit between myself and Andrew. He reached into his pocket.

"I managed to get the vice-boy cigarettes," Richard said, handing out marijuana joints. These were lit up and circulated.

Richard was 25 years old and a Grenadier Guard. Blond, a picture of health, intelligent, and in great demand apparently among the officer classes. Grammar school educated, he had no wish to go to university and soon joined the army. This I was able to establish whilst we were both still relatively sober.

Meanwhile, there was much fussing and fawning around the evening's guest of honour, a man whose unassuming name belied his distinguished military and political career. He was initially introduced to me as plain old Bill Sidney, but as the evening progressed and everyone became more familiar, I discovered he was Viscount William De L'Isle, a member of the landed gentry and a war hero. He'd been a Major in the Grenadier Guards during World War II and was briefly Conservative MP for Chelsea, until his elevation to the House of Lords following the death of his father. He'd even been Governor-General of Australia and, if that wasn't enough, Bill was a recipient of the Victoria Cross *and* a Knight of the Garter. He regaled the company with his tales of endurance as a soldier in the war, and his heroism in the face of the enemy. Even after having half of his arse blown off, weak from loss of blood, he had apparently repelled the Germans and saved the honour of the battalion. Here was a man who had been used to giving orders, to being obeyed.

His first order of the evening was for Richard and me to kiss slowly and intimately. His second order was for Andrew and I to take turns giving Richard a blow job. Richard then returned the favour on us. As a memento of the occasion, we were filmed with an 8mm camera, whilst some of the others took photographs. As drunk and drugged as I was, I kept telling myself there was no point in worrying about all of this. I had a funny feeling I wasn't going to live long enough to regret it. I downed more pills and more drink and smoked more dope. Richard, Andrew and I then removed all of our clothes and put ourselves at the disposal of the distinguished company. Bill assured Richard that, as a serving Grenadier, he alone would have the pleasure of mounting the Viscount's battle-scarred buttocks.

CHAPTER 12

The Firm

Sometimes I thought my handlers were playing sophisticated mind games with me, either with their choice of punters or the locations they chose for my assignations. To present me to the military was a case in point. They knew the dangerous position this put me in. A few words back home in Ulster could have been a death sentence for me. Perhaps, given some of the gangland and underworld connections, the plan was to compromise some of the very people I was being introduced to and then use me for blackmail, extortion and other purposes. Was I a pawn in some great game?

One Friday night, as I was taken to the Park Lane Casino Club on Hertford Street, Mayfair, wearing my tailored Rupert Lycett Green suit, Steve Harley sang to me:

It's just a test, a game for us to play
Win or lose, it's hard to smile

Next door to the casino was the Londonderry House Hotel. More mind games? We were led to a table in the bar area. Mr Fisher, Mr Hunter, Mr Raywood, Mr Machine, Mr Daly and, astonishingly, Detective Inspector John Legge of the Flying Squad made up the party. We were dressed impeccably, although Mr Raywood let the company down a little with his black shirt and white tie. When moving in more upmarket establishments, Malcolm's tastes in clothing ran to 1920s Chicago hoodlum elegance.

Three days earlier, Eve Stratford aged 22, who worked in the nearby Bunny Club, had been savagely murdered. Her throat had been slashed a dozen times. The men speculated about who may have murdered her, and why. Eve was actually the centrefold in the March edition of Mayfair Magazine. The Fruit Machine suggested that DI Legge use the centrefold as an information poster to encourage witnesses to come forward .

A barman informed us that the reception desk at the Londonderry had phoned to say that our guest was just checking in and would be joining us shortly. While we waited, Keith told us about the gentleman we would be meeting.

Mr Gerald Citron, ex-public-school boy, had gone to Manchester and taken up a career in law. He later moved to London and until last year had been one of the five biggest suppliers of hard-core porn to Soho. His biggest single customer was none other than Marjorie's old acquaintance Jimmy Humphreys. Gerald had made a fortune, bought a farmhouse with a swimming pool, and married a glamorous model. He invested money in a wine-importing business because he was shrewd enough to realise that the sheer scale of the illegal porn business in Soho could not last. He knew it would all come crashing down.

Gerald had been caught with 18 tons of obscene material at his farm, awaiting distribution. He was fined £50,000, but he absconded to the South of France and then moved to California. He never paid a penny of the fine. He'd apparently flown back to the UK the previous night, arriving incognito at a regional airport, to arrange some transatlantic business and tie up loose ends, before flying out again in a few days.

Gerald was greeted with hugs, handshakes and big smiles. Then the drink started to flow. Keith had warned me earlier to go easy on the booze, to pay attention and to learn. He said it had taken some persuasion to get the Fish to allow me to join them. He went on rather cryptically to say that Charlie Hornby had arranged, with the Fish's consent, for me to mix business with pleasure that night.

I excused myself and went to the gents for a dexie supplement. On evenings like this I hoped for the best but prepared for the worst. My greatest fear this evening was to end up in a hotel room on my own with this squad from Playland. Rent had a collective urban memory. Stories were passed down and became part of Dilly mythology. One of Damie's favourite cautionary tales took place in the Swinging Sixties.

The story went like this. Ronnie Kray had to go into hiding for many weeks to avoid having to appear in court as a witness to police corruption. Ron had an insatiable appetite for young men, and a fresh boy was brought to him every night. He had a sadistic streak and particularly liked boys who had never had experience of men. He liked breaking-in the first timers and teaching them what to do. Ron even threw money at straight boys to take their girlfriends out, on condition that they'd sleep with him the next night.

But he was also prone to delusional episodes and violent mood swings. One boy who had been delivered, and who was more than a little drunk, made a joke that Ron took to be a slight on his manhood. Ron smiled, took the boy to bed and went to work on him. During the "sex play" that followed, the boy suffocated. His body was disposed of under a motorway construction. Some time later, Ron's driver, a young man, tried to blackmail him about it. He also disappeared, like ice in morning sunshine. I thought about that rent boy's last moments. I thought about Billy Two-Tone again. My experience with Charles and Keith had been just a few weeks ago and the fear and sense of helplessness I had felt then were as raw and real as ever, which was why I drank and medicated myself into numbness.

During the course of the next couple of hours, I sipped my drink and listened to stories about the good old days, the Soho boom years for the porn and sex industry, from '69 to the summer of '72. I learned about the players, the business practices and the lingo of the trade.

Keith, who I felt was trying hard to woo me and take me firmly under his wing, had already explained the background to the Firm's involvement in Playland. Local gangland figures usually offered "protection" to enterprises like Playland. They threatened physical harm to staff, management and their families, or engineered traps to compromise anyone who was well known in the business community or active in local politics or such like: an individual's weaknesses would be found and exploited. Damie, my guide and mentor to all things Dilly, had taught me the term "badger-trap", which referred to a scam using either female prostitutes or rent boys.

"OK," he said. "I pick up a punter and take him to a room. During sex, an accomplice, 'my big brother', walks in and goes crazy to find his vulnerable little brother being sexually assaulted. The punter pays up a lot of money to keep this out of the courts and out of the papers."

When it came to businesses, most just rolled over after the first visit from the gangsters and accepted the inevitable. Businesses that dug their heels in would have hassle from bent coppers on the payroll of the gangsters. Plate-glass windows would be smashed, a mysterious fire might break out.

A man called Bernard Briggs had been pointed out to me in Playland one evening, a tall, chain-smoking barrel of a man with the look of a kind and dependable uncle. His title was managing director of Playland, but really he was just a respectable front for the enterprise, a kind of sponsor, as he had been in the jukebox and fruit machine industry for years. He owned his own company,

Modern Enterprises, and was also chairman of the Phonograph Operators Association, with its 153 member organisations.

Having been strong-armed into cooperating with the Firm, Bernard Briggs introduced the Fish to Bruce Eckert, a brash New Yorker or, as Keith described him, "a loudmouthed fucking wanker". Mr Eckert had a criminal record in the USA dating back to 1961 involving smuggling, bribery and tax evasion, and so the Fish felt that he and Mr Eckert were going to get along. Eckert became the actual manager of the arcade. The Firm got a piece of the Playland fruit machine takings.[24] The place was a goldmine. There were 125 gaming machines and 75 pinball machines. The average gaming machine in the West End took between £200 and £400 per 16-hour day, but the prime location of Playland meant around £700 per machine. With the number of machines in Playland, they were raking in over £87,000 per day, seven days a week.

As a sign of how much Keith was taking me into his confidence, he revealed that the "Bag Man" who collected the takings from Playland every night for the arcade's owner was a 65-year-old American named James Humpert, a director of Piccadilly Enterprises. He said only he and the Fish knew that – and now me.

As the arcade also happened to be a pick-up spot for rent boys, the Firm also took control of and organised that. They set about expanding the operation by introducing more boys into the business – or livestock, as Mr Fisher called them. The

---

24 The involvement of the underworld in Playland wasn't particularly unusual. In 1967 the Kray twins took over control of fruit machines across the West End, including Playland. They also moved in on and took a cut from the importers and wholesalers of pornography. What differed in 1975 was the extent of the Firm's involvement in Playland. This was down to the amount of money that could now be leveraged for "protection" and the money from the organised prostitution of boys and young men.

owners of Playland ran the machines and the Firm ran the boys. Everyone was making good money, including the Old Bill.

So the Fish knew all there was to know about blackmail, extortion, prostitution and armed robbery, but he knew nothing about the porn business. He was here to be educated by Mr Citron. As was I, apparently. We learned that the soft-porn magazine market functioned like any other publishing trade.[25] The big money, however, was in hard-core magazines and movies, most of which were imported from Scandinavia, Germany and the USA. As this material was completely illegal, the producers needed to shift the material quickly, rather than have it stored in warehouses. The public would pay anything to get their hands on hard-core and specialist pornography, so the shops dealing this stuff, in effect the middleman, could charge pretty much whatever they wanted, usually between £5 and £10 per magazine.

As the businesses were not registered, no tax was paid (actual ownership of the premises was cloaked in a labyrinth of dodgy companies and trusts). The bookshop managers or "bucks", most of whom had criminal records, were paid £50 a week, while rent was about £100 a week. After the cost of buying stock, an average Soho "bookshop" could clear between £7,000 and £10,000 a week depending on location. That amounted to at least £364,000 a year. The bookshop next door to Playland was one of a few owned by the Firm, but they were making nowhere near the amount of money that others in the heart of Soho were making.

The business had its own terminology. Scandinavian porn was called "scans"; blue movies were called "rollers", still pictures were called "smudges" and there were "straight smudges", "gay smudges", and "juve smudges", depicting children. Cine films

---

25   By 1975 the UK was saturated with soft-core porn. The magazines of about 12 publishers were distributed through eight distribution centres and 400 wholesalers, who in turn supplied 20,000 shops including most corner newsagents.

were the most expensive items in the shops; £15 for 200 feet in black and white or £30 for the same length in colour.[26] There was more money in porn than in the professions, which is why Gerald had moved from the practice of law to the provision of porn.

I also heard about "Big Jeff" Phillips, a trained accountant who imported Danish rollers and was now, at 33 years of age, reputed to be Britain's first blue movie millionaire. Big Jeff drove a white Rolls-Royce, and owned two blocks of flats, a few houses and a mansion in Berkshire. He took vacations in Monaco and the South of France. His background in accountancy proved useful. In addition to managing his own business accounts, he also organised payments into Swiss bank accounts for senior police officers in the Dirty Squad (his personal contribution to this "porn pool" was £15,000 per annum).

Big Jeff had broken new ground by offering a service whereby more wealthy clients could actually star in their own rollers. A cinematographer, a sound man and a lighting technician would be provided, as would costumes, props and "actors".[27] A high-rolling Playland punter could have cowboys and Indians, slave boys, schoolboys, or little girl-boys, and could star in and direct his own fantasy feature. Total cost including the original master print of the 35mm film, in colour and with sound: £1000. Unfortunately for Big Jeff, his personalised film production business was short-lived. He had been busted following an exposé by the *Sunday People* of his corrupt dealings with the Dirty Squad. He had started an 18-month sentence in January 1974.

Listening to them talk business, with Keith providing explanatory footnotes, I became increasingly uneasy. It troubled

---

26   The screening of blue movies was popular with guests at a few high-society dinner parties. The rollers introduced a risqué dimension to the proceedings and encouraged some guests to follow the movie with a live performance.
27   Girls were paid £30 and the boys £10 or £15 for starring roles in locally produced movies.

me that Keith thought he could trust me, treat me as one of their own. This insider knowledge was an additional burden I had to carry. Keith might consider me to be an asset now, but I knew I could easily become a liability. What then?

They then started discussing the recent spate of convictions. DI Legge wanted Mr Fisher to understand these had nothing to do with his team, since porn was the responsibility of Obscene Publications. Gerald was outraged. "The Dirty Squad alone are getting about £250,000 a year from Soho. Plus holidays, cars…"

Mr Fisher brought a fat cigar from his pocket. "So why the fuck did it all go tits up? Why is Bernie Silver in the nick?"[28] He took a moment to light up and spoke between puffs. "Why is Jimmy Humphreys in the nick? Why is Big Jeff in the nick?"

Keith leaned forward. "Jimmy fucked up big time. He was paying a fortune to his mate Ken Drury, but with Drury's expensive lifestyle it was only a matter of time before the pair of them attracted attention."

Keith turned to me and explained, "Commander Drury was only the Head of the fucking Flying Squad. The press got wind that Jimmy had taken Drury and their wives to Cyprus, all expenses paid. Papers had a fucking field day." He signalled to the barman for a refill. "Drury said he'd been over there looking for Ronnie Biggs, but he was finished. That was in '72, the year Mark took over the Met." He was referring to Robert Mark, who became Commissioner and was known for his anti-corruption campaign.

---

28   Bernie Silver, an ex-paratrooper, was known as the Godfather of Soho and was described by the Sunday People as one of "the two most evil men in London". Bernie had been active in Soho since the 1950s and had built up an empire dealing in prostitution, gambling, illegal drinking clubs and porn. Some people called Soho "Silver City". The Playland Firm was actually part of Silver's syndicate: a 'Firm within a Firm'. Similarly, the corrupt officers in the Met were also considered to be a 'Firm within a Firm'. At Silver's trial it was said that up to £50 million had passed through the Silver syndicate's hands.

I was sure I'd heard the name Ken Drury before. One of those nagging little moments of recognition, but I couldn't place it.

Malcolm Raywood looked squarely into DI Legge's eyes. "I believe you had a little jaunt abroad with Jimmy yourself, the year before that." He radiated one of his menacing little smiles. "Ibiza, with two strippers, wasn't it?"

DI Legge shifted in his seat and blushed a little. "Yes," he admitted, "but I paid my own way."

"Yeah, course you did."

DI Legge downed his whisky. "That holiday's going to cost me, I know it. Do you know how many forced resignations there have been since all this kicked off? Three hundred officers, from the top to the bottom."

Gerald shook his head. "All you lot had to do was turn a blind eye. But you bastards actually become one of our biggest suppliers."

Malcolm nodded vigorously. "Yeah, Jimmy Humphreys used to go Holborn nick and collect tons of porn from the wire-mesh vaults. You recycled it back into Soho. It was the same with the drugs."

Mr Fisher raised both hands like a referee and brought them slowly down onto the table. "Gentlemen, gentlemen, please remember why we're here. We need to look to the future. Silver and Humphreys and most of the fucking senior officers in the Met are going to go down for a long time. But this presents new opportunities." He sucked on his cigar. "So, Gerald, my son, you have your finger on the pulse, you are one of the smartest geezers I know. Where do we go from here?"

Gerald Citron took a moment to consider the question. "There's a power vacuum in the West End now, and that ponce Paul Raymond is cleaning up. The fucker is buying up Soho, building by building, while all the properties are run-down and undervalued. He'll increase the rents for legit tenants till they have to move out. The porn dealers, the racketeers and the clip-joints will move in: we're the only ones who'll be able to afford it. Now, Westminster City Council are talking about demolishing most of Soho, but if they rebuild, Raymond will be sitting on land worth a fucking fortune for redevelopment. He wins both ways."

The conversation stopped as a young waiter delivered a tray of drinks to the table. Malcolm patted his ass as he leaned over the table. The embarrassed young man retreated with the tray under his arm. Malcolm raised his glass. "Bit of competition there, Pretty Boy," he sniggered.

Gerald went on, "Our biggest threat is that Parliament makes hard-core porn legal."

"What?" said Keith. "You're kidding. How's that a threat?"

"That would make us irrelevant. Just think about it. If every street corner newsagent could sell hard-core, the bottom would drop out of the market. It'd be the kiss of death for Soho. If Parliament does what Denmark did, we're screwed."[29]

"Pretty's new friend would be in favour of that," Malcolm said.

"Who?" I said, wondering what I'd missed. "What do you mean?"

"Your new pal, Sir Keith Joseph. He thinks porn should be freely available to anyone that wants it."

"I think we all know," said Gerald, "there are big changes coming. The Greater London Council wanted to end film censorship so that people could screen *anything* in the city. Anything. Thank God for Mary Whitehouse and her campaign."

---

29   Between 1969 and 1979 Denmark legalised the production of all kinds of pornography, including child pornography.

There was a moment's silence as everyone took a drink.

"Never mind the porn," Gerald continued. "Your little operation is over. Playland is finished. You've fallen into the net of the big clean-up just like Bernie Silver's prostitution flats all over Soho, Jimmy Humphreys' bookshops, and my distribution operation. All under surveillance thanks to Commissioner Mark."

I knew from Keith that Bruce Eckert had been trying since late 1974 to persuade the Firm to vacate.

"Who the fuck does this guy think he is?" the Fruit Machine had demanded. "This fucking crook comes into *our* town and now wants *us* to clean up *our* act?"

The Fish gazed at Gerald, then at his associates. "Look, a handful of coppers had us under surveillance last year. We had a few arrests, Malcolm here is out on bail. There'll be a trial, maybe. Big fucking deal. So we grease a few more palms, drop a few of our client's names. When they find out who really owns Playland and who some of our punters are, the shit'll hit the fan. Worst case, some of our guys might do a little time for vice, a few months maybe. But we are fucking going nowhere. Playland is here to stay and so are we."

"I'm not so sure," said Gerald.

"It's all very well for you to say cut and run, Gerald," Malcolm whined. "You've already made it big."

Gerald sat back in his seat and crossed his legs. "Yeah, well, the way I see it, Playland will be gone. There's no way the fucking gaming licence will be renewed if there's a vice trial. And as for the Bishop, that fucking joker Gleaves, his hostels will be shut down and you're going to have all these boys running wild on the streets."

There was silence as Gerald's depressing assessment continued to sink in.

"Look at it this way," DI Legge said, trying to offer a little hope. "If you're determined to stick with it, and if by some miracle Playland is *not* shut down, but Gleaves' hostels *are* shut down, there'll be more potential rent packed into the Dilly than there are tourists."

"Now you're living in dreamland," Gerald cut in. "Look, Playland is finished. Milk porn for all it's worth, sure, while it lasts. But all these bookshops will at best have a few years to run. After that it'll all be mail order. It'll be tough, worse if it's legalised. The Soho we know is finished. It'll be an upmarket gentrified little village before you know it."

"Glad you brought all that sunshine with you from California, Gerry," said the Fruit Machine, always a man of few words.

"You could think about a merger," Gerald suggested. "There's always the legitimate entertainment business. Either negotiate with Raymond or use other means to muscle in."

Mr Fisher had been deep in thought. He hadn't been given the job of managing Playland rent for nothing. He was a shrewd businessman. I knew from Keith that the Fish lived modestly, supported a wife and three kids and kept a low profile, but that he was "worth a fucking fortune. He could buy and sell those wealthy wankers who were sleepwalking into prison."

"I think we can kill two birds with one stone here." Mr Fisher spoke quietly, his words measured. "We get control of all the Gleaves rent, *and* get into porn production big time."

"Fucking right," said Keith enthusiastically, "and I'm talking gay porn and juve stuff: that's where the business growth is. Copenhagen is always looking for new talent. We can rent them some fresh bunnies. We see more runaways arriving in London all the time, and they're getting younger." His eyes widened as he considered a brave new world. "Production *and* retail. We could open the biggest fucking sex shop in the West

End." He emitted a guttural laugh. "We shut down Playland and reopen as Pornland. We could be the Foyles of the porn world." He nudged me in the side.

"That's worthwhile diversification," Mr Fisher mused, before addressing Keith directly: "I think the Wolfman would have a problem with Pornland."

"Who the fuck is the Wolfman?" Malcolm asked.

Mr Fisher simply touched his nose. Everyone else apart from Keith looked mystified. Then they all just laughed. I laughed along, hollowly.

"Well, I wish you well, but as for me," Gerald said with finality, "I'm going into the movie business in the USA. Super hard-core, bondage and bestiality, but strictly adult stuff, no kiddies. I'll be exporting and if Big Jeff behaves himself he could be my biggest customer. The great British public will not be denied their simple pleasures in these bleak times."[30]

"Right," Keith announced with a broad smile, "time for some fun."

Everyone stood up and I felt my guts twist. The Fruit Machine put his vice-like arm around my shoulder. "Are you feeling lucky?" He gave me a little push towards Keith.

Keith lightly brushed my shoulders down and straightened my tie. "We're going to play in the casino, and you, Pretty Boy, are going to play in bed."

Malcolm stood beside me. "Derry is going to Londonderry," he said enigmatically.

"You're going next door, the Londonderry," Keith explained. "He'll have arrived by now. Just ask for Eden at reception. They'll

---

30   Gerald Citron returned to the United States. Repeated attempts to have him extradited failed. The Flying Squad Officer, Detective Inspector John Legge, subsequently faced 14 charges of corruption but he was acquitted after Jimmy Humphreys gave evidence in his favour. Humphreys testified that Legge was the only police officer who took him out to lunch and paid for the meal.

be expecting you. You'll be collected in an hour and a half. I hear he likes to take his time."[31]

When the men entered the casino, I went quickly to the bar, bought a large vodka and downed it with more dexies. As I walked over to the hotel, I paused and looked up at the sign above the grand doorway – Londonderry House Hotel. Then it came to me. Kenneth Drury, disgraced head of the Flying Squad. I knew why I remembered his name. I'd heard about him in Derry, six years earlier. Chief Superintendent Kenneth Drury, as he was then, had been sent over from London to investigate the vicious attack by the RUC on a civilian, Samuel Devenny, which had led to his death. His report into the killing had still not been made public.[32]

---

31 The punter was Nicholas Eden or, to give him his title, Viscount Eden, the son of the former Prime Minister Anthony Eden. Handsome, charming, and fastidious about personal hygiene, he would die of AIDS in 1985.

32 Mr Devenny was a 42-year-old father of nine children. He, a couple of neighbours and his children were attacked in his home in the Bogside by the RUC in 1969. He later died of a heart attack. An investigation by the RUC was found to be completely inadequate and the subsequent investigation by the Metropolitan Police was met by a "conspiracy of silence" and obstructed at every turn.

CHAPTER 13

The Conscience of the Rich

With a few exceptions, the more prominent men I was introduced to had no problem revealing who they were, what positions they held, what their opinions, interests and hobbies were and what they thought of other people. They often boasted about their wealth and their connections. Some could be incredibly indiscreet and seemed to get a kick from telling me things they knew they should be keeping to themselves. They would talk about their wives and children, their worries, their problems and fears. Some would gossip and recklessly pour secrets into my ear. I was hearing things I didn't need or want to know. As well as being corrupted by their sexual demands, I felt I was being corrupted by their secrets and their knowledge. It was a kind of foreplay for some. For others it would come with a cigarette after they'd sated themselves. Exhaling smoke with their revelations and disclosures, forbidden knowledge in return for forbidden sex. The perception was that they were so powerful, so well connected, there was absolutely no way I could ever pose a threat to them. Normal rules didn't apply here. Discretion was only the better part of valour in the company of equals. I was too far down the food chain to worry about. They were unassailable and untouchable.

Some used silly nicknames at the first introduction but this soon disappeared with the alcohol and they'd reveal their real names. They loved to listen to me speak, to hear me say their names with my Derry accent. My background and my accent seemed to add novelty to their encounters with me, and perhaps a heightened sense of risk too. Given the Troubles in Ulster and the IRA activity in London, associating with Irish rent was considered dangerous by some and thrilling by others. Some punters considered sleeping with the enemy to be a reckless but exciting forbidden pleasure. The fantasy of the honey trap turned them on.

* * * * *

Simon Hornby had become my most regular punter. He picked me up in Charing Cross Road one day after work. We spent some time browsing in the second-hand bookshops in Cecil Court and I tried to impress him with my knowledge of the antiquarian book trade. He admitted that many of the valuable books he bought were more for decoration than reading and invited me to value his book collection sometime.

"Are you familiar with P.G. Woodhouse?" Simon asked as he leafed through a first edition of *Joy in the Morning*.

"No," I shot back, "but I'll bet you Christina Foyle knows him."

Simon laughed. "I meant have you read him?

"No."

"He's one of my favourites. I adore his work. Such good fun, such humour. He was actually Sheran's grandfather. He died just last month. Three days after your birthday, as a matter of fact."

When we first met Simon had asked what age I was. When I told him I had just turned 20, he smiled mischievously and remarked that I was on "the edge of consent".

"Charming man. Wonderful writer," he continued.

I was ravenous and suggested we go for a pizza or a hamburger in Leicester Square. Simon wouldn't hear of it and suggested a nice restaurant in Soho for a Chinese instead. I wasn't really into exotic food (a curry was considered an exotic dish in Derry), so we compromised and went to the Iceland Steakhouse on the Haymarket. He treated us to the most expensive bottle of red wine on the menu. Simon didn't consider it to be expensive at all, but it cost more than I made in a week.

Simon confessed to not knowing much about the Troubles in Northern Ireland and asked me to explain what it was all about, which I tried to do as objectively as possible. He was surprised about the level of violence on the Loyalist side. All he'd heard in London was that the IRA were fighting the British Army.

"So essentially," he said, "it's all about Boyne water on one side and holy water on the other."

I smiled. Simon knew more about Irish history than he let on.

He also wanted to hear about the old Derry, before the Troubles, what it was like growing up, my education and interests. I told him about Agnes in Lowestoft and how I was crazy about her and planned to meet up with her again. He looked a little deflated, disappointed that I had a love interest, and worse, the object of my desire was female.

"Then why are you…" the question trailed off. Was he wondering why I was doing what I was doing? Didn't he know? Didn't he know that his brother drugged and raped me, was blackmailing me? Didn't he know I was attacked in his home? Broken in his bed? Surely he must know I was being forced to do this. Was it possible he didn't know? He'd ignored my remark about recognising his brother in the wedding photo. What was he thinking? Should I tell him everything? The moment passed. I couldn't find the words. Couldn't ask the questions. Perhaps I didn't want to know the answers. I liked him and enjoyed his company. He was charming, intelligent and could be very funny. The more time I spent with him, the less I'd be spending with others. He was becoming the only one of my clients I could trust myself to stay reasonably sober with. I knew he definitely liked me. He liked me a lot. If I had to play their game, then maybe I could make up some rules of my own. I felt I could use him. If I played the adoring acolyte and fawned over him, perhaps he'd want to spend even more time with me? But I felt guilty about taking advantage of him, about using him. And yet wasn't that exactly what they were doing with me? I felt confused.

Simon told me a little about his childhood, about Eton, about growing up and his time at Oxford University. But unlike some, he seemed to be wary of telling me too much, afraid perhaps that he'd inadvertently let slip something that he'd later regret. Perhaps his business background had fostered a cautious and guarded nature. Or more likely, he probably felt he couldn't fully trust me yet.

When the conversation moved on to his hobbies and interests he opened up like a sunflower. He was a man of many passions and could clearly afford to indulge them. He jumped enthusiastically back to his childhood, remembering how he used to help his parents in the garden at Pusey House in Oxfordshire. He inherited a love of flowers and gardening from his mother. One of his most memorable moments at Eton was escaping over the wall, making his way to somewhere called the Savill Garden and being astonished by its beauty. Recalling the lush, vivid colours and scents of the garden, he animatedly described the blue Himalayan poppies and the largest primulas he'd ever seen. I told him I thought all poppies were red, but he assured me these were blue. He was not amused when I asked if he'd been on LSD at the time.

"I didn't need drugs," he said wistfully. "The sight of that garden was intoxicating enough for me." He rested his elbows on the table and joined his hands as if he were about to pray.

"I used to steal seeds and try to get them to grow in our garden, polyanthuses and such like. I felt as if I was plucking forbidden fruit from the Garden of Eden."

As the conversation digressed, he eventually returned to his love of books. He explained how, after he'd married Sheran, they drew up reading lists to fill any gaps in their knowledge. He said this was essential if one was to remain interesting and relevant at the dinner table.

I told Simon I thought he was a true renaissance man. He thanked me but said he preferred to be thought of as an aesthete.

"I appreciate art," he said. "I love beauty in all its forms – architecture [he was an expert on Venetian art, culture and history], trees, gardens, paintings, porcelain, marble, music, the beauty of the young male body."

He paused, and his eyes traced a path from my hair, my face, to my shoulders and along my arm to my hand, which held a glass of wine. He followed the glass to my mouth and I took a nervous sip, feeling the intensity of his gaze upon me.

He sensed my discomfort and smiled. "The beauty of a healthy balance sheet." The renaissance man became a businessman.

I had to smile.

"The beauty in the works of Oscar Wilde," he continued. "The beauty in the world around us. The beauty of…"

Almost involuntarily Simon's musings on beauty reminded me of Blake. I cut in and recited, knowing it would impress him:

To see a world in a grain of sand
And a heaven in a wild flower,
Hold infinity in the palm of your hand
And eternity in an hour

That stopped him in his tracks.

"Goodness," he exclaimed, "I have found a literary gem. An Irish jewel. That was beautiful; you are beautiful."

The aesthete looked a little emotional.

"It's not all beautiful, Simon." I pointed at him and continued with the verse.

"*Some are born to sweet delight.*" I then pointed at myself. "*Some are born to endless night.*"

"Oh, please don't say that."

The mood changed and he looked upset. I could see sadness in his eyes.

"I've had a lovely time, I really have," he said.

"So have I, Simon. Thank you for the meal. It was lovely."

I regretted having said the last two lines of Blake. It was an unnecessary dig at him. It was meant as a gentle poetic rebuff. I really hadn't intended to make him feel bad. It had been the wine, me showing off again, and it had backfired. He wasn't paying to have me insult him. He was a sensitive man and I'd thrown his kindness back in his face. If Simon complained to Charles, or worse, to Keith or to Malcolm Raywood, I'd be dead.

He shifted in his chair and looked perturbed. "I think it's probably best if we don't meet again. Our acquaintance has proved to be more intense than I had anticipated."

"I'm really sorry, Simon."

"Why don't I arrange to have you taken home? You can have an early night."

"No it's ok, honestly, Simon. I want to do a bit of shopping. I'll make my own way home later."

He waved to a waiter and asked for the bill, paid and left.

I nodded my head in disbelief. *Shit.* I thumped my hand down on the table. A few heads turned. So much for me taking advantage of a punter. *Now what happens?*

* * * * *

I walked alone in Soho and went to Dean Street Records. It was the first time I'd felt like an ordinary person in a long time. I lost myself in the store, indulging my passion for film music. Most of the LPs were foreign imports and were quite expensive, but I could afford anything I wanted. I'd already earned more money than some people earned in a year. Sin paid well. I bought two Morricone soundtracks, for *The Hornets' Nest*, an Italian-American film starring Rock Hudson, and *The Red Tent*, a Russian-Italian venture starring Sean Connery and Claudia Cardinale.I walked out of the shop into bright sunshine, feeling chuffed with myself. Then I realised I didn't have a record player. That was my next purchase.

Easter was approaching, the highlight of the year for the Catholic Church, and I was trying desperately not to think of home. I looked at the calendar with dread, knowing I was going to feel very alone and vulnerable. In an attempt to bolster my spirits, I decided to send my mother a little gift for Easter, maybe a piece of jewellery, and try to write a letter. But that wasn't going to be easy. I had nothing to write home about.

I had nothing much to write to Agnes about either. I had been writing to her every week, but my letters had gradually become less frequent and much shorter. At first, I had tried to tell her how much she meant to me, but I was finding it ever more difficult to write about my thoughts and feelings. The letters quickly became very matter of fact: emotionless to the point of being impersonal. I was no longer writing love letters, I was writing reports. I became very anxious when she asked when I was going to visit her. Then I stopped writing altogether. Her letters went unanswered.

* * * * *

The sun was sinking in the early evening and I'd showered and dressed up again for tonight's appointment. I was dropped off in Mount Street in Mayfair and stood despondently outside Scott's seafood restaurant and oyster bar. I hated seafood.

"This way, sir."

I was led to a quiet corner at the back of the restaurant. I felt a jolt of nerves when I saw my client. Sir Keith Joseph sat at the table, which had been set for two. He appeared to be partially submerged in the shadows. He gave me the slightest hint of a smile and motioned for me to sit.

"Drink?" he asked.

"Red wine."

"With this menu?" he asked dubiously. "Have a look at the menu. I've already chosen."

I studied the menu, aware that he was studying me. I felt his eyes on me. The first bead of sweat rolled down my back. I was feeling very uncomfortable. The waiter appeared.

"Red wine for my friend, please," Sir Keith said.

"Certainly, sir." The waiter smiled at me. "What would you like?"

"Anything. You choose."

"Very well, sir, I will. A glass of red wine it is."

"No, a bottle of red wine," I corrected, safe in the knowledge I had a few uppers in my pocket. We ordered. Fish.

Sir Keith looked troubled, pained even. My wine was delivered and he raised his glass. He sipped abstemiously and our eyes met.

"Cheers," I said.

"I suppose I'd better come directly to the point." He toyed with his napkin. "I feel that I owe you an apology. No, I know I owe you an apology. I apologise."

He was clearly uncomfortable and ill at ease. He studied my face as if trying to interpret my expression.

"That party." He paused. "What I did was unforgivable and yet here I am asking to be forgiven." He shifted in his chair a little, looked at his glass, then lifted his head to me. "My behaviour was beastly. Beastly is the correct word. I was like an animal. We were like animals. I am truly sorry. I was drunk. Very drunk. I was insane. They joke you know, some call me mad. That party was madness."

If he was mad, I thought, he was in good company at that party. The Bard came to mind and I recast Joseph as Hamlet at the Monday Club feast: ... *Sir Keith... is mad and sent into Whitehall... 'Twill not be seen in him there. There the men are as mad as he...*

There was a strange quality to his delivery, as if he were reciting poetry or speaking the words of a song. His words had a rhyme and a cadence. He sounded as if he'd memorised the entire conversation he'd planned to have.

The man sitting in front of me was indeed a different person from the inebriate I'd first encountered. There was no doubting his sincerity. His eyes looked tired and pleading, and yet there was something about his features that made him look angry or conflicted. There appeared to be an internal war raging within him, as if he were trying to restrain some inner demon.

Considering what Peter Morrison and the other man had subjected me to at the Monday Club party, and given what I'd been through since, I thought Sir Keith had little to apologise for. In the divergent spectrum of exploitation, his inept, drooling, drunken fumbling between my legs didn't even register on my personal barometer of sexual abuse.

I looked into his sad wounded eyes, and pictured a halo around his head. A political martyr – not Sir Keith, but Saint Keith – like Joseph of Arimathea. The thought made me smile. "I accept your apology."

"Thank you so much," he whispered.

The absolution seemed to take a little of the burden off his shoulders. He offered an enigmatic smile. I didn't have much choice about the apology. There was little else I could do, or say. I was here to make him feel good, and no doubt would later be required to make him feel even better. To make him smile properly.

I waited for the inevitable request.

"Tell me a bit about yourself."

I delivered the by now well-rehearsed introduction to my life, beginning when I was 13, when the Troubles started, up to and including my arrival in London. I expected a question about Derry or the Troubles. I didn't get one.

"Didn't you know how impossibly expensive London is to live in? Or had you planned to supplement your income… in this way?"

"No I didn't know," I answered. "Love is blind, and as it turns out necessity is the mother of strange bedfellows." I filled up my glass. "My life choices have become somewhat restricted."

I could feel the wine taking effect, giving me an edge, a confidence and an eloquence that could easily be interpreted as impertinence, even contempt.

"My life choices have also become somewhat restricted," he sighed.

"In what way?" I asked.

"It's complicated. It's politics." He smiled again. "But I won't bore you with the details."

I thanked my lucky stars – a politician who didn't want to talk about politics.

The food arrived. Fish.

As we ate, he told me about his childhood, and how, at the age of eight, he was sent away to Lockers Park boarding school.

"Christ," I said, "don't rich English parents like their children? I can't imagine ordinary people sending their children away. I'd have been devastated."

"It's rather a kind of privileged abandonment. I hated it. I'm an only child. I missed my mother and my home so much. Perhaps that's why I lived with her until I was 33. To reclaim all those lost, lonely childhood years. I felt I would never be able to leave home again." He paused as if waiting for me to say something. I didn't.

"In boarding school it becomes a question of survival. One has to blend in, conform and obey. I received a little more attention than I'd anticipated, from some of the older boys."

"You were bullied?"

"A Jewish boy in an English boarding school? Why, of course. My father took the view that if I became more English than the English, my Jewishness might become less of an issue, less of a burden." He delicately patted a piece of food from the corner of his mouth.

"Then there were other forms of abuse. You wouldn't think to look at me now, but I had good childhood looks. I was the youngest in the class throughout my time at Lockers Park. I attracted some most unwelcome advances."

It was happening again. Here was a man opening up and telling me things I didn't need to or want to know.

"These experiences are of course, were of course, very unpleasant, very impressionable, very formative."

Was he now trying to provide some justification, some rationale for his tastes and more recent behaviours?

"I remember nearing the Christmas holidays, just before my 11th birthday. Things had got particularly bad. My academic record went through the floor. The teachers thought I was suffering from some kind of illness, and I suppose I was.

I didn't lead them to believe my problem was anything other than an illness."

Sir Keith's eyes rapidly dropped to the table, as if he had suddenly remembered something, or had forgotten something. He looked startled for an instant, and then returned from his out-of-body experience. He folded his arms tightly, almost as if trying to embrace himself. His head tilted back a little. There was something slightly camp about him, sometime mildly effeminate about the way he held himself.

"Actually, I did become ill and it could be blamed on my experiences. I developed a frightfully nervous disposition. I became very anxious and this I believe led to digestive problems, which I've suffered from all my life. I've been a very moderate drinker as a result. A few years back I had rather serious surgery on my stomach, which brings me full circle back to that infernal party."

His frankness was typical of my other encounters. No subject was out of bounds for these people, including their troubled childhoods and their medical histories. These men unburdened themselves emotionally and sexually. They confessed their sins in the course of committing more sins. They expected their escorts to be both priest and prostitute.

He leaned back in his chair, sitting perfectly upright, uncoiled but tense, his frame stretched to breaking point.

"It had been a particularly difficult few weeks, this whole election thing for the party leadership."

I knew it was too good to last. *Here comes the politics*, I thought.

"I had been under considerable strain and was drinking too much. Never was a party goer, not even in university, but I let myself go at that party. It was the first time I felt relaxed in a long time. I felt… happy."

He raised his glass, studying the contents. "Vinum exhilarat animum." He touched his glass against mine. "The truth is, the thing that has been really troubling me, is that I have a son who is the same age as you."

I was wrong, this wasn't politics. This was guilt.

"I haven't been able to stop thinking, what if it had been him at that party, doing those things with those men. How would I feel if he was engaged in those activities?"

"You've been feeling sorry for me?" I asked.

"Well... yes. You just seemed so different from those other youths. You looked out of place. Lost. This is going to sound awful, but in a way I think I'd wanted to cheer you up. Get you to loosen up and enter into the spirit of things. Of course, I now realise my behaviour was quite appalling."

That he had sexually assaulted me out of pity was not a justification I would have expected. He leaned forward and studied my face. "What would you like me to do?"

"In what way? I'm not sure what you mean."

"Is there anything I can do to help? To make amends, so to speak." He looked compassionate, yet sounded irritable. "*The Conscience of the Rich.*"

"Excuse me?" He had lost me.

"It's the title of one of my favourite novels. C.P. Snow. The title seems appropriate. Working in a bookshop, I thought you would have known that." He sounded a little peeved.

"No. I don't think so. But thanks, anyway."

We ordered dessert and as he had mentioned a novel, we talked books. He enjoyed political and historical works as well as some biography, and managed to get through a book a week, unless he waded into one of those protracted Russian novels. He preferred to read French literature in the original language (Proust was a favourite). We moved from literature, to his trying to explain the rules of cricket, back to education.

Sir Keith told me he continued to experience a little bullying at Harrow, but he made some good friends, particularly in his final year. When it came to developing relationships at school he admitted to being painfully shy and could never make the first move. He revealed, however, that his final year in Harrow was one of the happiest of his life, spent in the company of a few "very intimate friends". He then asked me an unexpected and rather shocking question.

"What's it like working the meat rack?"

"I wouldn't know. I've never done that."

"Oh," he said, sounding disappointed. "One hears about the excitement, the risks, the danger."

He could see that I was getting upset, was sensing my discomfort. "Sorry, I was just wondering what it's like to be in the centre of that world, so to speak."

"No," I said sarcastically. "I sell my arse on St James's, Pall Mall, Knightsbridge and here in Mayfair. Not under the arches, so to speak."

It was this attitude that had landed me in trouble with Simon Hornby. I'd clearly still not learned my place or my manners. I was too easily upset and, as Charles Hornby had reminded me, obviously too parochial. Sir Keith had suddenly turned the conversation to the Dilly, the meat rack and the rent, as a reminder of the real reason for our "date". I had no doubt that Sir Keith would manage to forget about his son for an hour or so. It also dawned on me that I'd forgotten to take the dexies. I'd actually found the conversation with Sir Keith so engaging that I forgot how the evening was going to end. I'd have to wait for an opportunity to down the tablets with a discreet cough.

He looked at his watch. "Oh dear, is that the time? A car will be outside now, ready to take you home."

"Really? I thought we were…"

"Then you have not been listening to me." He handed me his card. "Remember; contact me if there's anything I can do for you. Or you for me, for that matter." He tried another weak smile.

I couldn't believe my ears, or my luck. There was such a thing as a free meal after all. We both stood up. I wanted to hug him out of thanks and gratitude, but couldn't bring myself to do it. We shook hands awkwardly. Half way to the door, I turned and glanced back. The surface of the table was still illuminated by a little candle, but Sir Keith appeared to have moved back a little and had become lost in the shadows.

CHAPTER 14

Party Animals

There were two aspects of my experiences in London which caused me particular anguish. The first was the involvement of the military; the second was the involvement of young children. Whilst the first was disturbing and unsettling, the second was so shocking and horrific it's never left me.

It was made clear from the beginning that Charles Hornby had ideas about how I'd be used, but it was also becoming obvious that Keith Hunter had his own plans for me, and that these two sets of plans might be taking me in entirely different directions.

A few days after the meeting in the casino with Mr Fisher and Gerald Citron, Basil dropped Keith and me off at a flat somewhere around teatime. I had no idea where. I asked Keith if he lived there, but he ignored my question. We sat on a sofa and he poured drinks for us. He opened a pack of Benson & Hedges Gold and we lit up. He revealed to me why he'd invited me to that meeting. Keith wanted me to gain some insights into the business and reflect on the changes that would be coming. He reminded me about all the Soho "big shots" now in prison. He said that more arrests and prosecutions would inevitably follow and that there would be gaps left in the Firm. There was a power vacuum in Soho and the bent coppers were running for cover, but there'd also be opportunities and at some stage in the future there would be openings to run some of the Soho bookshops.

He told me more about Playland. Things I really didn't want to hear. The Firm wanted to get in on the gambling scene and was running a small-scale operation to see how things worked out. Playland was operating well beyond the parameters of its gaming licence, and high-rollers could play poker from early evening until dawn upstairs. The booze would flow and cigars would burn. Serious sums of money changed hands and the winner, if so inclined, could claim what they called a Bonus Boy.

Keith also revealed that the owners of the Playland arcade were involved in money laundering. He didn't know the scale of it, but he knew for a fact it was happening. With the owners of Playland up to their eyes in financial crime, they were hardly in a position to complain about the Firm's rent-boy operation. Playland was a hive of criminal activity.

"So who is the Wolfman?" I asked.

Keith smiled. "He's the Daddy, he's Mr Big. Mr Very Fucking Big."

"But who is he?"

"Pack in that shitty job in Foyles, come and work with me full time and I'll tell you."

I was silent.

"Listen, mate," Keith said, his voice harsh and gravelly, "the Fish, me, everyone, we are the little piggies. Not only could the Wolf blow down our houses, he owns the fucking houses!"

Keith said he liked me, said I was a good kid and that he wanted to help me develop and grow and reach my full potential. If I left Foyles, he could arrange for me to cover a few afternoon shifts at first and learn the ropes, before managing a number of

the outlets. He said I should consider it management development, and in the evenings I could be entertaining a number of
Playland's more important clients.

"Charlie Hornby thinks you're an intelligent young man,"
he said. "I can see what he means about working you upmarket,
but I think we can do more. You could go far in the business.
Why would you want to be surrounded by dusty old books? You
belong in a proper bookshop."

"Are you saying I should be surrounded by tits and arse
instead of Austin and Brontë? That's very cultured." I smiled
and tried unsuccessfully to blow a smoke ring. The neat vodka
was taking the edge off my defences already. I allowed myself to
sink back in the sofa.

"Well, now that you mention it, the stock would be a hell of
a lot more exciting than the books in that mausoleum you work
in." He laughed loudly, then coughed.

I filled our glasses again.

"Charles tells me he showed you some magazines."

I thought for a moment, then remembered. "Oh yes, those."
I laughed awkwardly.

Charles Hornby had once taken me into a newsagent on the
Tottenham Court Road. A regular newsagent shop. He picked
up two glossy magazines, which were on display among the other
usual publications. They were called *Boys Exclusive* and featured
black-and-white and colour photographs of naked pre-teen boys.
"For Keith," he had said, with a disapproving look on his face. "A
little on the young side for me."

I was shocked. "How can they sell that stuff here?" I asked.
"We're not even in Soho."

We returned to the Mini. Charles explained something to me,
which now of course is unimaginable. In those days, there was no
specific statutory offence against taking or distributing indecent

photographs of children.[33] The law was a shambles when it came to regulating pornography. Charles opened the magazine at the middle centrefold. "Is this obscene, is it pornographic? Or is it erotic, a work of art? Is it educational? Keith subscribes to the educational interpretation. He uses these as training manuals for his fresh bunnies."[34]

"So, what did you think?" Keith asked.

"Of what?"

"The magazines, of course," he laughed.

I said nothing.

"You did look at them?"

I remained silent.

"Well?"

He went into a room and returned with a brown package. He sat it on my knee and I took out a magazine and opened the cover.

"Hard-core juve smudge." Keith smiled. "The finest scans you can get this side of the Channel."

His eyes widened as I flicked through the magazine. He was feeding off the shock that was registering on my face. I threw the book aside but the images were still in front of me. Imprinted on me. As much as I tried, I could not displace the pictures from my mind. I felt as if the blood in my brain had been polluted. I poured myself another drink.

It seemed there was another secret layer of sexual activity that was taking place in the underbelly of Playland, the Dilly

---

33 It was made an offence by the Protection of Children Act 1978. Even after the Act was introduced the courts took a very lenient view on the matter. In 1979 Mickey Perrin, an aggressive porn merchant, was given a suspended prison sentence for selling child pornography.

34 The Head of RE in one London school also took an educational view. He had invited a guest speaker into the school to show slides that illustrated the difference between pornography and erotica. The headmistress cancelled the visit. "It would have helped the students to make rational judgements, to have discriminating tastes," the RE teacher reasoned.

and the rent-boy scene. This was an underworld that Keith had hinted at a few times through a guarded comment or occasional subtle reference. When entry was granted through this portal, it opened up a domain offering sex with children. Very young children.

'Fresh bunnies ', Keith explained, were boys aged around 10 to 13. They were scarce and expensive. These boys were picked up at the big train stations around London. They were runaways from abusive fathers or negligent mothers. Some were running from care homes. They would be practically snatched from the trains on arrival, before they could be spotted by the transport police and returned home. Their welcoming "uncle" would offer them food and shelter and lead them, all smiles, from the station with a protective arm around their shoulder. Rarer still was the "candy floss", boys aged between five and 10. These were pre-arranged deliveries and always accompanied.

The Firm's bookkeeper, a man known as the Butterfly Collector, liked them young. But, in his own way, Keith said, he was kind to them. He had a soft spot. "Better for a boy to live with a loving paedophile than a violent alcoholic father." Keith said that the bookkeeper had even adopted a particularly bright 10-year-old boy, had him privately tutored, sent him to a public school when he was 13, and was now supporting him through university.

A few of the Playland youths, Keith explained, were making good money by appearing in "juve smudge" and "rollers". But most who had a choice in the matter, he said, were reluctant to have a photographic record of their activities produced. Since Big Jeff's arrest, local production was quite limited, which is why so much juve material had to be imported from Denmark.

I then realised that Keith was leading me step by step into the depths of perversion. He was grooming me, preparing to take me down to the next level of degeneracy. The more he could corrupt, the more he could control.

* * * * *

In 1975 the legal definition of a young person was someone under the age of 17. Anyone under the age of 14 was a child.[35] The first children I came into contact with looked at most 13. Two schoolboys in their school uniforms. Black trousers and white shirts but without a tie or blazer. It was teatime and dark outside. I was in the sitting room of small flat, waiting for a punter to arrive. His name was Tony Hetherington and I had been told that he lived in a house full of women, but that he liked to dabble from time to time. I understood that he was a senior civil servant and worked in some legal capacity.

Opposite me, across a table that had on it an array of beers, spirits, soft-drinks and crisps, the two boys sat on either side of a man in his mid-30s. He had his arms around the shoulders of both boys, who would giggle, laugh a little, share a little secret and laugh again. The man stared directly and aggressively across at me, cold eyes fixing on me with scornful contempt. He ruffled the hair of one of the boys and kissed the other gently on the forehead. He possessively pulled the boys close to him so that their heads rested on his chest. They whispered to each other and giggled again. They threw furtive glances at me and smiled at each other and giggled again, like the custodians of some little secret. The only thing I could pick up from their whispers was St Paul's. They mentioned St Paul's two or three times.

I was aware of a muffled conversation coming from one of the other rooms. A bedroom, I assumed. The man lowered his

35   Philips, Richard et all, De-Centering Sexualities: Politics and Representations Beyond the Metropolis. (London and New York: Routledge 2000)

head and whispered something to the boys. They looked across at me and chuckled faintly, before kissing the man on each of his cheeks. He glared defiantly at me and I looked away. I poured myself a large drink and awaited the arrival of Mr Hetherington.

* * * * *

Another encounter that broke my heart occurred at a party I was sent to. It was at the same damp, unwelcoming house in Essex that Charles Irving had taken me to, but this time it appeared completely different. I couldn't believe it was the same place. Where before it had been cold, dark and empty, now it was a hive of activity, with lights glowing from every window. Music and laughter carried on the night air. The house seemed to pulsate with energy and activity in time to the music of Johann Strauss, and I felt as if I were about to enter a grand Viennese music hall where ballgowns would swish and glide across the floor.

The reality was somewhat different. The house was full of old men. They looked to be in their 50s and 60s, maybe even a couple in their 70s. The Dilly boys were also out in force that night, mingling and eyeing up the prospects for the evening. Probably taking note of any small but expensive movable items that might make their way back to London in the morning, while elderly statesmen slept off a night of wild and drunken sexual abandon. I was dressed down but tanked up, already high on a cocktail of barbiturates and various other substances, but not nearly drugged up enough, I feared, to get me through this geriatric assembly.

I saw James Molyneaux, the Ulster Unionist MP for South Antrim, standing among a group of men. I felt an irrational flush of embarrassment, as if he could possibly recognise me, before

I realised that the notion of familiarity was of course one way.[36] Then I saw Charles Irving and decided to attack. Bottle of wine in hand, I marched straight up to him and kissed him on the cheek and put my arm around his waist. I was watching and learning from the rent boys about how to make a move and stake a claim. Charles would be my defence against this elderly rabble. Better to bed the devil you know.

"My Lord," he said, "whatever happened to the shy boy I dropped off in London a few weeks ago?"

"He turned over a new leaf," I said drunkenly. "I've been brought to book. I've seen the error of my ways."

Charles smiled politely. "I see." He looked a little disappointed. "I think you've had too much to drink."

"Not at all," I slurred. I rested my arm on his shoulder and he put his arm around my waist to steady me. We mingled and chatted our way around the room and I made a point of never leaving Charles's side. I made a show of flirting with him, clinging to him, of sending out an "I'm taken" vibe.

Charles excused himself and parked me beside a couple of rather interesting gentlemen. One was an exceptionally gentrified Northern Irishman called Knox Cunningham. It turned out he was Jim Molyneaux's predecessor for South Antrim. The other gentleman was Anthony Chenevix-Trench, headmaster of Fettes College in Edinburgh. In Ian Fleming's novel *You Only Live Twice* it's revealed that Bond attended Fettes after being removed from Eton. Anthony Chenevix-Trench had actually been headmaster of Eton and, like Bond, had also been asked to leave. He freely admitted he had a penchant for caning boys across the bare

---

36   In 2016 an openly gay man, Christopher Luke, revealed that in 1984 he had met James Molyneaux at a gathering of the Monday Club in London. Chrissie was 17 at the time and James was 64. "The connection was instant." The pair met regularly at Mr Molyneaux's London flat and they developed "a personal relationship beyond politics", which lasted for 30 years.

buttocks in his private office, often for minor offences. Although Eton had a long and distinguished history of corporal punishment, Chenevix-Trench took it to an unacceptable level. In these more discreet social circles, he was known as Tony Trench, or simply TT. Clearly he was here to secure the services of a boy who would submit to some punishment.

Mr Cunningham and TT had never met before but were getting along famously. By a fortunate coincidence, Knox had also attended Fettes himself. Before he lost consciousness, Knox enquired after the Maiden City and informed me that he was a member of the Apprentice Boys of Derry, but that he hadn't marched the walls since Kennedy was assassinated. He had fallen into a deep sleep before I could enquire further. I downed another drink, thinking that I would enjoy a sleep myself.

The background music had changed during the course of the evening from the classics to the big band sounds of World War II, then to '50s crooners, and now to sleazy, seductive saxophone jazz. Four leather settees were positioned around a large carpet, boxing in what would be a performance area. The Dilly boys were directed to the carpet, where they began to kiss and undress each other.

I was pulled from my chair, as were a few others who had been engaged in conversation with the punters. We were led to the centre of the room. I closed my eyes and drunkenly let myself be drawn into the action on the carpet. I felt hands and mouths on me as my clothes were removed. Then it became violent and frenzied. I felt as if I were being torn apart by a crowd of zombies. I started fighting back before I lost control and submitted myself to a full-on orgy. One or two of the men would disentangle a body and drag him over to a settee, where another bout of passionate activity would ignite more lust. Ripples of heat, as if generated from a chemical reaction, spread out from the centre of the room like invisible fire. The men ripped off each other's clothes as if they were burning.

Sometime later I awoke. The violent lust had finally calmed down and everyone lay exhausted. Some, myself included, like survivors on a battlefield picked our way through the living dead, found our clothes and got dressed. I sat on the floor, my back up against one of the settees. I rolled my tongue over my bottom lip and tasted blood, whether mine or someone else's I did not know. I was numb, shocked at what had happened, but most of all I felt intense shame. I looked around me. The room resembled a slaughterhouse. Naked bodies lay everywhere. Young and old. The room stank with sweat and cigarette smoke. I could hear an audible click and hiss of the stylus of a record player looping, as it searched for music it would never find at the centre of a revolving LP. I could not comprehend what I had just done. I felt sick.

Someone tapped me on the shoulder and a hand reached down. I was helped to my feet. I didn't recognise the man.

"Upstairs," he said. "Let's go."

I pleaded with him, told him I couldn't, that I was exhausted. He ignored me and gripped the top of my arm and led me up the stairs. As I was led down a corridor, a man was approaching with a boy. He had short fair hair and was wearing jeans, a shirt and a sleeveless pullover. He couldn't have been older than 12. Like me he was being held by the arm and being led to a room. He had not been at the party downstairs and was far younger than the Dilly boys, who were asleep in the drawing room. As we passed I could see a look of desolation and helplessness on his face. I sensed the fear behind the tears that were brimming up in his wide brown eyes. He was shivering. I tried to offer him a look of reassurance and compassion.

What had become of the boy's father, his mother? Why weren't they there to protect him? What journey had that boy been on that led him from his home and from his mother? What circumstances had brought him to this house on this cold bleak night? My heart bled for him. I was pushed through an open doorway and into darkness. There was another man in the room. His English accent may have been posh but his language wasn't.

A voice said, "Take off your clothes, you fucking Irish bastard."

I undressed in the darkness and wept silently for the boy next door.

CHAPTER 15

Depraved

I decided to buy my mum a gold chain and a crucifix and post them over, a gift for her at Easter. I selected an expensive gold chain and then asked to see a crucifix.

"What is 'crucifex'?" the Eastern European female assistant asked.

I crossed my index fingers. "A cross."

"Aaaaah, a cross, I know that." She smiled enthusiastically. She looked at me with big sympathetic eyes. "You want one with nothing?"

"I beg your pardon?"

"You like an empty cross, or you want one with a little man on it?"

"Jesus Christ," I uttered, under my breath. This was both in answer to her question and in astonishment that the Lamb of God, the saviour of mankind – who had suffered a humiliating and excruciating death through crucifixion for our sins – had now, in this heathen capital, been reduced to "a little man".

She produced a couple of occupied crosses and I selected one.

Later that evening, just before I was collected from Hope House, I put the chain and cross around my neck. It was best to keep it safe with me, I figured, until I posted it. As usual it was dark outside and was pouring down. I was surprised to find Keith sitting in the back seat of the car.

"I have to do a quick collection and a drop off before we deliver you," he explained.

After a while we arrived at a large two-storey building, fronted by lawns and set behind tall railings.[37]

"I won't be a minute," Keith said, as the car came to a stop beside a gate.

He returned, umbrella held high, with his arm protectively around a young boy aged about ten or 11. He ushered the boy in beside me then climbed in himself.

"That's us, Basil."

We drove off.

Keith smiled at the boy then gently stroked his cheek and rested his hand on his leg.

"Good boy," he said quietly and reassuringly.

The boy was silent, had a rather blank expression but appeared to be relaxed.

Keith unbuttoned his overcoat and settled back in the seat. He pointed to his groin and the boy immediately slid from the seat, knelt down and undid Keith's zipper. Keith held the boy's head and stroked his hair affectionately.

"That's it, good boy," he repeated over and over.

I watched in disbelief and horror as the boy silently and obediently satisfied Keith.

When the boy had finished, he turned to me and reached for my zipper. I gently took hold of his hands.

"No, it's ok," I said and helped the boy onto the seat. He wiped his mouth with his sleeve.

---

37   Looking back, I am of the opinion that this address was a children's home.

"Go on," Keith whispered. "Let him do it. Let yourself go, free yourself. Do it, you know you want it."

Keith gently smoothed down the boy's hair. Stroked his cheek. Traced his lips with his finger.

"He wants you." Keith's eyes seemed to glint in the darkness of the car. He turned the boys head so that he was facing me.

"You like him, don't you, sweetheart?"

The boy nodded obediently. I was stunned. Was this the result of Keith's so-called training manuals? Was this what he could reduce a child to? He had brought me down easily enough and he seemed keen to take me down even further. Was my corruption a game to him or part of some twisted plan? The further he dragged me down, the more securely I felt he could lock me in. Every party I'd attended, every person I'd been with, felt like another door being locked behind me. Deeper into the labyrinth. Would I ever get out?

We pulled up outside a terraced house.

"Here we are, Robby boy. One sec."

Keith ran to the front door, which opened immediately, and he disappeared inside a dark hallway. I took the chain off my neck. "Here, Robby, take this."

I put the crucifix in the boy's hand and closed his fingers over it. Keith suddenly opened the door, startling me.

"Let's get you inside, Rob. They're waiting."

Just as the boy manoeuvred past me to exit on the pavement side, Basil reached from the driver's seat and grabbed the boy's arm. He squeezed until Robby opened his hand.

Keith looked at the chain and cross, puzzled. "What have we here?" He lifted the chain and let it dangle in front of his face, then reached over and dropped it in my lap.

"We don't bring God when we're going to dine with the Devil, do we Robby?"

Keith clutched Robby close, the umbrella held protectively over his head. The precious cargo was safely delivered and Robby vanished into the shadows of the hallway. The door closed behind him. I was then driven on to the home of my next client.

* * * * *

When I think back to those times, I'm filled with horror and distress. I'd buried these memories and didn't want to revisit them. I'd experienced terror and shocking violence in Derry, but it never touched me like this. Child abuse was something else. Sitting in that car as the rain drummed the roof, I knew I was in the presence of evil.

I didn't have to wait long until I was dining with the Devil myself, or perhaps more accurately, a few of his disciples. It was Holy Thursday, and yet I could not have been in the company of more unholy individuals. I'd posted the chain and crucifix to my mum the previous day. A car had dropped me off at the Prunier Restaurant in St James's and the familiar commissionaire advised me that my co-diners were already inside.

I brought the number to nine as I took my seat between Keith Hunter and Malcolm Raywood at the dining table. I looked at the other guests and smiled politely. I'd never seen the other men at the table before. All middle-aged, various degrees of balding, most overweight. They looked as if they'd just come from a head teacher's convention. Their eyes fastened on to me as I sat down and I tried to put on a brave face.

"Good evening, gentlemen," I said.

If I sounded confident it was because I was already fired up on psychoactive stimulants. Even so, I was still feeling an odd nervous twitch in my stomach.

Keith had told me I was having a night off and that this would be a social occasion. He warned me to lay off the drink and drugs. Fuck him, I thought. If it's a social occasion, all the more reason to indulge. I wondered how he even knew I was taking drugs. Not to worry.

"Good evening, darling," one of them replied.

This little gathering had decided to go for the silly little names routine. One man was presented as Myra (Mr Hindley, apparently), another as Wendy. Wendy saw the disbelief that registered on my face.

"No really," he said, "my name's actually Wendy."

The others around the table sniggered.

Sitting opposite me were two men I assumed were brothers, they looked so alike. They were the same body size, with the same bald pattern and the same sunken malevolent eyes, the same sinister smile. One was called Rabbit and the other Grass. Another guest was introduced as Twist and another, a German, was called Man, or was that Mann?

Wine and food was ordered and I was largely frozen out, ignored as the conversation progressed. General chitchat about politics, the economy, absent friends. I defiantly drank wine, tasted caviar for the first time and started to relax. My defences, my anger, my contempt for these strange old bastards dissipated as I drank more alcohol.

Mr Grass nodded in my direction and asked Keith if I was OK, to which Keith replied, "I can assure you, gentlemen, that young Mr Daly here is the soul of discretion."

The tone of the conversation became more hushed and conspiratorial. No wonder, given the sensitivities inherent in the subject matter. They were talking about sex with children. It soon became evident that Keith had his fingers in a number of pies, the Paedophile Information Exchange being one of them. At the first mention of PIE I thought it had something to do with the food we were ordering. I zoned back into the conversation with a jolt when it dawned on me what they were actually talking about.

Mr Rabbit – Peter Rabbit, evidently – was giving an overview of where things currently sat with regard to PIE. Up until that month their sole purpose had been to produce a newsletter. Now, however, they wanted to bring more structure and organisation to the group. They'd established that most current members and potential subscribers were adult men with an interest in boys aged between eight and sixteen. It was therefore likely that PIE would develop in favour of this demographic. It was agreed that thought would need to be given to spelling out the aims and objectives of the group and that they would need to become much more pro-active. It was like listening to them discuss a business plan.

Mr Grass, another Peter as it turned out, discussed the finer points of political lobbying and of putting reasoned argument in front of legislators regarding the current discriminatory age of consent. Peter Rabbit cited a number of ongoing academic studies in the fields of social and behavioural sciences that were emerging. These would undoubtedly result in papers and articles supporting the benefits of child/adult sexual relationships in the context of consensual and loving relationships.

"We must stand up and demolish these myths about childhood sexuality," he stressed. "How people gratify their bodies with consenting others is their choice alone."

"I agree," said Keith with conviction, "it's no one else's goddammed business."

Mr Grass, bald, with thick black eyebrows, bore a striking resemblance to the Hood, the arch villain in *Thunderbirds*. He raised his knife and cut the air with gentle swipes. "The law has to change, it's an absolute ass. As things stand, a paedophile is treated more harshly for giving a boy sexual pleasure than a man who would savagely beat him. It's simply absurd. It *must* change."

"It will change, darling," Wendy said, "And we are the ones who will do it. Consider the support we have. We have some very well-placed friends in key positions. They stand by ready to support our position in any way they can, albeit discreetly, but nonetheless effectively. We must learn lessons from our dear friends in the wider gay community. We must attach ourselves to the gay rights and minorities' agendas. I'm telling you the time is right for change, there's a real appetite for it. The next few years are critical. We must attract the best people to our ranks, the best minds among the like-minded."

They didn't seem to pick up on my body language – the eyes raised to heaven, the fingers drumming on the table, rolling the wine in contemptuous swirls around the glass. These bastards weren't having a conversation, they were giving speeches. They were rehearsing for PIE party political broadcasts!

"Bravo," said Mr Grass, gently clapping his hands.

The others politely joined in and raised their glasses.

I could feel their elation, their determination, as though a surge of electricity had passed between them. Myra began to quote Shakespeare's "there's a tide in the affairs of men" speech.

Shakespeare! That was my queue. I'd teach them not to ignore me, to take me for granted. I looked over at Myra. "Julius Caesar, Act 4, scene 3."

Grass clapped his hands again. "Well, well. Bravo, Mr Daly."

I immediately regretted having drawn attention to myself.

"And where do you stand on the debate? Have you ever initiated a boy into the pleasures of lovemaking?"

I felt myself blush uncontrollably. His eyes bore into me and for a moment there was an awkward silence.

"No," I replied emphatically.

Rabbit smiled at me. "Then you will not be in a position to have an educated opinion on the matter." The sarcasm practically oozed from him.

I tried to shift the argument back onto him. "So what about the age of consent?" I offered weakly. It was all I could think of to throw at him.

"By jove, he's got you there, Rabbit," Grass mocked. "Kids apparently need to be protected from their own sexual impulses, you know."

Rabbit's eyes remained locked on me. "The question is not what the best age of consent might be, but rather ought we be thinking about an age of consent at all? Children find the exercise of natural bodily functions pleasurable. They naturally reach out and seek physical reassurance and affection, hugs, kisses, more if it is offered."

"You're talking about seducing children," I said, shaking my head in disbelief.

"Keep your fucking voice down," Malcolm warned.

"I'm sorry," I said. "I just think…"

"It's not seduction. It is initiation, it is negotiation. The boy, the young man consents each step of the way. If they don't enjoy the experience or feel uncomfortable or indeed feel discomfort, it stops. Mutual consent, always."

"What do you think, Herr Mann?" Wendy asked. Herr Mann was 30-something, professorial looking, short with a light frame. His turtle-like head sprouted from a white polo-neck sweater. He wore a pair of round spectacles with a thin wire frame.

"Your British laws governing the age of consent are a fallacy, a lie," he said with a thick accent. "It is essentially paternalistic. It is denying children their sexual freedom by imposing these protective restrictions upon them. Society needs to stop pretending. Adults and children can and should enjoy sex together."

Keith turned to me. "Let me put this to you, mate. Take little Robbie in the car the other night. I noticed, by the way, that you couldn't take your eyes off him as he administered the most exquisite oral sex. He enjoyed giving me pleasure, I enjoyed receiving his pleasure. Robbie was then pleasured by a few men in that house. He enjoyed the evening. I can assure you it was all consensual." Keith smiled at the others as they nodded their heads in agreement.

I was beginning to feel nauseous. I could feel the blood pounding in my temples. "Excuse me," I said, rising from the table, "I need to use the gents."

I rushed to the toilet and doused my face with cold water, before downing two bennies. These bastards were getting the better of me, pulling me down from my pharmaceutical cloud. I looked at my troubled reflection and took a few deep breaths.

I returned to the table, determined that I would not say another word. I listened as they laid out all their plans, their strategies: to lobby, to infiltrate, to identify and recruit those who shared their passions and beliefs. Where necessary, Keith suggested, they could use some Playland rent to arrange badger-traps, then blackmail and suggest ways in which targeted individuals might be of assistance to PIE.

Grass was somewhat concerned at these tactics. "Gentlemen," he reminded the company, "we're British. Our cause is honourable, as are we. I am quite sure we can garner the necessary support and funding to further our ends, without having to resort to underhand methods."

"We are a liberation movement," Myra stressed, "the emphasis being on liberal, not radical. We need to play the long game, take it step by step. Remember, we are fortunate, but there are many sad and lonely paedophiles out there, who, because of the stigma society has put on them, see themselves as sick pathetic individuals who are under the influence of uncontrollable sex drives. We must reach out to them and offer a positive and alternative life-affirming belief system about paedophilia."

Another fucking speech, I thought, but I couldn't help but be impressed at the way they laid out what they saw as their reasonable and rational arguments. They were passionately, idealistically and compellingly trying to justify the unjustifiable. All of them, at the table apart from Malcolm and Keith, were erudite, scholarly men. I felt hopelessly out of my depth.

One man present, Mr Twist, hadn't said a word. He remained silent throughout the meal. The only parts of him that moved were his hands, his sunken hollowed eyes and his slow chewing mouth. The others behaved as if he wasn't there. It was all very peculiar. Mr Twist was a dark, brooding, scary individual.

Malcolm kept his pearl of profound wisdom until the end. "At the end of the day," he said affably, "it's just grownups and kids having a bit of fun together."

* * * * *

I was then told that we were going to see "the best show in London". We were taken in three cars to Notting Hill and delivered to a flat in a quiet street. There were a few men in the dimly lit living room, smoking, drinking and chatting quietly. Respectful greetings were exchanged. Background music was so low it was practically inaudible. Fruit Machine was there. The furniture was arranged around the walls, leaving the carpeted area empty in the middle of the room. Six dining chairs were arranged beside a couple of armchairs. Most of those present had a seat, but some chose to stand by a wall. Inexplicably, no one was sitting on the large settee, which was pushed tightly against the curtains of the far wall.

I was sitting just inside an open door between Keith and Malcolm on the dining chairs. I turned around and saw that the Fruit Machine had taken up a standing position behind me. He winked at me and patted my head. There was an air of hushed anticipation in the room, an unnatural tranquillity for a group of men at what I assumed was a party.

We were offered drinks, spirits only, and I took vodka, delivered in a plastic beaker. It was then that I noticed everyone was drinking from plastic or colourful paper cups. Even the plates containing the crisps and nuts were disposable. I looked at the plastic cup in Keith's hand, a questioning look on my face. He leaned over and whispered in my ear, "It can get a little messy if there's too much glass around."

It looked as if adults only had come to a children's party. Until, that is, two small boys were brought into the room. Each was holding the hand of a man who led them to the middle of the room. The murmuring stopped. Apart from the distant beat of the music, the room was in complete silence. The boys and the man were wearing matching white bath robes. The boys' robes trailed across the carpet and although the bulky sleeves had been folded up a few times their small hands were barely visible. They looked like little magicians about to put on a magic act. I was deceiving myself, this was never going to be a magic act. It was going to be a sex act. The man gently removed the robes from the boys. They were naked.

"Brothers, aged eight and 10," Keith whispered in my ear. "Enjoy."

The boys were obviously drugged, their movements were lethargic and unsteady. Their eyes were glazed and fixed, and they blinked slowly and irregularly. The man positioned the boys like mannequins into various postures on a rug in the middle of the floor, then stood back to let everyone watch the various sex acts they performed on each other. I shifted uneasily in my seat.

Keith patted my knee. "Just relax," he said softly.

The man then took sets of handcuffs from his pocket and handcuffed each boy's arms to his legs. He lifted the older child to the settee and placed him in a kneeling position, his head and shoulders placed down before a vibrator was inserted into him. The boy barely made a sound or moved. The man then dropped his robe and it was only when he forced himself fully into the boy that the child gave a few groans. Two other men then took turns slowly sodomising the boy.

I glanced at Malcolm. He and a few of the observers were masturbating. Four other men then stood over the child, who remained on the carpet. One of the men produced a candle and a box of matches. "It's the little one's birthday today," he announced. I had by now moved to the edge of the seat. I became aware that the Fruit Machine was restraining me, holding my shoulders. Keith was firmly gripping my arm. Nothing could have prepared me for the utter horror of what they did next, and yet I was powerless to intervene. The treatment of these young children at the hands of these animals will stay with me forever. The scene before me started to dissolve as tears ran from my eyes. I jumped up.

"You're all sick bastards," I shouted. I strained against the Fruit Machine's steely grip and fell forward awkwardly onto my knees. Chairs fell, and Keith was on his feet, pulling my hair and gripping my neck. I felt an intense blow to my lower back as I was either kicked or punched. The breath left me for a moment and I was dazed. Keith punched me on the side of the head.

A couple of the men joined in the attack, slapping and raining down punches on my head and shoulders. Someone was shouting, "pacify him, pacify him." I'd been thinking about it being Good Friday the following day, and maybe this is why what I thought I heard was "crucify him, crucify him!" I was getting flashes of images from my childhood: Jesus on the cross, the blood. An elbow glanced off my nose and I felt blood flowing. I was restrained in a kneeling position. Malcolm and another man were masturbating in front of me. One of them was smearing blood across my face with his penis, which he then forced into my mouth.

Either the noise was subsiding or I was losing my hearing. I was pushed face down onto the floor. I felt more hands on me, heard my shirt being ripped, wondered what Charles Hornby would say.

I heard Malcolm's voice: "This fucker needs to be taught a lesson."

My trousers were pulled off. Hands were pressing on my head, my neck and my back. I was having difficulty breathing and could taste blood and semen in my mouth. I started to gag and choke.

The older child was lifted from the settee and placed on the floor beside his little brother. The last thing I saw before I passed out was some of the men encircling the two boys and then descending on them like vultures.

Holy Thursday, London, March 1975:
It's just grownups and kids having a bit of fun together.

PART 2

Eternity in an Hour

For we wrestle not against flesh and blood,
but against principalities, against powers,
against the rulers of the darkness of this world,
against spiritual wickedness in high places.
Ephesians 6:12

You were the prettiest of playthings,
the most fascinating of small romances.
Oscar Wilde

CHAPTER 16

The Long Good Friday

I awoke gasping for breath and drenched in sweat. I was in my bed in Hope House. I couldn't remember how I got there after being entertained at "the best show in London". I was aching from head to toe and my lower back was in agony. It was extremely painful just turning onto my side and sitting up. Easing myself slowly off the bed, I hobbled to the mirror. My right eye, nose and lips were bruised and swollen. Dried blood was caked into my cheeks, mouth and chin. My shoulders, back, arms and legs were covered in bruises. It could have been a lot worse. They could have killed me. I looked at my watch. It was 11:00am. So much for work. Today was Good Friday. It didn't feel good. Foyles would probably be busier than usual. Too bad. I didn't care anymore. I'd survived another night and was alive. That was all that mattered.

After showering, I dressed in my Brutus jeans, white T-shirt, tan boots and a maroon zip up jacket. I looked in the mirror, my wet hair falling in curls over my eyes, face swarthy but battered. Since childhood I'd looked more Italian than Irish and I'd been listening to Morricone for so many years and learning Italian from LP sleeve notes that at times I even *felt* more Italian than Irish. Now I was looking lean and mean, like a street fighter. I could have been Italian rent, rough trade. I was transforming before my eyes, becoming one of them. *Che cosa hai intenzione di fare Pretty Boy?* I asked of my reflection.

One of the nuns stopped me before I reached the front door. "How are you feeling now Tony?" There was a look of concern in her face.

"I'm fine," I said, forcing a weak smile. "The only part of me that's not sore is my hair, but I'll live."

"You looked in a bad way last night when they brought you in."

"Who?"

"The two gentlemen. They said you were drunk and got into a fight at a party and they brought you home. You need to watch the drinking, Tony, it's not good."

I felt ashamed. If only she knew the drinking was the least of my worries.

"Father Paddy has asked to have a word with you. He's over in the church. Why don't you go over and see him now?"

I felt a stab of nervous anxiety on hearing that the parish priest of the Church of the Sacred Heart wanted to see me. Did someone tell him something? Had he found out how I'd been spending my evenings? I walked over to the church and found Father Paddy Hackett standing by the altar directing the efforts of a couple of women and a caretaker. The church was being prepared for the solemn Good Friday services and the joyous Easter celebrations.

Father Paddy was tall and thin with prematurely greying hair, which blended in with his equally grey complexion. He had been active in the running of the Irish Centre in London (Hope House was just one of their properties), but he'd retired from that management role due to ill health and had been parish priest of this church for four years. Gesturing for me to take a pew at the front of the church, he sat down beside me.

"Who's been in the wars then?" he laughed.

"I'm sorry, Father, I got into wee bit of bother."

"Are you all right?"

"What do you mean, Father?"

"Do you need any help?"

He seemed to be preparing the way for me to tell him something. "We can go into a confession box and make this sacramental, confidential."

The invitation to confession carried the implication that I'd sinned. That I was sinning and needed forgiveness. I was now becoming more ill at ease. What did he know about me? I didn't respond to his invitation.

He sat back against the pew and brushed some dust off his sleeves. "I want to tell you a story. I'd like to confess something to you and then maybe you can confess something to me – only if you want to, of course."

I was now feeling quite sick. He must know *everything*. Should I now just open up and explain what had happened to me, reveal my predicament? What could he do to help me? Could he protect me or my family? I doubted it.

"This very day last year, Good Friday 1974, I was in the church here, doing what I'm doing now, preparing for Easter. It's one of the busiest times of the year for us. A man called Ken Lennon, he was from Newry, came in here begging me to help him. He wanted me to arrange for him to see a guy called Brendan Magill. Magill runs an Irish record shop in Kilburn and he's a prominent member of Sinn Fein. Ken told me he was an IRA informer, working for Special Branch. He was trying to break free from the police. He'd given a lengthy statement to Larry Grant, a legal officer at the National Council for Civil Liberties. Then he went on the tear, ending up in Ronnie Scott's Jazz Club, where he poured his heart out to George Melly, of all people."

"George who?" I asked.

"Never mind. Ken pleaded for me to help him. He said the police were after him and he wanted to escape from their clutches and to sort things out with Sinn Fein. I told him I was far too busy, what with it being Good Friday and all. I told him to come back on Monday and I'd go with him to meet Magill. Ken told me that if he left the church he'd be walking straight into the arms of the police." Father Paddy leaned forward and rested his hands on the pew.

I edged forward and mirrored the priest's half-sitting, half-kneeling position. "So were you able to help him?"

Father Paddy sighed heavily. "On Monday morning I read that Kenneth Lennon's body was found dumped in a ditch in Surrey. He'd been shot three times in the head. I've never forgiven myself. I was too busy thinking about religious services, instead of assisting a man in desperate need of help."

"But you weren't to know…" my half-hearted effort to make him feel better faded away in the silence of the church.

"I promised myself I'd never let anything that like happen again. Which is why I want to help you."

"I'm fine Father, really, I don't need any help. If I did, I'd ask for it."

"We are living in very dangerous times, Tony. We, the Irish, are the enemy, especially here on British soil. I was listening to the radio the other day and the presenter told his listeners to report anyone they heard playing Irish music. People are becoming paranoid. Hope House is under surveillance, did you know that? We are being watched. The phones are bugged. We've been raided a few times. Did you know that? They've been photographing people who come and go." There was a hint of accusation in his voice.

"I didn't know any of this. Wow."

I was taken aback, worried that Special Branch could have photographs of me leaving Hope House every night of the week and coming home late.

"We've been getting harassed and intimidated ever since that business last year."

"Ken's murder?"

"No. The other business. The bombing in Guildford. Last September we took in two new residents: Paul Hill and Gerry Conlon. They were later picked up and charged with the bombing. Conlon was in Hope House, at least 10 people saw him that night of the bombing. They're both innocent. They're being stitched up, caught up in this hysteria."

Now I was feeling even more vulnerable. I remembered Keith calling Hope House "the Paddy hostel, the den of terrorists". Two residents of Hope House were facing trial for mass murder and would probably spend the rest of their lives in prison. I was beginning to feel I was in the middle of a web that I couldn't even begin to understand. A web of businessmen, politicians, paedophiles, gangsters and rent boys.

Father Paddy looked directly into my eyes. "Tony, I have to ask you this. Are you involved?"

"Involved?" I was breaking out in a sweat.

"Involved with the IRA?"

"God no, Father, I swear, I…"

"I didn't think you were. Are you involved with the police or the intelligence services or anything like that?"

I was speechless that he could even think such a thing.

"It's just that you look out of place here. You're different."

"I work in a bookshop, Father."

"We've had people here who have tried to…" he searched for the right word, "… infiltrate the hostel. They go around asking questions. They stick out like a sore thumb and I've asked them to leave."

He put his hand on my shoulder. I was feeling guilty, exposed, sick.

"You certainly dress differently, and you appear to have a very active social life. You're never here when we have the bomb scares. They're phoned in by the police. We have to evacuate and they come in and take the place apart – sometimes bedrooms and always the offices."

He studied the bruises on my face. "I just can't figure you out. You are a sore thumb. Sorry."

I shook my head from side to side, willing him to believe me. "I swear to God, Father, I'm not involved in anything like *that*."

He looked at me solemnly. "These are crazy times, Tony. The Metropolitan Police think Hope House is a staging post for the IRA. Nothing could be further from the truth, of course. They don't have a clue about the enemy they face. The IRA bury themselves deep and keep to themselves."

Father Hackett brought a hand to his forehead and rubbed it down over his tired features. He covered his mouth and closed his eyes for a moment as if in deep contemplation.

"If the Provos had to depend on the likes of Conlon and Hill, they would have packed up and gone home long ago. We only took the pair of them in because they showed up on the doorstep like drowned rats. We felt sorry for them. They are in deep shit now. Pardon my French." He looked at the cross on the altar and blessed himself.

"Ah, Tony," he said with a note of finality. "You have to laugh sometimes. The last time the police raided us they went through all the admissions cards and took note of all our residents. One of the officers came across a list of names in a desk: Dietrich Bonhoeffer, Hans Kung, Michael Quoist, Karl Rahner, Edward

Schillebeeckx. They thought they had struck gold, thought that we had links to a ring of international terrorists. I'll never forget the look of disappointment on their faces when I told them these men were some of the century's leading theologians."

Father Paddy stood up and I followed him into the aisle.

"So you're sure I can't help you with anything then, Tony?"

"Really, Father, I'm fine. I just happened to end up at the wrong party with the wrong people last night." I touched my swollen lower lip. "It's nothing to write home about."

The priest pointed to his right eye. "And there's more to you than meets this," he laughed.

I walked towards the door.

He called after me, "So, I won't be reading in Monday's papers that you've been found face down in a ditch?"

I shook my head and laughed, but didn't look back. I didn't want him to see the fear on my face. An image of the butchered Billy Two-Tone flashed before my eyes. As I stepped out into the chilly brightness, Father Paddy called after me, "I'll offer up the three o'clock mass for you."

* * * * *

I decided to go underground for a while. Literally. I needed some time to think. I got the Tube and embarked on some random subterranean travels, jumping stations when the notion took me. I reflected on the horrific events of the night before and thought about my conversation with Father Paddy . Hope House was under surveillance. Was I being watched? Was I being followed? I looked at my fellow passengers. They all looked normal, but what did normal look like? I was no longer normal. What if I was accused of a bombing, or a murder? What if someone passed information to the IRA, giving them my details and telling them

I was an informer? I wondered how much longer I could survive this. I was going to have to do something before I became more trouble than I was worth, do something before I was either imprisoned or killed.

Holy Week was proving to be surreal. I felt as if I was a stone skimming across a dreamscape. Each contact with the surface was a different kind of experience. Tuesday had felt like a parade day in Belfast, with pounding drums and singing and chanting, when 2,000 policemen flanked a large National Front rally in Islington, the NF protesting against European integration. That evening I had witnessed some nasty confrontations and fights breaking out in a pub I'd been dropped off at. On Wednesday I had stood in Leicester Square and watched The Who, Elton John, Eric Clapton, Rod Stewart, David Essex, Lulu, Britt Ekland and Ken Russell arrive for the film premiere of *Tommy*. A couple of minutes later I was in Playland watching some real pinball wizards, before being driven to my next gig, a threesome involving an MP and his banker boyfriend. Thursday, I was being wined, dined and beaten unconscious by paedophiles. It was now Good Friday, and I was a lost soul travelling in the underworld. The Catholic guilt was heavier than usual to carry around today.

I got off at South Kensington and kept walking. I walked and walked, passing the V&A and finally stopping outside the Brompton Oratory. It was the hour of the Passion of the Christ and I decided to poke my head in and have a look.

Inside, the Church of the Immaculate Heart of Mary was packed. The full Latin liturgical weight of the Roman Catholic Church was being brought to bear on this most solemn of occasions. No other religion in the world could put on a show like this. Not even the West End could compete with it. The stage lighting was spectacular, tall candles adding to the ethereal illuminations from the main altar, where priests in their fabulous robes directed the performance. The heavy ancient fragrance of incense blended with the smoky atmospherics. Gold and marble gleamed and appeared to slice through the thick air. The congregation looked spellbound, entranced. Nowhere else would crowds like this flock to see a show where the main star never made a personal appearance.

There was a series of individual chapels built along the length of the walls that led to the main altar. These chapels were dedicated to different saints. I walked respectfully up one of the aisles and there, standing by one of the columns, was a life-size statue of St Anthony of Padua. The saint I was named after. My granny's stories of the angels and the saints came flooding back. I lit a candle at his feet and knelt and prayed, for my family and for myself. I looked into his tranquil face. If only I could experience peace like that.

Heading back to the pews, I crossed over to the far wall on the right, where one of the priests offered a chant to the altar in Latin. The London Oratory Choir and the Oratory Junior Choir replied by singing a mournful response, also in Latin. The singing was beautiful, heartbreaking. I moved closer to another chapel to the right of the entrance; the chapel of St Patrick. The altar was Neapolitan and the walls around it were made of Irish marble. I looked at the central picture of the altar and felt as if a blade had been driven into my homesick heart. There beside St Patrick was St Columba and St Brigid. These were the saints I'd looked at countless times in my childhood. They were like sentinels who had guarded and looked after me. Had an unseen hand led me to them here in London? Was this a sign? It had been five years since I'd last been in St Columba's Church in Derry. Good Friday 1970.

It was all too much for me to take in: the building, the incense, the Latin choral music, the saints I'd grown up with. My senses were overwhelmed. I fell to my knees in the Irish chapel and wept pitifully.

After a moment a hand gently rested on my shoulder. "Are you all right, son?"

A woman in the congregation had come over to me. I wiped my tears, and feeling like a child, told her I was lost. I couldn't look at her face. I felt like an outcast, a leper, a sinner.

"Where did you want to go?" she asked sincerely.

"I don't know." I apologised and walked to the exit.

I cupped my hands into the holy water font, doused my face and slicked back my hair. I then reached into my pocket and pulled out a wad of £20 notes. I folded a few into the collection box, hoping I could buy some redemption.

Once outside I made my mind up. Rather than wait for divine intervention, I was going to ask for help of a more practical nature. The man I was going to ask lived a 10-minute walk from here. I was going to ask Simon Hornby if he could do anything to help me.

CHAPTER 17

West End Boys

I didn't know and didn't care if Sheran Hornby would be home. The door of 8 Ennismore Gardens was opened by Simon. He stepped back a little when he saw me, surprised that it was me and shocked by my appearance. He looked at me in horror, but also anger. He studied my battered face for a moment. For the first time I saw anger in his face. I waited for him to tell me to go away, but he led me into the hall and quickly closed the door, having looked around the darkening street to see if anyone might have observed my arrival.

"Oh my God, what have they done to you?"

I was relieved that his anger was directed not at me, but at those who'd attacked me. He put his arms around me and held me close. I closed my eyes and, in the darkness, felt my feet lose contact with the floor. I surrendered to the exhaustion. The mental and emotional strain I had been under seemed to drain away. Either I was floating or I was being effortlessly lifted. A sense of relief washed over me and for a reason I could not understand, I felt comforted. I felt safe. I slept.

Later, we sat in the drawing room, the same room where I'd been plied with drink and drugs before being raped. I told him everything that had happened to me since my arrival in London, everything except the part about being raped by his brother in his bed. I told him about Playland and the Dilly, the punters, the violence, the children. I talked and I cried. I told him about the things I'd seen and what they'd made me do. I let it all out. I pleaded with him to help me, to get me away from the Firm.

Why was I willing to confess to this man and not to Father Paddy? The reason was simple. Because this man was more powerful. The man of business could do more than the man of God. If Simon had feelings for me, maybe he would help me; maybe I could use him – and I'd let him use me in return.

Simon knew a lot more than I had expected. He finally admitted that Charles was his brother. He explained that it was never supposed to be like this. Things had got out of hand. He told me he couldn't go into detail, but that Charles was having some personal problems and had been forced to step away, to take a back seat for a while.

"Charlie's plan was to deploy you on an exclusive one-to-one basis," Simon said. "These criminals have taken you down a different path – paedophiles, violence. I fear Keith Hunter and his *fleshmongers* have been taking advantage of the predicament Charlie has found himself in."

Simon's anger took on a note of contempt. "Charlie had come to a financial arrangement with Mr Hunter regarding you. Charlie has been compromised. He's been betrayed. I can't say I'm entirely surprised, given the backgrounds of these people. No sense of honour, or duty to one's friends."

Simon looked at me intently and traced his finger across the bruises on my face. "Do you trust me, Anthony?"

"Yes," I had to say. I had no choice. "Can you help me?" I pleaded, shifting a little closer to him on the settee.

"Yes," he said firmly, "I believe I can. But in return you must help me. You must do what I ask. Let *me* introduce you to some of our friends and business associates. They are good and kind people. If you take care of them, I would love to take care of you."

It seemed Simon was keen to continue the work his younger brother had started and earn a decent return on the money Charles had invested in my grooming.

"I'll do anything," I promised. "Just get me away from Playland. Tell me what you want me to do."

"Then let's start over again."

He took me to bed. He was gentle, loving and caring with me. It was the first genuine affection I'd been shown in a long time.

Afterwards he cooked a meal and we talked for hours. I asked him about his marriage to Sheran. He explained that in his circle, it was the case that people of a certain class and breeding had to attend the right school, go to the right university, offer service to the country by joining the right regiment (Simon reminded me again that he had done his national service with the Grenadier Guards) and then pursue an appropriate career.

"The correct marriage is all important," he added. "If one were not married by a certain age, say mid-30s, questions would be asked. The lack of a spouse can have serious career implications, and be detrimental to one's standing in society. Of course, one can have male friends and companions," he said putting his arm around my waist as I did the washing up, "but marriage is the bedrock, the foundation of one's place in society. The tradition of one great family joining with another."

Sheran's father, Peter Cazalet, was the Queen Mother's horse trainer and her brother Edward was a close friend of Simon's. Edward and Simon met at university, where their main occupation, according to Simon, was riding. Edward was Master of the Heythrop hunt and Simon, like his brother, was an excellent horseman. They rode endlessly, hunting across country with the university drag hounds. We drank wine as Simon told me about his idyllic university days and life at Pusey: the summer parties, the cricket matches. It was bliss. But as the years went by, the "wife" problem had become a real issue.

Simon had known Sheran Cazalet for eight years. It was a match made in high-society heaven. A recipe for a happy, long-lasting marriage, one might hope.

"Where is she now?" I asked.

"In Oxfordshire. She prefers the country rather than here in London. I shall be joining her there tomorrow, spending Easter and returning to work on Tuesday."

We both got drunk and inevitably talked about books and authors, the joy of literature. Simon told me he was something of a Wildean scholar.

"Oscar, I presume?"

"Yes," Simon replied with relish. "His works, his words are a joy to read and to hear, when spoken properly."

I admitted that the only Wilde I had read was *The Selfish Giant* and *The Picture of Dorian Grey.*

"That's disgraceful, and you call yourself an Irishman? You shall have to rectify that so that we can have wild Wildean conversations," he laughed.

"That's a Derry expression," I said.

"What is?"

"Wild. We say it's wild weather, wild expensive, or 'that wean is wild cheeky'. Only in Derry we pronounce it wile." Simon looked utterly confused. Much to my amusement I got him to try and pronounce some other Derry expressions in his posh accent.

"Am goin upstairs day throw mayself down fir an hour," he repeated after me.

"Am in the middle a may dinner," he intoned.

"Try this one," I chuckled, "it's easy. The snotters are blindin may."

"That's horrid. You are a nasty boy," he scolded and pushed me down on the settee.

"No, not horrid, it's Harrods, you silly boy," I laughed, mocking his accent, "your corner shop."

We composed ourselves and I tried to be serious again. He showed me some of his first edition Oscar Wilde books. I was impressed, by the books and his knowledge of Wilde.

"Do you think I look like Oscar?" he asked.

I moved back a little for effect and looked at him. "I don't know. Maybe."

"Hold on," he said. "Wait here."

He returned a moment later with a journal in his hand. He opened it up. It was full of scribbling, writings, drawings.

"I've never shown this to another living soul. Not to Sheran, nobody."

He opened at a page and pointed to a paragraph. "Read that," he instructed. "Aloud. I've never had it read to me before."

I read aloud:. *"Tuesday 5th 1972. I was struck last night by the uncanny resemblance Simon Hornby bore to Oscar Wilde. A taller version, I suppose, though not much, for Wilde was about six foot two inches tall. He has the same sort of hair, the same liquid eyes, the same long oval face, the same lavish lips and the same elephantine hips. I never had the honour, of course, of being alive when the great Oscar was, but I've read endlessly about him and seen may cartoons and photographs."*

"Shit," was all I could say. "Who wrote that?"

"I am ashamed to say I copied that directly from the diary of the person who wrote it. He was quite drunk at the time and I happened upon it quite by accident. It was written by Richard Burton."

"Fuck!" I recoiled. "I mean wow. Is that good, I mean, or…?"

"It's fine, I suppose… mostly. But this is not." He pointed and I read.

"Wednesday 6th 1972. Lisa's birthday. Sheran is a snob and cultivates people only because they're temporarily in. I muse that if the Hornbys had a child, which seems to me to be unimaginable, it would consist of one enormous buttock. All ass and no forehead. Their two bottoms side by side would fill the Albert Hall. We discussed sycophancy last night and nothing is as crawly as Simon's having to play golf with the new director of WH Smith simply because he is the new director. He was also late for us at dinner and I cannot bear people being late. Except of course me."

"What a bastard," I said, but inside I was kind of sniggering.

"Yes, it is somewhat cruel, God knows what he's written about us since. The thing is, I go out of my way to be so civil to Burton, if only for Sheran's sake."

Simon went on to tell me that during the war, before he became a star, Burton used to go to London at the weekends to steal books from Foyles.

"He was particularly keen on the Everyman Library collection. Stole dozens of them." Simon raised his eyes to the ceiling. "The Welsh," he sighed.[38]

He took the journal from me and read. "'*One enormous buttock*', indeed." He chuckled and I could suppress myself no longer. I doubled over, laughing uncontrollably. Then Simon collapsed back on the settee roaring infectiously. It was a joy to hear myself laughing again. I rolled about the settee like a child. Simon took my arms and pinned me down.

"Behave yourself, Bosie," he smiled, then his face looked serious. "I can't remember the last time I laughed with anyone like this," he sighed, and suddenly kissed me.

---

38   Perhaps to ensure Richard didn't return to his old ways, Elizabeth Taylor gave Burton the 1,000 volume Everyman Library as a birthday present. She spent a fortune having the volumes rebound in leather, with lavish end papers and gilding on all edges.

I sat up, desperate to divert his sudden urge for more intimacy.

"Simon, do you think you'll be able to keep them away from me?"

"I believe I can." He drew me to him and kissed me again.

I leaned back. "Simon, do you know who the Wolfman is?"

"Where on earth did *you* hear about the Wolfman?"

"The Fish… Mr Fisher from the Firm, dropped the name."

"Well… I know of him, but I don't know him. He's American. You've heard the term a wolf in sheep's clothing. Well, he's a wolf in a business suit. As a matter of fact, I have a friend and neighbour who is a close associate of his. He's an American also, a man called Dick Stewart ."

He put his hand on my leg. "Will you stay the night, Pretty Boy?"

"Not-so-pretty boy." I touched the bruising under my eye and across my cheekbone.

"Don't be silly." He traced his thumb across my swollen lip. "Cuts and bruises on that face just look charming."

Christ, I thought, *there's an endorsement for violence.* I felt like telling him to punch me in the face a few times to make me look even cuter. Instead, I smiled endearingly. "But Simon, why is he called the Wolfman?"

"Goodness, you ask a lot of questions, but your diversionary tactics are not going to succeed." He laughed and moved his hand over my thigh. "I'm not going to give you a lecture on the big bad wolf archetype. You already know that in folklore the wolfman is a shape-shifting man/beast – part-man, part-monster. The wolf is also, of course, a creature to be found in fairytales, and in the world of finance, one who stalks the markets looking for prey. Perhaps the name originates from his business dealings, I don't know, but he does lurk in the shadows. He's a very private individual and by all accounts operates at the centre of a web of companies. They should have called him the Spiderman. Dick is very hush-hush about him." Simon laughed heartily, then the earnest look returned. "So, will you stay the night?" he asked directly. I knew it wasn't a request.

I felt what little energy I had within me drain away in an instant. I was crushed. I wanted to go home and crawl into my bed. My back was killing me again and I felt completely exhausted. I forced a smile. "Of course I'll stay the night, Simon."

I lay awake that night thinking about many things. Wondering who the Wolfman was and thinking about Bruce Eckert, the managing director of Playland, James Humpert the Bag Man and Simon's neighbour, Dick Stewart. All Americans. What was really going on in Playland? What was the American connection?

This was proving to be a very long Good Friday.

* * * * *

I got back to Hope House early on Saturday morning and went straight to bed. I slept until midday. Simon warned me to stay away from Piccadilly Circus and told me *never* to set foot in Playland ever again. He promised me he'd attend to any business matters with Keith after the Easter break. I trusted him. He'd sort things out, take care of me.

I rose and went straight to the Dilly, where I met Damie. I was relieved to see that he was wearing jeans, a white shirt, a grey cashmere sweater and a black bomber jacket.

His first words were, "Holy shit, what happened to you?"

"Holy Thursday," I replied.

We went to the Patisserie Valerie in Soho to gorge on cream buns and I told him everything. Told him about the young brothers I'd seen being abused. He said he'd been to parties where the youngest participants were about 12 or 13, but what I'd witnessed was off the scale.

"It getting worse," he said. "Punters want them younger and younger. I'd say you're too old in this game now if you're pushing 16. That's why I need to get out of this scene. I need to bag myself a sugar daddy."

He swept his hair back and I noticed how perfectly manicured his fingernails were. How perfect the eyes looked with their smouldering, smoky eyeshadow and mascara. How perfect the lips looked with the sheen of some subtle shade of lipstick that enhanced the natural lip colour. I had never met anyone like Damien McKenna before, had never studied the face of another boy like this before. He was like an exotic alien to me, provocatively suspended somewhere between being a boy and a girl. He scared me.

"I can't believe you've landed a big fish already," he said jealously, "and you've only been in London what... five weeks? Simon Hornby. Fuck, you don't know how lucky you are."

I couldn't believe my ears. I pointed to my face and reminded him of what I'd been through. "You call this good luck?" I said incredulously.

Damie brushed my protests aside.

"You're set. Simon is the kind of rich sugar daddy I've been hoping to find for years, except he's in the wrong line of work."

"What do you mean?"

"He sells books and newspapers. It's not exactly glamorous, is it? Don't get me wrong, you're into books and that shit, that's why you and Simon have hit it off." Damie looked dreamily out of the window and to a faraway place. "My sugar daddy will be a movie star. Or at least a TV star."

He then revealed something he'd never mentioned before. Although Damie was ostensibly working for Roger Gleaves and paying his Firm a percentage of his earnings, he'd also been doing a lot of freelance work on his own.

It started one afternoon. Whilst working the toilets around the West End, Damie had given a punter a hand job and then gone into a back alley to roll a joint. The back stage entrance to a theatre opened and some members of the cast of a play left following rehearsals. Damie was immediately propositioned by the director of the play, and so began his entry into the homosexual world of West End theatre land.

He built up a regular clientele of actors, producers and directors. He scheduled his activities around the end of daytime rehearsals, then did his usual Dilly work for Gleaves in the evenings. His plan, his dream, was for a star of screen and stage to fall in love with him and take him away from all this. He'd still not found the elusive leading man of his dreams, but at 15 years of age he was being taken to a number of parties, where he'd been passed around by pop stars, celebrities and people who worked in the movie industry. He had been given drugs, money and also syphilis. After two weeks of injections he was back on the game. It had never occurred to me before this conversation that disease was another risk I faced. Sexual diseases, condoms, gels, drugs, sex toys and the paraphernalia of gay sex were not topics discussed in Derry.

So, Damie was the darling of theatre land. Invariably, he was there on opening nights by special invitation to attend a free performance, and afterwards he'd be called upon to give his own performance at the after-show parties.

"Who's the most famous person you went to bed with?" I had to ask.

"Oh, I couldn't possibly name them, darling. Confidentiality is the key to repeat business in my line of celebrity work," he replied in a posh accent.

"Bollocks," I said.

"Ask me when I'm drunk. I have a tendency to be indiscreet if pressed."

"Speaking of getting drunk," I said, "I want you to round up a few of your mates. We're going to paint the town red tonight. Tell them I'm paying for their night off. I'm loaded, and I forgot to mention, Simon has very kindly agreed a weekly allowance for me."

"I'm telling you, Daly, you are one lucky bastard. Is your sugar daddy's name Simon Hornby or Simon Templar? Either way, the man's a fucking saint."

"Let's party tonight," I said, "and tell them to dress for the occasion."

"No need to tell rent to dress up, darling."

* * * * *

In late evening an amazing phenomenon occurred in the heart of London. Hundreds of thousands of starlings settled on every tree, roof and upper window ledge of every building. They covered every inch of available space between Piccadilly Circus and Leicester Square. The noise from the communal roosting of this invasive species threw a sonic canopy above the heads of the invasive species crowding the pavements.

We met up on the island, under the wings of Eros, and took flight across Soho. There were seven of us: Tiger (Damie); Dreamboat, an impossibly good-looking boy with cat-walk features, also known to punters simply as The Dream; Flash Gordon, the most outrageously dressed among us; Cherry, who swore he was 15 but looked younger; Skin Deep (don't ask); The Mouth, a boy from Liverpool rumoured to have taken the art of fellatio to a new level; and Pretty Boy, specialist in antiquarian books and antiquarian men. I'd already met The Dream, Flash and Cherry in Playland and had also chatted to them a few times in the Coffee House opposite the arcade.

We started off in the Cockney Pride Tavern, a few doors along from Boots, had a couple of drinks, then crossed the street to the Pronto Bar for a few more. Tempting fate, we practically ran past Playland. We had dinner in a pizza restaurant, where Tiger-Damie had insisted on applying some of his makeup on my face to cover up the bruises. He told me to sit still and stop being so bloody impatient as he applied the finishing touches, then finished off with a little brush to my eyelashes. "All done, Pretty Boy." I refused to look at my reflection.

He made a promise. The night would be punter-free, no matter how much they offered.

Staying in Leicester Square, we went into Spats, which was sparsely populated. Drinks in hand, we took turns doing a spot of cabaret on the tiny corner stage, performing party pieces as a DJ set up his gear. I recited as many verses as I could remember from *The Raven*, by Edgar Allan Poe. Flash, who was attending drama school, had us rolling about in laughter as he recited the words from *Make Me Smile (Come Up and See Me)* as they might have been delivered by Olivier's Richard III.

The DJ put on a single that had been number one and was still in the charts: an unusual number featuring a spoken-word version of the Bread hit *If*, recited by Telly Savalas. Tiger and The Dream (a brilliant name for a stage act) climbed up and started to mime to the song with a sleazy, provocative routine. At the lyric *You come, you come and pour yourself on me*, Tiger was on his back on the floor with The Dream straddling him as the act descended into pure pornography. The landlord offered to sign them up on the spot.

That night we christened ourselves the Westminster Babies, because each of us had been reborn into a different existence in the London Borough of Westminster. We looked amazing, an eclectic amalgam of fashion statements: two-tone fabric suits, blazers, fitted shirts, navy blue Crombie with red silk lining, shining brogues. Damie shimmered in his white silk blouse. We swaggered along, all attitude. I had blown money on a fitted black tux from Harrods, complete with bow-tie, and was wearing my white Turnbull & Asser shirt. I'd also bought a black raincoat, which I'd wear over suits and button to the neck so I could leave Hope House without drawing attention to myself. We turned heads. We also turned stomachs: one elderly gentleman spat at us and told us we should be hanged. A group of Japanese tourists thought we were a new British pop group and stopped us for photos and autographs. How I'd love to see one of those pictures now.

Mouth suggested we go to Chaguaramas, a gay fetish club in Neal Street, but Damie looked surprised at the suggestion. He gave Mouth a knowing look. I felt that some unspoken observation, some signal had passed from Damie to the others.

"I get it," Mouth said, looking at me. "Pretty Boy has to learn to walk before he can run."

I wondered what Damie had told his friends about me, and I felt uncomfortable for a moment. These were the only friends I had and I was slowly being absorbed into their world. I didn't know where I was going, didn't know what I was getting in to, but I trusted Damie. I knew he would keep me out of harm's way, even though there were times he couldn't keep himself out of trouble. He was inexorably drawn to bright lights: the Dilly, the theatre, the movies, the stars. He was the besotted moth, drawn to the flame of celebrity.

Coming as I did from a good Catholic home in Derry, I had no clue what "gay fetish" actually was, but as for Chaguaramas, I knew that, walk or run, I was *never* going to go to *that* club.

Flash recommended a new club off St James's. The Odyssey Club had just opened in January. Formerly known as the Westminster Ballroom, according to Flash it was the most ambitious gay venue London had ever seen. I paid the £7 entry fee for us. The interior was luxurious, with plush curtains draped everywhere. We watched a camp and cheesy cabaret artist murder some old anthems, and then we danced to disco and fought off the advances of old punters and patrons. Flash announced that his girlfriend was pregnant, so he'd be working the meat rack for longer than he had planned. We were totally shocked he had a girlfriend but delighted he was to become a dad. Flash was apparently gay-for-pay, or – as queer rent called them – a *bendy straight*.

More celebrations. More drink. More cigarettes. More pills. More powder.

After we were thrown out at 2am, we walked the short distance back to the Dilly and rested by the railings. By blatantly loitering here we were committing an offence. The meat rack underneath the arches in Piccadilly Circus had rarely seen such an in- your-face, defiant, sexually-charged fashion parade as this. Heads turned, cameras clicked, and cars slowed down to look at the magnificent seven.

Cherry suggested we go to Playland, which would be open until 3am, and earn some money.[39] So much for no punter promises. It was now Easter Sunday morning. Yesterday, Saturday, from teatime on would have been the optimal time of the week for juve rent at Playland: the minors, the fresh bunnies, seemed to come out of the woodwork at weekends. Anyway, there was no way I was going to set foot in there, especially after Simon's warning. I told them I was getting a taxi home but

---

39 Cherry told me that in the summer, Playland opened from 9am until 6am.

that they could go and pick up some early morning trade. We hugged and they thanked me for a great night.

I took Tiger to one side. "I forgot to ask. Give me a name of a movie star you've slept with."

He leaned in close to me and whispered in my ear. "Peter Finch."

"Fuck off," I said, laughing.

"Honestly! I swear." He sounded offended that I'd doubt him.

I waved to them as I was driven away in a taxi. We may have been a group of trapped, troubled, used, abused and confused young men, but we were like a family and we'd look out for each other.

Simon told me that Oscar Wilde had once written: "We are all in the gutter, but some of us are looking at the stars." That night we had shone across the West End. That night we owned the Dilly.

CHAPTER 18

Tainted Love

I have no idea what Simon Hornby did or what kind of arrangement he'd come to with the Playland Firm, but as each day passed, I was hugely relieved that Keith, Malcolm and the others stayed away from me. They made no attempt to contact me. It was as if they'd all been rounded up and put in prison. Had Mr Fisher sublet me to Simon? Was Simon paying the Firm money for exclusive rights to me? Or was Playland still calling the shots and telling Simon who to introduce me to. Maybe Simon was really Mr Big and in control of everything, telling Playland what to do? That was a ridiculous thought. I had no idea what the deal was and I didn't care. I wasn't going to ask questions and rock the boat. I felt as if I'd been rescued from Playland by Simon. I felt strangely grateful.

I had been in London a matter of weeks, but it seemed like months. The shy boy from Derry who loved books and film music had become Pretty Boy, the best dressed guy on the scene: cocky but knowledgeable and cultured. But Pretty Boy was also becoming addicted to speed and tranquillisers, and battling excruciating back pain on a roller-coaster of uppers and downers. He was starting to cough up phlegm and sometimes specks of blood.

I'd prepared myself to be sacked from Foyles for not showing up on Good Friday. I waited for the little note to arrive. Nothing.

Did no one notice that I'd not been at work? I wasn't sure how this made me feel. Then out of the blue and without warning, Christina Foyle glided into the Antiquarian Book department. This was the first time I'd seen her since she'd interviewed me. I practically jumped to attention. I was impressed that I was going to be dismissed in person by the woman who'd given me the job in the first place. That *had* to be special.

"Good afternoon, Tony. And how has London been treating us?" she enquired.

"All good, but a little tiring at times. I'm still getting used to life in the fast lane."

She studied my face. Tiger had given me a little makeup to conceal the bruises, but I may have over-applied the foundation somewhat.

"You look frayed around the edges," she remarked distastefully.

I was aware of the books I'd been looking at, laid out in front of me.

Please don't notice the books, I thought, willing her not to look down.

She looked down at the books and picked up volume one. She read aloud, *My Life and Loves* by Frank Harris.

Frank Harris was one hundred years and three days older than me, born in Ireland on 14 February 1855. He'd emigrated to America, studied law, travelled across Europe and settled in London to pursue a career in journalism. I'd been looking through his four-volume autobiography, published in 1931. The books gave a graphic account of Harris's sexual exploits, along with gossipy indiscretions about the celebrities of the day. They contained many drawings and photographs of nude women. His literary adventures had been banned in Britain and America for 40 years, but at that time, a copy could be picked up in Paris for a considerable sum of money. Very few people could afford to go to

Paris for a book, so the likes of Lord Randolph Churchill, Charles Stewart Parnell, Cecil Rhodes and others could sleep easy .

Christina reviewed a few of the chapter titles: Student Life and Love; Some Study, More Love; Hard Times; New Love, New Experiences. She gently sat the book on the counter. "Frank always was better in bed than in business." She smiled wistfully as some memory came to her.

"You knew him?" I already knew the answer.

"Yes, but don't look for me within those pages. Didn't know him *that* well. Frank once told me he opened a high-class restaurant in Monte Carlo. His partner was Lord Alfred Douglas."

"Bosie?" I asked, surprised.

"Yes, the great love of Oscar's life. The restaurant was a complete disaster. Frank ate all the oysters and Bosie drank all the champagne."

We laughed. I waited for the killer blow.

"Anyway, my hubby was asking after you. He wondered if you might nip upstairs and see him sometime."

"Of course," I said meekly.

She noted the look of concern on my face; even beneath all that makeup.

"You do want to learn the business, don't you?"

I wondered what business she was referring to.

"Antiquarian books and all that?"

"Yes, absolutely."

"Then make an appointment to see Ronald. He's the expert in the field. I'm sure he'll take you under his wing. No dreadful hurry, whenever you have time."

She said goodbye and walked to the exit. "He doesn't bite."

This reassured me no end, as there were still traces of Keith's bite mark on my shoulder. She left me with the scent of lily of the valley in the air and much to think about.

* * * * *

Simon had wasted no time in introducing me to his associates. In some ways everything had changed and yet nothing had changed. I was out almost every night, sometimes from very early in the evening until after 3:00am, returning to Hope House drunk, high and exhausted from relentless lusting. The main difference was that at least now it was a more civilised and less torturous form of abuse. There was no group sex, no child abuse and little violence. The encounters were one-to-one and the locations were upmarket. No more grubby flats or terraced houses. I was being entertained and exploited in the most luxurious hotels, restaurants and clubs in London. I attended champagne receptions at art galleries, publishers' book launches and other corporate bashes being hosted in exclusive premises in central London.

Occasionally, Simon would accompany me and show me off to what he called "the Mayfair Set". He beamed with pride when we'd enter a room filled with people, most of whom were men. I have to admit to feeling a little chuffed by the reception I'd get. Conversation levels would dip ever so slightly and I was aware that many eyes in the room would have discreetly noticed my arrival. These people may have had position and wealth but I had my youth and looks.

I learned a lot from Simon. I'd watch him work the room with effortless small talk, charm and perfect manners. Lord Back-Seat considered Simon Hornby to be the personification of his old college motto, *Manners Maketh Man*. I'd study him at the dining table. A seasoned raconteur, his voice was deep, rich and authoritative, though when he was alone with me he could be quite camp and effeminate. His fellow diners would cling to his every word, then he'd deliver the killer punchline and they would fall about laughing. On one occasion in a hotel restaurant, the piano player took a break. Simon jumped up from his dessert, made for the piano and started performing old music hall songs. Others joined him and an impromptu sing-along ensued before he returned to the table, to much applause. I looked up to Simon with genuine admiration. If only I'd had a father like *that*: intelligent, charming, talented… wealthy.

After dinner, one of two things would happen. Simon would either take me back home with him (I was at his beck and call whenever he required sex), or he'd leave me sitting or standing beside one of his gentlemen friends and would make his excuses and leave without me. That would be the signal. I was to be that person's companion for the remainder of the evening and I'd subsequently be taken upstairs to a suite in the hotel or driven back to the gentleman's residence.

Simon told me that if asked, I could give a client my Foyles business card, but that if anyone contacted me with a view to meeting again, I must tell him first.

One evening, as he applied the finishing touches to me before I was picked up, I asked Simon what the financial arrangements were. Was I to ask the clients for money up front or after?

"Goodness no!" came the horrified response. "Nothing so distasteful. No money is to change hands." Simon gestured for me to hold out my arms and fixed on my cuff links. "I'm providing you with a substantial weekly allowance. The companionship you offer my friends is a gift from me: a token of friendship and appreciation. In return, perhaps next week, next month, next year, there may be a requirement for certain services to be reciprocated: a business introduction perhaps, a kindly word in a Parliamentarian's ear, favourable consideration for a contract or a seat on a Board. These things are rendered in due course across the network."

"So I come gift wrapped, tied up with the old school tie?"

"You are a perceptive young man, Anthony. If you let me, I'll teach you how it all works. How the links that form the chain of the Establishment are forged and managed."

I shuddered, knowing that same chain shackled and enslaved me.

* * * * *

I was picked up outside Harrods by a shining black Mercedes and driven a short distance to the German Embassy in Belgravia. The Embassy was hosting a small delegation of businessmen from Berlin who were in London to explore investment opportunities. I was escorted to a bedroom occupied by a small but grossly overweight German businessman in his forties. He was bursting out of a three-piece suit, and he spoke little or no English. I'd been drinking in preparation and had consumed the necessary medication, but I was nowhere near high enough for this encounter. I wondered whether to make a run for it. He stared at me and mopped the sweat from his brow with a large handkerchief. Before I could attempt any kind of greeting, he attacked me and pinned me to the bed. His weight pressed down on me and I was submerged in the mattress. He tried to kiss my mouth but I turned my head to the side and he slobbered into my ear as he whispered "lustknabe, lustknabe" over and over again.

He rolled off me and I leapt up and headed for the drinks tray. I wasn't sure I was going to be able to get through this. I poured a large vodka and cupped a few bennies and painkillers into my mouth before he led me to the bathroom, where some little bags of white powder sat on a glass-topped table. Gesturing that I should help myself, he turned and went back into the bedroom, returning a moment later minus his trousers and jacket. Standing there in his shirt, waistcoat and underpants, he looked ridiculous.

He saw I'd arranged some of the coke on the knuckle of my left hand and was attempting to sniff it off, the way I'd seen my granny take snuff.

"No, no… all wrong," he admonished, licking the coke off my knuckle and sucking the remaining residue off my two fingers.

He cut the coke into a line on the table and, handing me a small plastic tube, showed me what to do. I sniffed up the powder and then sat on the edge of the bath as he fixed himself a line, knowing I'd crossed another line. It was the first time I'd ever taken cocaine. It would not be the last.

He led me to the bed, stretched me out and undressed me. I felt on top of the world, fired up and without a care in the world. I'd never felt a release like it, nothing mattered anymore. I laughed joyously, reached for his waistcoat and ripped it open, buttons flying everywhere. He slapped me on the face, hard, and I laughed senselessly. I slapped him back, and tried to slap him again but he blocked my hand and caught my wrist.

"Lustknabe like it rough, no? Lustknabe want to play hard?"

He straddled me, crushing the breath from me, pinned my arms above my head and spat in my face. I giggled again, floating on air. He slapped me again, then disappeared between my legs.

"Let battle commence," I shouted. I was out of my mind.

Then Germany declared war on me. He flipped me over onto my belly and climbed on top of me. As he forced himself into me and hammered me into the mattress, I wished he'd pull my head back and cut my throat from ear to ear so I could watch my blood splatter over the nice white sheets. I lay there and died inside, letting that fat fucking German destroy me.

* * * * *

The next time I saw Simon he told me he'd received an offer from my client at the German Embassy.

"An offer?" I was intrigued

"Yes. He wants to buy you. Actually, buy you and take you back with him to the Fatherland. The message was, 'How much for ze lustknabe?'"

I shook my head in disbelief. "What exactly is a lustknabe?"

"Well, I'm unsure of the exact translation, but essentially it means pleasure-boy."

* * * * *

After the elation of my first experience of cocaine came the self-loathing and grief for another part of me that was gone forever. I hated myself for days afterwards and had wonderfully liberating thoughts of taking my own life. I carried my anger into their beds. With some punters I was now showing an aggressive streak, pushing a little too hard, wrestling with them a little less playfully, giving bites that hurt, whispering insults and obscenities into their ears. Inciting them, half-hoping I'd provoke one of them into beating my face to a pulp. Then, no more Pretty Boy. I fantasised about me and Billy Two-Tone lying together in each other's arms, dead. In a ditch, both of us butchered, at peace.

In spite of my reservations about using harder drugs, the prospect of having to entertain clients soon turned my thoughts to the euphoric oblivion and blissful indifference induced by cocaine. In the children's book *Is* by Joan Aiken, there is a magical, place called Playland, a place described as happy and gay and so perfect that even apples don't have cores. Cocaine took me to Playland.

Damie introduced me to the Prophet. He was the hippy that time forgot, a long-haired leftover from the pseudo-psychedelic world of Carnaby Street during the summer of love. The Prophet was a Soho drug dealer. During our visit he talked about his personal drugs odyssey. He'd been just a pill-taker until he met Dr John Petro, one of a small group of notorious "junkie doctors" who prescribed heroin to addicts and curious thrill-seekers in the West End. Dr Petro lived in various hotels and employed a stripper as his receptionist. He ran his "surgery" from the buffet at Baker Street Station, before moving to Coventry Street, where he dispensed his goods from Playland and the all-night coffee bar opposite. When it became very difficult to get heroin, Dr Petro and a fellow physician, Dr Christopher Swan, began prescribing injectable methedrine, which was unregulated. It was an instant hit.

"1968," the Prophet said, "was the year of the needle – the golden era." He dragged on his joint. "Dr John Petro was the Mother Teresa of the Dilly."

We paid the Prophet and he handed over the cocaine. "It's all true, man," he intoned, "you won't find Petro and Swan in the history books, but those two dudes started a fucking revolution. It's all true, man."[40]

* * * * *

Simon surprised me in many ways, often with unexpected little gifts, or taking me out one Saturday morning to visit venues not far from his home: the V&A, the Natural History Museum. One of the biggest surprises came when he took me to Kensington

---

40   In January 1968 Dr Petro was arrested after appearing on *The David Frost Show*. He was fined £1,700 and eventually struck off the medical register in 1968. He continued dispensing and in November 1969 the *Daily Telegraph* observed him giving injections to addicts in the Dilly.

High Street and led me off into a tiny secluded little square, one of those small gardens of tranquillity that only Londoners know exist. We sat on a bench. He stared into my face intently.

"How would you like to visit your lady friend in Lowestoft?"

I waited for the catch, the punch line. None came. "Alone?" I said, incredulously.

"Of course. I don't think it would be entirely appropriate if I went with you."

* * * * *

I got the train to Lowestoft that afternoon. I'd phoned Agnes and given her the travel arrangements. She met me at the station. We kissed, but both felt and acted awkwardly. I checked into a B&B and she showed me her digs (she had a room in a convent). That night we went to a pub and she introduced me to some of her English friends.

As the evening progressed I became more and more agitated. All I could think about was what I was doing in London, and with whom. I felt uncomfortable to be in her company, in female company. I was acting the role I'd learned to play in London, but with a female, a girlfriend. It all seemed false and contrived. I just couldn't find the person I'd been, the real me. It was time for the mandies. I needed to calm down and chill out. I drank too much.

We were invited to a house party. I drank more and passed out, waking briefly to see Agnes in the arms of another man, kissing passionately. A sense of relief washed over me. There was one less complication to worry about. It had been clear from the first moment we met at the station that the spark had gone. Now the pressure was off. It was over. I went back to sleep.

We kissed goodbye at the station the following morning, tears in our eyes. I wondered if she could see my inner turmoil, read the secret thoughts in my head. I hugged her tightly, kissed her on the lips and whispered in her ear, "I love you."

I walked to the train, my heart breaking. I waved goodbye from the window. The magical Christmas romance we had shared was over. Had I been naive to think that the bells ringing out that Christmas for Agnes and me might one day be wedding bells? Our love had become tainted. A life that might have been faded away in the morning mist.

* * * * *

A broken boy returned to London.

I went to Simon. He looked surprised and delighted to see me.

"Well, how did it all go?"

"I've lost her," I choked, "it's over."

I walked to him and put my head on his chest. He embraced me and I wept uncontrollably. I couldn't speak. My shoulders heaved as I cried like a heartbroken child. He held me tightly.

"There, there, it's all right. Don't cry, Pretty Boy."

He led me to the bedroom.

"You came back. You came back to me." There was emotion in his voice. Had all this been a test? Had he given me the opportunity to break away? It hadn't even crossed my mind that I could try to escape. The thought never occurred to me. I had unthinkingly and instinctively returned to London. Simon was convinced that my returning to him was proof I wanted to be with him, learn from him, earn from him.

Later, we walked down to Harrods and Simon bought more clothes for me. A little something to cheer me up, but also something I could wear that evening when I would be taken to meet Sir Michael Havers.

* * * * *

Sir Michael sent a car to pick me up and I was dropped off at the Garrick Club in Covent Garden. The driver told me the club was a favourite with actors and writers. As Sir Michael was neither, I wondered about the venue, but then realised that QCs must be very good actors, performing as they do in court. Sir Michael greeted me at the bar and offered me a scotch. I told him I didn't drink whisky.

"You're Irish, for Christ's sake, of course you drink whisky, don't be such a girl." I seemed to be attracting a lot of attention from some of the theatrical types at the bar. But as I was in the company of a man who was 32 years older than me, I assumed everyone knew what I was there for.

After a couple of drinks, we went upstairs to one of the bedrooms. A bottle of Scotch awaited and Sir Michael began to unwind. I quickly found out he was a talker. If politicians can talk (and they can), politicians who also happen to be barristers can *really* talk. He was incredibly indiscreet and no one was spared from his caustic tongue: Lords, commoners, the judiciary, the police… all were subjected to his disdain. Most of all, though, Sir Michael loved to talk about himself, particularly after he'd exhausted himself in bed. He even incorporated his monologues and the use of props into the sex acts as he talked himself to orgasm by fixating on someone who'd fallen foul of the law, or better still, had fallen through the trapdoor of a gallows. He seemed to get off on crime and criminals. Murder was an aphrodisiac for him. I found it difficult to concentrate on the task in hand due to his continual rambling.

On this occasion the preselected subject of his fantasy was Ruth Ellis, the last woman to be hanged in Britain. Lying naked on the bed, I noticed with some trepidation that Sir Michael had placed a cardboard box on the table on his side of the bed. Once he'd finished undressing, he opened the box and put on a long tattered-looking judge's wig. He moved down the bed and proceeded to give me a prolonged blow job. I looked down and watched in disbelief as the horse-haired creature bobbed up and down between my legs. He then lay on his back and directed me to do the same for him.

Then the talking commenced again, as he waxed lyrical about Ruth Ellis's crime. He was breathing heavily and running his fingers through my hair.

"It's good, boy, so perfect... It's so... natural. She died and you were born. You come from 1955, the year they killed her, don't you see the connection... past and present. But that's not all."

He was holding my head, forcing me down on him.

"My father sentenced the bitch to death. He was the judge at her trial. My father, Justice Havers, was wearing this wig that very day, the day he pronounced death on her. You see? The past with us in the present. Me and my father, you and the bitch; 1955 has become 1975; all four of us are in this bed together."

He cried out and fell back as the smooth, wave-like motions pulsed and faded away. A shiver ran down my spine. A few punters I'd been with were into role-play and I indulged their fantasies, but I was quite freaked out by Sir Michael's grisly and twisted sexual imaginings.

We drank more whisky. He pulled the sheets up, put his arm around me and rested my head on his chest. And he talked. He told me that back in 1964, at the age of 41, he'd been named as Queen's Counsel, the youngest ever barrister to receive the accolade. He explained how the law works, and told me about famous trials, the inside stories, the courtroom dramas. I remember him telling me how in 1967 he'd defended Mick Jagger and Keith Richards. Keith's house had been raided during a drug-fuelled party. The case had become the *cause célèbre* of the era. A report at the time alleged that when the police stormed past Keith they found Mick with his head buried between the legs of Marianne Faithfull, eating a Mars Bar.

"All I can say is that when I had a look around Redlands after the raid, I did come across a stash of Mars Bars."

Sir Michael lit a cigarette and laughed.

"Anyway, I got them out of prison on bail the following day. I went to the appeal court. They overturned Keith's conviction and gave Mick a conditional discharge."

"I was never much of a Stones fan," I said. "I love the Moody Blues, though. They're not your typical rock stars. Not controversial like Mick."

"You'd be surprised. I dined a few times with Mick and co during the trial. Mick told me he and a few of the Stones, a couple of Who members and the odd Beatle went to parties at a house in Richmond Park leased by the Moodies. They partied hard."

It was impossible for me to take in the fact that this old 52-year-old dinosaur was, after having sex, still talking about sex, drugs and rock and roll in the 1960s.

"I'm not the old fogey you think I am," he said as if reading my mind. "I do miss the 60s though. I was the most expensive lawyer in the country. Then I became an MP five years ago and it all became rather boring. Things are, however, looking up again." He pointed to his erection and directed me towards him. Then he began to talk once more.

"Mick presented me with a poster advertising one of their early gigs in Guildford. He'd got the band members, Marianne and a couple of Beatles and other musicians to autograph it for me. You can have it if you like. A little gift from me. It's hidden away at home. I'll look it out and give it to you on our next meeting."

"Thank you," was all I could manage. If I got the poster I'd give it to Damie. He'd appreciate it more than me.

"Speaking of Guildford, there's going to be big trial arising from those ghastly bombings. I'm told the trial will be held later this year, September possibly. Now there's a trial I'd dearly love to get my teeth into. Get back into the spotlight. If I get to prosecute the case would you come and watch me perform? It would please me to know you were looking at me. I could arrange that."

"Maybe. I'd have to ask Simon or Christina Foyle to get off work."

We dressed. I helped him put on his salmon-and-cucumber club tie.

"The club has a wonderful library specialising in all things theatrical. I've arranged for you to be given a look around before you go. I'm led to understand that you like that type of thing. I could get you into the House of Commons library also, if you wish."

He reached for his wallet.

"There's no need for money or anything," I told him.

He counted out five £20 notes and patted my head.

"I know, but you are very good. Just a little tip."

"Thank you, Sir."

He insisted I call him Sir.

CHAPTER 19

The Illustrious Client

If nothing else, my punters were very interesting people and thankfully took personal hygiene seriously, as I was expected to do. Though Simon never let me call them punters.

"They are your clients," he would correct me. "Business etiquette and protocol are all important in these interactions, as indeed are civility, good manners and a sense of humour. Just remember, for all you know you could be dining with royalty."

I passed a very illuminating evening in the company of Noel Annan, the Provost of University College, London. The event was a rather intimate afternoon tea affair at the Dorchester, a bookish, educational gathering of sorts. Noel had given a brief talk to polite applause and he then took me from Simon and introduced me to some guests, a couple of whom, he said, had been apostles. I didn't want to think what the *apostles* reference alluded to. I was given a weak handshake and a graceful nod of the head by Brian Sewell, an art expert who'd worked for Christie's for many years. He in turn introduced me to an old friend and mentor of his, a tall gaunt half-blind professor called Sir Anthony Blunt. He seemed to pick up on my accent immediately and peered at my face impassively as if trying to focus, trying to see if he recognised me. "Are you a graduate of Kincora?" he enquired.

"Kincora?"

"Belfast," he prompted.

"No, I'm from Derry."

"Oh, I see. My mistake, do forgive me."

A waiter handed me another glass of champagne. Noel politely introduced me to a small group of academics discussing the parlous state of education. I made no attempt to embarrass myself in this distinguished company by offering an opinion. One of the men, John Rae, who was headmaster of Westminster School, talked about the need to stamp out bullying. He recounted a particularly unsettling conversation with the father of a pupil at his school. The man had told him his son, a bright but small and under-developed boy, had been systematically bullied at his prep school. Other boys had urinated on bread and forced it into his mouth. The father was being posted overseas and was understandably worried about his son. Mr Rae said he'd assured the father as best he could that his son was not being bullied at Westminster, but admitted to us he had no idea what was going on.

I was deeply affected by this story and my heart went out to the little boy. I wondered if the same horrors that I'd witnessed through Keith Hunter could be happening in other boarding schools or to children in care. That orphans with nothing and the children of the rich could be suffering equally in different institutions was a chilling thought. I remembered the schoolboys I'd seen in the Notting Hill flat and the boy at the house party in Essex. But I also thought of the little Jewish boy, Keith Joseph, seemingly equally abandoned.

As afternoon turned into evening, the small group of people who remained started drinking quite a lot of spirits. I began to feel anxious again. I always felt safe when Simon was around, but experienced feelings of vulnerability at these events once he left. I was becoming emotionally dependent on him, and on drugs. Despite Simon's reassurances about his associates, my clients, all being gentlemen, a recurring fear nagged away at me: of being taken on my own, without any Dilly support, to a hotel suite by a group of men. Before he left, Simon came over to see how I was doing. Perhaps he saw the worry on my face.

"Everything OK?" he asked.

"Yes, I'm fine, Simon." He patted my shoulder affectionately and smiled proudly.

"I'm planning a little surprise at the weekend, but I'll see you before that."

He winked at me, before leaving to go straight to the Adelphi Theatre for the opening night of Stephen Sondheim's *A Little Night Music*.

Damie had a date with one of his theatrical luvvies and was also going to see the musical. Damie would no doubt be attending the after-show party and I felt jealous that Simon might also be attending, but without me. He'd let me listen to a song from the musical that Sinatra had sung on his *Ol' Blue Eyes Is Back* album. It was called *Send in the Clowns*. The song could have been written about us. Simon sang along:

Isn't is rich?
Are we a pair?
Me here at last on the ground.
You in mid-air…

Noel took me to the lounge area (making my entrance with my usual flair), where we joined another few men, all in their 50s or 60s. More talk of the war. Sir Anthony remained aloof and detached from the conversation, as if he'd heard it all before. He and Brian Sewell largely kept to themselves. Mr Sewell seemed very protective of Mr Blunt.

The group then started to reminisce about the goings-on in a flat in Bentinck Street, Marylebone, during the war. Whilst at Cambridge, Noel had been recruited into the Cambridge Apostles, a secret intellectual society of sorts, which included a gentleman called Guy Burgess. Blunt and Burgess shared the flat and Guy would bring back a succession of boys, young men, soldiers, sailors and airmen, who would be put at the disposal of politicians and civil servants who visited the place. The flat was legendary among the homosexual underworld of London. As the conversation progressed I heard it variously described as a "homosexual bordello", a "male brothel" and an apparent "den of Soviet sympathisers and spies".

Once Mr Blunt and Mr Sewell called it a night, the conversation became raunchier and explicit. Noel, obviously speaking from experience, described Bentinck Street as a 24-hour party. He said a staggering number of people used to call in and then stagger out in the mornings.

"It was quite comical, chaotic and constant. An endless stream of visitors. People sleeping on floors during the black-outs, ration books going missing, housekeepers going missing." Everyone laughed.

"Blunt bedded his way through politicians, writers, actors, soldiers and choirboys. You have to give it to the old boy, he was magnificent in his day."

The men regaled each other with their tales of debauchery, from the 1940s onwards, of their flings with foreign diplomats, other civil servants, politicians and rent boys. Everyone seemed to have been sharing beds with everyone else, particularly during the war.[41] Later that night, Noel observed to me that during the war, the situation for homosexuals had become better, more tolerant. The all-male environment of the forces provided countless opportunities for same-sex liaisons, within and between the ranks, and the officer class brought their public-school expertise in the matter to a new environment.[42] Now Noel offered a toast. "Old friends… remembered with affection and an erection."

As the laughter subsided, I decided to throw in a question.

"What is Kincora?" I asked innocently.

The conversation stopped dead. Knowing smiles were exchanged.

"Well…" Noel explained hesitantly, "it's a residence in Belfast, nothing like Bentinck Street, of course."

A little laughter broke the ice that I had inadvertently created.

One of the other men, a senior civil servant type, who seemed to be knowledgeable about Northern Ireland, said, "Let's just call it one of the last No-Go areas."

Another man changed the subject. "It seems a few Belfast men like yourself have made it to London to pursue their careers."

"Well, I'm from Derry, not Belfast," I said sarcastically, not really knowing what point I was trying to make.

Noel brought the conversation to a halt, sensing tensions starting to build.

41　In his book The Naked Civil Servant, Quentin Crisp said that the Blitz turned London into a "paved double bed. People talked to everyone – even to me," he wrote. "Voices whispered suggestively to you as you walked along; hands reached out if you stood still…" Being less discreet than others, Quentin had stood still for too long and was arrested by two policemen in Coventry Street (Playland had opened in 1935). He was charged with soliciting, however the magistrate released him.

42　Joshua Levine devotes a chapter of his book The Secret History of the Blitz to what he describes as "the first sexual revolution". He demonstrates that homosexuality was unofficially tolerated during the war, with some soldiers already "well versed in the arts, while others had no other outlet for their sexual frustration". Tolerance of homosexuality ended with the war. When Alan Turing pleaded guilty to gross indecency in 1952, he was one of 3,757 people convicted of homosexual offences that year – compared to 956 in 1938.

"Well, if they're anything like you, Anthony, send over a few more from Derry – that's what I say."

It appeared that I'd be spending the whole night in the Dorchester. All-nighters were very unusual and made me worry about getting to Foyles the next day. I worried about what I would be wearing and what I would look like if I was up all night. Noel had pre-booked a luxuriously appointed suite. He proved to be surprisingly agile and possessed of a strength and stamina I had not anticipated in one I had considered old.

After sex, he spoke quietly and sincerely. "It's an utter disgrace that what I have just done in this bed with a lovely young man is considered a crime. That I should have to crawl off to a room I paid good money for and that you should have to follow at a discreet distance is a great injustice."

Like everyone else, Noel talked. In fact he kept me awake most of the night. He told me that in spite of the prejudice and hostility he knew he'd face, he'd joined a group in the late 1950s that had been fighting for homosexual law reform. It had a lot of unspoken support in both Houses, he explained, but a combination of convention and hypocrisy held back progress for years. He talked about the double-lives that homosexual MPs had to lead. Noel was enraged by a newspaper article that had revealed that attitudes seemed to be hardening in the Home Office against any further reform of the age of consent for homosexuals, which was 21.

"May I ask what age you are, Anthony?"

"I'm 20."

"And I am 59 years old. Have you consented to come to bed with me?"

"Yes."

"Yet in the eyes of the law you are underage and your consent is meaningless. We are both criminals."

Under any other circumstances I would have said Noel was a sincere, generous and intelligent man, but I could not be entirely objective. The situation was not as simple as Noel portrayed it. Although I'd consented to sleep with him, I had not really been exercising my free will. But he didn't know that. All my punters probably thought I was a free agent willingly engaging in illicit sex. Many probably assumed I was over 21. I may have been on the "edge of consent", age-wise, but I was not really giving consent. My predicament was complicated.

Noel questioned me about Simon. How was he doing? How was I getting on with him? Was he treating me well? Paying me well? I was immediately suspicious of his questions and I made my answers as non-committal as possible. "You could do better," he said after a thoughtful pause. I wasn't sure if he meant I could have made more of an effort to answer his questions, or that I could do better than work for Simon.

I asked Noel if he had ever heard of Playland. "Ah... Playland – a den of dirty amusements and dirty secrets." Noel spoke cryptically, yet sounded sober and scholarly. "In the world of intelligence, secrets are a valuable commodity. They can be bought and sold, they are what make people loyal and obedient. The Establishment is obsessed with secrets."

We turned onto our sides facing each other, our noses inches apart. He stroked my hair, my cheek. "Most of all, secrets are an aphrodisiac. Indiscretion is such an exquisite pleasure. Telling secrets to someone like you gives old men like me a hard on."

"Tell me your secrets, Noel," I whispered in his ear. The drugs I'd taken were insinuating their way into my bloodstream. My inhibitions and feelings of guilt were being flushed away in a rush of toxic elation.

I was getting good at this, taking just the right amount of drugs to shut down parts of my conscience while firing up other parts of my brain. I was able to manipulate punters, giving them whatever they wanted and taking what I wanted, which usually meant obscene amounts of money, on top of the weekly allowance Simon was giving me, but also information. The secrets flowed like forbidden honey, from the seasoned intellectual to the innocent youth. In bed, nothing was out of bounds for these people. They would tell anything, do anything, to enlighten, to enchant, to seduce… to corrupt.

"But what about Playland?" I prompted.

"Playland. It's just a boy business. What else can I say? There is nothing that special or unique about it, apart from the management and some of the clients, of course. Keep well clear of it."

Noel went on to tell me, almost in a whisper, that he had been a spy and worked for military intelligence in France and Germany. He told me that the Bentinck Street flat where Blunt and Burgess had lived was actually owned by a good friend of his, Victor Rothschild.

"One of Victor's passions is rare books. He's a wonderful man, you'd love him. I could try and arrange for you to meet. Strictly business, of course," he reassured me. "Flog him some old books from Foyles. What a name with which to start your own client list," he smiled.

"Who is he?" I asked. "Is he in the book business?

"No, he's in the bank business."[43] Noel threw me a knowing look. "And another good friend of mine I'd also like you to meet, perhaps more intimately, is Gordon…"

I didn't wait for Noel to finish. I put my hand over his mouth for a second, then sat up and straddled him, pushing him down flat on the bed. I needed to end this conversation.

---

43   Victor Rothschild was the chairman of NM Rothschild & Sons, a multinational investment banking company.

I felt that he was trying to pull me away from Simon and take direct control of me himself. I had suspected that there was something underhand, sinister even, about this all-night arrangement, but I was not going to allow him to start planning introductions for me. For reasons I could not fully comprehend, I was determined that I would stay faithful to Simon, even if I wasn't sure quite what that meant. I was unsettled and confused but felt a certain pride that I was being loyal to my master, the man who had saved me from Playland.

I went in for the kill. Noel didn't last long the second time. Sexually, I was beginning to take control in the bedroom. Chemical courage. Damie had given me a few pointers on technique so I could get a "man overboard" quickly. Simon told me he'd been getting great reports about how good I was. Clients were telling him I was passionate and enthusiastic in bed, but they were mistaking passion for anger and self-loathing.

As Noel lay there breathing heavily, but looking wide awake, I knew more indiscretion was inevitable. "It's the same in Northern Ireland. Homosexuals are well represented in the higher echelons of Ulster Unionism: Knox Cunningham, Jim Molyneaux, James Kilfedder and others. And they have like-minded friends across the border in the Republic. Sometimes even political enemies can find a common cause because of a shared sexual orientation."

"How do you know all this stuff?"

"I'm a member of the House of Lords, the best grapevine in the land. And I take an interest in what my kindred spirits get up to in the provinces."

He pulled me close to him and reached between my legs.

Noel knew an awful lot about Northern Ireland. He told me things I could scarcely believe. He said that Bernie Silver, the Godfather of Soho, had been asked by Detective Chief Superintendant Ken Etheridge to help him gather information about the IRA. Bernie was told his co-operation in Belfast would make his life easier in London. So, he flew to Belfast and met Etheridge. He helped to set up a couple of discreet "massage parlours" there. The girls, who were chosen for both their looks and their brains, had to sign the Official Secrets Act. The plan was to compromise influential punters with tapes and photographs. Noel went on to say that in 1971, Etheridge asked Bernie to help him with his inquiries into the brutal murder of three young off-duty soldiers. Noel's mouth was now at my ear. "This information came out at Bernie's trial last year," he whispered. I felt Noel's hot breath in my ear, followed by his tongue.[44]

I somehow extricated myself from him and went to the bathroom. I had a headache and suddenly felt sober and nauseous at the thought of Noel feeling me up whilst chatting nonchalantly about murder and the involvement of Soho criminals in Belfast brothels. I fought the urge to throw up. His voice followed after me, as his reminiscences turned to books, sex and censorship.

Many clients thought that because I worked with books all day, I'd be interested in listening to them talk about books all night. I suppose they were trying to be polite, pretending to give a damn about what I did, but I preferred as far as possible to keep my two worlds apart. I didn't want to talk about books with clients in bed, any more than I wanted to talk about sex with customers in Foyles.

---

44 In 1974 Bernie Silver appeared in court charged with "conspiring to live off the immoral earnings of prostitutes". A number of police officers appeared for the defence. Detective Chief Superintendant Ken Etheridge provided a glowing reference, telling the court, "I was serving in Northern Ireland assisting the RUC and the army over the murders. I asked if he would assist me in a certain way. He agreed to do so." The prosecution chose not to enquire as to the specifics of Bernie's assistance. In spite of his services to the Crown, Bernie was found guilty and sentenced to six years. He was brought back to the dock the following year and charged with murder.

This illustrious client was an academic, an intellectual, so I suppose in his case it was only to be expected. As he rambled on about literature once considered obscene and corrupting, I stood by the sink in the bathroom staring at my reflection in the mirror, trying to find the person I used to be. There was no sign of him.

"Speaking of pornography," Noel called out earnestly, "I've been trying for years to get my hands on a copy of a biographical novel of sorts called *The Sins of the Cities of the Plain*. I heard about it years ago from one of my friends. It was published in two volumes in 1881. It's incredibly rare. There's supposed to be only one copy in existence, kept under lock and key in the British Library, which can only be read under close supervision, but I've heard rumours that there are other copies in private collections. See if you can track down a copy for me and I'll reward you handsomely."

I returned to bed. Noel waited for me to ask him what the book was about, but I'd heard enough for one night. I turned onto my side, facing away from him.

"I'm really tired," I said, yawning.

He ignored me. "As a work of homosexual pornography, I am told it has never been surpassed."

I pretended I'd fallen asleep.

"That book is the holy grail, something of a *locus classicus*." His hand moved under the sheet, between my legs. He held me again but failed to get the desired response. He shifted and I felt his erection press against me. Baron Annan seemed to have an insatiable appetite, but he finally got the message and rubbed his hands across his bald head.

"God, I'm tired also. I need to sleep."

I heard him sigh and breathe through his nostrils.

"You may be hearing from James."

"Bond?"

"No, Kilfedder, of course. He's the one who will only misbehave in London, never in Ulster. He's already been with a few other Irish boys. He may be curious to meet you."

Noel switched off the bedside lamp and yawned.

"He told me he has a fondness for home-grown produce." He then added through another yawn, "Your name came up in the conversation."

I lay there waiting for more. But there was silence. And then snoring.

I stared at the ceiling, as wide awake as I'd ever been.[45]

---

45   I never did hear from James Kilfedder, but on 20 March 1995 the *Belfast Telegraph* ran a front-page story revealing that OutRage!, the radical LGBT rights group, had targeted 20 MPs in an open letter inviting them to come out. One of the recipients was an Ulster MP. As he travelled by train from Gatwick Airport into London that same day, Mr Kilfedder died of a heart attack.

CHAPTER 20

The Story of a Soldier

The time came to see Ronald Batty about my future development in the world of antiquarian bookselling. I couldn't even climb the stairs anymore because of the pain in my back. It hadn't been the same since the kicking I got at the gathering where the two young brothers were abused – so I took the creaky old lift up. The thick green phlegm I was coughing up was now streaked with blood. The pain really was excruciating, to the extent that I was having difficulty breathing and, as I couldn't take hard drugs at work, I was eating a lot of painkillers – but to no avail. The near-constant pain was getting difficult to bear, but I hoped in time it would subside.

Mr Batty was very welcoming and offered me a seat beside him. He even poured me a cup of tea this time. He asked me how I was getting on and I lied through my teeth about how I'd been settling in, had made lots of new friends, and was loving the work in Foyles, which of course I was.

He asked me how come a young man my age could be so interested in old things. I was unsure if he was referring to the books or my clients. I told him of my passion for literature and said that, to me, antiquarian books presented two forms of art, the art of the writer and the craft of the bookbinder. This seemed to please him. He asked further book-related questions and I felt as though I was being interviewed again.

"Well, Anthony, I would like to teach you all about the art of retailing. By all means have affairs with these beautiful objects, but don't fall in love with them. Don't get too attached to them. This game is all about selling pretty things and making lots of money."

I forced out a little laugh. Ronald could see I was looking a little tense. His position in Foyles and his power intimidated me. I tried to relax and settled back into the settee, expensive china cup and saucer in my lap.

"It's important to have a career plan. Think about what you really want out of life. Be prepared to invest in the things that really matter to you. Be prepared to make sacrifices, because success comes with a price."

"I understand that," I said. I needed him to understand what working in Foyles meant to me. "I've left my home, my parents and my brothers and sister to come and work here. I've left everything behind. I'm paying *that* price."

"I understand, Anthony." He moved a little closer. "You're a very special young man. Not many people your age show that kind of determination. Christina and I never had children. Foyles is our family. You are now part of that family. I'll be your mentor," he said, giving my leg a little pat. "There is an awful lot to learn. I can teach you things. It's a very specialist side of the business, but like everything else we'll take it one step at a time."

I felt my heart hammering in my chest. I sat the tea on the table and stood up. He looked surprised.

"What on earth is the matter?"

I backed towards the door. This was my refuge, the place where I was safe and secure. There was no more Charles or Keith coming in and threatening me. It was the one place in London where I didn't have to think about my other life. If that vile and perverted world entered in here, what little was left of normality would be over. My life would be over.

Ronald stood up with a look of genuine puzzlement on his face. "What is the matter, Anthony, are you unwell?"

Maybe I was mistaken, perhaps I'd completely misread the situation, misinterpreted his gesture of friendliness. But the damage was done, there was no going back. I reached the door, my heart pounding.

"I'm sorry," I said, "I'm just… so sorry, I can't…"

I walked out and closed the door on my future in bookselling.

* * * * *

I waited outside Prunier on St James's Street. It had become something of a regular pick-up point for me. It was within walking distance of the gentlemen's clubs on that street and along Pall Mall, which lay beyond St James's Palace. I had a chat with the commissionaire, with whom I was now on speaking terms.

"How's business?" I enquired.

"I was about to ask you the same question," he smiled.

As I waited to be picked up I was approached by a strikingly blond, good-looking young man. I recognised him immediately. It was Richard, the 25-year-old Grenadier Guard who'd been at the party with the old battle-scarred Viscount.

"Good evening," he said, all smiles. "You are required to come with me."

"Where?"

"It's not far, walking distance."

"A party?"

"No, just you and I."

He took me to the bottom of the street where a Rolls-Royce Silver Shadow was waiting.

"Fancy," I said.

"Quite."

"Who owns it?"

"Military secret," he winked at me. "A benefactor, an old soldier. Your first time in a Roller?"

"No."

Simon had made appearances in a chauffeur-driven Rolls-Royce a few times, but I had played it all cool and didn't ask Simon if he owned it, if it belonged to someone else, or if it was leased by WH Smith. I was impressed but didn't want to show it.

"Are we going to a party?" I asked again.

Simon had assured me there would be no more group stuff, so I was alarmed at being picked up by military rent and driven off to an unknown location.

"No, just you and I."

The car pulled up outside the Guards Club at 16 Charles Street in Mayfair. We were greeted politely by a gentleman in the reception area. He discreetly placed a door key into Richard's hand and in turn Richard put something in the man's hand. Richard led me upstairs into one of the guest bedrooms.

"Just relax and have a drink." He pointed to a tray of drinks.

I poured two drinks and prepared a line of coke. "Want some?" I said nonchalantly, as I demonstrated my newly acquired dexterity in the art of chopping a line of coke.

"Nah, better not. Early start in the morning. What else have you got?"

"Bennies?"

"That'll do."

We took the drugs and went to the bed with our drinks, sitting upright against the headboard. I closed my eyes and greeted the dopamine rush as the happy hormone flooded my body. Damie had warned me not to take alcohol with coke because it produced cocaethylene in the liver and this could cause a heart

THE STORY OF A SOLDIER

attack and sudden death. I didn't believe him. It sounded too dramatic. One of those urban myths. I sipped my vodka.

A few moments passed as I waited for Richard to make the first move.

"Now what?" I asked.

"We wait," he smirked.

"For what?"

"You'll see."

I turned on a radio. Ralph McTell was singing *Streets of London*. I tuned into something a little less depressing. My feelings of anxiousness evaporated the instant my contaminated blood carried its good tidings to the 86 billion nerve cells in my brain. A few drinks and some idle chat later, there was a tap at the door. Richard let in a man wearing a tattered suit. He looked about 40. His black hair was plastered down and he had a little pencil moustache. He looked like a 1940s hack from central casting.

"Evening, gents," he breezed. "All right are we?"

I ignored his question, as I was a little puzzled to see he was carrying a large suitcase, which he placed on the bed. He sprung open the catches. I leaned over and looked inside, expecting the worst. The case contained three cameras and various photographic accessories, all set into foam compartments.

He shook our hands.

"Call me Harry. One moment, gents, this won't take long."

He set up a tripod, then opened a large black umbrella, which was silver on the inside.

"I'm looking for a nice soft glow," he said as he readied the cameras. "Black and white and colour," he advised, taking out a little notebook.

"So then, gents. Richard and Anthony I believe."

He wrote the names down.

"I can't say if they'll actually use these names. That won't be up to me."

As he adjusted the lens on one of the cameras, he glanced up.

"To use a military term, you two have been mentioned in dispatches." He laughed. "Black on blond looks striking in black and white." He laughed again.

We downed more drink as he gave us directions.

"OK, it'll be the usual stuff, nothing too heavy. All right, gents. And try and make it look convincing, like you mean it. Folks will be paying big money for this. It could be your big break, boys. Hollywood could be calling."

"Hold on," I said, "I need more coke."

"I changed my mind," said Richard, "give me a line too."

As Harry directed us and snapped his way around the bed, long shots, medium shots and close ups, he treated us to a lecture on the gay sex life of Guardsmen. He reckoned up to 20 per cent of all Guardsmen made themselves available for rent. The London-based Guards Regiments had a long and distinguished reputation for being "TBH", meaning To Be Had. Many punters targeted the new young recruits who did not realise their own true value, and got themselves a bargain. The most popular pubs to pick up a Guardsman, according to Harry, were the Golden Lion, the Grenadier in Wilton Row, the Horse & Groom in Belgravia and the Paxtons Head in Knightsbridge. The parks and squares around Knightsbridge and St James's were also notorious cruising grounds for those looking for "a bit of scarlet".

When the shoot was over Harry carefully packed away his equipment.

"I've been asked to give you both a tip." He counted out £80 each for us, then shook hands and said goodbye. "The room's been booked for the night," he said. "It's all yours, enjoy yourselves."

After we showered and dressed in bathrobes, someone knocked on the door. I opened it and a waiter wheeled in a trolley with soup, sandwiches and a bottle of champagne.

"Compliments," he announced, and withdrew.

Richard and I looked at each other and devoured the food and hit the champagne. We talked for hours.

"Is all that true? What Harry said about the Guards?"

"Yes, probably, but I can only speak for myself. When I joined it was talked about quite openly. We were told just don't get caught.

Richard said he hadn't had the chance to go looking for punters. He was sexually assaulted by a senior officer within weeks of joining and then forced to provide sexual favours on request by other men he was taken to.

"I was the pretty boy of the Company. I had no choice in the matter. I've been looked after and well paid, but it would be nice if I could choose who I had sex with."

I told Richard everything that'd happened to me since my arrival in London. He was shocked. In many ways we had a lot in common: we were both being forced into doing what we had to do. The pressure was being applied in different ways but we were both trapped.

This had not been his first photographic session. During the last one he had to dress in full Guardsman uniform before having sex with a man who was into bondage and punishment.

"I was his dream come true. He got off on blond hair, scarlet tunics and pain."

"His name wasn't Chenevix-Trench, was it?

"No," he laughed, "I'd have remembered that."

As we drank champagne and listened to the radio, it turned out we had a lot more in common than we could possibly have imagined. What he told me was staggering. He had served two tours of duty in Derry with the Grenadier Guards. He started to tell me about them.

"Hold on," I said, reaching for a sheet of notepaper and a pen. "Do you mind if I write this down? Just the dates and stuff. No one is ever going to believe this."

"I don't give a fuck, mate," Richard said indifferently. "It's not like you're going to write a fucking book," he laughed. "And as you say, who's going to believe you, anyway?"

He rattled off when and where the battalion had been stationed in Derry, including the Brooke Park library. "Thanks to you lot taking over the library, the Provos burnt it to the ground," I said.

It had broken my heart to see the burnt-out ruins of the library, that beautiful stately building where I had spent so many childhood hours reading. "I never thought the IRA would destroy a library," I said. "I think museums and libraries and archaeological sites should never be targeted in warfare."

"Fuck's sake, it was just books. People on all sides were dying."

"Yeah, I know, but still." I realised I was sounding like Christina Foyle when she mourned for the millions of books destroyed in London during the war.

Richard talked about the sniper and bomb attacks, the endless patrols, the removal of barricades, which seemed to spring back up every night.

His sexual services were called upon in addition to his military services. One evening a week or so before the tour ended, he was taken from his base to Piggery Ridge, and from there flown by helicopter along with two other soldiers to some kind of stately home – possibly Hillsborough Castle in Belfast, or some other residence near the border or across it in the Republic of Ireland.

There was a banquet in progress. The three soldiers were taken to a room where two teenage boys had already been delivered. A spread of food and drink had been laid on and a butler was in attendance. He told them that the banquet itself had been attended by some local Unionist and British politicians, and top brass from the military, together with all their wives and a couple of religious ministers.

Richard then described a scenario similar to what I had already witnessed here in London. After most of the guests had departed a small group of men joined the soldiers and boys for some group interaction, before they were paired off and taken to separate bedrooms. One image had stuck in Richard's mind. Just before the heavy drinking and the sex started, the butler took a loaded gun off one of the guests and took it away for safekeeping. That night Richard ended up in bed with a member of the House of Lords known as "Boofy".

The Battalion returned home but he returned to Derry for another four-month tour. This time his Company was in Piggery Ridge, which, I told Richard, was very interesting... "because I was in Piggery Ridge four days after you arrived."

"You're kidding, how come?"

"Because you bastards arrested me on my way to work that morning. I was taken in for questioning."

There was a look of shock on Richard's face. "Fuck! Are you in the IRA?"

"Yes, of course I am. I'm over here on counter-intelligence, Active Rent Unit. Don't be stupid."

We both laughed.

I never knew I had been lifted by the Grenadier Guards until now. As far as I was concerned it was the British Army – I couldn't distinguish the regiments, except of course the Parachute Regiment. It was an unbelievable coincidence that we had both been in Derry and were now both here in London.

"Jesus, that was a tough tour. There were no fatalities, thank God, but a sergeant was shot in the back by an Armalite, a guy lost an arm, another lost an eye. We were told at that time that there were more shootings in Creggan than in the rest of Ulster put together." Richard topped up our glasses. "We also received more visitors than anywhere else. Members of Parliament and the House of Lords."

"Did they keep you busy?"

"What – in the Land Rovers or in the beds?" He laughed. "Both, I suppose. There were the occasional encounters. Some of them welcome. Going four months on tour in Ulster of all places without sex can be tough. I'll never forget, one guy started chatting me up in the Telstar Bar one night."

"I choked on my drink. You were in the Telstar Bar?"

The Telstar Bar was a noted Republican watering hole.

"Yes, we were ordered to go in and check everybody's ID, not that they had any. A guy started coming on to me. He was taking the piss of course, his mates were falling off their bar stools."

Richard and I talked until dawn and then slept for an hour or so. Taxis were ordered. We shook hands outside.

"Do you ever get to see any of the photos Harry takes?"

"Never. Why, do you want a copy?" He smiled.

"Never."

* * * * *

I arrived at Foyles feeling terrible and hungover. Still, I'd be able to get a little snooze during the day in the stillness and tranquillity of the antiquarian book department.

When I entered the room there was a young lady from administration, looking at some of the books.

"Can I help you?" I asked.

"Hello," she smiled. "No, I was sent down to tell you that you're being transferred to another department."

"What?" I was stunned.

"Yes, you are being moved to the classics department. It's on the…"

"I know where it is," I snapped. "Why?"

"Goodness, I have no idea. Just passing on the message."

Moments later I was standing behind a little desk in the classics department on the ground floor. I felt like a fish looking out of the large shop-front window onto the madness of Charing Cross Road. The glass door there was one of the busiest entrances into Foyles. The classics department was little more than an annex leading into the massive fiction department. In terms of customer footfall, it seemed to be as busy as Piccadilly Circus.

CHAPTER 21

The Endless Game

The hamlet of Pusey sits in a tranquil corner of the Vale of White Horse, between Charney, Bassett and Faringdon, 15 miles from Oxford. My chauffeur-driven journey out of London to Oxfordshire was the little surprise Simon had been planning for me. I was delivered on Saturday afternoon to the Hornby family home.

Lake House was a solid-looking, late-Regency property built of stone, with a slate roof. I walked up the steps to the front door, where Simon greeted me with a hug and delivered his second surprise by introducing me to his wife, Sheran. She had been cut from the same cloth as Christina Foyle: prim, proper and immaculate, with hair regally swept back. She was a small woman and Simon, being Simon, towered over her.

"Ah, the book boy," she said, smiling, but a tad dismissively as she shook my hand. Her greeting was like the weather that day, sunny but a little chilly. She excused herself and retreated to the kitchen, where she was directing operations for the get-together planned for the evening.

Simon was wearing cream trousers with a faint stripe and a pastel lemon T-shirt – a stark contrast to the double-breasted suits he wore at work and at social occasions in London. "Keep your coat on," he said as he grabbed his own coat. He turned me on my heels and pushed me out of the door again. "I must show you the gardens."

His face lit up as he led me around the house to what he called his "little cottage garden". It was at least an acre. "Did I mention that I've been working on this since 1970?"

"Yes, I think you mentioned that, Simon."

He led me along his flowerbeds, borders and little terraces, rhyming off plant names in Latin. I tried to show some interest. "What's your favourite flower?"

"Never mind about that," he replied with uncustomary curtness. "I wish to make you a proposal."

"But Simon, you're already married."

He laughed loudly. "I'm being serious. I want you to come and work for me."

"But I already…"

"In WH Smith," he cut in.

I wondered if he'd heard about my difficulties in Foyles, of my demotion to the ground floor.

"You know more about books and literature than most of my managers. I could get you on a fast-track management development programme. Teach you the business. You'd be managing your own shop in no time." He paused. I didn't respond. "What do you think?"

I looked at my surroundings. "I think you're leading me down the garden path."

Simon looked a little hurt.

"You're going nowhere in Foyles. You must know what she's like. You'll be out the door in no time. Your future lies with me."

"And means lying with your friends also."

"No. Look, this is not easy for me to say, but I've fallen for you. I'm starting to realise you mean a lot to me. This *other* business, entertaining my associates, it's complicated. It's a game,

269

I've always called it the 'endless game', but you won't have to be a part of it for much longer."

We walked and talked. Had Sheran been curious about her husband and me, she might well have gone upstairs to spy over the garden. What she would have seen was a young man strolling by Simon's side, listening intently, his hands held behind his back as the older man gestured with his arms, explaining it all, laying out the workings and the extent of the network.

What Simon called the "endless game" involved interactions between the pillars of the Establishment: politicians, judiciary, police, the military, the intelligence services, businessmen, the church – in fact, any large organisation with financial or political clout. He considered it a web of kinship or brotherhood. I wondered if this included Masonic or Orange Lodges. Simon's game involved fostering friendships and building and strengthening his contacts, his "strands", as he called them, within the network. The game was all about exploiting mutually beneficial contacts, but it was also about mutual help and support.

There were many common interests across the professions within the network, including not only the desire to make money and attain power, but also to satisfy sexual tastes. Some members of the network were homosexual, inevitably, and some had a fondness for younger men. Those with the contacts in this particular area not only facilitated introductions, but also helped those who had got into a spot of bother by bringing some influence to bear on the relevant authorities. Some of the most powerful individuals in the network had contacts in both Parliament and the London underworld. At these two extremes, paper or even people could be made to disappear.

Simon stressed that the game was not hidden like some illegal poker game. The endless game was played out in full view. It was rather like the rent scene in the Dilly, visible only to those who knew what to look for. If any kind of business deal was done, any arrangement made or any favour provided for someone in the network, it was called "giving them cake". Simon had been given a lot of cake over the years. More recently he'd been returning favours and was now giving cake to politicians, businessmen, barristers, the military and friends in publishing. I merely happened to be the icing on it.

"I've been doing a lot of thinking," he said reflectively. "I've decided to take you off the market. I've already received two offers for you."

"What does that mean?"

"It means I've been an old fool. I didn't realise what I have. Two of my associates want to set you up for their exclusive use and give you a flat and an allowance. They're both willing to split the costs and share you. I must confess to feeling jealous at that thought."

"Who are they?" I asked.

"It doesn't matter. Suffice to say you've met them both."

"Are you saying I don't have to do it anymore – with your associates, that is?"

"Well, yes, soon. I have certain obligations to fulfil, certain promises to keep. I've given some very important people guarantees. Give me a couple of weeks. Can you do that, Pretty Boy?"

"Yes. What about your 'game?'"

"Well," he smiled, "the game continues. You'll just have to find me another pretty boy to take your place. I want you all to myself."

We returned to the house and Simon showed me his impressive book collection and his equally impressive wine collection in the cellar. His knowledge of wine was yet another thing about Simon that impressed me. He promised he would teach me all about fine wines. He made a few recommendations and let me select the red wine, as I whispered, "Am I staying here the night?"

"Yes, of course."

"Where?"

He pointed to a black metal ring on a wall. "Well, I was actually thinking of having you chained up here," he smiled.

I spent an entertaining evening with the Hornbys and some of their friends. Among their guests were a few ladies from Sheran's social circle and some of Simon's old university pals. A fellow director from WH Smith was also present. It didn't take long for Burton and Taylor to enter the conversation. On one occasion they'd borrowed Lake House for a few weeks and this had enabled Burton to fulfil one of his great ambitions, to teach literature at Oxford. One of Simon's friends, who held a professorship at Oxford, had sat in on one of Burton's classes. He shared his views on Burton's teaching, describing it as idiosyncratic and unconventional, but inspiring.

I enjoyed the discussions and held my own in the various debates about literature, music and film. Simon was a joy to behold, at once amusing and frivolous, then fiercely intellectual and knowledgeable.

As if a secret signal had been given, the ladies went to the kitchen to talk lady talk. Meanwhile, in the living room, by a blazing fire, as the wine flowed so the conversation flowed towards Oxford. The recent gossip, the scandals. The men reminisced about the Arcadian passions and pleasures of the past. The conversation, the mannerisms, the company seemed to assume rather homoerotic undertones. It was all very *Brideshead Revisited*. I felt I'd been allowed access to another corner of a privileged world. During all this talk of boating, hunting and cricket, of country estates and exclusive parties, I felt I was being educated but also strangely corrupted.

Most of the guests had gone by midnight. When I got a chance, I silently mouthed to Simon, "Where am I sleeping?"

He pointed to the ceiling.

After a while one of the domestics appeared and announced that my room was ready. I excused myself and was directed to a bedroom at the back of the house overlooking the garden and the black countryside beyond. I lay in bed, in the darkness, listening to muffled laughter coming from downstairs. I wondered where Simon would sleep. Who would he choose: me or Sheran? I couldn't understand why I was thinking like this. Would I feel let down if he spent the night in bed with his wife? I'd begun to question my sexuality. I had not been able to connect on any level with Agnes in Lowestoft and now was having these thoughts. What was happening to me? Steve Harley, my inner conscience, was at my ear, *Resist, resist, it's from yourself you have to hide.* What the hell did *that* mean, anyway?

After a while I heard doors closing. Then other doors. Car doors? The house became quiet and I drifted off to sleep. I don't know how long I was asleep, but I heard my bedroom door open. Simon slipped into the bed beside me.

* * * * *

I went looking for Damie in the Dilly. We'd agreed a time and a spot to meet. I wondered if he had heard Pilot's new song, *Call Me Round*. It could have been written about us. But there was no sign of him anywhere. I looked around every corner and waited for him to appear. I couldn't stand still too long. If you did, and you were young, you'd invariably be approached by a punter or a cop. Any cheek or back-chat to the police and they'd be on you like a ton of bricks. Sometimes they put a lot of effort into removing drug dealers from the Dilly, other times the focus was on removing boys.

The police also sometimes fielded young, good-looking plain-clothed officers who, as agents provocateurs, would prowl the Dilly, the Underground concourse and the public toilets around Soho. They would send out all the right signals and invite an approach, try to incite acts of indecency and then nick the offender. Some rent boys who were arrested were released on condition that they offer sexual services to the arresting officer. The pretty police were Piccadilly's blade runners.

I looked in the cafes and fast-food outlets. No Damie. I took my chances on the meat rack for a while and still there was no Damie. I headed for Soho and visited all the usual haunts and the back entrances to the theatres. No luck. On my way back, I spotted The Dream and asked if he'd seen Damie.

"Damie who?"

"Tiger. Have you seen him anywhere?"

"No, I haven't seen him around. He hasn't been in the Dilly for a few days."

I took The Dream into a Wimpy Bar for tea and jam dough-nuts, and we sat by the window looking out for our friend. If he'd been picked up by a punter, he'd have been back in the Dilly by now.

"Maybe he's met the big movie star he's always on about and been whisked off to Hollywood."

"No," I said, "he wouldn't just vanish without telling me, or his friends here."

"Maybe he ended up in the Romper Room."

"That's not funny."

The Romper Room was another urban Dilly legend. It was said there was a bedroom on the floor above Playland, with a large bed, a cabinet full of drink and drugs, and another cabinet full of bondage paraphernalia. A punter could book the room for a whole night and it was said to have been used primarily by those with a taste for fresh bunnies or candy floss. The charge for this service was £5,000, but that meant the customer could do absolutely anything he wanted, with no boundaries, no limits: indulge in his wildest fantasies. The price included insurance cover: if the livestock was broken or damaged beyond repair, everything would be taken care of. The mess would be cleaned up, no questions asked.

The Dream apologised. "Yeah, you're right. Where do you think he is?"

"I don't know. I think I'll try that place in Brixton where he lives."

"That would be the last place I'd go. You might not get out alive."

I was now getting worried. I wondered if Damie had been arrested. I didn't know what to do anymore or who else I could ask. I did a final circuit of the piazza and ended up standing beside a newspaper vendor. I tried to remember what day I'd last seen him. I didn't even know what today's date was. I picked up one of the newspapers. It was Wednesday 9 April. I thought for a moment about everything I had seen and done during the endless torturous month of March. As I waited, I glanced over the front page. A report in the bottom left-hand corner carried the news that the trial had started of three men from the Roger Gleaves Firm, accused of the murder of Billy Two-Tone.

* * * * *

True to his word, Sir Michael Havers had dug out the Rolling Stones poster for me. It advertised the concert in the Civic Hall Guildford and had autographs scribbled all over it, by the Stones, Marianne Faithfull, George Harrison and others. I'd been delivered to his home on this occasion and arrived coked up and running on high-octane fuel. I drank his whisky and did his bidding.

During his lustful role-plays and afterwards as we smoked, I became reacquainted with his manic garrulousness. Then, out of the blue, he asked me a question which jolted me.

"Were you in Derry on Bloody Sunday?"

This caught me by surprise, as moments before he'd been mulling over where he might go on holiday this year. It sounded like an accusation, rather like being asked if you were present at the scene of a terrible crime. I told him yes, I'd been at the anti-internment march. He immediately perked up and asked me to tell him everything I'd seen. He'd never heard a firsthand account of the massacre. I told him about the events of that awful day and what I'd seen.

"But what did you actually feel, what were you thinking?"

I wondered if he was going to get some sick sexual kick from this and incorporate it into one of his sexual monologues.

"I'd genuinely like to know," he pleaded, "about your *experience* of it."

I told him of the unfolding horror of it all, the sickening realisation and disbelief about what was happening, helplessness in the face of high-velocity fire as unarmed civilians were targeted and brought down.

"It was rather a dreadful business, wasn't it? I spoke to John about the matter a couple of times."

"John?"

"Widgery. He told me that Heath was most reluctant to deploy the Paras."

Like everyone, I knew that Lord Chief Justice Widgery had taken the side of the army over Bloody Sunday, blaming march organisers for the deaths that occurred. Sir Michael went on. According to him, the military view in London was that 8 Brigade in Derry were a bunch of softies. All they ever did was fire CS gas to disperse rioters, whereas in Belfast the response was much tougher. The existence of Free Derry was an affront to the top brass, who were offended that army maps showed a big black dotted line – the containment line, over which police and army hardly ever crossed. They were infuriated by the five o'clock follies that happened every day at "Aggro Corner", with troops just standing there being bombarded with stones and other objects. Sir Michael told me that the army commander, Brigadier Ford, had asked Heath's permission to use the Paras to target these hooligans that Sunday and teach them a lesson.

"The idea," Sir Michael explained, "was just to give Derry a bloody nose. Heath was put under considerable pressure to approve the operation. Skeletons were being rattled in Downing Street cupboards." Sir Michael lit up another cigarette and placed an ashtray on his chest.

"He was furious after the killings. The Home Secretary and army intelligence ran around like headless chickens doing a damage-limitation dance. He never forgave himself for Bloody Sunday. It broke him in many ways. In any event, Widgery has put the whole matter to bed. Probably best left alone now." He squeezed me in a comforting hug. "Sorry, old boy."[46]

I needed a shower. I felt unclean and polluted. I also needed the bathroom to take more drugs. I felt much better after I'd washed away the sweat, sex and political gossip. I returned to the bed, a bath towel around my waist. He could see the talk about Bloody Sunday had disturbed and unsettled me. The couple of bennies I'd taken would soon change that.

---

46   In April 1972, Edward Heath confirmed that the plan to conduct an arrest operation, in the event of a riot during the march on 30 January 1972, was known to British government ministers in advance. He never admitted that he personally had given final approval to use the Paras. Giving evidence to the Bloody Sunday Inquiry, Heath said he had no notion of the army's intention to send troops into the Bogside area of Derry, then a "no go" area, and no explanation for why people were killed. Heath pointed out that on the evening of 30 January he was entertaining the crew of his yacht and said he was thoroughly shocked by the news emerging that evening from Derry.

In an attempt to cheer me up he told me another one of his legal stories, one concerning Widgery. He said that just the year before Bloody Sunday, three editors of the satirical magazine *Oz* were prosecuted because of the *Schoolkids* edition of the magazine, which featured contributions by three teenage students. The magazine was undoubtedly explicit and controversial, but not by 1970s standards. One boy aged 15 had skilfully pasted the head of Rupert Bear onto a rapist featured in a series of sexually explicit cartoon frames. Page 10 featured a drawing of a schoolmaster with his trousers down, masturbating whilst groping a young boy – one of his pupils.

The editors of *Oz* – Jim Anderson, Richard Neville and Felix Dennis – were charged with the archaic offence of "corrupting public morals", which had an unlimited punishment. The prosecution argued that *Oz* had promoted homosexuality, lesbianism, sadism, perverted sexual practices and drug-taking. After the longest obscenity trial in British legal history, the three had their heads forcibly shaved and were imprisoned. Yet another *cause célèbre* ensued. During the appeal, which he was hearing, Lord Chief Justice Widgery sent his clerk to Soho and instructed him to buy the hardest porn he could find.

"John had for some time been dying to find an excuse to get his hands on some porn to see for himself what all the fuss was about, so this presented the perfect opportunity. The porn was, of course, for research and comparison purposes only." Sir Michael chuckled.[47]

"Because of his Soho purchases, one of the Lord Chief Justice's staff members called him, somewhat predictably, Wanker Widgery. Behind his back, of course."

---

47 Widgery's "review" of the Soho porn proved that *Oz* magazine was tame in comparison to what the police were openly allowing to be sold in Soho. The editors were freed and Home Secretary Reginald Maudling ended up with a lot of egg on his face as it was revealed that the police were targeting hippie magazines whilst turning a blind eye to the filth on sale in Soho.

Sir Michael had surpassed himself on this occasion with his indiscretions. Just as I was starting to climb to a new high and get the urge to drink more of his whisky, it was time for me to get dressed and go. The car had arrived. Before I left, I was determined to ask him about something. Simon told me that Sir Michael always referred to me as Christine when talking about me or requesting my company. I thought this was perhaps a reference to my working for Christina Foyle. So I asked him about this as I was heading to the door. He laughed.

"When we were in government, Ted was obsessed with some sex scandal bringing down the government. Profumo was still fresh in everyone's minds. It's my little joke. You are my Christine Keeler."

It was raining heavily outside and I ran to the car. I'd never heard of Profumo or Keeler so I had no idea what Sir Michael was talking about. Ten minutes into the journey home, I realised I'd walked out without the poster. Never mind, I'd get it next time.

CHAPTER 22

Old School Ties

There are some things you learn to live with. A deep sense of shame is one. Physical pain is much harder, and I was struggling to cope. The short distance I had to walk down Charing Cross Road was now taking much longer. I shuffled along like an old man, the pain in my back so unbearable I was forced to stay drugged up during the day on the strongest painkillers I could buy. In the evenings, I tanked up on the harder stuff. Anything to kill the pain, kill the emotions, kill the bookseller and let Pretty Boy surface and work the night shift.

I had been coughing up so much green-black phlegm and blood it was scary. In an act of desperation and in the hope of medical salvation, I had even phoned my doctor in Derry that morning and described my symptoms. For an instant I thought about asking him to get a message to my family, but I couldn't risk it. Holding the telephone receiver felt like holding a gun to my head. Dr McCarty suspected acute bronchitis and perhaps other complications and advised me to see a doctor in London immediately. I pleaded with him to send me a prescription in the meantime and he agreed to post a script to Hope House. I wondered what effect an antibiotic supplement would have on top of the mandies and amphetamine martinis I had been taking.

* * * * *

As the spring buds began to flower, I couldn't say I felt the same sense of renewal in my life. I felt corrupted and decayed beyond caring. I was numb, obedient and eager to please. I wanted to make a good impression. I wanted people to like me, maybe even show me some sympathy instead of their wallets – but then how were they to know why I was doing this?

I was ordered like a carry-out to a business meeting in the Shell Mex building on the Strand. Simon tried to explain to me in simple terms the deal that was being hammered out there. It concerned the terms by which Shell would be able to break away from the joint Shell/BP marketing company in the UK, which in effect would mean the transfer of 182 petrol stations from Shell to BP. The stakes could be quite high in Simon's endless game, but I was nothing more than an entertainment expense.

On this particular evening, negotiations had been fraught. Tempers were fraying. A gentleman who was prominent in Simon's network had been attending the meetings in some consultancy capacity, and I'd been dispatched to keep him company for an hour whilst business was adjourned.

We ended up out on a balcony beneath the giant art deco clock overlooking the Thames. As I went down on the punter, he said, "If Winston Churchill could see us now." Churchill, he revealed, had stood on this very balcony during World War II and watched the planes fly low over the river as they went off to fight the Battle of Britain. When the punter said he could do this all night, Pretty Boy replied, "Put your money where my mouth is." Pretty Boy was becoming more self-assured, more mercenary. I was losing myself in the role.

Another night, another venue. I was taken to a club over on St James's Street and introduced to "Boofy", a man I'd already heard about from the young Guardsman, Richard. Boofy's name was actually Arthur Gore, and he proudly revealed himself to be the 8th Earl of Arran. When I told him I worked in Foyles, he said he understood why I needed to supplement my income by other means. I wondered if he'd been speaking to Sir Michael, because he started talking to me about the 1960s and pop stars. He told me that in 1964 he'd attended a Foyles literary luncheon at the Dorchester Hotel, where the guest speaker was none other than John Lennon, there to promote *In His Own Write*.

"Lennon was an embarrassment," Lord Arran grumbled. "Bloodshot eyes, hands shaking. He was terrified or hungover, or both. He stood up, mumbled a few words and sat down. Some of the guests booed. I was sitting beside his mortified wife, Cynthia. Epstein saved the day somewhat by jumping in and saying a few words."

Lord Arran believed that sex was better in the dark and it was only when the lights went out that I recognised his voice. He was the man in the bedroom at the house party in Essex who'd called me a "fucking Irish bastard" and ordered me to undress. He was more pleasant on this occasion.

* * * * *

I must have made a bigger impression in the Dorchester than John Lennon had, for I was requested back. This time I was met by a serious-looking man in a suit. He led me to the lift, escorted me to the top floor, then ushered me out, before descending back down in the lift. At the end of the corridor a similarly dressed man stood outside a door like a guard. He opened the door for me and waved me into the bedroom. I dreaded the door openings more than anything else. These were the moments of intense anticipation and anxiety and fear. What waited for me on the other side of the door?

I was warmly received and given a friendly welcome by a balding man, who would have made a great stand-in for Bernard Lee, the actor who first played M in the Bond movies. He had politician or senior civil servant written all over him. He had a certain touch of class. Smart single breasted suit, hanky popping from the pocket, slim dark tie. He shook hands. Not many shook hands. The suite was large and luxurious. I took in the furniture and the fittings. The room glittered and shimmered with glass, crystal and mirrors. Lots of gold fabric, silk bed sheets, all high quality stuff.

"Make yourself at home, Anthony. Drink?"

Like the clothes he was wearing, his accent was also upmarket. His demeanour was posh and privileged.

"Vodka."

"So tell me," he said as he fixed the drinks, "what name have they given me?"

"I beg your pardon?"

"Smith, Jones, Johnston? Hotel reception, who were you told to ask for?"

"No one, sir. I wasn't given a name. I was met in the foyer."

I felt compelled to call him sir, he was friendly but formal. Sir seemed strangely appropriate.

"Ah, very well, I see. Truth is I'm not really supposed to be here."

"In the hotel?"

"No," he smiled, "in the country. I'm retiring this year and I want to see what retirement might look like. I'm in London for a couple of days to meet old friends."

He took off his jacket and tie, opened a bottle of Cristal Champagne and we toasted "the undiscovered country." After a little small talk with the lights turned down, he stood over my chair and fed me oysters from the palm of his hand. I washed them down with the champagne and resisted the urge to throw up.

"Parlez-vous Français?" he asked.

"Juste un peu, ce que j'appris a l'ecole," I attempted hesitantly.

"J'aimerais que vous me parler en Francais dans son lit."

"Excuse me?"

"I said I would like you to speak French to me in bed."

"I'm sorry I'm not really that good."

"What, at speaking French or having sex?" He laughed. "Not to worry, Anthony, I've spent years in France. Let's go to bed. I'll give you all the French lessons you'll ever need." He kissed me fully on the mouth and I felt an oyster slide between my lips, followed by his tongue. Once again I swallowed and resisted the urge to throw up.

* * * * *

One evening a few days later, on the recommendation of Lord Arran, I was presented to the Vice-President of the Campaign for Homosexual Equality, an elderly gentleman called Ian Harvey. Simon told me his tragic story.

In 1958 Mr Harvey, who was then the Conservative MP for Harrow East and a Foreign Office Minister, had been found in the bushes of St James's Park with a Guardsman in full uniform. Married with two daughters, Mr Harvey was 44 at the time; the Guardsman was 19. The scandal ruined Harvey. He resigned his seat in Parliament and resigned from his clubs. He took to heavy drinking, suffering from depression, and his marriage ended. He was left a broken man, out in the political wilderness from that day until this, but he'd found a role to play in actively fighting for gay rights. Not only was Mr Harvey very well respected by the political gay community, he was even considered something of a hero, a martyr to the cause. He'd been replaced in the Foreign Office by John Profumo.

Mr Harvey was very pleasant but very drunk, but then so was I. For a 61-year-old, he was direct and to the point. There was no small talk. He was already naked when I entered his room. He impatiently removed my clothes and we went to bed. Once we had dressed, he informed me he was an Anglo-Catholic and asked if I'd pray with him. We knelt by his bedside and prayed for forgiveness, not for him, but for those who had shunned and persecuted him. He was sitting on the bed when I left him, a sad lonely figure.

"His name was Anthony also," he said softly as I walked to the door.

"Who?"

"He had fair hair, he was slim, beautiful. I can still see his face. We stood together in the dock, humiliated. That boy I was found with. The best my associates could manage was to keep us out of prison – but not out of the papers. We were each given a £5 fine for breaking park regulations. Anyone else might have got five years for indecency. I paid his fine, of course. That was just a down-payment. I've been paying all my life."

I felt as if I were closing the door of a cell when I left. Mr Harvey had indeed been given a life sentence.

In some ways he reminded me of Sir Keith Joseph. They had a couple of things in common: both circumcised, for a start, they were also both tortured, circumspect, and strangely compassionate. Another working week had passed. The endless game was not getting any easier.

* * * * *

Simon liked to ask about my clients and their bedroom habits: what they got up to in bed, the pillow talk, the secrets. He'd store up people's gossip, their business plans or troubles, their indiscretions, political ambitions and opinions on others. All the little bits of information were gathered and put away for future reference. Intelligence was a currency to trade when playing the endless game.

I spent a Saturday afternoon with him. He read the newspapers for a while, browsed through business reports and correspondence, then looked at gardening magazines. I knelt on the floor and looked through his record collection which consisted mainly of classical music. Simon's favourite composer was Mozart. He loved the adagio movements and considered them to be the most beautiful music ever written. Mozart, he proclaimed, could write anything from heavy masses to light entertainment. Simon was also into more contemporary light entertainment in a big way, but as I flicked through his George Gershwin, Irving Berlin and Cole Porter LPs, he stood up solemnly and burst into *Cavatina* from act II of *The Marriage of Figaro*. He sang in Italian for a moment before dissolving into laughter and collapsing back in the chair. I flipped through the LPs, stopped at Mantovani and placed it onto the turntable. The lush strings covered a few classics and some instrumental versions of songs from movies. While that was playing I flipped through some more: old crooners like Sinatra and Matt Monro. I stopped at the bespectacled grin of Nana Mouskouri and threw Simon a questioning look. "Nana Mouskouri, Simon, really? He just shrugged his shoulders and said, "She's Greek, she's nice… really."

We joked about how the record shops labelled some music as easy listening, as opposed to difficult listening. I played *Sleepy Shores* by Johnny Pearson, then *Cherry Pink and Apple Blossom White* by Eddie Calvert. That made me think about the young cherub-faced rent boy Cherry, then I thought about Tiger and I wondered if Damie had appeared back in the Dilly. First chance I got I was going to go looking for him again.

"Why, Simon, you old rocker." I held up *F.B.I.*, a Shadows single, then put it on and side-stepped across the room playing air guitar and trying to get Simon to join in. He wouldn't entertain it.

Mid-afternoon he made tea and sandwiches and we chatted. We talked of our childhoods, years apart, miles apart and classes apart. He stirred his tea with a little silver spoon.

Simon said he'd been painfully shy until he was about 16. He also revealed that his indomitable mother Nicolette, who was a cousin of the Earl of Dudley, had had an affair with the 11th Duke of Blanford, when he was young, which had made him very insecure. Nicole was aloof and frosty and rather a bully. She could intimidate, even terrify people.

Simon's twice-married maternal grandmother was the Baroness Irene de Brienen. He called her Eny. He spoke affectionately about granny Eny, a remarkable woman who had died the previous year. In 1973 Simon had attended her 90th birthday party at his parent's house in Pusey. There were 50 guests in the dining room and there was Eny holding court, sitting between the Duke of Westminster and the Duke of Beaufort. After lunch, a helicopter landed on the lawn and whisked her off for a jaunt around the Oxfordshire countryside. Eny's ashes were buried in the tiny graveyard of a Georgian church at Pusey.

Something else that troubled Simon whilst still at school was the failed marriage of his elder sister, Susan Hornby. She had married John Spencer-Churchill, 11th Duke of Marlborough, and Simon said he'd felt so sorry for their children, who were just six and three when their parents divorced. It was another reason why Simon would never have children.

"James, is your age now," he sighed. "God, where do the years go? When I was your age I was a 2nd Lieutenant in the Grenadier Guards."

"Let's go out," I said unsympathetically, failing to appreciate the trust he was showing in me. But I was bored listening to the domestic problems of his privileged family.

"Where do you want to go?"

"Anywhere. Let's just get out."

We walked down to Harrods and he bought me some chocolate. Sometimes I felt like a child when I was with Simon. He was causing me to regress, to become more dependent on him. We ended up at the Houses of Parliament and walked towards the Embankment.

"Simon, can I ask you a question?"

"Of course."

"How does it work? I mean if a man wants a young man or a boy, how does he know who to ask? Who makes the introductions, who arranges things, assuming of course that the person is famous or important and doesn't want to risk going to the Dilly and picking up rent?"

"Well, there are many ways, but I'll give you one example."

Simon then delivered a lecture on the subject of boy procurement.

"If the person has never dabbled before and has say, an interest in boys, it's all conducted very civilly and discreetly. It's all about little signals being sent out, little messages being communicated." He pointed back towards the Palace of Westminster. "There might be three or four people in there, in a bar, or it might be in a gentleman's club or some other social gathering. The man will drop his fishing line into the pond by reminiscing about the old school, about the romantic yearnings, the passionate attachments between the boys. Every house had at least one "tart", as he would have been known, in effect a prostitute, not to put too fine a point on it. This little angel would have provided sexual favours for older boys and would in return have been showered with gifts or privileges."[48]

I offered Simon an exotic chocolate, but he waved my hand away. I munched on the expensive confection as he continued with my tutorial.

"When I was at Eton, I heard of a pupil who used to prostitute his little brother, made an absolute mint. So anyway, our man might actually admit to having been a recipient of the services of the school tart and joke about it, saying he'd like to relive that experience all over again. This would be after a few drinks, of course. If he's lucky someone in the group might continue the conversation in this vein, all the while laughing and joking. But then, depending on the company, one of those present might drop a hint that such a boy might be had. Or the man might be approached later when the topic might be explored a little more earnestly, a little less humorously. An invitation to a party might be offered or a more private introduction arranged. Money or the promise of a favour, some cake, might be expected in return."

"But where do the boys come from?"

"I can speak only of London," he said. "Depending on the tastes of the man in question, a boy can be brought from Playland, care homes, foster homes or schools. London is teeming with waifs and strays, urchins and orphans. Read Dickens. Read between the lines. It's both explicit and implicit. Don't forget, Oliver was sold. Fagin may have sent his boys out to steal, but he also sent them out to sell."

---

48   Simon also revealed that the Eton Society, the self-electing body of prefects collectively known as "Pop", were entitled to avail of the sexual services of the prettiest boy in the school, who was referred to as "pop bitch".

We walked along the Embankment as the light faded and the Thames turned black.

"Have you given my offer any thought?" Simon asked.

"Yes, but I'm considering another offer as well," I teased.

"Really?"

"Yes, I've been offered a management job in Soho, managing a bookshop or maybe a chain of bookshops."

His booming laughter turned a few heads.

"Do you know something funny? The owners of those bookshops know when they are about to get a raid by the police, because the police tell them. They phone the person managing the bookshop and give a code. The code they use is WH Smith."

Now I laughed. "Why WH Smith?"

"It means get the hard stuff out of the shop. WH Smith is whiter than white. We won't even stock *Private Eye* in case we are jointly sued for libel and we don't stock material like *Gay News*. We know who our customers are and we don't want to offend them."

We walked a little further. "And, of course, your Playland contacts and the porn barons work hand in hand."

"I know," I said nonchalantly.

"I've heard of some rent boy being offered money to look after one of these bookshops for an afternoon. A tip-off had come the day before that a raid was planned. The Playland cohort let the raid go ahead, leaving all the hard-core material in the shop. The rent boy went down for possession. You can imagine how popular he was in prison. He was never seen in the Dilly again."

I wondered how Simon knew about the Soho porn business and its sordid and ruthless dealings.

"I suppose the porn was picked up at the police station the next day and brought back to the shop."

"Very probably. So you see, you should consider your options very carefully. A job at WH Smith may be the lesser of two evils!"

"I'll think about it," I said, smiling.

The Thames shimmered and reflected the lights of the city. The skinny naked branches of the trees reached for the stars and the night air became crisp and cold. We made our way anonymously through the crowds. We were an odd couple. I asked him questions about many things and he answered, patiently and thoroughly. I'd never had a conversation like this with my father. I listened and learned, clinging to his every word.

We stopped for a moment and Simon looked back across the London skyline, gazing at the dark silhouetted spires of the Palace of Westminster, the radiant reassuring face of Big Ben, marking this moment in time, the bridges reaching across the Thames. He became a little emotional and his eyes brimmed with tears.

"God, Anthony," he said sincerely, "at moments like this, when I think about our history, our institutions, our literature… I feel so proud to be British. To be a Hornby." He gave my arm a little squeeze. "To be with you."

The only thing needed now, I thought, was an orchestra sitting by the banks of the Thames playing Elgar's Nimrod to accompany the slow movement of the river, to enhance the emotion, to swell the pathos, to bath us in patriotism.

When I was with Simon, at times I felt like laughing and at times I felt like crying. We walked on together. It was a little bit pathetic, but also a little bit romantic. I liked Simon. I liked him a lot.

CHAPTER 23

Teach Me Tiger

Damie had still not been seen around the Dilly, so I decided to go the hostel he was staying at. After work I got a taxi from Charing Cross Road to 58 Branksome Road, situated just behind Brixton High Street, the HQ hostel of Roger Gleaves. The street was dark and shabby, and every other street light seemed to be broken. When I found the hostel it was in darkness. A couple of the windowpanes were cracked and tape had been crudely applied to the dirty glass. Other windows had filthy lace hanging in tatters. I was about to knock on the front door when I noticed it was ajar. I pressed my hand to the letterbox and the door swung silently open. The hall was in darkness, but the light from outside now threw shadows on the walls and floor. I moved to the bottom of the stairs. The atmosphere was dank and mouldy. There was a smell of neglect and decay. I entered a room where odd bits and pieces of furniture seemed to have been strewn around, knocked over in a struggle perhaps. Had someone broken in and been disturbed? I stood listening in the silence. Then I heard it. A scratching sound. It was coming from above. I peered up at the tall ceiling, where the plaster-work had disintegrated, creating a deformed gargoyle. There it was again, the same low scratching noise, like a rat slowly clawing at something.

I returned to the hall and switched on the light. The low wattage bulb emitted a weak pulse of light, went out and flickered on again. I tried the landing light. It didn't work. I slowly walked up the stairs, heard a faint cough and froze to the spot. Then snoring. Someone was in one of the bedrooms. I reached the landing and looked around. The snoring was coming from behind a closed door. The door of another room, which would have been directly above the room I'd been in downstairs, was open. I walked to the doorway and strained to see inside, waiting for my eyes to adjust. Lamplight from the street fell on the floor. I slowly made out the shape of a body lying on the bare floorboards in the middle of the room. The unnaturally white skin of the face seemed to glow in the darkness. The teeth were clenched and the eyes shut tightly. It was Damie. My heart hammered blood to my temples and my throat constricted in horror. His body was twisted to one side and his right arm was missing, as if removed from the shoulder. It was not beside the body.

I forced myself to take a step forward. The floorboard creaked. Damie's head slowly rotated. The mouth closed and the eyes opened. I staggered back and banged into the door.

"Jesus," he hissed quietly, as his missing arm slowly emerged from underneath a missing piece of floorboard.

He extracted his hand, which was holding a brown paper bag. He then stuffed this into a small suitcase.

"You scared the living shit out of me," he whispered.

I was still in shock, speechless. He pushed me out of the room, holding his finger to his lips. "Quietly."

We descended the stairs and he led me into an office and flicked on a desktop lamp. It looked as if it the office had been ransacked, papers strewn everywhere.

"Nothing worth nicking here," he said, rifling the drawers of a desk. "Too late. Shit!"

I looked down as I walked over the scattered sheets of headed notepaper. I scooped up a handful. The stationery looked to be amateurishly printed and carried different headings: The Old Catholic Church Community Service Department; The Voluntary Service Department; The Guild of St Dismas. A name printed on the paper jumped out at me. I was stunned – it was my grandfather's name, Frederick Burder.

"Leave that rubbish." Damie pushed me through to the kitchen as I folded the paper into my pocket.

We went through to a kitchen. He grabbed a carrier bag and swiped his arm across a shelf, dropping in some tinned food. He then took some utensils from hooks on the wall.

"Right, let's get out of here."

We fled from the hostel and made our way to Hope House. I sneaked him into my room.

"Where the hell have you been? I've been worried sick."

Damie explained that people had been looking for him. A man called Peter Chambers, who managed Gleaves' Osterley hostel, had warned Damie he was in danger. Gleaves was still, to a certain extent, directing operations from prison through his more loyal henchmen and he wanted to take care of a few loose ends. Damie was a loose end. He'd not been paying the Gleaves Firm the agreed percentage of his earnings. In fact, he'd been giving them nothing of what he earned from his "theatrical work". Gleaves' little empire was slowly imploding. The DHSS money was drying up and the boys were stealing anything that wasn't nailed down in the hostels and moving on.

"What was in the envelope under the floor?"

He opened it for me to see. It was stuffed with cash.

"How much?"

"I don't know. I haven't counted it. I can't believe the fuzz missed this when they were searching the place."

"Maybe it was put there after the search," I said. "Damie, there must be a hundred quid there. Billy Two-Tone was murdered over the £60 Hyland stole. Are you mad?"

"I didn't know there'd be this much. That bedroom was Gleaves'. When I was his favourite for a while I saw him hide money when he thought I was sleeping."

I remembered about the stationery and looked at it properly in the brighter light of my bedroom. The name on it was actually Frederick Burden, not Burder. He was Conservative MP for Gillingham. Another patron whose name appeared on the stationery was none other than Lord "Boofy" Arran.

I let Damie stay the night. I didn't really have much choice.

He quickly made himself at home and as I undressed and climbed into bed, he cast a critical, distasteful eye over the clothes in my wardrobe. He dismissively flicked his hand across each shirt and jacket. He shook his head despairingly at the ties. He lifted one out and held it near the bedside lamp, as if holding a dead kipper by the tail. He let it drop to the floor and, smiling, rubbed his fingertips together.

"You cheeky little shit," I said, laughing. "So let's see your Spring collection then. I looked at his battered suitcase. "Where do you actually keep all your clothes and stuff?" He shrugged his shoulders. "Damie, you don't live out of that... do you?"

"My wardrobes are strategically located across the West End." He smiled, but sounded a little defensive. I wondered if Damie was being secretive because he was embarrassed about the reality of his existence.

Sometimes listening to Damie talk about his punters and his theatrical luvvies, you'd think he was leading a charmed life. He projected the image of a cocky, streetwise hustler. He may have been good-looking and clean and shiny and fashionably dressed, but he was sleeping in a slum and living out of a suitcase. His "strategically placed wardrobes" were the shops he stole his clothes from: places like C&A in Oxford Street and Big Biba in Kensington High Street, where he picked up some of his more daring and decadent outfits.

Every time I tried to probe into the harsh reality of Damie's life in London, he changed the subject. His diversionary tactics this time were to light up a joint for us to smoke, delve into his suitcase and extract a little bundle of 45s. He put a single on the turntable, *Teach Me Tiger* by April Stevens. He said it reminded him of his mum, that the record was the only possession of hers that he had. He told me he used to sit on her knee as a little boy and she'd pretend to pounce on him and tickle him with her tiger claws. She called him her baby tiger. I'd assumed that Damie had called himself Tiger because he saw himself as a predator in the Dilly jungle, not one of the hunted. A typical hustler mindset. But maybe he simply used the name to remind himself of his mother, of the child he used to be, and to remember happier times.

For a song that had been released in the mid-1960s it was one of the most sexually suggestive things I had ever heard. Damie began to sway his hips and mime to the words, as if the sultry soul of Stevens had possessed him. He pouted his lips, ran his fingers through his hair and caressed his body. He slowly rotated and gyrated as he transformed into the Siren that was so irresistible to punters. The song captured Damie's rent persona perfectly: it projected innocence interlaced with a yearling sexuality. Damie became Tiger, the boy who made people go weak at the knees. He undid some of the buttons of his white silk blouse. He crawled onto the bed and knelt over me, his fingers curled like the claws of a tiger, waiting to strike. He took a long drag on the joint and put it into my mouth and mimed to the song. He moved his head until his nose was an inch from mine – *"What must I do to make you my very own?"* I had never been subjected to Tiger's beguiling charms before. I was confused and intimidated. Was this a confessional seduction or a cry for help? I looked directly into his eyes, trying to figure out who he was and what he wanted: sex, love, friendship, security… what? *Vorrei poter leggere la storia nei tuoi occhi Damiano.* What would Pretty Boy do if he were here? I reached over and knocked out the light.

April Stevens sang in the darkness…

Teach me tiger how to tease you wah wah wah wah wah

Tiger, tiger I wanna squeeze you wah wah wah wah wah.

The following morning, we parted company outside Foyles. I warned him to keep away from the Dilly and to lie low. I told him to meet me outside Hope House at 7:00pm and if he'd still not found anywhere else, I'd let him stay there for just one more night.

* * * * *

Foyles bookshop had by now become a place I truly hated. All I wanted was peace and quiet, a chance to rest after sleepless nights. Instead, I was constantly being asked for directions to the other departments. I was a bloody tour guide in this book-cluttered death-trap of a shop. The days seemed endless, standing in that little classics department. I felt I was working in a tomb surrounded by dead authors. How the world had turned since the day I'd been interviewed and was told I'd got the job. I'd stood on the pavement outside this very door, filled with pride at my achievement, looking at my grinning reflection. Look at me now. I had become that distorted reflection of myself. I had become the ghost I had seen in the window of the classics department. I was a wreck, stooped over at times from the recurring pain in my back, choking at times on phlegm or blood.

I went to see the Prophet to get something for the pain. He assured me that heroin was not only the ultimate in pain relief, but that the "opium lady" would also bring euphoric bliss to my troubled soul.

"All that fucking pain, all your problems will just float away, man."

He even offered to cook it and shoot it up for me. He waved a little bag in front of my eyes. The Prophet got his heroin from the Triad gangsters in Gerrard Street, where they had been firmly ensconced since 1970. It was they who first imported a new novelty product from Hong Kong – powder heroin. They filled the vacuum in the UK market when liquid ampoules became difficult to get hold of following the demise of the "junkie doctors". The Prophet said he'd take good care of me, take me to the promised land. I reluctantly declined his offer. Thankfully, that was one line I did not cross.

At five o'clock I walked, or rather shuffled, to Westminster, where I was picked up by Lord Back-Seat. On this occasion he was much more chatty. He told me he was a good friend of Simon's. Like Simon, he had been to public school and Oxford. He and Simon had many common interests, including education – they shared concerns about levels of literacy among the young. He gave me a small boxed gift, a token of his appreciation for the joy I brought into his life, and the life he could bring into my mouth. It was an expensive fountain pen. I appreciated the gesture.

* * * * *

I never did get around to taking Dr McCarty's prescription to a chemist, so I had no one to blame but myself when I became so ill that I had difficulty breathing at times. I'd lean over a bookcase at work and try not to panic, forcing myself to slowly inhale through my nose and breathe out of my mouth while trying to control the back pain. Finally, one afternoon I decided that it might be better to actually see a doctor rather than just speak to one on the phone. I asked Father Hackett if he would drive me to casualty. He took me to the Whittington Hospital. I was seen by a man who was either Indian or Pakistani and who was either a very poor doctor or a very ambitious hospital porter. Either way, he was as useful as the Ukrainian in Foyles who spoke no English but looked after the medical books department in the basement. The doctor/porter gave me a cursory examination and looked at me rather suspiciously, then sent me away with instructions to rest and take painkillers.

What do you do when you know you're dying but a doctor tells you you're fine and just need a little rest and some tablets? When you're a confused, troubled, drug-dependent, brainwashed, sexually exploited 20-year-old who's suffering from sleep deprivation, you obediently do as you are told. I went away feeling desolate. I apologised to Father Hackett for wasting his time. He suggested that now might be a good time to start taking the antibiotics Dr McCarty had prescribed.

What do you do when you know you are slowly dying and feel you're wasting what little time you have left standing in the classics department of a large bookshop? You write a little note to Christina Foyle telling her that you're making no contribution whatsoever to the business, and you fire yourself.

I left the note with administration on the fourth floor and advised them I was leaving forthwith. There would be no week's notice. I couldn't work in Foyles anymore. I admitted defeat. The day job had to go. I was simply too tired, too ill to stand in a bookshop all day. I gave up. I surrendered myself, surrendered what normality had remained, to the inevitable. There was no going back. *Fuck it*, I thought. They can have all of me. Pretty Boy would burn brightly day and night from now on, until the light in him flickered and went out. I didn't care anymore. I didn't matter anymore. Pretty Boy would sacrifice himself on the altar of Eros.

CHAPTER 24

Devil in the Brain

I didn't tell Simon I'd left Foyles and I felt bad about deceiving him, but during the day I was now a free agent and I spent most of my time with Damie. The good news was that Damie had sorted out a place to stay. The bad news was he'd be sharing a bed with a member of the Playland Firm, a guy in his late 20s called Andrew Novac. Damie told me he and Andrew had worked together in the past, setting up badger traps.

There was an unwritten and unspoken code among rent boys that governed their behaviour. Badger-trapping was frowned upon because it frightened away some punters and a case might come before the courts and generate a lot of negative publicity. Blackmail gave rent a bad name. Something else that really pissed off rent was someone offering themselves below the going rate. This was usually new younger boys who didn't know any better and were taken advantage of. They were soon put right by the other boys, and if they didn't up their prices they were harassed off the Dilly. In any case these youngsters, who arrived in London with nothing but the clothes on their backs, soon looked dirty, tattered and torn. They were the ones who were most abused and exploited by the Playland Firm or by unscrupulous punters. They were the ones who were easily picked up by gay bashers and beaten to a pulp, or who caught diseases and soon disappeared back to wherever they came from. The Dilly was brutal and unforgiving.

Damie and I went on the rampage. We drank from early morning, smoked dope and bought Montecristos from Robert Lewis of St James's, where many of my clients bought their cigars. The shop was almost opposite that regular pickup haunt of mine, the Prunier Restaurant.

One day when we had ignited the rich brown tobacco, we went for afternoon tea in the Savoy in the Strand, only to be refused entry at the door by two uniformed commissionaires – doormen to you and me. We protested indignantly but one of the men discreetly asked for a word in our ears.

"Fuck off out of it, you poofters, or I'll call the Old Bill."

We received a warmer welcome in the Scandia Room, a large restaurant in the Piccadilly Hotel. Damie had been here before, he claimed, in the company of a group of actors. He said he had spoken briefly to a lovely man and a fellow Glaswegian, an actor called John Fraser. Mr Fraser had coincidently played Bosie opposite Peter Finch in *The Trials of Oscar Wilde*.

The restaurant was very nice but virtually empty, the atmospherics not conducive to the spirit of social inclusiveness we had been seeking. Nonetheless, we had a pleasant afternoon tea before spending a rainy night in Soho enjoying some rather more welcoming and inclusive but uncivilised activities. We threw money around, literally. In the early hours of the morning we retreated from the precinct, folding money into the pockets of the sleeping children huddled up under cardboard in doorways.

I also began to familiarise myself with some of Damie's clientele, including his swooning circle of luvvies from the theatrical world. Damie had recently been introduced to a very attractive American in his late 20s who had been an original cast member of *Jesus Christ Superstar* when it opened in London in 1972. Paul was back over from the States on a brief visit and was able to get us in backstage at the Palace Theatre on Cambridge Circus, where the show was still running. He suggested Damie and I join him for a threesome in a nearby apartment. He was offering £100 in return for some amateur dramatics, but we declined. Damie had briefly considered an invitation to return to the USA with him, but concluded that whilst the artist was attractive and multi-talented, he wasn't rich enough.

Late the following night, having left a client, I returned to the Dilly and met Damie at the Wimpy. He dragged me along to a party in a rundown docklands loft. I lifted a bottle of vodka and escaped to a quiet room, where I collapsed fully clothed onto a bed. A short time later I was joined by a man with intense eyes and Gallic features, who looked like a French hitman. He was in fact a 33-year-old English artist-cum-stage designer called Derek. He thought I was Italian, so we were both surprised when we introduced ourselves. He seemed sober, sensible and charmingly softly spoken.

Derek sat at the foot of the bed. He talked about his artistic pursuits and I talked sluggishly if not incoherently about mine. He said he was planning his next project and, assuming the modest funding could be raised, he would be directing his first feature film the following year. Set in Italy, the picture would be about the martyrdom of Saint Sebastian. He had been casting his recruitment net around the Dilly and the toilets of Central London in his quest to find a few select extras, and he asked me if I would like a part in the movie. I was about to tell him I'd never acted before, but then realised that I was an actor, one who played a leading role every night in the West End. All the same, the prospect of having a bit-part in a bargain-basement biblical epic did not appeal to me. I reached into my jacket pocket and gave him my Foyles business card. I asked him to phone me if he decided to make a spaghetti western instead.

Derek stood up and placed his hands across his heart and rolled his eyes towards heaven in supplication. He struck a saintly pose for a moment, then fell dead-like on top of me. He fixed me with those piercing hypnotic eyes and gingerly removed the vodka bottle from my grip.

It proved to be an all-nighter.

The following morning I extricated Damie from a bed that he had shared with a 26-year-old fellow Scot called Ian, who was preparing to make his debut on the West End stage. We made our way to Soho for breakfast. As we talked about Paul, Ian and Derek, we couldn't know that all three of them would die from AIDS within a few of years of each other in the early 1990s.[49]

One of Damie's regular punters from the world of politics was a gentleman called Tom Driberg. Having nothing else to do that afternoon, I accepted Damie's invitation to accompany him to Tom's small flat in Mountjoy House in the Barbican development. Damie told me that 70-year-old Tom was convinced that teenage semen had medicinal qualities, which, if consumed frequently, could extend life. He therefore availed himself of a steady stream of willing donors, stretching from the East End to the West End, who would deposit their tonic in him.

Tom had the kindly face of my old primary school headmaster, a smooth, tanned complexion and slightly drooping

---

49 The three men went on to become major successes in their respective careers. Paul Jabara appeared in films and TV shows and was a pioneer of the disco movement. He also wrote and produced songs for Barbra Streisand, Donna Summer and Bette Midler. He won a Grammy for a platinum-selling album, and an Oscar for best original song. Derek Jarman got to make his film about the venerable St Sebastian and went on to become one of the most radical avant-garde film directors in British cinema. Coincidentally, Ian Charleson made his film debut in 1977 in a film directed by Derek and a few years later became an international celebrity after starring in a couple of multi-Oscar-winning films.

jowls. We spent a very interesting afternoon with him, discussing politics, religion, books, sex and black magic. I told Tom about my Northern Irish upbringing, and how I'd worked in a bookshop since I'd left school. He was surprised and delighted when I told him I'd worked in Foyles. He said he'd known Christina Foyle – an old and dear friend – since she was a teenager, and enthused about what an incredible woman she was. I felt uneasy about all these links and connections between people I'd been introduced to. I worried about this network of powerful and influential people, and the extent to which their tentacles reached into the place where I'd worked. Who exactly knew what about me? Who was pulling the strings?

In spite of all these concerns and reservations, I surprised myself by being very open about my indecent London adventures. Tom was disarming, he had such a warm and trusting way that it was easy to relax and talk to him. He was fascinated by my story and appreciated that I'd been so open. But my concerns about an elite community, tightly knit together by wealth, position, power and knowledge, were confirmed. Not only did Tom know Christina, he also knew Simon, and Simon's parents. He had visited Pusey on numerous occasions.

"Everyone knows Simon," he proclaimed.

Simon Hornby and Christina Foyle, the two people I worked for, albeit in different capacities, seemed to know everybody. This whole class of people in their ostentatious social circles were orbiting the capital in the steady, predictable trajectories of their careers, constantly interacting with one another. Some were attracted by the gravitational pull of the Dilly, sending probes to bring back the precious celestial bodies they longed to explore.

Tom had retired the previous year, having been a Labour MP for 30 years. He said he expected to be elevated to the House of Lords soon. He was a man of many parts: a politician, a practising Anglo-Catholic, a Communist, and a homosexual who had flaunted his sexuality all his life, not particularly concerned that it was illegal.[50]

Tom was equally open about his own past and sexuality. He was regularly being supplied with Playland rent, so he also knew the people behind the arcade business and the porn business. Given my insignificant and harmless status in the food chain, Tom was being as indiscreet as any of my clients, but his stories were more interesting. He relished telling us about the highlights and lowlights of his sexual indiscretions. He'd been having sex with men and boys since he was 13.

"The pursuit of sexual pleasure," he said, "has been the driving force of my life. I'm 70 years old and still a sexual being to the core."

Tom was a long-time friend of the Kray twins and had used his political influence to try and help them, not only in the past but even now, when he was trying to make life easier for them in prison. He'd attended Ron's notorious all-male parties and together with Lord Bob Boothby (who was also still being supplied with Playland rent), would feast on the boys who had been procured for the evening. Tom was also a very good friend of the American author Gore Vidal, and he reminisced explicitly about their sexual exploits in Italy.[51]

I mentioned my experiences with Richard in the Guards Club, and Tom said he too, aeons ago, had had sex on a sofa in

---

50   It was said that when Tom was first elected to the House, the Conservative MP Chips Channon had taken him on a tour of the most important room in the Palace of Westminster, the gentlemen's toilets.

51   One of Gore's admirers at that time, the young journalist Christopher Hitchens described how in Rome, Driberg and Vidal would pick up "rugged young men from the Via Veneto". Back in their apartment the young men would "be taken from the rear by Gore and then thrust, with any luck semi-erect, into the next room where Tom would suck them dry".

the Guards Club. But then, he said, he had had sex in just about any place one could possibly imagine, including the back seat of Louis Mountbatten's car. This happened during the war, when as a war correspondent he had journeyed with Mountbatten from Ceylon to Singapore. On the night he had arrived in Mountbatten's HQ, in a place called Kandy in Ceylon, Tom said he was presented with a young Burmese boy also called Candy. With a sense of the exotic and the erotic, Tom chose to have sex with Candy on the spacious white-leather back seat of Mountbatten's Dakota. Tom reminisced that the closest thing to heaven he'd experienced was sharing an old cross-channel steamer in 1944 with 500 Guardsmen. He spoke of blissful nights in Paris with British and American troops.

Tom surprised me by raising the infernal and eternal "Irish Question". He surprised me even more with his knowledge of the conflict. He said at first he had thought the troops wouldn't be in Ulster very long. Now he had his doubts. I agreed with him. Although an IRA ceasefire in Ulster had started the day before my interview with Foyles, I thought that the Troubles would probably be as endless as Simon's *game*. I told him about my one-time crush on Bernadette Devlin and he laughed. He considered Bernadette to be one of the most eloquent speakers he had ever listened to, her maiden speech in the House the finest he had ever heard. We talked about Bloody Sunday. He was moved by my account of the killings. He said that the week after Bloody Sunday he had spoken at a demonstration in Newry alongside Bernadette.

"I've always been of the opinion that the real terrorists are in Stormont and Westminster. Why in the name of Christ would you deploy an elite Parachute Regiment at a civil rights march simply to arrest a few hooligans? Whoever made that decision is responsible for the killings. Even if there were a few nuts among the rioters, there was no justification for using a sledgehammer."

Damie tried to steer the conversation towards the reason we had visited. He said he was feeling tired and he went to Tom's bedroom. I expected Tom to follow but he sat on and continued to chat over a bottle of wine. We must have spent a couple of hours talking about books, boyhood and bothers. I told Tom that my father was also called Thomas and that we had never had a proper father-son relationship. I told him about the drinking and the violence. His sympathy turned to shock when I told him that when I was 13 years old I decided to kill my father.

At that age my interests had shifted from the thrilling stories of Sir Arthur Conan Doyle towards the occult. I used to spend hours every week scanning the library shelves or sitting in the reference room looking through encyclopaedias, and I started to borrow various books on witchcraft and demonology. On one occasion the assistant turned the book cover to face me with a disapproving look. "My father," I said, shrugging my shoulders, matching her disapproval.

My younger sister, Faustina, and I had come to the unfortunate conclusion that our father needed to be removed from our lives. In tomes on the supernatural I had read about a book called *The Key of Solomon the King*, attributed to King Solomon, but influenced by medieval Jewish kabbalists and Arab alchemists. I found a modern reprint copy for sale in the books section of the *Exchange & Mart* and sent off a postal order. The section I was interested in contained conjurations, invocations and curses to summon demons and spirits of the dead and constrain them to do my will. My intention was to put a curse on Thomas and kill him. However, my plans were dashed when I discovered that not only did the spells have to be carried out at an appropriate astrological time using specific magical symbols, they also required substances including cuttings of hair and fingernails from a man who had been hanged at a crossroads. Thomas was going to be around for another while.

Tom laughed heartily at the thought of my murderous intentions.

"I knew Irish Catholics prayed for divine intervention but I never heard of anyone, let alone a child, take a more direct approach."

His expression changed to one of sadness.

"What a troubled boy you must have been." For a second his eyes glazed over with a faraway look. "I wish I could have been there to help."

He sipped his wine.

"Have you ever heard of Aleister Crowley?" he asked.

"Of course," I shot back. I knew all about Crowley. He was a legendary black magician and was considered by many to have been 'the wickedest man alive'. "The Great Beast," I proclaimed with theatrical verve.

"Well, the Great Beast and I were great friends."

"Shit! Really?"

"Why yes. We met many times and developed a close relationship. It was his intention that I be named his successor as 'World Teacher'."

I was mesmerised. Tom told me stories I could scarcely believe. The hair stood on the back of my neck. I hadn't felt quite like this since I was a child sitting in Sloans Terrace listening to my granny's stories of the supernatural. I felt bewitched and excited to have made a direct connection to Crowley through Tom.

"He left me his books and manuscripts when he died."

I sprang out of the chair. "Please let me see them!"

"Sorry. I'm afraid I sold them."

I dropped to the floor, then sat up, my back against the book case. I had a sudden urge for some chemical stimulant. It was approaching teatime but I felt I could use a fix now to provide some early fortification for the night ahead. I was to meet the chief of an insurance company that evening. I lifted a book and used it as a makeshift surface.

Tom continued as I prepared my compound. "His manuscript diary was beautiful, bound in red morocco, encased in silver. And within, all his magic, all his sex, all the details. I sold it to Jimmy Page."

"Led Zeppelin?"

"Yes."

"Fuck!"

The desire to kill my father by conjuring up spirits and employing black magic had long since passed, so Crowley's spells would have been of little use. Still, I'd have loved to have seen those books.

"Two years ago I auctioned all his other books at Christie's, made a lot of money."

Tom's story made me realise why I loved old books. It wasn't just about the books. It was about their owners, their stories.

It slowly dawned on me that Tom was trying to seduce me. He had spent the afternoon impressing me, flattering me, casting his line over the river of my life: my interests, my books, music, family, my troubles, *the* Troubles. I was finally hooked and he was reeling me in. He told me shocking tales about his friend the Great Beast, of degeneracy and the corruption of youth. He talked of magick, explained what the spiritual philosophy of Thelema was. He dropped names of the rich and famous at my feet like rose petals, intoxicating me with the scent of his forbidden knowledge. I swallowed his poison like a trusting child. I was enchanted by his dark charisma. Tom was a magician all right, a charming and disarming rogue.

He offered me his hand and helped me to my feet.

"Why don't you and I join Tiger in the bedroom?"

"I don't think that's a good idea, Tom."

He started to sway and sing *That Old Black Magic*. Simon had a Frank Sinatra LP with that song on it. I couldn't help but laugh.

"No, Tom, I really need to be going."

"I'd like to put a spell on you," he smiled mischievously.

I felt like he already had, although it may have been the powder I had snorted, or the wine, or both. My head spun for a moment and I had the strangest sensation of feeling the blood slithering through me, of the skin crawling off my body, of sensing the devil in the brain. I went into the bedroom to make sure Damie was OK. I touched his shoulder and shook him gently.

"Damie, Damie, wake up, I need to go."

Damie rolled onto his back and stretched out luxuriously on the bed.

"I really have to go now."

Damie held out his arms and I reached for his hands to pull him up. He gripped me and pulled me down on top of him.

"Fuck sake, Damie, stop messing around, let me go." I laughed drunkenly at the ridiculousness of the situation.

"I'm tired," Damie moaned, "stay with me."

He looked drugged. I raised his head from the pillow and shook him.

"Have you taken anything?" I asked. I felt stoned myself. His head rolled back onto the pillow.

"*Ho ho ho,*" Damie whispered. "*It's magic.*"

I heard the bedroom door close. I looked over my shoulder. Tom was approaching the bed.

"It may be magic, but I need something stronger to drink," he said with affected yearning. "But which first, Scotch or Irish?"[52] [53]

---

52   In spite of Tom Driberg's reckless sexual behaviour during his long career in politics, including the years when homosexuality was illegal, he seemed to live a charmed life. He was untouchable. The establishment never failed to protect him. An account given by John Symonds, a young Met officer in the 1950s describes an arrest he made while on "Queer Patrol" in toilets at Covent Garden. He caught Driberg buggering another man and arrested him. Tom offered him £5 to let him walk away, but Symonds took him to Bow Street station. Tom made a phone call and another Labour MP arrived at the police station and demanded to see Chief Superintendent "Bones" Jones. A short time later both MPs departed in high spirits. Symonds's pocket book was confiscated and he was warned that the incident never happened. The following month he learned that Driberg had a reputation as "a notorious predatory homosexual" who was a repeat offender. He handed in his warrant card and resigned in disgust. This pattern of institutionalised collusion in protecting VIPs has been evident throughout the last 40 years in other cases involving prominent people. Investigations by the IPCC into historical cases of misconduct by the police are ongoing. Symonds re-joined the Met in 1959 but was drawn into a web of corruption himself. He fled the country in 1972 to avoid a trial and was subsequently recruited by the KGB as a spy.

53   I agreed to visit Tom again, socially but not sexually. As by this time I had left Foyles and was free most mornings, I would call and we'd have tea and talk about many things; his life, his loves, his political beliefs, his exploits as a journalist and as a spy. We chatted about everything from science to socialism; from sex to Satanism. I think he appreciated the novelty of being able to meet a young person and have interesting conversations, rather than simply pay them to put their cocks in his mouth. Tom said he was looking forward to his 70th birthday the following month. Later that year he was granted a life peerage. He tabled a motion in the Lords calling on the government to consider the withdrawal of troops from Northern Ireland. He died from a heart attack the following year.

CHAPTER 25

Some Kind of Freedom

It wasn't long before I was back in Soho, dressed to kill with my looks and medicated to kill my pain. I was dining at Mirabelle with Simon and one of his old friends, Pat Gibson. Pat was rather bald and small with spectacles. He was softly spoken and unassuming. He came across as simply a charming old man. In fact, he was anything but. Pat was a giant in the world of publishing. He was chairman of Pearson Longman, a director of Westminster Press, a director of the *Economist*, and in 1972 had taken over the chairmanship of the Arts Council. Listening to Pat and Simon talk about their associates moving in and out of directorships made it sound like a game of corporate musical chairs.

Some publishers came to see Simon on their hands and knees, begging him to read a manuscript. If they couldn't get an agreement for WH Smith to stock the books, they wouldn't publish. Simon drove a hard bargain. Pat was different from other publishers. He met Simon on equal terms. Pat was also a *player*. Like Simon, he had connections and clout. They both came from good families and had made good marriages. They were friends. They shared cake. As a gesture of that friendship, Simon was also sharing me for the evening. There was a strange dynamic on occasions like this, when I was in the company of privileged men. They somehow made me feel privileged to be in their company, which meant we were all privileged. Everyone was happy.

There was genuine warmth between Pat and Simon as they chatted away. I politely answered Pat's questions, but found it difficult to contribute to their conversations. Some of their stories were incredible, and Pat told one that was the stuff of movies. Predictably it concerned the war, a tale of courage, hardship and endeavour. Unexpectedly, at its heart was a gay love story.

Pat had been fighting against the Italians in North Africa. Captured in Libya in 1941 and taken to a PoW camp in northern Italy, he'd met a young man there called Eddie and they immediately became good friends. Eddie was a fluent French speaker and had served as a liaison officer with the Free French, until he was captured while making his way back to British lines from the battle of Bir Hakeim, south of Tobruk.

They were both moved and ended up in the same camp. They spent two years together in captivity. As roommates they became close and on the rare occasions when they had a chance to be alone, they shared intimate moments together. When Italy surrendered to the Allies, the camp commandant received instructions to hand the PoWs over to the first Allied troops to arrive. One day, Pat and Eddie heard two guards talking about the war being over. They then turned their backs and let the two prisoners cut their way to freedom and take their chances in the open countryside.

They headed for nearby woods and were given food and civilian clothes by locals. The pair then set off on a trek south, travelling the length of Italy. Week after week passed. They depended on each other as never before.

"I have never come to know or love, or depend on another human being in quite the same way." Pat's smile conveyed an expression of loss and regret. "We scavenged for food, nursed one another when we fell sick, motivated one another when one wanted to give up. We cried and laughed together, bled together and made love under the stars."

Some of the details of Pat's account were harrowing and brutal, two young men struggling to survive under appalling conditions, and yet he told his story in a wonderfully uplifting way. Pat's experience was spiritual, biblical.

"We walked for 81 days and travelled 500 miles. We looked down on the river Sangro from the Abruzzi Mountains. The Allies faced the Germans across the river.

"Eddie had taken a bad fall and I'd carried him." Pat's voice cracked with emotion. "I left Eddie by the river bank and waded across alone in the dawn light. I came across a British officer shaving. I told him my friend was injured and that I needed a stretcher. The stunned sergeant just said, 'Certainly, sir, we'll get him right away.' We'd made it. We were saved."

Simon raised his glass and solemnly toasted his old friend's heroic tale. I was quite moved myself, but as Simon hadn't asked what became of Eddie I couldn't bring myself to enquire if he was still living or dead. Pat must have read a look of expectancy on my face, as he then provided a brief epilogue.

"We spent some time together in hospital and then went our separate ways. In the world that was then, we could never have gone on. We took our memories with us and a lost love that dare not speak its name."

Outside, the Rolls pulled up and took us to the Savoy on the Strand. Much to my delight the same two doormen who had turned Damie and me away were on duty. I took great satisfaction in linking arms between Simon and Pat as we walked through the doors, which they held open for us.

"Good evening, gents," they fawned.

I acknowledged their greeting with great satisfaction and solemnly nodded my head as we passed them. I just knew they were looking after me as I swaggered into the foyer between Simon and Pat.

We sat in the American bar for more drinks. Simon loved the Savoy, not least because all his heroes had stayed in it, including of course Wayne, Streisand and Sinatra. Oscar Wilde had conducted his affair with Bosie at the Savoy and the hotel had featured prominently in Oscar's trial for gross indecency. At times I felt that Simon was trying to recreate the past through the present. Oscar had been a frequent user of Dilly rent. I couldn't help but feel I was becoming Bosie to Simon's Oscar.

Simon revealed that the Hornby family also had close business links to the Savoy. Simon's old uncle Sir Antony Hornby, who had been a senior partner at Cazenove, the most prestigious stockbroking firm in the City, had also been President of Savoy Hotel Ltd as well as a director of Claridge's and the Berkeley. Simon said the old man was now 71 and that I'd be getting to meet him soon. I prayed the meeting would be purely social and not sexual.

When we finished our first drink, Simon asked me if I'd mind giving Pat and him half an hour to discuss some private business. He suggested that I have a look around the hotel, but to go to reception first and pick up the key to a room.

"Whose name is it under?"

"Tell them that there's a reservation for a Mr Smith, Mr WH Smith."

I felt as if I were a child being told to go and play while the adults talked. I retrieved the key, checked out the bedroom, then walked around briefly, got bored and went back and sat alone at the bar. I asked the barman to make me up the strongest cocktail he could make without breaking the law.

"I don't want to know what you're putting in it. I'll guess."

I glanced down occasionally at Simon and Pat. They looked very focused and serious in their deliberations. Simon caught me looking at him and he threw me a little smile.

Later in the bedroom I made Baron Gibson of Penn's Rocks in the County of East Sussex smile. An hour later, his innermost thoughts and secrets revealed and the burdens of corporate responsibility eased, he produced his wallet.

"Simon insisted on no money, but here's just a little something." He counted out £60. Tell Simon I'll phone."[54]

I found Simon reading a newspaper down in the bar. He smiled at me and patted me on the back like a proud father. "Pretty Boy," was all he said. I was glad I could make him proud of me.

On the journey home Simon asked for all the explicit details, what I did to Pat, what he did to me, all his secrets, soaked up by the pillow like a sponge. I felt a sense of achievement if I could surprise Simon with some private personal or business information I had been able to extract from a client. I would be rewarded with a tender hug or a conspiratorial finger traced across my lips.

"Mum's the word," he would say. "One of the things I love about you, Pretty Boy, is that you know when to open that beautiful mouth and when to keep your lips sealed tight. He tapped the end

---

54   The following month Lord Gibson made his maiden speech in the House of Lords. A lively debate focused on the Problems of the Theatre and the Cinema. Lord Gibson argued passionately for public funding for the Arts Council and support for the theatre. Lord Longford and Lord Beaumont differed on the subject of censorship. Longford complained about the number of "revolting films being shown" and the dangers of being exposed to this "flow of filth." Beaumont, however, who was President of the British Federation of Film Societies, stressed that the Federation was totally opposed to censorship of films and bitterly regretted that the GLC's motion to ban film censorship in London had been narrowly defeated.
In a rare example of the Lords being prescient, the notion of a fourth television channel was raised and the concept of pay-per-view television suggested.

of my nose with his finger as he recited my virtues and attributes. "Handsome. Irresistible. Intelligent. Discreet…"

I proudly repeated what Pat had said to me in bed. "Pat told me he had never met a rent boy who could quote Shakespeare and Blake or discuss the symphonies of Beethoven and Mahler." Simon gasped. "Dear God! Don't ever let anyone call you a rent boy." He was genuinely shocked. "You, Anthony, are an escort, you are a companion. Never forget that."

We both started to talk at the same time, "I have something to…"

"Sorry," he said.

"No go ahead, you first, age before beauty," I laughed.

He reached down the side of the seat and handed me a very slim gift-wrapped present.

"What's this?"

"Open it."

I tore it open. It was a thin hard-back book. I read the gold title on the black cover. *The Romance of a Bookshop 1904-1938*. The bottom right-hand corner said FOYLES. I carefully opened the book. There was a handwritten inscription inside. Simon had written:

To Anthony
Yours ever
SH x
4/75

I instinctively leaned over and kissed him on the cheek. "Thank you so much, Simon. Where on earth did you get this?"

"It was nothing. I got someone in the antiquarian book trade to find me a copy."

I turned to the title page. The book was privately printed by Foyles in 1938, the year Christina Foyle and Ronald Batty were married. It was written by Gilbert H. Fabes, who'd worked in the rare book department of Foyles at that time. This book was rare and very valuable and he'd obviously gone to a lot of trouble and expense to get it.

"Why the gift?"

"Because you make me happy, you make me smile." His expression grew serious. "I have something else to tell you."

"What is it?" I asked, feeling unexpectedly nervous.

"Pat Gibson."

"What about him?" I was now feeling sick in my stomach.

"He was the last one. You're out of the *game*."

I choked up and broke down. I covered my mouth with my hands, tears running down my face.

"You mean I don't have to do it anymore?"

"Yes."

I threw my arms around him and cried. I couldn't speak. Now Simon had tears in his eyes. We cried and smiled at each other and laughed and cried again.

After a few embarrassing moments he composed himself and said, "You were about to tell me something."

"Yes. I wanted to tell you that I've left Foyles. I want to work for you, for WH Smith, I mean. I want you to teach me everything you know about the business of bookselling."

I said this because I wanted to make Simon happy. I knew I'd never work at WH Smith because I knew I didn't have much longer to live. Simon slapped his hands on his knees and threw his head back, "That's just wonderful. It's perfect. I'll teach you everything you need to know about retail." He clasped his hands together and fluttered his eyes. A little of the camp he tried so desperately to conceal sprang from his core.

As I was being driven home, I studied the date Simon had inscribed: 4/75. The arduous weeks of April were, like the

Vietnam war, finally drawing to a close. A new phase in my own war had unfolded. Simon was removing me from the battlefront, but I didn't know if I was being rescued or captured. Was I now to be Simon's own personal prisoner of war? I put fear and doubt to the back of my mind. If I was out of the game surely that *had* to be some kind of freedom.

The Rolls dropped me off in Kilburn High Road. I couldn't very well be delivered to the front door of Hope House in a Silver Shadow.

"You'll be moving out of that horrid place. I'll have to find you somewhere where you can be near me. Ennismore Mews, perhaps."

I leaned in through the door. "OK, if you want to. I meant to ask you, Simon, do you know what ever happened to Pat's friend Eddie?"

"Of course I do. The old soldiers had a reunion recently. You've already met Eddie."

"What?"

"Yes, you met him a couple of weeks ago in the Dorchester."

"You mean the man with the bodyguards?"

Simon smiled. "They weren't bodyguards, just assistants. Yes, that was him. That was Eddie, or Edward. Edward Tomkins. He's retiring from his job soon. He's the British Ambassador to France."

CHAPTER 26

The Crypt

Damie had managed to get himself into more trouble. Serious trouble. He'd been picked up by a nervous punter, a first-timer in his 30s, married, two kids, bisexual. He was in London for a business meeting and had a couple of hours to kill before a train took him back to a life of domestic deception. The man had been in Leicester Square buying some souvenirs for the wife and kids. He'd strolled over to Piccadilly Circus to check out the boys beneath the arches that he'd heard about.

He was approached by Damie in a sugar-coated request for a light. Damie knew an easy touch when he saw one. Tiger suggested they go for a meal and he enticed his prey to Chinatown for expensive wine, hot curry and the prospect of even hotter sex. They flirted by candlelight as the aroma of exotic spices and lust hung thick in the air. They binged their way through the narrow streets of Soho at the expense of the novice punter. They exchanged stories about life's hardships and the joy of finally discovering one's true identity, the bliss of finally finding a soul mate. The novice punter missed the train and phoned his wife from a grimy phone booth with a sorry tale of transport trouble involving buses, trains and bloody trade unions. By 10pm that evening he was declaring his love for Damie and making plans to leave the wife and kids.

Damie took his prey to a special place he had access to, courtesy of a theatre director with whom he had an "arrangement". He gained entry to St James's Church in Piccadilly and descended into the Crypt. There in the gents' toilet, where it was warm and dry, the couple stripped naked and had sacrilegious, drug-fuelled sex, before they both passed out.

The next day Damie awoke and quickly dressed. The punter was still sleeping. Damie slipped the man's wallet out of his coat pocket and put it in his own, but the punter had just opened his eyes and he scrambled unsteadily from the floor. Damie shoved him down, snatched the man's trousers and bolted for the exit. The crypt was used at times for theatrical rehearsals, and on this occasion cast members had assembled and were rehearsing for a play. Running with the man's trousers, Damie skirted around the group of actors and bolted for the stairs. A few seconds later the frantic punter, fumbling with his shirt, zig-zagged between the startled thespians. The ensemble stood open-mouthed before collapsing in uncontrollable laughter.[55]

Whilst there may have been laughter down in the crypt, out on the street it was a different matter. Damie ran straight into the arms of a policeman, who'd been alerted by the shouts of a half-naked man running towards him. Damie kicked the cop hard between the legs and escaped through the lanes and back streets that he knew like the back of his hand.

The punter told police he'd been forced to strip at knife point before being robbed. Damie was well known to the police as Dilly rent and as a frequent visitor to Playland. To make matters worse, the punter was related by marriage to a senior police officer in the

---

55   Those present in the crypt included Judi Dench, Sian Phillips, Daniel Massey and the play's director, John Gielgud. The play was appropriately called *The Gay Lord Quex* by Pinero. It opened in the Albery Theatre (now The Noel Coward Theatre) in June 1975.

Met. Such a flagrant breech of the peace had to be responded to, and not knowing what else to do, the police came down hard on the Playland Firm. Mr Fisher was beside himself with rage, furious that Damie had brought down so much heat on Playland, especially "as the little bastard worked for the Gleaves Firm and was not even Playland-controlled rent". An order went out and a price was put not on Damie's head but on his balls.

"I want that fucking little bone-smoker castrated," the Fish had screamed at the Fruit Machine.

The Machine knew Mr Fisher wasn't kidding. He would not be content until Damie's scrotum was laid out before him in a Tupperware box. This was just the sort of assignment the Fruit Machine relished. Down the street from Playland, the latest giant neon sign defacing the façade of the London Pavilion advertised a new film, *Bring Me the Head of Alfredo Garcia*. Fruit Machine suggested the sign be changed to *Bring Me the Balls of Damian McKenna*. He certainly had a sense of the dramatic. He was said to have promised that if the police ever came looking for him, he'd be standing on the roof of Playland, armed to the teeth. He would go out in a blaze of glory.

The Dilly was horrified. Word on the streets was that Damie was wanted. His balls were now worth more than rent would make in a month. The Fruit Machine was throwing his weight around, intimidating the boys, and the police were also giving them a hard time. But even though they were angry that Damie would rob a punter and cause so much hassle, they'd never betray one of their own, especially not Damie, who had served his time behind the prison bars of the meat rack for so long and against all the odds.

Damie vanished and then reappeared in my bedroom in Hope House after I offered him refuge for the night. There was no way he was going to talk or rent himself out of this one. He was going to have to get out of London and far away from the Dilly. I couldn't believe he could be so stupid and reckless and told him so. I was also devastated to be losing my best friend. Damie had been my mentor and my guide to Soho and the Dilly. He'd taught me how to swim with the sharks and to survive. Damie was a hustler, a thief, a dreamer, a survivor and a lost child. He could embarrass, shock and amaze me and it broke my heart that he'd be gone for good. We lay in bed, facing each other in dim light, our silent thoughts keeping us awake. I had to break the silence with questions I hated to ask.

"Where will you go?"

"Back to Scotland. As far away from here as I can get and I intend to take my balls with me."

"What will you do?"

"Don't know. Get a job, I hope."

"What would you like to work at?"

"You mean *who* would I like to work at?"

"Give over. You're smart, Damie, do something with your life and stop dreaming about sugar daddy movie stars."

"Your dream came true. You've met your sugar daddy, you're set."

"My dreams are down the drain, Damie. I don't know what I'm doing anymore. Simon isn't my sugar daddy, he's my…"

"You're a lucky bastard, appreciate what you've got."

I touched his cheek and felt the tears.

"I don't know what I'm gonna do," he sniffed. "I don't know anything else." He broke down and cried like a child. "I miss my mum so much."

I held him to me. "It's OK, it'll be OK." I'd never had to comfort someone like this before. I didn't have the words. I fought back my own tears. Damie pressed himself tightly against me. He clung desperately to me, yearning for comfort, for reassurance and for the love only a mother could give him. He kissed me.

"No, Damie," I said gently, and turned over onto my back. "You have to be strong. We have to be strong. We'll get through this."

"I'm gonna miss you, Pretty Boy."

"And I'm gonna miss you, Tiger."

"Will you be able to survive without me?"

"Probably not." I couldn't tell Damie I thought I was dying. Couldn't tell him that without the pharmaceutical cocktails I was living on, it hurt to breathe. We lay in silence again for a while.

"It was funny though," he said.

"What was funny?"

"That punter chasing me and his trousers down Piccadilly. You should have seen the look on his face."

Damie recounted the crypt episode again with a humorous spin to it. He said he had learnt the "nick the trousers" routine from the older boys in Queen Street station in Glasgow. They'd talk a man out of his trousers by promising him the sexual earth, then flee with his coat, trousers, underpants and, hopefully, wallet.

I had to laugh, but this latest stunt had ended Damie's career in London.

"My replacement has arrived," he announced unexpectedly.

"What do you mean?"

"There's a new face on the Dilly, and *what* a face. All the boys are talking about him."

"Who is he?"

"The boys took him for a drink, got him drunk and he opened up. He came from a good family, went to a good school. He was the best voice in the school choir, sang in church, left the congregation in tears every time. His mother died of breast cancer and his da hit the bottle, lost his job. He and his two little brothers were taken into care. Those bastards took really good care of them, I bet. He's a runaway. They're already calling him The Fallen Angel. I've seen him. Jesus, he's beautiful. He'll be popular. With a face like that he'll make a fortune."

"What age is he?"

"Fifteen."

Charles Hornby's favourite age, I thought. I often wondered where Charles had vanished to, not that I missed him. Maybe if I waited long enough Simon would tell me.

Damie had regained his composure and perked up, his defences reconstructed.

He started to sing softly, "If a picture paints a thousand words, then why can I paint you…"

"Damie, go to sleep."

"The words will never show, the you I've come to know."

"For God's sake, will you go to sleep, you've a long journey ahead tomorrow."

Damie put his mouth to my ear. "Come and pour yourself on me," he whispered. I laughed and elbowed him to the far side of the bed. Minutes later he was asleep. I studied his child-like face. There was always a restless intensity about him, but this was the first time I'd seen Damie looking truly relaxed. He looked peaceful. I'd only known Damie for about 10 weeks. It seemed like 10 months. We'd formed an incredibly strong bond, a connection. Maybe it was an Ulster-Scots thing. I knew I'd give my life to keep him safe, just as Billy Two-Tone had sacrificed his life to keep Jim Hyland safe. I kissed his forehead. I thought about running away with him. The two of us could be fugitives, hiding out in the highlands together. But, in the real world, going where, and doing what? In my heart of hearts I knew I was never going to run. I couldn't risk the consequences. I would have to stay, just for a little while longer before I died. Then I would be truly free.

I thought about The Fallen Angel. The latest act to join the circus. How a lovely family could simply fall apart. How easily the boy with everything could lose it all: parents, security, himself. His congregation would now be predatory older men and the choirboy would use his mouth rather than his voice to bring them bliss. Eros had a new recruit. Now the Dilly had two fallen angels.

The next morning, Damie and I said goodbye. I gave him £100 to add to the stolen Gleaves money, which he readily accepted. He refused to tell me exactly where he was going, partly because he didn't know where he was going and also because if I didn't know, I could never tell anyone. He promised he'd find a way to make contact with me and let me know he was safe. There were tears and embraces as he boarded the train. He pressed his mouth to my ear and whispered, "I love you."

I was never good with goodbyes. The farewell played out like the departure scene with Agnes, only in reverse. I was the one left standing on the platform. I had never felt so alone. My already broken heart now felt like it had been crushed to a bleeding pulp. My chest hurt with the pain of loss and separation. This unending emotional turmoil and sexual confusion was tearing me apart. I couldn't find the courage to tell Damie that I loved him.

I never heard from Damie again; never saw him again.

CHAPTER 27

The Ritz

True to his word, Simon introduced me to his uncle, Sir Antony. Simon had promised him a belated birthday celebration. The wider Hornby family always seemed to be so busy that they rarely got the chance to see each other. Simon said he intended to make a point of catching up with his father Michael soon and that I would get to meet him. I wondered why Simon wanted me to meet the Hornby grandees. It was not as if he was going to make some big announcement about him and me.

Simon and I arrived together at the black-tie event in the Ritz Hotel. A member of staff took my raincoat and Simon beamed with pride and admiration as he straightened my bow tie, happy also that I had taken his advice and parted my hair at the side before slicking it back with oil. Apart from a few painkillers, I'd stopped taking other drugs and was determined to stay sober and behave at what Simon said would be a formal but friendly celebration.

A private dining room had been booked and about 20 places set at a magnificent table, lavishly laid out with gleaming crystal candelabras and silver cutlery. The company was all male and mostly middle-aged, apart from four other guests who looked about my age. They were definitely not Dilly rent. They projected a confident upper-class bearing and a polite, sophisticated manner. Sir Antony arrived to polite applause. He had difficulty walking because of an old war wound. Like the other gentlemen around the table, he looked immaculately groomed and very dignified. Simon and Antony sat together and I sat opposite them beside a tall, handsome, aristocratic-looking gentleman who introduced himself as Gordon Richardson. As the guests arrived they were offered New York Dry Martinis. Gordon had insisted on showing the barman how to make the cocktail, which was one of his specialities.

It soon became apparent I was in the company of finance men, for though the meal was wonderful, the talk was of stock-broking, asset management and other financial matters, which I found very tedious. After dinner we stood, champagne glasses raised, and toasted Her Majesty the Queen. Simon gave a very humorous speech in praise of his esteemed uncle. He then called upon Gordon to say a few words.

Gordon offered an apology on behalf of Victor Rothschild, who had to cancel at short notice. He then talked light-heartedly about his role in turning around Schroders, an investment bank. Gordon was undoubtedly the guest of honour, and the alpha-male at the table. The other diners showed him great deference. I felt honoured that such an obviously important man took the time to engage me directly in conversation. He said his friend Noel Annan sent me his regards, before questioning me intently about the Troubles. He listened carefully to what I told him, fixing me with his steely-blue eyes. He told me he'd worked in law before switching careers for a job in the City, and joked that he now had a boring job working behind a desk in a bank. He was remarkably charming and friendly, making me feel that my opinion was important.

I studied the other guests; bankers, stockbrokers and financiers including Major John Gouriet and Adrian Stanford, both of whom I had met before. Stanford was the boyfriend of an MP who was a member of the Shadow Cabinet. There was even an author there; George Kennedy Young – GK to his fellow diners. A few months ago I'd been working in a bookshop in Derry. I could barely believe I was now sitting in the Ritz in London with such distinguished company. I smiled across at Simon and raised my glass. He smiled back. Gordon excused himself and went to the gents.

For the first time, I allowed myself to contemplate what my life would be like if I survived this illness and stayed with Simon. There was a reason I had not taken the antibiotics that Dr McCarty had prescribed for me. I had a death wish. Now, for the first time, I considered the other option that was open to me: life. I was now out of the endless game. I entertained thoughts of leading a charmed life, living in luxury in London, dining in places like this. Could I ever forget the person I really was and let Pretty Boy live my life from here on?

One of the younger men coughed and pointed at me with a cocktail stick. I snapped back from my reflections.

"You need to go to the gents, Anthony," he said directly.

"No, I'm fine."

A couple of minutes later he spoke again.

"You really need to go to the gents."

"No, really, I'm ok."

A couple of the men stared at me with disapproving looks. I looked across at Simon, questioningly. He looked serious and troubled. He nodded towards the exit. I walked to the gents and a cubicle door swung open silently. I stepped inside. Gordon reached behind me and locked the door.

"You kept me waiting."

He slapped me on the face, more with contempt than force.

"Go to work, you little cocksucker."

He put his hands on my shoulders and pushed me into a kneeling position in front of him. Pretty Boy was back in business.

When Pretty Boy was done, Gordon Richardson dropped £50 on the floor and walked out.

There may have been five £10 notes on the floor, but I felt worthless. Pretty Boy had been given no time to prepare for the role. He'd been dragged onto the stage naked and made to perform. There'd been no warning, no drugs and not enough alcohol to suppress my old self. The truth was painful. I realised it wasn't Pretty Boy who'd knelt in front of Gordon, it was me. I moved to the toilet and threw up. I gave a raw cough, wiped blood from my lips and wept.

I took my seat back at the table.

"How was dessert?" someone asked.

* * * * *

Later, in the car, Simon apologised.

"Fuck off," I screamed at him. "You said I was out, that it was finished."

He looked hurt and helpless. "I didn't plan for that to happen."

"But you fucking let it happen. You let him use your fucking whore rent boy."

I was crying uncontrollably. Simon tried to put his arm around me. I pushed him off.

"Please, Pretty Boy, I'm so sorry. It will never happen again. I give you my word."

"Stop calling me fucking Pretty Boy, my name's Tony. They all know about me, don't they? They know what I am."

"I will never let that happen again. I promise. I don't care who they are."

"Yeah right, until the next Gordon comes along expecting you to hand me over. Now I know why you call it the endless game."

"I didn't expect Gordon to… I was taken by surprise."

"I'm the one who was taken by fucking surprise."

"I'll never let that happen to you again. Gordon is… a powerful man."

"Aren't all your friends?"

"Gordon's different… he's very useful… he's the Governor of the Bank of England."

I stormed out of the car.

"You forgot your raincoat."

I ignored him and walked to Hope House. A nun at reception gave me a surprised look. "Good evening, Mr Bond," she said in a melodious Cork accent. I ignored her and went to my room.

Up until that night I had, for some reason, always thought of the network as being Simon's network, had imagined that he was the lynchpin. After what had happened at the Ritz, I realised that the network could equally well be Gordon Richardson's network, Noel Annan's network, Pat Gibson's network, Sir Michael Havers' network: it was everybody's network. Simon was just a bookseller. Others in the network were movers and shakers, men with real power, real money and political influence. Simon had told me that the network did not have a leader in the sense of a conventional organisation. He had said that the network was a matrix of interconnected equals, where everyone brought something to the table, brought different flavoured cake to the feast. But if Simon genuinely hadn't known what Gordon had planned to do with me, then it indicated a pecking order, a hierarchy where the most powerful members could take someone else's "boy" and use them as they liked.

If the ages of the individuals I had encountered was anything to go by, this "network" had been in existence since at least World War II. It was now infused with the blood of new generations, men who had known each other since public school, attended the same universities, served in the same regiments. These were professionals bound together by tradition and honour and secrets.

I undressed and threw my clothes on the floor. I padded around the room in my underwear like a restless animal before picking up my diary. The daily reality, the horror was all there: dates, locations, names, abbreviations, codes for sexual activities and services rendered. On the back pages was my crude bookkeeping. A record of who'd given me money, who'd paid for my body and soul. I read the diary again and started to cry. The entry for Tuesday 25 February, my second day in Foyles read, "Feel so proud to be working in the best bookshop in the world!" The entry for Monday 14 April read, "Feel like I'm working in a tomb, surrounded by dead authors. This shop is a fucking fire hazard + a death trap." It was the same shop, but the person working in it had changed. They had taken everything from me, including my future.

It occurred to me that I hadn't read a book during my whole time in London. The only book in my room was the Bible. I retrieved it from the bedside locker. I flicked through the pages, seeking the Word. I stopped at Mark 13:22: "False prophets shall rise and show signs and wonders to seduce." That just about summed up Simon Hornby. He had led me through the streets of Babylon; showered me with money; promised the earth; purchased my soul. I thought about Keith Hunter taking me to the roof of Playland and telling me that the spoils of the great citadel would lie at my feet, if only I pledged allegiance to him and followed his dark path.

I rolled over to the other side of the bed, where Damie had slept, and reached under the bed for the plastic bag he'd brought from his hostel. I was missing Damie so much. Missing Agnes. Missing my family. I opened the vodka and drank. Then I found tablets. What would happen if you took dexies and mandies at the same time? Would the uppers cancel out the downers? Only one way to find out. I swallowed the tablets. I leafed the pages of the Bible and contemplated eternity. I thought about the man who in Oxford Street had thrown the dice across my path. I had played a game of chance. I had gambled and oh how I had lost. Destiny? I looked at the Bible again. Then I attacked it. Ripped pages from it. Tore them into tiny pieces and scattered them over the bed. How could God have let this happen to me? I needed to blame Him, defy Him, provoke Him. Life or death? Let Him decide. What would happen if you also took pain killers? I swallowed a handful. We'll soon see. My mind clouded over and invisible fingers close my eyelids. I had one friend left in London and he shouted at Simon on my behalf:

You spoilt the game, no matter what you say.
How come you tell so many lies?
There's nothing left. There ain't no more, you've taken everything.

Some time passed. I awoke, disorientated. Mr Twist, the silent stranger from the Prunier restaurant at the Holy Thursday meal, was standing at the foot of my bed. His coal-black eyes fixed on me as he slowly crunched on something in his mouth. His chewing made a strange metallic grinding noise that sounded like the gates of hell being unlocked. I felt dark fire in me as the shadow of death hovered over the bed.

I awoke again. Had I been sleeping? I didn't know. Inexplicably, I felt hungry. Was this a side effect of the drink and medication? Reaching into Damie's bag I found a tin of beans and, thankfully, a tin opener. I scooped out and ate some of the cold beans with my fingers. I needed to hear Morricone, so I wiped my hand on the bedspread and put on *The Red Tent* soundtrack. It was one of the most beautiful, moving and yet uplifting pieces of music I'd ever heard. I wished Jackie Duddy were here to listen to it with me. Jackie would have loved this. I propped up the pillows and listened to the music. Then I closed my eyes and was transported to the Dilly. The boys were working the rack, patrolling the piazza and the underground concourse. Moving between the shadows, stepping out from under the arches for a moment, their beautiful faces changing colour in the saturated neon. Morricone gave them a soundtrack. It occurred to me that in Leone westerns the final big gunfight always takes place in a circular arena of some sort. Did this represent the cycle of life and death? Maybe that's the way this should have ended. Gunfight in the Dilly. The place where the good, the bad and the ugly come to play.

I looked at the lid still attached to the tin of beans and twisted it off. I knew I could do this. It was time. I'd lived through seven years of war in Northern Ireland. I'd survived shootings and bombings, but I'd been in London for a few months and was reduced to this. I needed to release Pretty Boy but I had to kill myself to set him free. I would do it for him.

I held out my left arm and brought the lid to the skin. I visualised a thin line appearing and then a trench opening up as the flesh separated and the blood overflowed. My stomach turned at the thought and the vomit erupted from me splattering the sheets and running down my chest. I looked down, surprised by the violence of the projection and bemused by the sight of tablets, beans, the partially digested remains of the Ritz's fancy food and fragments of Bible pages. I fell back, half-sitting, half-lying. Unconscious.

* * * * *

I awoke. Daylight stung my eyes. I was shocked not only at the state of the bed and me in it, but of the room itself. It looked as though I'd been burgled. I showered, stripped the bed and took the sheets to a launderette. I got a taxi to Simon's house. He opened the door and I collapsed in his arms. I awoke again later in a bed in the spare room. He made me soup and was clearly shocked at the state I was in.

"I wanted to phone an ambulance, but I thought it best not to create a scene." He nodded to the window. "The neighbours," was his excuse.

"Simon, you have to let me go. I need to go home. I'm dying. This is killing me."

He studied my face for a long time. "But I love you. Every time I look in your eyes…" His words trailed off.

"Then let me go."

He looked distraught, his mind in turmoil as he raced to consider options. After a while an expression of resolve softened his features.

"All right," he said finally. "I want you to go home and get better, then come back to me. We'll go to Europe for a few weeks. I'll see Pat Gibson. We can stay in his villa in Italy. Will you do that for me Tony?" This was the first time Simon had ever called me Tony. Hearing him use the name everyone in Derry called me by was disconcerting, as if he was talking to someone else. The name seemed strange, out of place here, disconnected from this reality. I wasn't that Tony anymore. Anthony and Pretty Boy lived in London. I didn't answer him but I realised in that moment that Pretty Boy was the dominant one. Like Simon, he towered over me. He suppressed me and I knew that it was for my own good. He shielded me. I stood behind him and he did all the dirty work. What would I do without him? Would I ever be able to let him go?

Simon lay beside me on the bed and rested his head on my chest. It was heavy and made it even more difficult for me to breathe.

"Will you do one thing for me?" He sounded emotional. "I need to hear you say the words. Please tell me you love me."

There was a strained silence.

"I love you, Simon."

His head moved a little and I knew he was crying silently. I put my arms around him.

Finally, he released me. He let me go. He opened the front door for me. I hugged him and said, "Thank you Simon."

At first, I thought his parting words were a compliment, but later realised it was an insult. "You were the prettiest of playthings," he whispered, "the most fascinating of small romances."

* * * * *

Hope House. I couldn't remember returning there. Next morning, I was so ill I stayed in bed all day. I didn't eat. The silence was unbearable. I had hoped to die in my sleep. That would be peaceful, and less messy. But I did wake up. It was dark. I wept and slept.

* * * * *

I didn't die. The following day I didn't know which was worse, the hunger or the pain. Unbelievably, I was missing the Dilly. Every time I set foot there it was like an energy transfusion. I may have bought my drugs there but the place was a drug in itself. I needed a fix. I needed painkillers and I needed to breathe that neon-charged atmosphere. Petula Clark brushed Steve Harley to the side for a moment and sang *Downtown* to me: she stirred childhood memories of longing to escape from my father, from Derry; of yearning for pretty neon lights and city traffic, of bustling sidewalks where I could lose myself, forget about cares and troubles.

I ate alone in Soho in the afternoon. The light soon faded and as much as I tried to fight the urge, I was drawn to the Dilly. The gravitational pull of the place was like a black hole, only this hole was full of blinding colour, a supernova in the heart of a dark city. I went into the Pronto Bar. This, I told myself, would be my last-ever drink in the Dilly. One for the boys and one for the road. I didn't see any rent I recognised. I went to a quiet corner and hid, wondering if I was trying to make some statement, some symbolic gesture to get as close to Playland without going inside.

I thought back to that first weekend in London, when I'd walked penniless out of Playland. How I'd been picked up by Keith Hunter. How Damie had followed me out of the arcade after my first meeting with the management and how, at the meat rack, he'd invited me for a bite to eat. I finished my drink and walked towards the Dilly for one more look at the neon lights.

"Well, fucking well," a voice behind me said. "Look who it is."

I turned around. Malcolm Raywood and the Fruit Machine each placed a hand on my shoulder, big grins on their faces. They frogmarched me down Great Windmill Street along the side of the London Pavilion. We crossed the street, past the rear entrance to Playland and through a nondescript arched entrance, into a small enclosed yard.

"You look like shit," Fruit said. "Are your big rich friends not taking care of you anymore?"

Malcolm pressed his nose against mine. "Pretty Boy ain't so fucking pretty anymore."

"Well, don't you worry," Fruit said, as he licked my cheek. "Malcolm and I still love you. We'll take real good care of you."

He grabbed me by the throat and banged my head off the wall. Malcolm gripped my balls and I tried to scream out in pain, but couldn't breathe.

"Where is the little bastard?"

"I don't know, I swear."

"I think you and your little boyfriend are inseparable. Now where is the thieving little toe rag? If you know what's good for you, you'll fucking tell us."

The Fruit took his hand from my throat. "OK, Irish, here's what I'm gonna do. I'm gonna give you a chance to find out where he's hiding himself. That little shit has been warned before. Now he has two fucking Firms who want him."

He dusted off my shoulders and patted my cheek. "I want you to forget all the shit you've seen in the movies with guys getting tortured and not talking. All that dramatic shit, just forget it. People talk for me. I've learnt at the feet of the fucking masters." He took a pencil out of his pocket. "This is all I need." He felt between my legs. "You see what I do is, I sharpen it up and put the full length inside your dick. I poke and probe around a little in there. You'll talk, take my word for it. I once lost a full pencil in a guy. He talked, but he needed to go to hospital to have an HB2 removed from his bladder."

Malcolm was in my face again. "Find out where that little fucker is and come here. Twenty-four hours, then we come for you. We'll spend a night in the Romper Room, have a little threesome together. We'll give you a night in bed you won't forget, and that's even before the pencil fun begins."

Fruit flung me to the ground and I defensively curled into a ball as Malcolm punched and kicked me several times. After much swearing and threatening and returning for a final kick, they walked away. I lay for a while until I found the breath to stagger to a wall and stand up. I walked with great difficulty and had to sit down on the steps outside Playland. I could hear the deep booms and metallic crashing of the machines inside.

After a short while, I stood up and walked over to the Dilly. I got a taxi home.

* * * * *

I washed my face and cleaned my teeth. I looked at myself in the mirror.

"Well, Tony," I sighed, *you've done it all, you've broken every code.*

I hurriedly gathered up a few belongings, the gifts I had been given: Simon's *Romance of a Bookshop,* a copy of *A Man for all Seasons,* given to me by Sir Michael Havers, the fountain pen from Lord Back-Seat, and various documents and papers, including business cards and Houses of Parliament-headed notepaper on which various instructions or words of appreciation had been inscribed by some clients. I raised the lid of the record player and saw that Damie had either forgotten to take his 45, or had left it as a gift for me. Something to remember him by. I carefully placed April Stevens, Steve Harley, Ennio Morricone and my diary in the suitcase. The only clothes I took were the ones I stood in, nothing else. The next occupant of my old room would be surprised to find a record player and collection of very expensive clothes at his disposal. I hoped they'd fit him. If not, I was sure he'd sell them.

I then extracted all the money from the various hiding places in my room and counted out the notes on the bed. I couldn't believe the amount that had accumulated over the long weeks. The cash that had been thrown at me night after night had been added to the weekly allowance Simon had given me. But all this dirty capital had been meaningless. I had squandered most of what I had earned in the first month in Playland. I couldn't part with it quickly enough. Since then I had been giving it away, snorting it away and pissing it away. Apart from buying drink, drugs, clothes, a record player and a couple of records, I never really had a chance to spend it – properly, as it were.

I stuffed a wad of notes into an envelope and addressed it to Father Hackett. I then evenly distributed the rest of it in the pockets of my coat and trousers. I had paid a few weeks' rent in advance, so I simply left the envelope with one of the nuns at reception and walked quickly from Hope House. Inexplicably, I felt like a thief. It was actually Pretty Boy who had earned that money and I was robbing him.

The Piccadilly line was my escape route to Heathrow. I phoned my aunt Doreen from the airport and told her when my flight was due in. I boarded a British Airways shuttle flight to Belfast and was met by my brother Fred in Aldergrove. I had to walk right up beside him and look into his face. He didn't recognise me. We drove to Derry, to Creggan and I walked into my home in Circular Road. The house looked so small. So did my mum. She didn't smile or laugh or cry, she just looked into my haunted eyes and tried to figure out where her son had gone. She hugged me tightly. I stooped down and rested my head on her shoulder, closing my eyes. I was home, but in a strange way I felt I'd left Pretty Boy alone in London.

It was over. Or so I thought at the time. I had no idea that some influential people in London were determined to make sure I kept my mouth shut. People with enough clout to get the army in Northern Ireland to deliver a message to me.

PART 3

Time's Fickle Glass

There are people in their manor houses
and luxury flats, holding important positions
in society, who were behind this case.
Alan Campbell QC, Playland Trial, Court of Appeal hearing 1976

There is clear evidence of a sordid underworld network,
the extent of which cannot yet be measured.
Harold Wilson, Prime Minister 1964-1970 and 1974-1976

CHAPTER 28

Surveillance

Police Sergeant Geoffrey Bredemear, Police Constable Victor Coates and Police Constable Maurice Maylin were dressed in plain clothes and were part of an eight-man undercover surveillance team working observation shifts in the arcade. At 4:50pm on Thursday 30 May 1974, they spotted Malcolm Raywood talking to four schoolboys aged about 13, all wearing school uniforms. Malcolm chatted to the boys for about five minutes, then left Playland and walked to the Piccadilly Bowl on Shaftesbury Avenue. PS Bredemear and PC Coates followed him.

Malcolm went to the restaurant area of the bowling alley, where he was observed talking to a man in a dark suit, aged about 55, and a boy aged 15 or 16 and wearing a distinctive plum-coloured suit. At 5:55pm Malcolm and the boy left together. They walked west and entered the Sandwich Bar on Shaftesbury Avenue. PC Maylin followed them in. Malcolm went to the counter to buy drinks and then stood with the boy.

"I've got to go soon," the boy said.

"Stay on for a bit," Malcolm urged. "I'm meeting some of my mates later and then we'll get some booze and go to my place for a piss-up."

"No, not today," the youth insisted. "I've got to go home. We'll make it another time."

They chatted for a while longer, then left at 6:20pm and walked to the Underground. The boy went through the barrier and waved goodbye to Malcolm. In the police witness statements, Malcolm Raywood is designated as "C".

Later that night at 11:50pm, PS Bredemear saw another man who had been under surveillance, referred to in the records as "J". He was about 25 years old, five foot seven, with dark hair. He was sitting in the driver's seat of a blue van parked on the pavement in Great Windmill Street. In the front passenger seat was a boy aged about 16. Five minutes later the rear doors of the van opened and four boys also aged about 16 jumped out. The youth in the passenger seat got out too. A few moments later "J" drove off.

We don't know who the boys were or where they had been collected from. We don't know who they met, where they went or what they did. The reason we know nothing more about that midnight delivery to Playland is because the next four pages of PS Bredemear's statement have been extracted from the file held at the National Archives and will remain sealed until January 2065.

PC Maylin's account of that day ends with the boy in the plum suit waving goodbye to Malcolm Raywood at Piccadilly. The next 10 pages of his statement have been extracted. The first 28 pages of PC Coates' statement have been removed, so there is no account at all of the events of 30 May from his perspective.

In total, I have seen 130 documents relating to Playland, but 802 pages will remain closed until 2065 – 90 years from the date of the trial. A further 73 documents will remain sealed until 2066. The entire record of the actual trial proceedings is among the closed files. It contains exhibits and photographic evidence, including prints from seven rolls of film developed by Scotland Yard Photographic Department.

It is unfortunate that the vast majority of the Playland archive will remain closed for so many years. However, with the limited release of some of the documents, we are able for the first time in 40 years to read some of the police accounts of what they saw going on in the arcade.

* * * * *

The surveillance operation came about because a disenchanted member of the Playland Firm had walked into the *News of the World* offices a few months earlier and asked to speak to Peter Earle, their chief crime reporter. Earle was old school and had fostered contacts within the London underworld, but he also cultivated friendships within the Met. His visitor sat down and started to tell him about Playland and rent boys. Then he dropped a few names – very big names – who were sexually abusing young boys. Earle saw unfolding in front of him the biggest scandal since Profumo, a story he himself had exploited by publishing Christine Keeler's story. He grabbed his Gannex raincoat and led the man out into the street and up the stairs to the top bar of the Tipperary on Fleet Street. Sipping his usual large Scotch, Earle scribbled down all the incredible details about the Playland vice ring, the boys, their clients, the pimps and the profits.

Earle then arranged to bring the informer to see Commander David Helm at the West End Central station in Savile Row. A major investigation was launched and Playland was put under prolonged police surveillance by a small team of vice squad officers, led by Chief Superintendent Malcolm Ferguson from West End Central.

Most of the police evidence was gathered between 13 May and 24 July 1974. The movements and activities of men in and around Piccadilly Circus and Playland were observed. Additional evidence was also gathered relating to a range of specific offences committed between 1 September and 3 December 1974, less than three months before I arrived in London.

In particular, the police were tracking the moments of 18 men aged between 22 and 60, each of whom was identified by a letter. Only Malcolm Raywood ("C") and Charles Hornby ("T") are named in the records, and only six out of the 18 men would subsequently be charged and appear in court.

The last line of the opening page of PC Maylin's statement reads, "The following are descriptions of the men." Unfortunately, the next two pages have been removed. However, page 1A of PS Colin Lloyd's statement does contain one-sentence descriptions of each of the men, apart from Hornby and Raywood and three other men whose descriptions have been redacted. At 43, Raywood was the oldest of the defendants to stand trial, but we know that at least six of the men who had been under surveillance were older than that, somewhere between 46 and 60.

The police witness statements describe the constant activity of men patrolling the arcade. They target and proposition boys, give them money to play the machines and sometimes take them across the street to the Coffee House. The men were rejected most of the time and returned to Playland to begin the process again. The following accounts give examples of the comings and goings at Playland, snapshots of the Firm's foot solders working collaboratively to recruit teenage boys into a world of prostitution.

* * * * *

"C", i.e. Malcolm Raywood, was observed as he walked along Great Windmill Street and stood on the steps of Playland. A

50-year-old man in a grey silver suit came up and spoke to him. Malcolm pointed into Playland and the man nodded. Malcolm went in and returned a few minutes later with a 19-year-old youth wearing a black shirt. There was a brief conversation and the man reached into his pocket and gave money to Malcolm. The man then walked off with the youth, up Great Windmill Street to the junction of Shaftesbury Avenue. They stood chatting on the pavement for a few minutes. The man hailed a taxi and they both got in and drove off.

In the meantime, Malcolm had gone back into Playland and was standing next to the cash desk talking to a 15-year-old boy who was wearing a yellow shirt and blue jeans. Malcolm put his arm around the boy's waist and they were both laughing and joking. Malcolm gave the boy money and the boy started playing on one of the machines. Malcolm stood behind him and leant over the boy and whispered something in his ear. The boy pushed Malcolm away and walked off. Malcolm then slowly walked around Playland talking to boys and other men.

* * * * *

On Wednesday 10 July, at 9:25pm, "L" was talking to a 15-year-old boy wearing a blue-patterned shirt. "D" was playing a game with another boy, a 16-year-old wearing a red jumper and blue jeans. As the boys were playing, "D" said, "These two are on holiday with their parents, so I wouldn't bother."

"L" replied, "Then I'll leave it and call it a day." He walked out into Coventry Street.

About an hour-and-a-half later Malcolm walked into Playland. He spoke to various men and boys. After a while he went and stood behind two boys aged 15 or 16, both wearing denim jackets and jeans. He struck up a conversation with them.

"How does London compare with your place?" Malcolm asked.

"We like it," one of the boys replied.

Malcolm smiled and said, "Have you seen our sex shops?"

"Yes, we have been next door tonight."

"Have you got a gay scene over your place?"

"What does that mean?" the boy asked.

"Free loving for men," Malcolm laughed.

"We are not interested in that. Please leave us alone."

* * * * *

Malcolm was joined by "D", who had just entered by the Great Windmill Street entrance. Malcolm pointed to a 16-year-old boy wearing a dark jacket and jeans who was playing pinball near the entrance, then went to join the boy and started chatting. He gave the boy money and the boy played the machine again. Then he moved closer to the boy and said something. The boy answered, "Yes. I don't mind going back with you. I could do with something to eat."

"Let's go then," Malcolm said.

Malcolm and the boy left Playland via the Great Windmill Street exit and walked to the end of Coventry Street. "D" left immediately afterwards.

PS Bredemear and PC Coates lost sight of Malcolm and the boy as they descended into Piccadilly Tube Station. At 12:15am, the two police officers arrived at Malcolm's home in Garratt Lane, Earlsfield. There were no lights on in Malcolm's flat above the butcher shop. They hung around until 1:30pm, then left.

* * * * *

"B" was in Playland, chatting to a boy aged about 17 with blond streaks in his hair and a gold earring in his left ear. He was wearing black trousers and a white silk blouse. Could this have been Damie? As the boy moved from game to game, "B" kept feeding him money. When he was finished playing, the boy took coins to the cash desk and exchanged them for a packet of cigarettes. "B" then led the youth to the Great Windmill Street exit and they turned right into Shaftesbury Avenue. The 45-year-old "B" hailed a taxi and they climbed in. The taxi did a U-turn and as it pulled away, "B" leaned over and kissed the boy on the mouth.

* * * * *

"D" was talking to a 15-year-old boy outside the rear entrance of Playland. The boy had long fair hair and was wearing a black jerkin, black trousers and a yellow shirt. "D" had his right arm around the boy's shoulder. After a short conversation the boy shook his head and walked into Playland. "D" stepped inside the door and stood next to a 45-year-old man in a grey suit, wearing glasses. He turned to the man and said, "No chance."

"D" and the grey-suited man were joined by a 16-year-old boy with long black hair, wearing a green vest and dark green slacks.

"Where have you been hiding?" "D" said.

"I've just come back from the coast."

"What was it like?" the older man asked.

"Fucking lousy, it pissed down most of the time and the place is dead."

"D" smiled at the boy. "How about coming back with me then?"

"It'll cost you."

351

"I'm not paying anybody fuck-all," "D" said contemptuously. "I've had better for nothing."

The older man laughed, and the boy turned to him: "I don't know what you have to laugh about, you old cunt." The boy walked away into the main body of the arcade.

* * * * *

"L" noticed a 16-year-old boy in a light brown jacket and blue jeans walking around the machines pressing the reset buttons and putting his fingers in the coin trays to see if anyone had left money behind.

"L" approached the boy and took him across the street to the Coffee House and bought him a cup of tea and a roll.

"I daren't stay up town tonight because my folks won't know where I am," the boy said.

"Give them a ring and say you're staying at a friend's place."

"We ain't got no phone."

"Well, just come back for an hour or so."

"No, I daren't, I've got to be home by 11:00."

"If you can't say up here this week, give them some excuse that you want to see a pop show or something."

"I'll see what happens at home. My old lady doesn't like me hanging around here."

"L" and the boy sat in silence for several minutes, sipping their drinks. Finally, the boy said, "Well, I've got to go or I'll miss my train."

"Don't forget," "L" said, "if you can make it, I'm always around."

The boy left and "L" returned to Playland and walked slowly to the rear exit. He then walked to the Haymarket and caught a No.159 bus.

* * * * *

Another night in Playland… Three Americans were chatting to two boys. Malcolm was in attendance.

"All right, I'm game," the older boy said.

"No I'm not going," the younger boy protested. "I've got a punter later."

One of the men took out a business card and wrote something on the back of it. He handed it to the boy. "Well, come along later."

The boy shrugged his shoulders and returned to a pinball table.

Out on Great Windmill Street, the boy stood between two of the men while the third paid Malcolm and gave him a business card. The boy walked with the three men to Shaftesbury Avenue, where one of the men hailed a taxi. All four of them got into a taxi, which drove off east and turned right into the Haymarket.

* * * * *

At 11:05pm one night Malcolm was doing his usual rounds in Playland. He walked around the cash desk and spoke to men and boys he knew. He then approached three 16-year-old boys, two with blond hair and one with dark hair. The boys laughed and joked together. Malcolm and the three boys were joined by Charles Hornby. They chatted for several minutes before leaving via the Great Windmill Street exit and turned right. All five climbed into a red Mini (registration number redacted). Charles and Malcolm got into the front and the three boys got into the back. Charles then drove off and turned left onto Shaftesbury Avenue, then left again at the lights at Piccadilly Circus.

* * * * *

In January 2016, the National Archives opened some of the files relating to the Playland affair. The documents mainly consist of typed witness statements from four of the police officers involved in the surveillance operation – those named above and also PS Colin Lloyd, whose statement commences on 1 July 1974. Approximately 60 per cent of the numbered pages have been removed,[56] but it's not easy to know how many exactly because we don't know how long the statements were in total: the last page present is probably not the last page of the statement.

For example, the last page of PS Bredemear's statement ends with him sitting in Detective Inspector Dick's office with Malcolm Raywood on 25 July 1974. DI Dick reminds Malcolm that he is under caution and says somewhat intriguingly, "I understand you want to speak to us?" Has Malcolm voluntarily come forward to assist the police in their enquiries? The rest of the pages have been extracted.

* * * * *

I submitted a Freedom of Information request to the National Archives and requested that all the remaining Playland files be opened. I received a reply advising that they would have to conduct a public interest test in consultation with the Ministry of Justice, as it was they who had transferred the files to the National Archives. I subsequently received a detailed

---

56   Of the 61 numbered pages of PS Bredemear's statement, 44 have been removed. There are two statements by PC Maylin, 17 pages have been removed from a statement that runs to 29 pages; and 41 pages have been removed from his second statement of 60 pages. Of the 28 numbered pages of PC Coates' statement, 16 have been removed and 30 pages have been extracted from the 46-page statement made by PS Lloyd.

response to my request, but regrettably it was decided that the information in the files should be withheld from the public domain. It was however suggested that given my involvement with Playland, I could make a request to the MoJ and ask for privileged access to the information. They might allow me access to the documents for a limited period, in a private area at the MoJ Headquarters in London, though the information would remain classified and could not be made available to the wider public. I would be allowed to see, but not allowed to speak or write about what was in the files.

CHAPTER 29

Trials

The trouble had begun for Charles Hornby in 1974 when he had been seen collecting boys from Playland, two or three at a time, and taking them to his home in Montagu Square. There he had sex with them and photographed them committing "acts of gross indecency" with each other in a bath. He also took them to parties and introduced the boys to other gentlemen within his social circle.

Following the surveillance operation, on 30 July 1974, Charles was arrested. His flat was searched, and police removed various items. These included a penis-extension piece, a Prinz Jupiter camera with flash attachment, a black loose-leaf address book, plus several pieces of paper with names and numbers written on them, books including *The Kama Sutra* and *Dreams of Empire*, and gramophone records including *Great Moments in Wagner* and *Horowitz in Concert*. Bed clothes were removed, and the list of exhibits presented to the court also included tubes of cream, tubes of jelly and a whip.

Charles was released the following day and remained on bail throughout the committal proceedings at Lambeth Magistrates' Court, which lasted from 30 January to 24 February 1975. Their purpose was to determine if there was sufficient evidence to proceed with a full trial at the Central Criminal Court – the Old Bailey.

The police had been rounding up the rent in their dozens and taking statements. In fact, 152 boys had been interviewed, and some were giving evidence at the committal hearings. In desperation Charles made contact with a few of the youths, one of whom had given a statement to the police on 19 November 1974. Using bribes and subtle threats, Charles paid the boy to deny the allegations that had been made against him. The boy was instructed to say "no comment" to every question put to him in court. If shown his original statement, he was to say he had been bullied by the police into making it. A taste of the high life was arranged by way of reward – but also to ensure the boy went through with the agreement – on 19 February 1975. Charles booked a room at the Kensington Hilton Hotel under an assumed name and deposited the boy there for the night. The following morning Charles arrived and had breakfast with the boy, briefing him again as to what he should say in court that morning. He even drove the boy to court and dropped him off. The boy performed admirably under cross-examination and did exactly as he had been instructed to do. He said nothing that could incriminate Charles.

This must have given Charles some hope that he might evade conviction. He approached other boys, and even tried to meet with the father of one of them. Unfortunately for Charles, the volume of evidence against him was overwhelming. On 24 February 1975, my first day at Foyles, he was committed for trial at the Central Criminal Court on counts including procuring the commission of an act of gross indecency by a boy aged 14 with a male person under the age of 21, and committing buggery with a boy aged 16. The other defendants facing trial were Malcolm Raywood, Basil Andrew-Cowen, Andrew Novac, David Archer, and another man we shall call Mr X for now. All were released on bail.

The boy who had refused to implicate Charles at Lambeth Magistrates' Court was arrested and interviewed again, this time under caution. He admitted he had been bribed to change his evidence. Charles, who had met and ensnared me during his time out on bail, was re-arrested on 22 May 1975 and this time remanded in custody.[57] When interviewed by the police, he said, "No one is perfect. We are all evil. Fortunately or unfortunately, I have done things that are evil." On the basis of further statements from boys he had tried to bribe, Charles now faced a further two counts of attempting to pervert the course of justice.

* * * * *

The sensational Playland Trial began on 20 June 1975, with Judge Alan King-Hamilton presiding. Charles Hornby pleaded guilty immediately, I believe in order to protect his brother Simon and the other VIPs in the network. Mr X also pleaded guilty to all charges, which meant that the indictment of 38 counts to be tried, including five separate conspiracies, could be reduced to 19 counts, including one conspiracy. Even with 19 counts to consider, this was going to be a very long and complex trial. Prosecution alone produced 70 witnesses, including 30 youths.

The Playland trial was heard in QB VII, Queen's Bench room seven at the Old Bailey. Down the corridor in QB II the trial of the Guildford Four had started four days earlier. I dread to think that if I had refused outright to do what Charles Hornby and the Playland Firm had asked me to do, I could have been one of the Guildford Five. Gerry Conlon, Paul Hill and I were all

---

57   As Charles entered prison on remand, the accountant and porn-film baron Big Jeff Phillips exited prison. Big Jeff, who had provided film services to some of Playland's VIP clients and who might have had relevant testimony to offer at the trial, committed suicide by drug overdose shortly after his release.

20 years old when we went to work in London and we all stayed in the same hostel. I ended up being passed from bed to bed, but they ended up being transferred from prison to prison. In many ways I'd had a lucky escape. And that wasn't the only awful fate I avoided. Billy Two -Tone never lived to see his 20th birthday.

Defence counsel for Charles was Mr Robin Simpson QC supported by Mr Richard Du Cann QC. Mr Du Cann had been part of the defence team at the *Fanny Hill* and *Lady Chatterley's Lover* obscenity prosecutions, and in fact the previous year he had represented United Artists in another obscenity case involving the film *Last Tango in Paris*.

The court heard about Charles's marriage to former debutante Amanda Fitzwilliam Hyde and his three children. They learned that he'd been told about the rent-boy scene in Piccadilly Circus by a colleague at Lloyd's,[58] and that two months after his daughter Camilla was born, Charles decided to have a look. During the summer of 1973, he picked up a young man in Half Moon Street, just off Piccadilly and another in Shepherd Market, a small square in Mayfair.

Charles admitted that he had quickly become hooked by the risk-taking, the adrenalin rush and the forbidden pleasures of consorting with rent boys. Oscar Wilde had described the thrill of propositioning Dilly rent as "feasting with panthers". Befriended by the pimps of Playland in August 1973, Charles had easy access to a stable of teenage rent. He indulged himself, feasting enthusiastically until his arrest on 30 July 1974.

It is timely to reveal here that a month before proceedings at the Old Bailey began, Simon Hornby had actually given me a letter to hand deliver to Sir Michael Havers. He didn't tell

---

58   That colleague was possibly fellow underwriter and old Etonian, Francis Cory-Wright, an active paedophile who in 2011 was found guilty of having sexually abused a 10-year-old boy in 1976.

me what was in the letter, but Sir Michael, being Sir Michael, did. The letter requested that he try and use his good offices in regard to a forthcoming trial, the outcome of which was of some importance to their mutual associates. Much icing on the cake was promised in appreciation. Sir Michael was dismissive and muttered, "Some bloody people think I'm the Attorney General. I'm a bloody Shadow." In the circumstances, he didn't think much could be done. When he later did become Attorney General, he was able to wield much more influence.

The Playland trial lasted a total of 46 working days and cost £250,000 – over £2.3 million in today's money. It took the judge four full days to sum up. He sent the jury out early in the morning of Friday 19 September. Surprisingly, given the volume of evidence to consider, the jury returned their guilty verdicts later that afternoon.

The sentences were handed down on Monday 22 September 1975. Addressing the defendants, the judge said that one of the most nauseating aspects of the case was that those in the dock had tried to suggest that they were only helping the boys. "All of you are completely obsessed with boys," he said. It was clear from the witness testimony that Playland was a marketplace and that "the boys were selling the only thing they had to sell: their young bodies ". The youngest boy involved in the Playland case was just 12 years old.

Charles Hornby was fined £1,000 (£500 for each count of perverting justice) and jailed for 30 months. The next month he received a "Variation of Sentence" stating that his term of imprisonment would be considered as having begun on 8 July 1975. He had served just 12 months of his sentence when he was released in July 1976. For reasons that have not been revealed, the count of buggery of a 16 year old boy had not been proceeded with. If it had been (as it was in the case of

Raywood), Charles would have earned a prison tariff of six years. Both Raywood and Basil Andrew-Cohen were jailed for six years; Andrew Novac, for six-and-a-half; David Archer, five-and-a-half years.[59] There is no mention of any sentence being handed down to Mr X, who like Charles had pleaded guilty. I believe that Mr X is the informer who went to Peter Earle and who triggered the police investigation, then gave evidence against fellow members of the Firm. He was probably released after the trial. His name has been redacted from the court documents I have seen at the National Archives.

Predictably, it was Charles Hornby, underwriter at Lloyd's, who featured in most of the headlines. Much was made of his background. As an officer in the army he had become aware of his feelings of attraction towards the same sex. Mr Robin Simpson had described the "secret shame" that his client never confessed to his wife or friends. Charles had been an assistant horse trainer and amateur steeplechase jockey. Known as "the Lanky Lancer" and "the gentleman jockey", he had two winners at Plimpton in one year. He had inherited the £300,000 country estate in Shipton Moyne, Tetbury, in Gloucestershire, where Prince Charles had been an occasional guest.

On the Sunday after the trial's conclusion, *The News of the World* declared: TOP MEN FACE CHARGES IN VICE ROUND UP. In what was presented as a devastating scoop, Peter Earle reported that dozens of arrests were expected following the Playland Trial. He revealed that some of the men involved were show-business celebrities and top names in the world of finance.

* * * * *

---

59 Archer requested that he be chemically castrated to prevent his reoffending, but the judge refused.

It was proving to be a busy summer in the courts. The trial of the Birmingham Six also started in June 1975. One of the Six, John Walker, was from Derry.[60] Then in July 1975, Bernie Silver, the Godfather of Soho, went on trial for ordering the murder in 1956 of Tommy "Scarface" Smithson, a tearaway from the East End who had been trying to muscle in on the West End. Two key witnesses failed to appear, but Silver was still found guilty and sentenced to life imprisonment.[61]

More directly relevant to the Playland Trial was the case of Roger Gleaves. In May 1975 Gleaves was sentenced to four years in prison for sex offences against boys. There wasn't enough evidence to try him on a conspiracy to murder charge in relation to Billy Two-Tone McPhee, whose killers had been identified from the horrific findings of the post-mortem.[62] However, during the sex offences trial it emerged that blood from over 40 different people had been found on the walls of his hostels. By the end of the month all the hostels were closed.

* * * * *

In the summer of 1975 two landmark television programmes were broadcast. The first, in June, was London Weekend Television's *The London Programme* which investigated a number of

---

60 The following year, their first application for leave to appeal was dismissed by Lord Widgery.

61 Both the verdict and the sentence were subsequently overturned on appeal. Bernie was back on the streets of Silver City in 1978.

62 This was reported by a young journalist called Jon Snow. In the early 1970s, Snow had been director of New Horizon, a day centre for homeless young people in Soho (John Profumo was a member of the management committee and had been working there to atone for his sins). In his autobiography *Shooting History*, Snow recalls comforting a 16-year-old rent boy who looked about 12: "He sat in my office telling me, in floods of tears, of the abuse he suffered on the streets. He named MPs, a minister and a priest as being among his clients. I had no reason to doubt him: he identified them so clearly."

senior police officers in Scotland Yard and their friendships with Soho club owners and pornographers. The following month Yorkshire Television broadcast a shocking documentary called *Johnny Go Home*. This programme presented problems for both the Gleaves and Playland trials. It was meant to be a one-hour film about homeless children in London. A lot of footage was shot in the West End, including round Piccadilly Circus and even inside Playland. The film followed the fortunes of a boy called Tommy Wylie and a cast of other children as they struggled to survive on the streets of London. One of the characters featured in the story was none other than Roger Gleaves, who was shown carrying out his missionary work on the platforms of Euston Station and inside one of his hostels.

Following the murder of Billy Two-Tone and the arrest of Gleaves, the film was extended to two hours to cover the ongoing investigation, but the producers had to wait until after the trial of Gleaves in May before a broadcast date could be set.

Two of the boys who appeared in the film were also witnesses in the Playland trial. The Judge asked the producers to postpone the showing of the film until after the trial. Ultimately, a compromise was reached and the sequence showing the two boys was edited out. Even so, it was decided that the Playland jury would not be allowed to see the programme because the general tone of the piece was prejudicial. They spent a night in a hotel with the TV prohibition being enforced by ushers.[63]

The broadcast went ahead on 22 July and was viewed by 10 million people. It caused public outrage and was debated in Parliament twice, where finally the endemic problem of young runaways and the homelessness crisis in London was acknowledged. In August 1975 the House of Lords debated the

---

63   The jury were treated to a special screening of *Johnny Go Home* after the trial.

subject of bogus charities and Lord Janner (father of Greville Janner)[64] urged his noble friend Lord Wells-Pestell to view the programme so he could appreciate the horrific nature of what had been going on for a considerable time.

Whilst *Jonny Go Home* highlighted the plight of homeless children and the dangers they faced, the programme was also deeply flawed in many ways. It perpetuated a number of myths, including the idealised notion of a safe family home, and it presented paedophiles simply as "homosexuals". Given the impact the programme had on public opinion, this set back the arguments for equalising the age of consent for many years.

* * * * *

On 17 February, while the initial committal hearings were going on, the board of directors of Trafalgar Novelties Ltd held an Extraordinary General Meeting in a property they owned in 16 Coventry Street. It is highly likely that the Firm was represented at the meeting. In view of the arrest of Hornby and others the previous year, and the ongoing court proceedings at Lambeth, they decided it was best to ditch Trafalgar. As the legal operator of the Playland amusement arcade, Trafalgar Novelties Ltd would be tarnished by the impending scandal. Bruce Eckert placed a notice in the *London Gazette* advising that the company was being wound up voluntarily and that a Liquidator had been appointed. A new company, Piccadilly Amusements Ltd, was formed. They resolved that no matter what, Playland, which had been in existence for 40 years and was something of a Dilly institution, must be allowed to keep its gaming licence and remain open. The goldmine would be protected at all costs.

---

64   Greville Janner was a politician and QC who was himself accused of abusing children, but died before the facts could be established in court.

During the Old Bailey trial, the "legitimate" directors of the Playland arcade made themselves scarce. Bernard Briggs took himself to Malta for a holiday, and Bruce Eckert returned to America and checked into a hospital. Briggs flew back to London for the conclusion of the trial. "Frankly," he said to the press with astonishment, "I feel indignation at all these accusations. My place a vice trap? You have got to be joking."

Playland's five-year gaming licence had fallen due for renewal at the end of June. When the licensing sub-committee of Westminster City Council met on 26 September, just four days after the sentences were handed down, they would have seen the newspaper coverage and read the salacious details reported beneath the colossal headlines. One councillor described Playland as a "neon-lit slum ". They voted unanimously not to renew the gaming licences of three of the amusement arcades in the West End. Charles and his co-defendants may have been given prison sentences, but Playland had been given a death sentence. During the trial a *Gay News* journalist had visited Playland but was prevented from taking photographs by the Fruit Machine and some other heavies patrolling the arcade. He reported that three police officers were posted at the rear entrance. Playland, he said, was largely empty.

* * * * *

The Birmingham Six were found guilty in August, the Playland defendants in September and the Guildford Four in October 1975. In all cases the weight of evidence appeared to be overwhelming. Who then would have believed that Playland would remain open, that its gaming licence would be renewed and that the Playland defendants, unlike the Irish prisoners, would all be free by the following Christmas? 1975 was a very bad year to be Irish.

CHAPTER 30

Cover Up

As they were driven off to prison, the old Etonian and the "four nobodies", as the press called them, probably knew that the Firm would start pulling a few strings and leaning on a few people. Friends in high places would mobilise and initiate an appeal against their convictions.

Just over a year after the original trial, in November 1976, the Court of Appeal delivered a very brief statement. The outcome of the appeal represented a remarkable turnaround. It stated that all of Raywood's convictions would be quashed, as would some of Novac and Andrew-Cohen's. Strangely, David Archer is not mentioned in this initial statement at all.

A much more detailed judgement was delivered on 15 December 1976. It makes for torturous, practically incomprehensible reading as it covers the deliberations and legalistic gymnastics performed over the various counts. Even the trial judge could not make sense of it all. In this later judgement Archer is given top billing and, in a breathtaking reversal of fortune, is portrayed as a victim, against whom police evidence was "devastatingly prejudicial", unfairly turning the jury against him. This is ironic, as Archer and Andrew-Cohen had previous form, having been tried and found guilty along with other men in 1972 for similar offences against nine boys aged between 13 and 15. Archer knew the Dilly rent scene inside out.

As a result of the appeal, David Archer walked free. Malcolm Raywood also walked free. Basil Andrew-Cohen and Andrew Novac were cleared of some charges but still had to serve three and three and a-half years respectively .

Given the complexity and duration of the Playland trial and the burden this put on the judge, especially during his mammoth summing up and direction to the jury, it was inevitable that an appeal would be launched. The prosecution had actually helped the defendants by throwing the book at them. Malcolm Raywood had even been charged with minor offences dating back to 1969, including stealing two Westminster Bank cheque books, dishonestly obtaining a pair of shoes and a Pifco hair dryer, and failing to return library books to Westminster City Libraries. All this was on the same slate as multiple charges of buggery with young boys, conspiracy to procure the commission by male persons under the age of 21, of acts of gross indecency with other men, and living on the earnings of prostitution of male persons. The indictment had been massively overloaded – and the more complex a trail, the greater the chance of an appeal being successful.

The Appeal Court judges were scathing in their criticism of the DPP and the prosecution: "We cannot conclude this judgement without pointing out that, in our opinion, most of the difficulties which have bedevilled this trial, and which have led in the end to the quashing of all convictions except on conspiracy and related counts, arose directly out of the overloading of the indictment. Even in its reduced form the indictment of 19 counts against four defendants resulted in a trial of quite unnecessary length and complexity."[65]

Judge King-Hamilton was not happy with the Court of Appeal's ruling, but he waited until he retired before expressing his discontent. In 1982 he admitted in his autobiography that he'd misdirected the jury on the topic of corroboration in relation to one of the defendants, but said that even he had difficulty understanding other rambling and incoherent parts of the appeal judgement. He complained that in April and June of 1976, in two other cases in which the facts were remarkably similar to those in the Playland case, the trial judge gave the jury directions that were practically the same as his, yet in those cases the appeals were dismissed. His strong implication was that the Court of Appeal had been unduly sympathetic to the Playland defendants.[66]

After his release, Archer announced that he would be presenting police with a dossier he claimed to hold, naming "millionaires and titled people" involved in the Playland affair. He believed that "there was a tremendous cover-up to protect these people". During the original trial, Judge King-Hamilton had remarked that not all the perpetrators were in the dock. At the appeal hearing, Mr Alan Campbell QC for Novak expanded on that comment, stressing that the most nauseating aspect of

65 The fundamental flaws made in the Playland trial were cited by a judge in a case before the Crown Court in Northern Ireland in 2007. A man was facing an indictment containing 85 counts involving sexual offences against girls aged between 12 and 19. Both defence and prosecution counsel requested the judge to conduct three separate trials with different juries. The judge agreed, referring to the judicial criticism made by the Court of Appeal about the overloading of the Playland trial.

66 Judge King-Hamilton spoke at a Foyles Literary Luncheon to celebrate the Jubilee of the Crime Writers Guild. Sir Robert Mark was also present and it was he who talked the judge into writing an autobiography. About the Playland case, the judge wrote: "With all due respect, I have found difficulty in understanding other parts of the judgement of the Court of Appeal. Moreover, I was not alone in experiencing that difficulty."

the case was something not apparent in the appeals. "There are people in their manor houses and luxury flats," he said, "holding important positions in society, who were behind this case."

One week after the Court of Appeal decision, Playland received a mention in the House of Commons. Mr Arthur Lewis, MP for Newham North West, asked the Home Secretary Merlyn Rees, "if he will arrange for an independent investigation into complaints made by Mr David Archer arising out of the Piccadilly Playland call-boy case". Rees refused to hold an inquiry but stated that the Commissioner of the Met, Sir Robert Mark, was arranging for an investigation of complaints Archer had made specifically against the police while he was in custody. Rees also said he would write to Lewis about "outstanding matters" raised in correspondence Lewis had sent him, about which one can only speculate.[67]

It is not known if Archer gave his dossier to the police. If he had used this as leverage to secure a deal, why then bite the Establishment hand that had fed him? Neither is it known what happened about his complaint against police behaviour whilst he was in custody. The same goes for the information supplied by the original Playland informant, which had given Peter Earle the confidence to write an article in the *News of the World* predicting that dozens of high-profile arrests would be made in light of a "detailed dossier" on "illegal homosexual activities", held by the DPP, Sir Norman Skelhorn.

I was very interested to find out if the names of any of the men I had been with were mentioned in either the Archer or Skelhorn dossiers. I therefore decided to submit a Freedom of Information request to the Met. I asked that they provide me

---

67 My very first client Mr Charles Irving was in the chamber at this time and, demonstrating his concern for the welfare of young people, questioned the Home Secretary on how many boys and girls had been remanded or committed to adult prisons following conviction in the previous few years.

with copies of David Archer's dossier and the one supposedly held by Sir Norman, as well as the outcome of Sir Robert Mark's investigation into Archer's complaints.

Months passed, and the Met repeatedly failed to meet their own deadlines for the provision of a definitive response. I complained to their Information Rights Unit about how my request was being handled. A review was carried out and the Met accepted that there had been a breach of best practice under the Freedom of Information Act. Six months after I had submitted my request, I finally received the following response: "Thorough searches were undertaken in order to answer your request and this involved the requesting of a series of files which were then manually reviewed. Unfortunately, having undertaken significant work we were not able to locate the information you have requested. To clarify, despite best efforts, we are unable to confirm whether we do or do not hold the information requested, we can simply confirm that in the time spent searching, the information pertinent to your request was unfortunately not located."

* * * * *

In the course of carrying out my research I came across a Court of Appeal case dated 13 July 1982. The appellants were none other than Malcolm Raywood, Basil Andrew-Cohen and another man, Brian Sheppardson. All had been found guilty in 1980 and 1981 of sexual offences against boys, one as young as 12 years old. Andrew-Cohen had also been found guilty in 1980 of an historical offence – four counts of indecent assault on a 13-year-old boy, which had occurred around Christmas 1976. The boy and his brother had met Raywood and Andrew-Cohen and gone to their flat at an address in Liverpool. This is surprising because Andrew-Cohen was supposed to have been in prison in

1976 serving the remainder of his three-year sentence. What was he doing out of prison?

I believe that both Basil Andrew-Cohen and Andrew Novac were quietly released at the same time as Raywood and Archer, probably in November 1976. Was a deal done, perhaps with the DPP, to suppress the names of "millionaires, and titled and influential people", and "top names in the world of finance and show business", in return for the release of the remaining Playland defendants?

Roger Gleaves, Malcolm Raywood and Basil Andrew-Cohen continued to abuse boys for many years. Basil had chauffeured me around London on a few occasions and I had considered him to be one of the more decent members of the Firm. He was laid-back, easy-going, friendly, the quiet one who never had much to say for himself. But by 1980, Basil had been before the courts six times for 44 sex offences dating back to 1970. It turned out that he, like Malcolm, was a prolific child abuser. However, when it came to abuse, Roger Gleaves was in a league of his own. He would spend most of his life in prison.

Piccadilly history kept on repeating itself. The problem eventually became so big again that it could no longer be ignored. Operation Circus was set up in 1984 to clean up the Dilly… again. Over the next few years more than 20 men, including Malcolm Raywood, appeared in court. During the course of the enquiry the names of MPs, celebrities and businessmen surfaced. Trevor Lloyd-Hughes, the Met commander who was leading the operation, had warned officers that if Establishment figures were found to be involved, this was to be ignored. However, the commander himself came under investigation when his home phone number was found in the address books of two rent boys. Lloyd-Hughes died of a heart attack during the investigation.

These periodic purges of the Dilly were having little effect. By May 1986 the *Daily Mail* was describing London as a magnet for international paedophiles, a European centre for organised sex with young boys. Some international magazines even carried adverts offering trips to London for sex with boys.

For Malcolm Raywood, the New Year's Eve celebrations of 1991 did not end well. He'd just been released from prison again, and was staying in a hostel in Islington. He left his digs looking for someone to pick up for sex. Edward Hillhouse, the 24-year-old Glaswegian he met and took back, stabbed Malcolm 12 times and smashed in his skull with a hammer. Raywood – Tony the Butcher – was well and truly butchered. His decomposing body was found a week later. It is very likely that Edward had been a rent boy for many years and had old scores to settle. I wonder if Edward knew fellow Glaswegian Damian McKenna.

* * * * *

Since he was so key to the Playland trial, it is worth briefly casting an eye over Sir Norman Skelhorn's tenure as Director of Public Prosecutions, between 1964 and 1977. His shadow has fallen across a number of questionable decisions relating to the prosecution of crimes of a sexual nature.

In March 1970, following an investigation by the Lancashire police into the alleged sexual abuse of boys by Cyril Smith, Sir Norman wrote to the police and advised that a prosecution would not proceed because the backgrounds and characters of the boys would render their evidence suspect.

In December 1970, police found a Mr Kenneth O'Neill in bed with a boy, and a Mr Prichodsky (who was a friend of Malcolm Raywood) in another bedroom. Both rooms were plastered with obscene photographs of boys, and Mr Prichodsky admitted taking the pictures. "Yes I took them. You may think it funny, but I like pictures of young boys and there are a lot of influential people of the same mind. You would be surprised if I told you some of their names."

The two men had been producing juve smudge and rollers: child pornography and blue movies. The trial judge described the material as hard-core pornography at its worst. He was surprised that the prosecution was charging the men with a single offence under the Obscene Publications Act 1959, relating to only some of the photographs, particularly as there were statements from young men who claimed to have been involved in unlawful homosexual acts with one or other or both of the defendants. The judge repeatedly questioned the prosecution as to why charges of indecent assault, acts of gross indecency, or possibly even buggery or attempted buggery were not brought. The prosecution, under the direction of Sir Norman, took the view that much of the evidence was weak and only a very limited number of photographs were actually being offered for sale. The judge passed the maximum possible sentence of three years, but naturally, the case went to the Court of Appeal and in June 1972 the appeal judges ruled that a sentence of 18 months would have been more appropriate. O'Neill and Prichodsky were released that same day.[68]

In 1972 Sir Norman decided not to prosecute Victor Montagu, a rightwing Tory MP for South Devon and member of the Monday Club, for sexually abusing a boy over a two-year period. Montagu admitted to every allegation put to him, including taking the boy to his London home, but Sir Norman choose to give Montagu a caution rather than proceed with a criminal trial on condition that he have no further contact with the boy. Montagu's own son,

---

68 Pichodsky and Malcolm Raywood appeared in the dock together in 1986 for sexually abusing children. They had been back in Piccadilly Circus picking up boys.

Robert, later revealed that his father had been sexually abusing him between the ages of seven and 11. He believed his father had abused as many as 20 other children. The paedophile activities of Montagu only came to light following an application under the Freedom of Information Act. The file on the case had been kept secret for 40 years.

It's interesting to note that Sir Norman, who had few qualms about either preventing or perverting the course of justice, also believed that the ends justified the means. When questioned in 1973 about torture, Sir Norman did not deny that torture had taken place in Northern Ireland and stated that, "When dealing with Irish terrorists, any methods were justified."

* * * * *

No sooner had Westminster City Council revoked Playland's licence than the solicitors for Playland Amusements Ltd announced their intention to appeal against the decision in the Crown Court. In preparing their case, they requested copies of all the depositions, statements and written exhibits presented at the trial. I have found a letter dated 20 October 1975 in which they write, "We wish to make it clear that none of the defendants in any of the cases has in any way been connected with or employed by our client..." Attached to this letter was a schedule of files requested, which included a "Bundle of Offences/Verdicts/Sentences for J.A. Kay". This name does not appear in any of the court documents nor contemporary newspaper reports from that time. I could be wrong, but based on the available evidence, I believe that J.A. Kay is the sixth defendant in the Playland trial and the member of the Firm who went to Peter Earle of the *News of the World*.

Bruce Eckert returned from the USA for the licence appeal hearing at Knightsbridge Crown Court. Playland Amusements

Ltd were represented by one of the best QCs money could buy, celebrated lawyer Jeremy Hutchinson. He was famed for his defence of clients involved in vice and obscenity cases, including Christine Keeler.

Bernard Briggs, the respectable front man for Playland, explained that, "people employed by him to watch the premises had failed in their duty to report what was going on". He said the first he had heard about the matter was when the case went before the Old Bailey. He was surprised that the police had not informed him about what had been going on. The police, he said, were, "encouraged to visit Playland".

Taking a more realistic perspective than his colleague, Bruce Eckert regretted the arcade's "unsavoury reputation", but he insisted that, "no one could find fault with the way the arcade is run now". They attested to increased surveillance at the arcade. A Playland spokesman had already made the following incredible press statement: "We do not admit anyone under 18 unless accompanied by an adult. The adult may not be a parent but perhaps an uncle." An "uncle" or a "guardian" might well, of course, be a pimp.

After a three-day hearing, which concluded on 7 April 1976, the well-named Judge Friend granted Playland a gaming licence for three years, rather than the usual five. He said: "We have considered the evidence and paid great attention to the arguments put forward. I find it difficult to describe the moral standard of some of the people who frequented the premises in 1974 and 1975". The reference to 1975 is significant because it shows that the goings-on in Playland continued after the police surveillance operation ended in 1974 and it was business as usual right up until the trial when the scandal was reported in the papers .

He did not give reasons for allowing the appeal and subsequently refused to comment on the matter. To be fair to the judge, any refusal of a licence would have to relate to a breach of the 1968 Gaming Act, such as having rigged machines or refusing to admit an inspector, or the suitability of the building.

A contrite and appreciative Bruce Eckert responded: "I hope it is in our power to maintain an outstanding reputation." However, Playland continued to make headlines and Piccadilly Amusements Ltd would be back in Court six years later, the "outstanding reputation" in tatters. Sexual exploitation of boys was one thing, but screwing the taxman was another.

* * * * *

The original police investigation into Playland in 1974 was very limited. It centred on the surveillance of a group of pimps operating on the ground floor of the arcade and failed to explore the gangland infiltration they represented or arrangements that might have been made with the owners of the arcade. The Playland investigation was managed out of West End Central police station, the most corrupt station in the Metropolitan area. It had responsibility for policing Soho, which in itself presented the most concentrated area of illegal gambling dens, nightclubs, casinos, prostitution and pornography in the UK. The corrupt senior commanders in the Met responsible for policing vice, obscene publications and serious crime, who were 'on the take', would have had little trouble influencing the scale and scope of any investigation on their patch. They might just do enough to please the Met Commissioner while ensuring that nothing was uncovered which might hint at organised crime.

During his time as Commissioner between 1972 and 1977, Sir Robert Mark fought with great success to root out corruption at every level within the service. He once called CID the "most routinely corrupt organisation in London". At the conclusion of the police corruption trial that took place in 1977, Mr Justice Mars-Jones said officers had engaged in "corruption on a scale which beggars description". The heads that rolled included DCI George Fenwick, Head of the Obscene Publications Squad, and his superior DCS Bill Moody, Commander Kenneth Drury, Head of the Flying Squad, and Commander Wallace Virgo, Head of the Serious Crime Squad. They were jailed for between 10 and 14 years each. In total 50 officers were suspended and a further 478 dismissed or forced to resign.

* * * * *

Although Playland was called the "biggest vice ring" ever busted, the investigation and subsequent trial merely peeked inside the can of worms and sealed it shut again, with just four of the Firm's foot soldiers and one upper-class punter being jailed. Charles Hornby was the sacrificial lamb. The Establishment had been given a symbolic slap on the wrist as a warning to the VIP clients of Playland. No other individual from the many hundreds of Playland's regular punters, never mind any of the really big clients, were arrested or charged. People might have had to be a little more careful subsequently, a little more discreet, but they would hardly have been dissuaded from indulging in the pleasures provided by teenage rent.

Such, was the combined influence of widespread police corruption, the power of Playland's owners, VIP clients and the Firm's determination to make money. While newspaper headlines may have implied a major scandal of government-toppling proportions, the small print simply recounted how four nobodies were sexually exploiting boys in Playland. After the trial, there seems to have been a desire by the Establishment to make the messy and embarrassing affair go way, with official records placed beyond reach for as long as possible – a desire to bury and to forget.

When I think back over my pilgrimage to London, I find it exasperating to try and unpick the threads of influence that were woven into the fabric of my experiences. It's easy enough to look back and think about the individual events: the people I met, the places I went, the things I did. But it's much more difficult to make sense of the structures, the connections and associations between the people, institutions and businesses. It is clear, for example, that the Playland Firm had connections to and serviced those in the Establishment. It was also linked to the wider London underworld community, in particular the porn barons of Soho. Via the arcade it operated from, it was also connected to dozens of other local amusement arcades and – via the Wolfman – to a syndicate whose dubious financial dealings stretched as far away as Panama.

Playland also had at least tenuous links to the Paedophile Information Exchange – through Keith Hunter and possibly others.[69] PIE's own tentacles stretched into social services via the residential children's care sector, the diplomatic service, academia and even the Home Office. Through Keith Hunter, the Playland Firm also did business with Roger Gleaves and his Firm, sharing resources and providing some older boys with guard dogs to fulfil security contracts, looking after warehouses. A unique and disturbing feature of Gleaves's empire of youth hostels, which like Playland facilitated the sexual exploitation of many homeless youngsters, was that it was funded by the taxpayer and received patronage from the great and the good.

---

69   A few months after I had been interviewed by the Met, they phoned me to say that other survivors had subsequently come forward and had named a man called Keith who was active around Piccadilly Circus in the mid-1970s. The Met were of the opinion that Keith was not his real name. Who then, was the Artful Dodger?

In spite of the scandals involving the sexual exploitation of children during the 1970s that resulted in high-profile court cases and terrible headlines, Playland's gaming licence was never revoked. Playland remained open until 1981, when it was finally shut down because of tax, not sex. Why? Who was protecting Playland's interests? It had to help that Playland was owned by one of the richest men in the world – who will be discussed in the next chapter – and that his syndicate had a long history of bribing and corrupting people in authority. Playland's immunity may also have been guaranteed as a result of the information (including photographic evidence) the Firm had on its VIP clients. The threat of blackmail and the resulting scandal would certainly have provided an incentive for the Establishment to keep the lid on the extent of VIP involvement. It also helped that there was such a sympathetic Director of Public Prosecutions, Sir Norman Skelhorn, with his singular and peculiar view on evidential matters and what might be in the public interest.

The network in which Simon Hornby played his endless game was primarily a business network with fringe benefits. The network had powerful political connections and links to financial institutions and the military. In particular, Eton College seems to feature in the backgrounds of many of the dramatis personae, as does Simon's old regiment, the Grenadier Guards.[70] I was introduced to two serving members of the military. That both of these soldiers had served in Derry seems quite a coincidence, though not one I think I can unravel.

---

70 Simon Hornby, Charles Hornby, Lord Gibson, Lord Arran (Boofy), Lord De L'Isle, Peter Morrison MP, and others were all old Etonians. Anthony Chenevix-Trench was the headmaster of Eton 1964-1970.

CHAPTER 31

An American
Werewolf in London

James Humpert, the Bag Man, was not just collecting money
from Playland. In fact, each night, he travelled from Clapham
Junction to the Edgware Road, Tooting to Kings Cross,
Victoria to Kilburn, collecting the takings from most of the
arcades in central London. He took the cash back to his luxury
flat overlooking Buckingham Palace, and each morning he
transported his haul of cash to be converted into notes at the
National Westminster Bank in Victoria. Every Friday morning
at exactly 9:00am, his wife, Susan, would leave their home with
a plastic bag containing at least £50,000 in notes and deposit it
in one of the three bank accounts she held in either Nat West,
Barclays or Lloyds. She never had a bodyguard.

High above the Humperts' flat, in a penthouse apartment
that occupied the 15th and 16th floors of Roebuck House,
lived the boss, the person some called the Wolfman. On the last
Wednesday of every month, the Wolfman took a business trip to
Zurich. This daily, weekly and monthly sequence of local and
international travel went on year in and year out. The entire
operation ran like a Swiss clock.

However, on 25 March 1981 Her Majesty's Customs and
Excise jammed a very large spanner into the works and the
entire operation ground to a sudden and unexpected halt. The

Wolfman was being accompanied by Simon Hornby's friend and neighbour Dick Stewart. The two men were about to board a Swissair flight from Heathrow to Zurich when they were arrested on suspicion of VAT offences. The men were found to be carrying £147,000 in £20 notes, and the Wolfman's passport revealed him to be one of the richest men in the world. His name was Martin Jerome Bromley.

* * * * *

Martin Bromley was born to Jeanette and Irving Bromberg on 9 August 1919 in New York. After high school he went to work at his father's business, the Irving Bromberg Vending Co., which became the largest distributor of coin-operated machines in the U.S. (Irving Bromberg was said to have brought the first pinball machine to New York). The family moved to Los Angeles and then Honolulu, where Martin and his father set up another company, Standard Games, joined by an old friend of the family, James Humpert. Both James and Martin, who had now changed his name to Bromley, were drafted into the U.S. Navy in the early 1940s. They were working at the shipyard in Pearl Harbour when the Japanese bombed.

By the end of the war, Bromley and Humpert had made valuable contacts in the Navy. Through exploiting these contacts they were able to install slot machines and jukeboxes into the bases. The military market became more successful than the civilian market, so they changed the name of the company to Service Games. Some years later, SErvice GAmes became SEGA, the firm that subsequently hired employees including Ray Lemaire, Richard Stewart, Bruce Eckert and later Scott Dotterer.

Honolulu police records show that in 1947 Martin was convicted for illegal possession of gambling machines in San Francisco, and the following year he was arrested for robbery.

But SEGA continued to grow. Then disaster struck. A moral crusade was sweeping the country and in 1951 the U.S. Congress passed the Gambling Devices Transportation Act, banning slot machines within the territory of the United States. SEGA was forced to look into other avenues to market and sell the machines.

They first expanded into Japan, via US military bases. Mechanic Ray Lemaire and salesman Dick Stewart set up a number of partnership businesses. They also opened a Honolulu bank account into which profits from Japan were transferred, and then used to fund outgoings for other companies in the group. The authorised signatories for this account were MJ Bromley and Irving Bromberg. The maze was being constructed, with Bromley operating under numerous names, including Peter Schmuck and Adolph Dixon.

In 1953 Martin Bromley moved his banking affairs to Panama. The coin-operated machines were now being smuggled abroad in Navy vessels and even in Air Force planes using counterfeit importation documents. All this was achieved using bribes and kickbacks. Within a few years, SEGA companies were manufacturing, distributing and servicing gaming machines across South East Asia.

In 1959, Bromley decided to begin exploiting the post-war business opportunities in London, where people were ready for some bright lights and amusements. He brought with him James Humpert and Dick Stewart.

He bought flats across half of the two top floors of Roebuck House in Victoria and converted it into a 4,768 sq ft. penthouse. He created a rooftop terrace and gardens with a retractable roof and had gardeners from Hampton Court and Kew Gardens attend to the plants. His neighbours included Sir Laurence Oliver and international arms dealer Adnan Khashoggi. He bought flat 15 for James Humpert, who would be his general manager, and flat 12, which would be their office. Bromley owned a blue Rolls-Royce with a personalised number plate: MB1. Like Charles Hornby, he also had a fondness for the Mini Clubman: he owned 10 of them, all registered to one of his offshore companies. Dick Stewart bought himself a luxurious apartment in Knightsbridge, and he sent his sons to Millfield School in Somerset, of which he became a governor.

* * * * *

Back in America, the U.S. Internal Revenue Service had prompted a Senate investigation into SEGA. The subcommittee heard accounts of numerous investigations by law enforcement officers relating to smuggling, fraud, bribery and tax evasion. In 1959 the Navy banned the company, its officers and affiliates from bases in Japan, and the following year from the Philippines. Fines were levied against the company, and against Scott Dotterer and Bruce Eckert personally. This did not impede the growth of operations, and production in Japan continued unabated. In 1969 Bromley and his associates sold 80 per cent of SEGA to Gulf & Western for nearly $10 million.

The Vietnam war provided Bromley with his greatest opportunity. His man in Saigon was William John Crum. Half-blind and crippled, he was an old China hand who had made a profit out of almost every war in Asia since 1941. In Vietnam he sold and leased amusement machines to U.S. military bases, as well as supplying liquor, frozen pizza (plus the necessary refrigerators and ovens), and civilian suits and dresses to military personnel. Since the U.S. Air Force had banned Bromley's companies from doing business with him in 1964, Crum founded Sarl Electronics to sell and lease Bromley's machines, under the close direction of Scott Dotterer, who was Bromley's Bag Man for the whole of Asia. Some of the most senior military officers in Vietnam were bribed to award contracts to Sarl Electronics. Crum bought a villa where he could entertain top brass lavishly, providing food, drink and women. The place was known as Chateau Saigon.

Not even the Mafia could challenge Bromley and Crum. American crime boss Santo Trafficante Jr of Tampa, Florida, had sent a young Mafioso called Frank Furci to Saigon. Malcolm Raywood would have loved Frank. He was a *real* gangster – intelligent, ambitious, proud and confident. Everyone in Vietnam's criminal fraternity – including the corrupt military and the Corsicans already operating there in narcotics – was impressed by Furci's frankness and willingness to cooperate with like-minded associates. Furci was exceedingly successful, diversifying into numerous areas, including black-market currency transactions. However, eventually his business activities clashed with those of Crum, when he started muscling in on the supply of amusement machines to U.S. army bases. Crum estimated that Furci had done him out of $2.5 million worth of business, and when word reached Bromley, the order was given to either buy Furci out or bring him down. The fight was short, and Crum won. He knew all about Furci's illegal currency transactions, and was paying a US general $1,000 a month for protection, which now paid off. Furci was convicted of fraud. He left Saigon, moved to Hong Kong and eventually opened a restaurant.

By the time Saigon fell, Crum had made $40 million. Because of Martin Bromley's intricate network of trusts, companies and offshore accounts, it has never been established how much he made out of the Vietnam war, but in one transaction alone in 1969, $7,000,000 was transferred from a Sarl Electronics bank account in Los Angeles to one of Bromley's accounts in Panama.

* * * * *

Martin Bromley's business plan for London was similar to the one for the Far East, albeit on a much smaller scale. The gaming laws in England had been liberalised and he intended to saturate the capital with amusement and gaming machines.

He started acquiring properties all over central London, and a number of companies were established, including Atlantic Amusements Ltd, Family Leisure Ltd, JWD Amusements Ltd and Aladdin's Castle Ltd. As usual, Martin Bromley's name never appeared as a director of any of the companies. Rather, it was his closest friends and associates who were listed as directors: people like James Humpert and Dick Stewart. Scott Dotterer, based in Hong Kong, owned 59,999 shares out of the 60,000 issued for Family Leisure Ltd.

The chairman of the Phonograph Operators Association, Mr Bernard Briggs, told Bromley about an arcade in Coventry Street called Playland. Although it looked a little shabby and had an unsavoury reputation, Briggs felt it had great potential, occupying one of the best locations in London, between Piccadilly Circus and Leicester Square. The syndicate acquired Playland. At first 99 per cent of the shares were owned by Briggs's company, Modern Enterprises Ltd, and 1 per cent by Bruce Eckert, whom Martin had withdrawn from the Far East after paying the fines for his tax fraud conviction in 1961. Eckert was given the job of managing Playland, the biggest arcade in London, as well as the Family Leisure arcade in the Strand.

Bromley recruited a businessman of Kenyan Asian decent called Hasmukhray Permshand Shah and installed him as a director of both Atlantic Amusements Ltd and Aladdin's Castle Ltd. As acting personnel manager, Shah recruited staff to work in the syndicate's arcades (most were from the Asian community, as they were prepared to accept the pittance of a wage offered). He also recruited his younger brother, Vasantkumar Malde, who ended up listed as a director of one of the companies.

The entire empire was commercially incestuous. The companies had very porous boundaries, with a structure on paper that was belied by the reality. Bromley's core team were woven into the fabric of all the enterprises. Playland was officially owned by Trafalgar Novelties, but the ultimate owner and main beneficiary of Bromley's British empire was being hidden behind a maze of companies. The accommodating financial regime in Vaduz, Liechtenstein enabled Bromley to establish a trust fund called the Tunalt Family Foundation, into which profits could be diverted.

There was the small matter of some thugs who had offered "protection" from other elements in the London underworld and from corrupt cops in the Met. However, Martin Bromley considered these hoodlums to be a minor inconvenience, small flies in a large jar of ointment. In terms of the money his arcades were generating, these two-bit criminals were taking just loose change.

A court case in 1972 created some adverse publicity for Playland, when five men admitted various sexual offences against boys aged between 13 and 15, who had been picked up in the arcade. This was followed by the surveillance operation in 1974, and the devastating trial the following year, after which Playland came very close to being shut down. Fortunately for the syndicate, the police investigation was limited to a handful of the Firm's pimps (plus one unfortunate VIP client, Charles Hornby), and not the legitimate owners of the arcade. The police conveniently failed to notice the biggest ever money laundering operation in UK history taking place right under their noses. No one ever questioned James Humpert about the goings-on in the arcade, even though they must have observed him leaving Playland in the early hours of every morning, loading up his car with sacks of coins. Neither did they think it relevant to examine the corporate governance of Trafalgar Novelties Ltd or look into the background of its directors. No one from the renamed company Piccadilly Amusements Ltd was called to give evidence at the Playland trial of 1975.

Had police investigators read the conclusions of a U.S. Senate subcommittee investigation published just three years earlier in 1971, they would have discovered that, "The Service Games operation including more than two dozen associated and subsidiary companies has had since its founding a history of corruption. Charges against the complex and its operations and employees have included many customs violations in many countries, the use of fraudulent military purchase orders, violations of military transport regulations, bribes, illegal gratuities to military and civilian personnel of the armed services, smuggling and many other irregularities in Korea, Japan, Okinawa, the Philippines, Guam, Vietnam, Thailand, Germany and other military stations." This syndicate was now running Playland and most of the other arcades in London.

Playland's licence was renewed and before long it was business as usual. We may never know who knew what in 1974/75, either about the Bromley syndicate's money laundering activities or about the Firm's rent-boy operation and its VIP clients. The millionaires who lived in London at that time were part of a very exclusive club. The syndicate was well connected and well informed. When, at the Court of Appeal hearing in 1976, Mr Alan Campbell QC said, "There are people in their manor houses and luxury flats holding important positions in society, who were behind this case," was he referring only to the VIP clients who used the arcade or also to Martin Bromley and his wealthy associates, the people who really were behind Playland? And another question needs to be asked, which is whether there were any connections between Bromley's syndicate and Simon Hornby's network. Bromley and Hornby did have a common friend in Richard Stewart, so it's by no means inconceivable.

* * * * *

By 1980 Martin Bromley had conquered the amusement machine industry worldwide. His business interests including manufacturing, distribution and ownership of amusement arcades now stretched from Dublin and Cork in Ireland, across Western Europe to the Far East and Australia. He was so powerful that he even muscled in on the mob's turf in Las Vegas. He contributed little to either the tax man or to the cultural life of London, where there were now more amusement arcades than bookshops. He had turned central London into Little Vegas. His personal wealth stood at more than £50 million.

At last, Customs and Excise began to take an interest in the syndicate's affairs. A major covert enquiry called Operation Nudger (named after the nudge button found on pinball machines) was set up to investigate the amusement arcades in London and Blackpool. One hundred undercover officers were involved. In one strand of the investigation, men seen around the arcades were placed under surveillance, the difference from the Met's investigation of 1974 being that this time the men being watched were clearly management. When customs officials realised that James Humpert, a director of Piccadilly Amusements and JWD Amusements, was also lifting the takings from arcades owned by Atlantic Amusements and Family Leisure, the link between the companies was uncovered.

Martin Bromley and Dick Stewart were arrested at Heathrow Airport on their way to Zurich. Officers then swooped on addresses across London including not just the arcades but Roebuck House, Kingston House and other directors' homes. The company directors were rounded up and when they appeared at Horseferry Road Magistrates' Court they were refused bail. With the managers of the syndicate in custody, Customs operatives were placed in the arcades and found out how much money was actually being made. They discovered a discrepancy between what was lifted and what was entered in the books. They also found that the office in flat No. 12 of Roebuck House was the business hub of global operations. They saw that weekly reports were being received on every gaming machine the syndicate owned across the world, and the results analysed. If any machine's earnings weren't hitting the projected targets, problems would be identified and remedied. It was a slick, sophisticated operation that evidenced superb business acumen.

As the scale of the fraud was emerging, the defendants appeared in the High Court before Mr Justice Stocker. Bail was set at more than £1 million and the men were released without a date being fixed for the next hearing. By the time the painstaking investigation had concluded, it was estimated that the suppression of takings by the syndicate amounted to more than £10 million. The defendants were facing very serious criminal charges. However, just when it was shaping up to be a titanic battle between the tax man and the Wolfman, something extraordinary happened. The Commissioners of Customs and Excise used their powers to stay criminal proceedings and prevent a trial in the High Court. These powers were rarely used but were for some reason considered appropriate in this case. The matter would now be dealt with back in the lower court, before the Horseferry Road Magistrate.

The settlement hearing took place on 20 August 1981. Appearing before the bench were Martin Bromley, James Humpert, Richard Stewart and his son Scott, Oscar Dotterer,

Alan Rawlinson, Hasmukhray Shah and Vasantkumar Malde. The Magistrate, Mr Edmond MacDermott, had been fully briefed on the terms of the deal, so that these proceedings were essentially a formality. An official from the cashier's department of Customs and Excise walked into the court, Martin Bromley casually signed two banker's drafts for the sum of £2.7 million, and then he and his associates were dismissed. Bromley put his penthouse on the market for £1.2 million. Although he continued to live in London, his new lair was a closely guarded secret.[71]

Ten weeks before this, an advertisement had been placed in *International Coin Slot*, a trade magazine, announcing the closing-down sale of a Piccadilly arcade. "Everything must go!" The machines were for sale at reasonable prices and a phone number was given for Mr Shah. Finally, on 30 June 1981, after 46 years, Playland closed its doors for the last time.

Bromley had lost his most profitable arcade and one of his best men, as Dick Stewart retired to the South of France, where he bought himself a £100,000 villa in Juan-les-Pins. But the businesses continued to thrive. None of the other arcades changed hands or were sold. Three years after the tax case, the Trocadero was redeveloped as an entertainment centre. It was expanded to occupy not just the old London Pavilion building but much of Coventry Street, including the Playland site. The Bromley syndicate still had shares in SEGA, which became the anchor tenant, and in 1996 a giant amusement arcade named Segaworld was launched.

Martin Bromley was found dead in his bed in Zurich in 2008. He was 89 years old, and was said to have died of a heart attack caused by an overdose of Viagra. A search of records held by

---

71 In 1982 the financial journalist Martin Tomkinson carried out a brilliant piece of financial forensic analysis following the Bromley tax avoidance case. He dissected the Bromley empire and revealed the extent of the syndicate's operations across the globe.

Companies House reveals that the syndicate still has companies operating out of Soho: Family Leisure Holdings Ltd, Atlantic Amusements Ltd, Funland Ltd, Big Game Ltd. Bromley's daughter Lauran now runs the syndicate's global operations.

CHAPTER 32

Notes on a Scandal

One of the men I had been introduced to in London went on to hold one of the most important and powerful offices in the land, that of Lord Chancellor. Sir Michael Havers was a theatre lover and he told me he had attended the original stage production of *A Man for All Seasons*. It was one of his favourite plays. He gave me his copy of the play (which I still have) and told me that I simply *must* read it. He was a great admirer of Sir Thomas More, one of his predecessors as Lord Chancellor. Since I will no doubt be accused of tarnishing the reputation of a good and honourable man, I think it is appropriate that I comment on Sir Michael's work and character.

Sir Michael Havers landed the big trial he wanted, that of the Guildford Four, and he was also given the Maguire Seven case to prosecute. Sir Michael therefore represented the Crown in two of the worst miscarriages of justice in British judicial history. Together with his old friend, the DPP Sir Norman Skelhorn, he colluded in presenting untruths and in suppressing alibi evidence that would have supported Gerry Conlon and Paul Hill's claims of innocence. He was also found to have suppressed statements from the IRA team known as the Balcombe Street Gang, who confessed to carrying out the Guildford bombings.

As Attorney General (a post he held from 1979) Sir Michael was more interested in protecting the Establishment than seeing justice done. In 1981, he warned Geoffrey Dickens MP not to name the British diplomat and MI6 intelligence operative Sir Peter Hayman as a paedophile in the House of Commons. Astonishingly, Sir Michael argued it was not in the public interest for this to be known. He said all it would do would be to cause Sir Peter shame and embarrassment. Sir Michael was defending the DPP Sir Thomas (Tony) Hetherington's decision not to prosecute Sir Peter, who was a member of PIE, for being in possession of a vast collection of child pornography, some involving the abuse of babies, and for carrying out obscene correspondence with others. Dickens accused Sir Michael of taking part in a "whitewash" and the "cover-up of the century". Sir Peter Hayman was the man who called himself Mr Grass. He was one of the men I'd witnessed abusing one of the brothers in March 1975.

Sir Michael also decided to suppress the fact that Geoffrey Prime, a former worker at Cheltenham GCHQ and a Russian agent, also just happened to be a member of PIE. He did so "to avoid embarrassing security chiefs". Prime was jailed for 35 years for his espionage activities and received three years for assaults on young girls. Then when journalists revealed in 1982 that powerful Establishment figures had been sexually abusing young boys at the Elm Guest House in Barnes, South West London, Sir Michael seems to have been behind a press blackout that was instigated following complaints by lawyers for the Guest House.[72][73]

---

72   This personal intervention may have been prompted by a telephone call he received from Margaret Thatcher, reported by a friend of the Havers family who was staying at the Havers family home one weekend. An MP had apparently been caught by the police with young boys. A car then arrived to take Sir Michael away. I was given a copy of an email that was sent to an MP in July 2014, detailing the specifics of this incident.

73   The CPS file relating to the police raid on Elm Guest House, including the list of suspects, was destroyed on 11 April 2007.

In 1984, following Cabinet level discussions, it was decided there would not be a full public inquiry into a similar scandal in Northern Ireland, concerning the Kincora Boys' Home. Instead, Sir Michael drew up highly restrictive terms of reference, which would only consider the administration of the hostel and procedures and practices within the system of residential care in Northern Ireland. Judge William Hughes, who led the inquiry, made a point of stressing its limitations and inadequacies, since it had not been able to scrutinise "the conduct of the police, or elected representatives, or clergymen, or military intelligence, or any other persons, who may have been in receipt of allegations, information or rumours relating to Kincora".[74]

That same year during the miners' strike, Sir Michael was accused of trying to influence the courts when he predicted that the NUM would be "brought to heel" by the High Court.

It was Sir Michael Havers who was responsible for the embarrassment caused to the government by the *Spycatcher* affair in 1986. As Attorney General in 1981 he had advised the government that there was no basis on which they could prevent publication of Chapman Pincher's book *Their Trade Is Treachery*, which covered essentially the same ground as Peter Wright's *Spycatcher.* Pincher made it clear that Sir Michael was one of the political figures who, over the years, had been passing secrets to him (which Pincher was in turn exchanging with Peter

---

74   In 2017 the Historical Institutional Abuse Inquiry chaired by Sir Anthony Hart found no evidence that the security agencies were complicit in any form of sexual abuse in Kincora Boys' Home, yet prefaced these remarks by stating that they had not been able to compel witnesses from the Northern Ireland Office or the intelligence services. The inquiry had been given fewer powers than an ordinary Coroner's Court. Theresa May, when Home Secretary, refused repeated calls for Kincora to be included in the remit of the Independent Inquiry into Child Sexual Abuse in London, which was given much wider powers than the Hart inquiry. Inaccuracies in the Hart report have already started to emerge. One commentator has referred to the report as Hart failure.

Wright). Sir Michael had been at the heart of the entire messy merry-go-round.

One of the salacious titbits that Sir Michael passed to Pincher, actually in the same year as the *Spycatcher* affair, was that Sir Maurice Oldfield, the Director of MI6 from 1973 to 1978, was a promiscuous homosexual and had for years posed a security threat by falsifying his positive vetting. He also revealed that the Prime Minister had withdrawn Oldfield's security clearance. In 1979 Sir Maurice was brought out of retirement by Margaret Thatcher and appointed Ulster Security Co-ordinator. Newspaper articles reported Sir Maurice's taste for lower-class down-and-out boys, or 'rough trade'.[75]

Sir Michael was a key legal adviser to the Thatcher government, but Margaret Thatcher's close friend and biographer Robin Harris considered Havers' credibility to be non-existent. He revealed in his book *Not for Turning* that Sir Michael "spent his lunchtimes telling journalists at the Garrick Club all the tastiest government gossip of the day". Harris believed that Thatcher (who had been in chambers with Sir Michael) let Havers keep his position because of their friendship.

In fact, she appointed Sir Michael Lord Chancellor in June 1987, which resulted in his pension being doubled. However, his tenure in the post proved to be very brief. Just four months later he suddenly and unexpectedly resigned on "health grounds".[76]

Also in 1987, Chapman Pincher became embroiled in investigations by the police amid allegations of treachery and his links to

---

75   In 1987 Margaret Thatcher finally admitted in the House of Commons that Sir Maurice had been a homosexual but insisted that he'd never posed a threat to national security. It has been suggested that his seeming use of rent boys was actually faked in order to discredit him, but other evidence links him to Kincora Boys Home.

76   I have however seen a document which suggests that Sir Michael resigned for a different reason.

a spy. He robustly defended himself during twelve hours of inter-rogation. During the course of his long journalistic career, Pincher had amassed thirty volumes of documents including cabinet papers which had been passed to him from various sources. In the updated and uncensored edition of his book *Treachery*, published two years before his death in 2014, he revealed that he had invited the police to take some of his files. "In particular I made sure they left with a rather fat folder marked 'Havers', concerning the former Attorney General. Those who had to read the documents would realise that I would be likely to divulge the information in my defence and the damage to the government would be catastrophic, with at least one high-profile resignation inevitable and Labour having a field day". He concluded that, "The witnesses I would have been required to try to subpoena would have included the Prime Minster, Sir Arthur Franks and, above all, Lord Havers".

Back in 1981 the IRA blew up Sir Michael's home in Wimbledon. He and his wife were in Spain at the time. I wonder if my Rolling Stones poster survived the explosion.[77]

* * * * *

After Charles Hornby was released from Wormwood Scrubs in July 1976 he retreated to his country estate in Gloucestershire. His wife, Amanda, had bravely stood by him throughout the trial, at which he profusely apologised for his behaviour. His fall from grace had been spectacular and humiliating. His reputation was ruined, his dignity lost. I find it easy to forgive many of the

---

77   In 1975 Sir Michael told me that the Rolling Stones had written a song about him. I dismissed this as wishful thinking, but recently out of curiosity I searched the internet and found a Stones Blog. Sure enough, the Rolling Stones did write a song called Havers Chambers. Like a lot of stuff about Sir Michael, it was never released.

people I was passed around because they probably knew nothing of the circumstances or threats that had led me into their beds. But Charles Hornby drugged and brutally raped me. Why?

He had been committed for trial just five days before Keith introduced me to him in the Golden Lion pub. Malcolm Raywood had also been there. No doubt they'd been discussing the outcome at Lambeth Magistrates' Court that Monday and the forthcoming trial – discussing options, making plans, getting drunk. I wasn't even his type. Charles liked them young, passive. Was I targeted and attacked out of some kind of rage, or in defiance against his committal? The police were still gathering evidence against him but it's highly unlikely he was still under surveillance, and even if he was, the police would just have seen him with a young man, having a drink, going for a meal.

Perhaps an unexpected opportunity presented itself and he identified me as someone who could be introduced into his brother's endless game. Charles blackmailed and exploited me by threatening my family, taking advantage of the untimely murder of a young policeman and the anti-Irish sentiment that was prevalent at the time. He may have been arrogant enough to believe his connections and position in society would protect him from a public trial, but Sir Robert Mark's crusade against corruption and vice saw the Playland case forced through the doors of the Old Bailey.

After leaving prison, Charles kept a relatively low profile for the rest of his life. He still entertained distinguished guests at Hodges, the country estate that his grandmother Eny had left him. Eny had promised him the estate and then changed her mind when she thought he had taken to gambling. But she changed her mind again and he inherited the grand house set in six acres after she died in April 1974, three months before Charles was arrested.

One of Charles's visitors to Hodges in 1979 was the promiscuous, bi-sexual, Irish-hating James Lees-Milne, who'd made an early conquest of Lord Arran, aka Boofy. Lees-Milne wrote that they had wined, dined and gone to bed. This encounter is interesting because history records Lord Arran as being the heterosexual peer who introduced the Parliamentary bill that decriminalised homosexuality in 1967. Perhaps Boofy's initiative was motivated by compassion in the wake of family tragedy: he had inherited the family title after his older brother the 7th Earl, who was gay, committed suicide.

Lees-Milne had written an "extremely sympathetic letter" of support to Charles whilst he was in prison. He now described Charles as a "silly young man with a weak face", whose "appearance has changed since I saw him last, before imprisonment".

In 1984 Charles joined the Queen and most of the royal family at the funeral of his neighbour, and his granny's old friend, the Duke of Beaufort. There were so many mourners that a large marquee was set up outside, as the pews in the church had been reserved for royalty and relatives only. Charles's mother, Nicole, horrified that she was being led to the marquee, lied and said she was related to the Duke. She got a seat in the church. "She always gets her way," Charles apologised later.

Charles continued to hold a number of directorships in a few companies associated with his estate. He continued his association with Lloyd's where, as a Name, he was pledged to underwrite different types of policies offering unlimited liability. In 1993 he was exposed to massive losses, and had to resort to selling off paintings. In fact, he came very close to having to sell his estate in order to avoid bankruptcy. Three years later he was dead. He was 57 years old.[78]

---

78 After I'd been interviewed by the Met in 2014 about my experiences in London, they made a point of tracking down Charles Hornby's death certificate. They wanted to make absolutely sure he was in fact dead. He was, though they refused to disclose the cause of death.

* * * * *

I decided to look into the incredible story Pat Gibson had told me about his escape from the POW camp with Eddie Tomkins and their long trek to freedom. Sure enough, the history books record that Tomkins overheard two guards saying that Mussolini's regime had been overthrown, and – unhindered by the guards – the men cut through the wire and escaped. Local Italian girls gave them civilian clothes. Eddie chose a brightly coloured shirt and took a hat from a scarecrow. He must have been the most flamboyant and highly visible escapee of the war. They walked 500 miles through mountainous terrain to reach the Allied lines at the River Sangro 81 days later.

But Pat had not been telling me the whole story. There was a third man with them – a young fellow officer named Captain Hugh (Hughie) Cruddas. Hughie had been wounded in the leg and captured in North Africa, then imprisoned in the same Italian POW camp. He was the son of a lieutenant colonel in the Indian Medical Service. On his return to London, Hughie got engaged to Juliet Heygate, a 24-year-old RADA-trained actress. However, the wedding was called off after Hughie met and fell madly in love with Robert Heber-Percy, reputedly one of the most attractive men in England.

Robert, known to all as the Mad Boy, was the lover of the wealthy and eccentric Lord Berners (who was nearly thirty years his senior), and they lived openly together at Faringdon House in Oxfordshire. Hughie was taken on as farm manager and live-in lover and his name was added to the estate stationery. Described by the many visitors to Faringdon as a gentle and sweet-natured young man, Hughie played a "wifely" role in the household. He excelled at flower arranging and by all accounts could mix a wonderful Bloody Mary. He continued to live there for many years until the Mad Boy dumped him for a younger man. Heartbroken and in constant pain from the old war wound, Hughie died alone in a nearby village.

Perhaps Pat didn't mention Hughie because his presence would have made their story less heroic, less romantic: a threesome on the run rather than a couple. Hughie's story and his death would also have added a tinge of tragedy to the tale. It would seem that Gibson, Tomkins and Crudass had been drawn together by shared sexual inclinations. Having decided to escape together and make their way to freedom, they apparently remained close friends for the rest of their lives.

CHAPTER 33

The Abyss of Shame

In the weeks following my return to Derry, I had cravings for the drugs I'd been taking in London and, inexplicably, I also had cravings to be back in Piccadilly Circus, to be fired up again by the neon, the noise and excitement of the place. During those same weeks I wondered if they would come for me. I felt like a convict who'd escaped from prison. I had nightmares about being dragged out of the house by the army and taken back to London, back to Playland and forced to relive the horror all over again.

My adventure in London had ended as quickly as it had begun. That blast of madness and noise and neon light and confusion and brutality and sex and anxiety and pain. Suddenly my life had become a silent vacuum. I had arrived in London a heterosexual virgin and returned as what? I felt like a stranger in my own body. Pretty Boy had now vacated and left this shell. I felt as if I had been possessed. And I had been. I had been told what to wear, where to go, who to meet and what to do. I would now have to claim responsibility for a body which for months I had not regarded as my own.

I asked myself many questions about what had happened. Why me? Was it my fault? How could I have done those things? How could I have been sexually assaulted yet sometimes physically gratified at the same time? The drugs and the drink had helped me switch off the connection between my mind and body. I had parked my sexuality beside their fancy cars outside the hotels and restaurants and luxury apartments, and I had developed a sexuality based on providing pleasure.

The person they had created, the shiny black-haired Pretty Boy, was everything a gentleman could ask for: impeccably dressed, mild-mannered, polite, intelligent, witty (after a few drinks) and obedient (after a few chemicals). Pretty Boy was an illusion, a sex object. During his time with Pretty Boy, a gentleman could go from being on a romantic date to engaging in unrestrained sexual degeneracy, without the usual interlude of a relationship. Pretty Boy was a thing to strip down, debase, defile and humiliate. And that boy confused exploitation for affection, touch for intimacy, pain for pleasure and lust for love. When he experienced any kind of warmth or kindness from someone, he was drawn to the charm of their magnetic deceptions. He wasn't even their friend; he was their fantasy.

Pretty Boy had made the best of a bad situation. He had become an actor, a chameleon. He could blend in with the milieux of Piccadilly Circus or St James's, Knightsbridge and Mayfair. He relished the few hours of luxury afforded him – the good food and fine wine, the conversation, the flirting, the teasing. Mingling with the great and the good, he experienced the dizzy intoxicating unreality of it all. And as the centre of attention, at times he felt privileged. But after the dates and the parties, he would be taken from the opulent surroundings and returned to his real world. It may have been Pretty Boy who partied, but it was the bookseller who fell into bed spaced out and exhausted, only to rise after a few hours and go to work.

Five weeks into his experiences in London, Pretty Boy had written in his diary, "What have they done to me? What have I become?" One evening a client, a director with Lloyds bank, told him exactly what he was. When Pretty Boy said, as he had been instructed, "No charge, it's covered", the client laughed gently. "No charge until the Hornbys come round looking for their cake and their kickbacks, for contacts or contracts, a seat on a board". He ran his fingers through the young man's hair. "No charge indeed," as he counted out a few £20 notes. "You're a good lad, but you're also a blank cheque. The Hornbys fill in the amount later. You could be the most expensive male prostitute in London." The word prostitute cut like a knife made of mortal sin. The young man could delude himself and project the glamorous persona of the escort or the companion, but those words cushioned the brutal reality of what he did. He could even think of himself as being rent, but never a prostitute. That word was hurtful and disgusting.

Once back home in Derry I was troubled, confused and racked with guilt and shame. I had thought I had principles, beliefs, values, yet my behaviour in London had contradicted everything I stood for. Psychologists call this cognitive dissonance. I call it psychological warfare, angels and demons doing battle inside my head. Also, I was having inner dialogues and thoughts about Pretty Boy, as if he were somebody else. It wasn't me but he who had suffered the abuse and the trauma. Psychologists have a term for this also: Dissociative Identity Disorder (DID). It's a disconnection between a person and their own thoughts, memories, feelings, actions and sense of identity.

My experiences in London had therefore not only left me physically diseased, but mentally disordered. The antibiotics had finally cleared up the chronic bronchitis, but I was experiencing bladder problems and I had scratches and bruises on my body and other internal injuries. I also had short-term but intense cravings for drugs. It was just as well that in Derry in 1975 it was almost impossible to get your hands on illegal drugs.

It's been said that rape is the murder of the soul. That's the third nail in the unholy trinity of abuse, the crucifixion of the mind, the body and the soul. If that wasn't bad enough, in 1975 the Congregation for the Doctrine of the Faith ruled that homosexual practices and all masturbation were "disordered" and constituted mortal sins. I therefore considered myself to be physically and spiritually fucked. This was one confession I was never going to make. How could I ever tell this to a priest, friends or family? I was damned.

Something else that occupied my mind was the opposite sex. How was I ever going to interact with them? The thought of what Pretty Boy might do to a girl in bed terrified me. The thought of him having to navigate the contours of a woman's body for the first time filled me with dread. A Dilly Boy with a Derry Girl just didn't seem right.

Simon Hornby had warned me all about women. "Keep well away from them," he pleaded after I had returned broken-hearted from Agnes. "You might want to get married, of course," he clarified. "But you know what I mean," he said, glancing down. The insane thing is, sometimes if I had a question in my head or needed advice, I would think, *I must ask Simon*. Then I would suddenly realise I couldn't. Ever.

As the weeks passed I began to relax and started to spend the money I'd earned. I bought a few hundred books from mail-order catalogues, some antiquarian but mainly new editions of the collected works of authors in fine bindings. I soon built up an impressive collection, which occupied a fully shelved wall in the little back sitting room. When I knew my mum was short of money, I'd slip her some cash. She never asked how her unemployed son could give her money and I never told her its source.

The more I tried to put my experiences in London to the back of my mind, the more it seemed the IRA was determined to keep reminding me. In October 1975 they bombed Piccadilly. The cutlery and glassware flew off the dining tables in the Ritz, injuring diners. Outside, a 23-year-old homeless man was killed. Twenty people were injured including two children. And on 29 January 1976, the day before the fourth anniversary of Bloody Sunday, 12 bombs exploded in the West End during the night. I wondered what effect all this was having on Dilly trade.

In February 1976, exactly a year since I'd started in Foyles, I was offered a job by the Western Education and Library Board as a library assistant. It was strange at first not actually selling the books people walked out with, but I loved working in public libraries. In late September, I took my first foreign holiday. I went to Malta and blew a lot of my dirty money with two friends, Martin Hegarty and Hugh Rooney. The Guinness cost a fortune due to the export costs, but what the hell, I could afford it. The big hit at the time was *Dancing Queen* by Abba and I couldn't help but think the song was a great anthem for some of the Dilly boys I'd known. I had a wonderful time and was finally starting to feel my life had returned to normal. But my feelings of security came to an abrupt end the week after I returned home.

At 4:40am on Sunday morning of 3 October 1976, I was awakened by a commotion downstairs. Before I could get out of bed a soldier burst into my bedroom and pointed a rifle at my head. I thought my worst fears were realised – they had come to take me back to London. What would they tell my parents? I was ordered to dress and get downstairs. I joined my family in the living room while the army took the house apart. A soldier called one of his colleagues into the back sitting room. They had not expected to see a book collection like *that* in a working-class housing estate in Derry. I noticed that the soldiers had removed the badges from their berets and any other identifying insignia from their uniforms.

The search ended at 6:10am. I can be precise about the times because the officer in charge filled out a search-damage claim form and entered the times on it. What he did not do was sign the form, as he was required to. After he got my father to sign the form, he asked for me by name and took me to one side. He tore the form off the pad and handed it to me. He beckoned me to him and whispered in my ear, "Consider this a calling card from your friends in London."

Then they left and we returned to our beds. I lay awake for a couple of hours and reflected on the warning. The message was clear. They could walk into my home and take care of me whenever they wanted. The communication had been delivered a couple of months after Charles Hornby was released from prison. Before I went to work I unfolded the search form and placed it inside the copy of *A Man for All Seasons* given to me by Sir Michael Havers. Because of what that officer said to me, I've kept it safe for over 40 years.

The day after the house search I discovered that the fountain pen Lord Back-Seat had given me, and the notes, the stationery and business cards I had brought from London, had been taken from a little storage box I had kept under my bed. Fortunately, I had kept my dirty money and my dirty diary in a Chinese box, which had been designed to look like a book and sat camouflaged among my book collection – hidden in plain sight.

* * * * *

In 1977 I met the girl who would become my future wife. I'd gone to a disco over the border with a few mates and I saw her ordering drinks at the bar. She looked amazing. I'd had a few drinks myself so I swaggered over to her, gave her my most disarming smile and asked her if she'd like to dance. She said no, that she was with someone, and walked away. Dejected, I walked back to my table and sat there alone most of the night, while my mates boogied on the dance floor with various girls. I looked on in envy at the other young men who were either chatting effortlessly to girlfriends around the bar or clinging to girls on the dance floor during the slow sets. *Why do I even bother*, I thought. Was there something about me that female intuition picked up on? I knew that there was a tender, gentle, sensitive and trusting side to me. That's what got me into trouble in London, where I had lost my innocence and had become damaged goods. I wondered if the damage showed. Did I no longer appear 'manly' enough to women? The blinding flicker of a strobe light suddenly hit me and cast the dancing, mocking shadow of Pretty Boy on the wall behind me. I went home on my own.

The girl I had fancied was called Dympna and, unknown to me, she actually worked with my brother Fred for the local council. Fred delivered a message from her to say she had dumped the guy she was with and that she'd be at the disco again the following week.

Scene one, take two. I walked up to her at the bar and asked her to dance. She smiled, took my hand and led me to the dance floor. We had found each other. We hit it off right away and started going steady. Little did she know, she just wasn't dating me, she was rescuing me, but I promised myself then and there that I'd never tell her about London. I had been hurting and hiding for so long, now was the time for healing. I broke free and detached myself from Pretty Boy. There was no room for him in this relationship. He was gone forever, or so I thought.

In May the following year I was appointed librarian in a newly opened high school. It was a job I loved. Not only was I working with books but I felt I was finally doing something meaningful. I was helping kids develop the skills to use a library, find information and experience the joy of reading and learning. I devoted a lot of time to working with fifth- and sixth-formers and I felt very protective of them, knowing they'd soon be leaving school and making their way in the world, knowing what had happened to kids their age in Playland. I became active in every aspect of school life and discovered a talent in assisting with the production of school shows. I collaborated with the head of the music department, Tony Carlin, and introduced him to the music of Ennio Morricone. He loved one track so much, a hymn called *Glory, Glory, Glory*, which Morricone had written for a film called *A Genius, Two Friends, and an Idiot,* that he taught it to the choir at my childhood church, where he happened to be choirmaster. Little did the choir or congregation know that they were singing music from a spaghetti western!

* * * * *

I was married on Easter Monday, April 1979. I was 24 years old. My big day didn't go particularly well, as when I dressed in my formal wedding suit, put on my bow tie and looked in the mirror, Pretty Boy was looking back at me. In fact, it was four years almost to the day when Pretty Boy, wearing his tuxedo, had gone on the tear with the wild boys of the Dilly, on that crazy Easter Saturday night. Was I misrepresenting myself to my wife-to-be? I took the Holy Communion and drank down my marital vows with the blood of Christ. It tasted of fear and self-doubt. I literally worried myself sick during the day, thinking about my activities in London. On what should have been one of the happiest days of my life, I couldn't quite shake off the burden of my past.

I had clearly not completely forgiven myself for being a victim, but finally and thankfully, I learned the difference between love and sex. It wasn't about the joining together of bodies, but the joining also of minds and souls. Unlike when in London, where there had never been real intimacy or commitment, I was finally able to make love with my heart. Life rushed in and covered the past like a tide. London was now beneath the waves, the memories washed away. I had other things to occupy me. After the tragedy of losing our first baby during birth, Dympna and I went on to have four beautiful children. We both worked hard over the years. Like every family we had laughter and we had tears, some sadness but mainly happiness. We experienced the joy of rearing the children, seeing them through the school years and then developing careers and having children of their own.

* * * * *

Eventually, the time came that I faced up to and re-lived the horrors of my sojourn in London. An article that appeared in the *Sunday Mirror* of 13 July 2014 was the catalyst. The front-page headline read: "I Supplied Underage Rent Boys for Tory Ministers". Anthony Gilberthorpe, a Conservative political activist at the time, revealed that at the 1983 Blackpool conference he was asked to procure young rent boys for "entertainment". His account was met with much scepticism from some quarters, and of course I have no way of knowing if the claims were true, but some of those named in the article were people I had personally had experiences with in 1975.

I first approached the kind-hearted Bishop Daly, and then at his urging told my story to the police, addressing at last the full import of what had been done to me. I did it for the sake of other young exploited people, as well as myself.

Some weeks after my police interviews, I was rummaging around in the attic. While sifting through bags and boxes my eyes were caught by the gleaming brass handle of a solid green storage box. I knew it contained all my old diaries dating back to when I'd left school. I hunkered down, removed the lid and started leafing through bygone years. I pulled out a Filofax-type ring binder diary from 1999 that smelt stale and mouldy, and as I looked through the last days of the 20th century, I saw some paper wedged into a pocket on the inside back cover. It was a little book. The covers had been torn off and half of it seemed to be missing. At first glance it looked like an address book. The first pages were blank. I turned them over and fell back against a beam. It was the 1975 diary, the one written in London. I had completely forgotten about it. Somehow it had silently followed me through the years and had escaped all the house-move purges, when one dumps the remnants of a life, possessions once considered important or sentimental, but which time turns to trash. How was it here? How was this possible? I wondered if my children had found it during forages when they were younger and placed it here. I climbed out of the attic and sat down at my desk to revisit the past.

I read the diary and wept. It was a shocking testament. It recounted a rapid descent into a hell of sexual exploitation. There were names and sometimes just initials of politicians, civil servants, military, prominent businessmen and people from the theatre and television. The initials of other names were also recorded but after 40 years I could not remember who some of them were. The diary also included, written in red ink, simple little codes for sexual activities. It was in parts pornographic in detail, brutally honest in its outpourings, in the thoughts and feelings recorded about the encounters, the drink, the drugs, the guilt and the shame. It was full of stinging self-criticism and self-loathing.

For a few weeks Derry had been buzzing with news that the Californian sculptor David Best was constructing a 75-foot-high temple from laser-cut birch plywood on Bards Hill overlooking the city. It was a community event. Children helped to design the panels of the temple and unemployed carpenters helped build the structure. It created a shared space where people could come to stand and reflect, it was a place of contemplation and of letting go. In just one week an estimated 25,000 people visited the site.

Within the intricate lattice walls they left personal mementos: photographs, locks of hair and letters to lost loves; memorials honouring lost lives, whether victims of the Troubles, of sickness or of suicide. The city brought its pain and its past to the temple. Former Loyalist paramilitaries brushed shoulders with Republican hunger strikers. It was heartbreaking to read some of the tributes etched into the wood. Strangers talked to each other and shared their stories.

It was during a visit to the temple that I decided to destroy the diary. My counsellor had been telling me that I needed to do something dramatic to shake off the flashbacks I was having. I was replaying scenes of Pretty Boy being abused over and over again. She explained that I needed to release that 20 year old, who in my mind was still trapped in the past. I was going to rescue him and set him free. I knew the temple was due to be burned, in an act symbolising healing through a cleansing pillar of fire. I decided to set Pretty Boy free by putting the diary in the temple and burning him out of the past. It may have been irrational, but by God it was poetic. More importantly, it worked. The flashbacks stopped.

I knew the diary had little value as evidence. There was never going to be a dramatic moment with it was presented in court, partly because there was never going to be another major criminal trial involving Playland Firm members, the Bromley arcades syndicate, or the VIP clients who were part of Simon's network. Everyone involved, apart from one man, was dead. In any case, a good defence barrister could have claimed that it was merely the deranged outpourings of a drug-dependent rent boy, all a figment of my imagination. Or, alternatively, that I had willingly taken advantage of, and accepted money from, troubled and vulnerable older men. It could even have been doctored with additional text in the blank spaces.

In any case, I was aware that somewhere out there was photographic and pornographic evidence from my time in London. I had been captured on film a few times in group photographs at events I was taken to. There were photos of me standing beside Simon and his friends, or sitting at a table, all smiles. I have spent many hours online searching for these pictures, though without success.

I do have one photograph. A picture of me with one of my punters from the House of Lords, though it wasn't taken in London. A couple of months after I was married, I unexpectedly received a visit from Lord Back-Seat in Northern Ireland. For legal reasons I still cannot name him, nor the reason for his visit to Ulster, nor how we happened to meet. He insisted on having a "trophy" photograph taken with me, as a memento to show "our mutual friends back in London". I wondered if this too had been a kind of warning, whether the whole thing had been set up to remind me that they could re-enter my life with impunity at any time, smile and softly say, "You never said goodbye". I expected him to pass on a message from Simon, but none was forthcoming. Bizarrely, I wasn't sure how I felt about this, whether I was relieved or disappointed.

The appearance of this man was surreal. The war was raging. It was no small matter for a Peer of the Realm to visit Northern Ireland, entailing a major security operation. The incident deeply troubled me, even more so than the raid on my house by the military three years earlier. Why bother? Any concerns about me talking were ill-founded, as I knew perfectly well that British intelligence could denounce me to the IRA as a rogue agent. The Provos didn't need clear proof before putting a bullet into someone's head. Neither did the British army, of course. Alternatively, Special Branch could have me arrested on any number of trumped-up terrorism charges.

Thinking one evening about the photographic session with Richard and me, and also of the photos and 8mm film that had been taken, I did a search of adult gay porn sites. Following link after link, I came across a few specialist sites featuring "vintage" and "classic" porn. I found a series of very poor quality photos taken from old film, photos copied from the 8mm film of Andrew, Richard and Pretty Boy. It was truly shocking to find and to look at images of my 20-year-old alter-ego engaged in this activity. Each still seemed to have been taken from his own personal Zapruder film, and showed his slow assassination in London, frame by obscene frame. These images are in effect photographs of a crime scene. I copied and sent the pictures to the Met.

I returned to the Bards Hill temple on the night of 21 March 2015 and opened the diary to see what Pretty Boy had been doing on the same date in 1975. It recorded that he had met up with Simon Hornby that Friday at teatime in Notting Hill. I closed the diary and put it in an envelope and wedged it behind a lattice frame.

Then the torchbearers came. They surrounded the temple and set it on fire. Thousands watched as the flames consumed the irreplaceable items that had been brought to the temple. I thought about Playland and the Dilly and I thought about Damie and the other lost boys. The Phoenix burned. All those troubled memories, all that pain was then transformed by fire into hope.

I felt the presence of Pretty Boy. He was standing beside me. I realised that in London he had never cried: he did what he had to do and he got on with it. He never complained. It was I who did the crying afterwards in Hope House. I now gave him permission to be human. I gave him permission to cry and accept love. I accepted him. Tears of joy ran down my cheeks. I had set him free, and so I had set us both free.

CHAPTER 34

Rent

During the Playland trial, prosecution counsel Mr Michael Corkery described five of the defendants as "homosexual touts" who supplied boys to Hornby and "other wealthy clients". In both the Gleaves and Playland trials the term 'homosexual' was used incorrectly to describe the defendants and the range of offences committed. The term was also used widely in the press. There was no distinction between being gay and being a paedophile. Lord Hailsham had published an essay denouncing homosexual practices as "contagious, incurable, and self-perpetuating." He likened same-sex attraction to heroin addiction and considered all homosexuals to be pederasts. The public perception, therefore, of the homosexual was of a sad lonely figure preying on vulnerable boys who, once seduced and corrupted, would also be 'infected' with homosexuality and doomed to wander the streets in search of young blood. A national opinion poll commissioned in 1975 by *Gay News* found that almost half of the population felt homosexuals should not be allowed to be doctors or teachers.

The word paedophile was not in common use and didn't enter the Shorter Oxford English Dictionary until 1976.[79] Ironically, we have PIE to thank for publicising paedophilia as

---

79   Philips, Richard et all, *De-Centering Sexualities: Politics and Representations Beyond the Metropolis.* (London and New York: Routledge 2000).

distinct from homosexuality. In 1975 Roger Gleaves was being referred to as a homosexual, but when he was later jailed for reoffending against boys in 1998 he'd become a "sex abuser" and "paedophile".

While homosexuality was still commonly reviled in the 1970s, another narrative that had gained some currency was that sex with children was not particularly harmful and not really a serious offence in the eyes of the law. This partly explains why PIE decided in 1975 to publicly launch and promote their agenda and why they were so successful in lobbying Government and in forming associations with other organisations, such as the NCCL and the Gay Liberation movement.

Judge King-Hamilton, in his summing up of the Playland trial, and after weeks listening to nauseating evidence of sex parties, sexual abuse and exploitation, was rather bizarrely of the view that none of the boys had been corrupted and that violence had not been employed. He had obviously not considered the *threat* of violence. Had I been a witness at the Playland trial I could have offered an alternative view on the use of violence.

The Board members of the Albany Trust, a psychosexual health charity, wrote to the *Guardian* complaining about the hefty sentences handed down to the Playland defendants. They felt that "the most pathetic aspect of the recent 'vice trial' was its revelation of the double life and self-deception which society still forces on the bisexual man and the sexually active adolescent".

In another trial that ended in June 1975, a child psychiatrist walked free when the jury accepted that he had touched a seven-year-old girl's "private parts" as he was "only trying to teach her not to be ashamed of her body". That same month an appeal was allowed on behalf of a convicted offender because "the girl was not without sexual experience and the intimidation had been mild". And, meanwhile, in the House of Lords, it was ruled that a man could be cleared of rape if he "honestly" thought the woman had consented.[80]

In the same week the Playland trial ended, the case of a 14-year-old girl who'd been sexually assaulted by five soldiers in the barracks of the Royal Irish Rangers in Wiltshire concluded. The girl's father said the experience had scarred her for life and that she'd tried to commit suicide. Judge Nathaniel Blaker, however, fined the men and released them. "I'm satisfied you are all good soldiers," he said. "I don't think it will do any good to deprive your country of your services. Go now and serve your country well."

The military continued to be implicated in scandal. The September 1975 issue of the gay magazine *HIM* carried a 'Sex and Violence' feature showing photographs of guardsmen from the elite Household Division in various poses – fighting, wrestling and undergoing punishment. Another page carried an advertisement offering pictures of soldiers for sale by post. The following month the *Daily Mirror* claimed there was a homosexual vice ring in the Household Calvary involving up to a hundred soldiers. Questions concerning national security were asked in the House and a full investigation carried out. Subsequently, 18 guardsmen were discharged from the army and an officer was asked to resign his commission. Seventeen others, all from the same regiment, were hauled before their commanding officer and given a stern warning that they could have been taken advantage of by the IRA!

Richard, the young Grenadier Guard I had been with on two occasions, was not the only soldier stationed in Derry who had been sexually abused and exploited during the Troubles. In 1987, a young soldier from Lowestoft, who was a raw recruit in

---

80   *From Anger to Apathy: The British Experience since 1975;* Mark Garnett.

the Royal Anglia Regiment and stationed in Derry, wrote to his father and told him he was being subjected to appalling bullying and sexual abuse. He said that it had got to the stage where he was more frightened about what might happen to him at night in the barracks than when he was out on patrol and facing the IRA. The Special Investigation Branch of the Military Police was called in to investigate. This was the second such complaint in Derry involving the same regiment. Despite rumours that many soldiers were being sexually exploited, the Ministry of Defence kept the findings of its report secret. Back in Colchester, it all became too much for the young soldier and he staged a siege with army weapons in the middle of town, firing shots down streets and narrowly missing a policeman. He was subsequently sentenced to five years in youth custody. His father went public about his son's abuse. One newspaper compared the abuse the soldier had suffered to that inflicted on the inmates of Kincora Boys' Home. The father was then warned to keep quiet because his campaign was "playing into the hands of the IRA".

He said his son had been a perfectly normal young man until he had been sent to Derry.

* * * * *

All the Playland publicity didn't discourage boys from pursuing a career in rent. In fact, after the *Johnny Go Home* programme was aired and the Playland trial ended, even more runaways made their way to London to make what they naively thought was easy money. One 16-year-old whose mother was taking all his earnings from a Saturday job, left home because he'd been "inspired" by the *Johnny* documentary. In 1974, 934 boys and over 300 girls between the ages of 14 and 17 were reported missing. Worse still, 350 boys and 264 girls *under* 14 were also missing. Police said most of them headed for London. One of the very few shelters that kept statistics recorded that in 1975 they'd accommodated 7,700 youngsters for a night or two. Of these, over 1,000 came from Scotland and 750 from Ireland, with others from the Midlands, the North West and the North East.

By May 1976 the *Evening Standard* was reporting that an estimated 400 teenagers from the suburbs and provinces had been reported missing and were suspected of being integrated into the West End vice rings. That same year the police believed there were now 25,000 children under the age of 17 living rough in London.[81]

The law of supply and demand ensured that business continued as usual. In fact, it began to experience a second boom, as the ages of the rent boys dropped even lower. By the 1980s most of the boys in the Dilly were under 14 and some were as young as 10. Because of this fresh youthful demographic, the meat rack was re-christened the chicken rack.

But the 80s brought AIDS to the streets in the shadow of Eros. It was estimated that up to a third of all rent boys had been infected with HIV. Those who survived the angel of death were driven off the Dilly with the proliferation of CCTV monitoring and relentless policing of the plaza in the 1990s. Rent moved off the street and went online. The Piccadilly rent boy became extinct, replaced by online escorts and gay-dating websites.

* * * * *

---

81   In April 2015 the *Evening Standard* reported that in London, a city of billionaires and millionaires, 72,000 children were homeless (one in 25 children). Having no permanent residence many were living in cramped conditions in emergency hostels and B&Bs, sharing beds with siblings and parents. Many were threatened with violence and regularly witnessed drug use. Eighty per cent of all homeless children in England live in London.

To the authorities, the rent boy was either a criminally delinquent mercenary who had to be punished and reformed, or a hapless runaway who had to be returned home or put into care. Public perception was similarly unsympathetic: the boys didn't have to run away, and there were surely easier ways to make money. As for the punters, some were seen as being degenerate middle-aged men, but many were viewed sympathetically, as ordinary people having marriage problems, or perhaps sexual, drink or work problems – or just moments of madness – and succumbing to temptation during a personal crisis.

Of course, many rent boys were homeless, vulnerable and being ruthlessly exploited – for them it was survival sex. Some of the older teenage boys I came into contact with in Playland had been in care homes when they were much younger. They had suffered years of sexual abuse and had been trafficked to London and forced into prostitution, then abandoned when they were too old for the tastes of certain particular clients. Some VIP punters considered themselves to be occupying the moral high ground by claiming that they only had sex with willing boys over the age of 16 (heaven forbid anyone should think them paedophiles), but they never questioned how it came to be that boys were selling themselves in the first place. It never occurred to them that many of these young men had been sexually abused as young children.

But rent could be out-of-work actors, students, confused teenagers questioning their sexuality or some who choose it as a profession. The bendy straights, some of whom were stereotypical delinquent youths, turned to prostitution as one of a number of illegal activities: a change from housebreaking, shoplifting or mugging.

For Damie it was ultimately about finding Mr Right. Mr Rich Film Star Right. The Dilly scene was a contrived fantasy world based on the sale of sexual pleasure. Youth sold it and age bought it. But the Dilly rent scene was also a brutal, sleazy, dangerous place. Only a very brave millionaire, politician, peer or celebrity would personally want to visit that marketplace (unless you were reckless like Jeremy Thorpe, who did pick up his rent in person). Hence the appearance of the middlemen who could take the bookings and deliver the goods; the pimps, the party planners and the pornographers; the specialists who could cater for expensive tastes, or forbidden pleasures. People you could go to if you wanted a sophisticated young man to accompany you to dinner and entertain you afterwards, or procure a 'fresh bunny', or 'candy floss' if you preferred pre-teen pleasures. Playland was an agency, a business. Homeless or not and regardless of age, it was about sex, not sympathy. With the possible exception of the Playland informer who went to Peter Earle, no one in the Playland Firm felt pity for the plight of the boys. As one of Bernie Silver's hitmen, Victor Spampinato, once said, "You don't build crime on tears."

* * * * *

The past reaches into the present.

In November 2015 I was sitting in a London cab, stuck in a traffic jam. I was late for a meeting and got chatting to the taxi driver. We talked about London, the past, the Dilly. I was taken aback when he asked if I'd been a runaway. I saw his eyes in the mirror, studying me.

"No," I said abruptly, feeling strangely offended. For me, the term runaway meant a troubled, desperate penniless teenager. I had been a sensible young man with a job, plans and prospects. But then I realised I *had* been running away from the Troubles. I had been a runaway.

His second question shocked me. He asked me if I had known Roger Gleaves.

"I never met him," I replied.

He went on to tell me his father used to run a pub, the St James Tavern on the corner of Great Windmill Street where it intersects with Shaftesbury Avenue and a stone's throw from Playland. He was 12 years old at the time and he used to help out in the pub. His father warned him that if he ever set foot in Playland he'd kill him. Roger Gleaves was a regular drinker in the pub. He'd come in and eye up the young men. One afternoon his father caught Roger chatting to his son in the gents' toilets. He dragged Roger to the bar, poured a bucket of ice cubes over his head and kicked him out into the street.

* * * * *

All those years ago I was caught and trapped into this world of pimps, perverts, rent boys and VIPs. I had found my way to the Circus and ended up as a star attraction on the merry-go-round of high society parties, drink, drugs and sexual exploitation, before finally being flung off, a sick, broken, troubled and confused young man. Shame and guilt are heavy burdens to carry, but at last I have set them down.

CHAPTER 35

Requiem: The Name
of the Rose

On a quiet Tuesday morning on 4 February 1992, parking wardens noticed a car parked in London's Chelsea Bridge Road, near Chelsea barracks, which was a high security zone. They asked the young man sitting behind the wheel to move on. His behaviour was so strange that the police were called. PC Alan Young from West End Central police station approached the car to deal with the trivial parking matter. The driver flew into a rage and jumped from the car. He levelled a hand gun at the terrified officer and pulled the trigger three times. The gun jammed and another officer, PC Ian Crawford wrestled with the gunman and disarmed him. The man was arrested and found to be in possession of LSD.

In November the "deranged" gunman appeared in court. He had been well groomed for the occasion and wore a fine single-breasted grey suit. The 23-year-old Jonathan Hornby, son of Charles Hornby, pleaded guilty to possession of LSD. The prosecution accepted his pleas of not guilty of possessing a gun and not guilty of technically assaulting PC Young with intent to resist arrest, on the basis that criminal intent could not be proved as Jonathon had been 'psychotic'. Consultant psychiatrist Dr John Cobb said that Jonathan had been "acutely disturbed" in 1989 and had suffered manic depression.

Mr Montague Sherborne, defending, said, "Jonathan is young man of unblemished character and comes from an excellent background. He realises there is a link between drugs and the psychotic condition from which he suffers and now knows he must not dabble any further with them". He offered his client's "sincere apologies and regret" for the terror caused to the police officers. PC Young had been on sick leave suffering from recurring nightmares since the incident.

Jonathan's uncle Sir Simon Hornby took the stand. He explained that his nephew was an Oxford graduate who was now working in one of his London bookshops. He presented a glowing testament in support of the "hardworking, diligent and gentle young man". Jonathan was placed on two years' probation on condition that he continued psychiatric treatment. The Hornbys left court with sombre dignity. Jonathan joined his uncle, Sir Simon, in the back of a chauffeur-driven Rolls-Royce, which drove off slowly and quietly, taking the Hornbys out of the limelight.

* * * * *

The Hornby family had been in partnership with WH Smith since 1892. Simon Hornby, like his father and grandfather before him, rose to the top of WH Smith. He became chairman in 1982. Over his 12-year tenure he transformed the business, increasing the group's profits year on year. Smith's became a more recognisable brand on the high street, building up a huge share of the newspaper and magazine market. They also had a 40 per cent share of the stationery market and at one point 30 per cent of all books bought in the UK were purchased in a WH Smith shop. Simon once told me the secret of good gardening and good business was diversity. In a WH Smith context he was referring to the diversity of the book stock, and he envied Foyles for its unsurpassed range of subjects and titles. He also told me that the branches of WH Smith stores were like little lifeboats in comparison to the titanic Foyles. But he believed that in time Foyles would sink beneath the waves, especially with Christina at the helm, and his little boats would make it to the shores and not only survive the dark days of the 1970s but grow and flourish in fertile soil ploughed and sowed by a Conservative government.[82]

As a keen collector of fine art, Simon used his authority as chairman of WH Smith to get the company to invest in some contemporary art. He bought a number of paintings and commissioned the sculptor Elisabeth Frink to create three life-size male nude bronzes, which were positioned around the retail division headquarters in Swindon.

On the afternoon when I sat on the drawing-room floor in Ennismore Gardens playing Simon's record collection, he said he'd always entertained the notion of opening a little record shop one day. Just over 10 years later he bought Our Price, making WH Smith the largest record retailer in the UK. WH Smith also bought Paperchase and even expanded into the DIY sector, establishing the Do It All chain with Boots. His aggressive business intention was to become market leader in every area they operated in.

Simon then decided he wanted to conquer the United States and despatched a young manager called Tim Waterstone across the Atlantic. The project was not a success and Simon sacked Waterstone, who used his £6,000 redundancy payout to open his own bookshop in the Old Brompton Road. That

---

82 I read a footnote in a book that stated that on two occasions Simon had stood as a Parliamentary candidate for the Conservative Party. This surprised me because when we talked about our dreams and aspirations, Simon had never expressed a wish to enter politics. Perhaps this was one piece of cake the network could not give him.

business succeeded in areas where WH Smith could not. They stocked a diverse range of quality books, put good literary authors in front-of-shop displays and employed well-read staff. Waterstones became a "different breed of bookshop" and expanded into a chain of successful stores. The year before Simon retired, after having built up a stake in Waterstones, he bought the company outright for £9 million. He finally owned the kind of bookshops he had always wanted. He expanded Waterstones from 19 to 120 stores.

Simon was a truly outstanding businessman, and over the years he landed an impressive number of directorships, including Lazards, Pearson and Lloyds bank. He also sat on the Boards of the National Trust, the British Museum, the V&A and many others. He became chairman of the Design Council in 1986, founded the National Literacy Trust in 1993 and the year he "retired" became president of the Royal Horticultural Society. The Renaissance man was much in demand. In 1988 he had received a knighthood, along with two MPs, Cyril Smith and Nicholas Fairbairn. That would have been the ultimate icing on Simon's cake.

* * * * *

In 1992, Simon bought an 18th century property called the Ham, set in 46 acres of land near Wantage, Oxfordshire, and started work on creating another outstanding garden. Four years later he was awarded an honorary LLD, a Doctor of Laws degree, by the University of Reading. I think he would have preferred a doctor of letters or literature, nonetheless the award was well deserved. But age was catching up with Dr Hornby, and if there was one thing Simon hated it was grey hair. He started dyeing his hair a luxuriant shade of auburn. His choice of clothing, checks and floral patterns became a tad more extravagant. Slowly but surely he became less concerned with the traditions and conventions that constrain "the older man". He became bolder, more daring. He started to channel his literary hero Oscar Wilde. Finally, he could be himself.

Simon's health declined and he developed Parkinson's disease. His eyesight slowly deteriorated and it became difficult for him to read. Simon once told me that he could read me like a book. The thought of him having difficulty reading the words on a page saddens me greatly. It must also have been distressing for him to see the colourful floral beauty of his garden, his years of planting, dissolve to a blur. At least he could still listen to his beloved Mozart. Sheran faithfully looked after him during his ill health.

I believe Simon came to terms with his sexuality and reached out in solidarity to acknowledge and support the gay community. In 2009 he joined the likes of Simon Callow, Julian Clary, Stephen Fry and Sir Elton John by becoming a patron of the Terrence Higgins Trust.

* * * * *

Every year around Christmas I couldn't help but pause for a moment and think about Simon. My wife's birthday was on the 28 December and his was the following day. At other times he appeared in my life in the most unexpected ways. He'd jump from a newspaper in the company of her Majesty the Queen at the Chelsea Flower Show, or he'd get a mention on radio in a business report. One night in late January 1989 I was in the kitchen when I heard the distinctive voice of Sir Robin Day coming from the TV in the living room. Then I heard another voice that I recognised instantly. Simon was a panel member on *Question Time*, and in his authoritative tones was offering comment on the issues of the day.

Every time I saw his face, or heard his voice, I thought again about what had happened to me in 1975. There were many unanswered questions. Why did Charles Hornby take me to Simon's home and "break me in" on Simon's bed? What was the significance of this location? Some twisted ritual before passing me to Simon? Did Simon know his brother had assaulted me? Did Simon get his friend and neighbour Richard Stewart to intercede on my behalf somehow with the Playland Firm and have me released from their clutches, perhaps even by asking Martin Bromley, the Wolfman himself, to use his influence? Was Pat Gibson really meant to be my last client? Had my abuse by Gordon Richardson in the Ritz been planned in advance and did Simon know that was going to happen? Was I really out of his endless game or would other encounters have been inevitable? How did the Playland trial and the imprisonment of his brother affect Simon? I wondered what Simon had really felt for me and what he truly wanted from me. What did he do once he realised I would not be returning to London? I needed answers to so many questions.

In 2010, Cardinal Sean Brady had admitted that he'd known about a cover-up concerning the sexual abuse of teenage boys in 1975. The Catholic Church was beginning to look like an ecclesiastical Playland of sorts. This was when I first decided I would try to get some answers for myself. Thirty-five years had now passed and 2010 – with its exoneration of the Bloody Sunday victims, too – was proving to be a good year for the truth.

On the 15th July I wrote a long hand-written letter to Simon in which I talked about our time together in 1975. I didn't wish to threaten or intimidate him in any way, so I started off by reminiscing about the wonderful conversations we used to have about literature, book-selling, art, music and history, though I did also admit that his passion for cooking and gardening bored me to tears. Keith Hunter had wanted to drag me down into a world of crime, violence and perversion, so I told Simon I didn't think of him so much as the man who had passed me around his friends, but as the man who saved me from the Playland Firm. I thanked him for letting me go, for setting me free, allowing me to return home. I even told him that in spite of being used to entertain his friends and associates in the network, I still thought of him with affection. I asked him if he wanted to meet. I never received a reply.

Two days after I sent the letter, Sir Simon Hornby was found dead in the grounds of his home. His beautiful gardens would have looked stunning at that time of year. The long summer evenings would have been mild and bright. It was said he had accidently drowned, and this was the verdict of a subsequent inquest. He was 76 years old.[83]

A memorial service was held in St Paul's Church, Knightsbridge, that October. Prince Edward the Duke of Kent and Princess Alexandra sent representatives. The Duke and Duchess of Abercorn and the Earl and Countess of Dudley were among the many noble mourners. Charles Hornby's widow Amanda and her sons Nicholas and Jonathan attended. The lessons were read by Sir Malcolm Field, a former Chief Executive of WH Smith, and Jonathan Hornby. The address was given by Mr Anthony Loehnis, who was two years younger than Simon and had followed in his footsteps from Eton to New College, Oxford. Loehnis had been a Foreign Office official and then a Director at Schroders, where in the late 1960s he was Gordon Richardson's personal assistant. When Richardson was appointed Governor of the Bank of England in 1973, he seconded Loehnis as his adviser.

---

83   Simon's personal wealth at death was in excess of £8.1 million. His home was worth an additional £6 million.

Also present in the congregation was Mary Cameron, still grieving the loss of her own husband, who had died the previous month. Mary's son, David, had become Prime Minister in May that year.[84]

The organ piped up and the choir of St Paul's sang beautifully, then a rather irreligious note was introduced as Simon's old musical favourites were hammered out on the piano: Cole Porter, Irving Berlin and George Gershwin. Simon would have loved it. So would I, had anyone thought to invite me.

* * * * *

A couple of weeks after I had visited Simon at his home in Oxfordshire, we were having early evening drinks in Mark's Club in Charles Street, Mayfair. He had been meeting a very good friend and business associate, who for legal reasons I am unable to name. I had been delivered at the appointed hour and was relieved to learn that Simon's friend was just a friend and not a client for me.

"You're all mine tonight, Pretty Boy," Simon said seductively.

After some chat about book business and gossip about boy business, Simon settled back in his chair. He looked a little puzzled, lost in contemplation, the way he did when he was trying to remember a quotation from a book or a line from a song; then his eyes widened and sparkled as if with some internal illumination.

"The rugosa Belle Poitevine," he announced with delight.

"I beg your pardon?" I had become much more cultured. In Derry I would have simply said, "What?" Either way, I was mystified.

---

84 Anthony Loehnis's son, Dominic, is one of David Cameron's closest friends. Cameron was best man at his wedding. On the weekend before Simon's memorial service, Dom was invited to Cameron's 44th birthday party at Chequers where, as he would later testify in the Old Bailey, Rebekah Brooks explained to him how a mobile phone could be hacked.

"You once asked me what my favourite flower was. The rugosa Belle Poitevine is undoubtedly my favourite," he proclaimed. "It produces large semi-double medium pink blossoms."

His flower choice did not entirely surprise me. A big pink blossom. That just about summed up Simon.

Maybe someday I'll place one on his grave.

Epilogue

I had assumed that after 40 years, telling the story of Playland would not present problems. I was wrong. In June 2015 my house was broken in to. I have lived in a tiny rural estate for 22 years and the area has been virtually crime free. The intruders were clearly well prepared and took advantage of a 30-minute window of opportunity when my wife left my daughter at work.

The intruders were not deterred by a 35kg Siberian Husky whose bed is in the kitchen. They removed the window in the utility room and tackled the dog, who was later found in the back garden with his dog collar broken. My study was wrecked. Desk drawers emptied onto the floor and papers strewn everywhere. Not only was a filing cabinet forced open and emptied, but a small home safe was ripped from a wall and completely removed from the premises. The safe contained highly-confidential documents and emails I had gathered during my research: information about Sir Michael Havers and others, as well as passports, insurance policies and jewellery. Strangely enough my desktop computer, a laptop, Kindle, and a mobile phone were seemingly untouched and left. The burglary appeared to have been executed with military precision.

The PSNI investigated the break-in but the crime remains unsolved.

Towards the end of February 2016 I was receiving some very disturbing news from contacts I had made in London. I was so concerned by what I was being told that I emailed my solicitor on 2 March and told him about the warnings I was getting:"Put another way I have been warned that they will do whatever they can do to destroy me, attack those close to me and ruin my reputation."

Five days after I sent that email, on 7 March 2016, a warrant to enter and search my home was signed. There does not appear to have been much urgency as the PSNI did not execute the warrant until over 10 weeks later on 17 May 2016.

The officer in charge said that they had received "intelligence" that linked my address to indecent images of children. When I asked him where the "intelligence" came from, he said that he could not compromise his intelligence sources.

This second intrusion into my home lasted a more leisurely three hours. Interestingly, everything of value the first intruders left – the computer, laptop, kindle, phones were removed on this occasion. They also took a couple of hundred Ennio Morricone film soundtracks I had recorded onto CDs. I didn't know whether to feel pleased that the PSNI had such good taste in music, or to feel angry that the collection was specifically targeted because they knew how much it meant to me.

I was arrested when the search concluded and taken to Strand Road police station where I was kept in a cell for some 12 hours. During a brief interview, in answer to a question, I told a Detective Constable and his colleague, that not only had I been shown child pornography in 1975, I also disclosed that I had actually seen children being abused. Neither officer batted an eyelid. One would have thought in the circumstances this would have prompted a line of enquiry – who were these children, where did this happen, who was abusing them, were you involved in the abuse... not a word. They returned to their script and continued the predetermined line of questioning. It seemed that the "intelligence" about the alleged indecent images was more important than the information I had about the actual sexual abuse of children. I asked one question during the interview: "where did the 'intelligence' originate from?" Again, I was told that for operational reasons they could not disclose the source of the intelligence. I was finally released on police bail around 1.00am.

The following day I noticed that *The Romance of a Bookshop*, the inscribed book given to me by Simon Hornby was missing, along with some old family photographs. Furthermore, the only photographs I took of the book, together with an early draft of the manuscript and much research material was on the computer. I therefore complained to the Police Ombudsman for Northern Ireland.

In spite of initial denials by the police that they had taken neither the book nor the photos, a PONI officer found the unlogged photographs in an evidence bag. There was no sign of the book. A subsequent PONI report recommended misconduct sanctions against an officer involved in the search.

I remained on police bail for a year and was interviewed again in May 2017. I was informed that a forensic investigation revealed that 11 indecent images of children were found on my computer, but they were unable to say when and how the pictures came to be there. I was then released without charge, but I was advised that because of the images found on the computer, the machine would be destroyed. This would mean that the only piece of photographic evidence linking me to Simon Hornby would, unfortunately, also be destroyed

The story of Playland continues…

Acknowledgements

Earnest Hemmingway once said there is nothing to writing; all you do is just sit down at a typewriter and bleed. Well, I bled a lot during the writing of this book, but I was sustained by transfusions of love and understanding, help and support and the encouragement of many people.

I want to thank Matthew Baker for his early encouragement and input and for opening doors that might otherwise have remained closed. Thanks also to Paul Gosling, Garbhan Downey, Julieann Campbell, Adrian Kerr, James J. Fox, Slawomir Kosmider, David Barlow, Gary Dunne, Mehta Ajay, Nickolas Urquhart, Jeremy Reed, David James Smith, Dame Judi Dench and Paul Frift.

I am grateful to the many organisations that assisted me, but in particular, the Metropolitan Police Service, the National Archives, the London Irish Centre, the Whittington Hospital NHS Trust, HM Revenue and Customs, and the Museum of Free Derry.

Sincere thanks to Liam Milligan who supported me through some difficult times and to Joan Doherty MBE for her practical assistance. To the officers of the Met who interviewed me over many hours: your courtesy, utter professionalism and support gave me the courage to tell my story and to confront, for the first time, ghosts from the past.

Very special thanks to John Stergides, veteran of the high street gaming business in London and to Freddy Bailey in New York, one of the 'Wolfman's' oldest and dearest friends; for sharing his memories, his insights, his contacts and documents from his private archive. When word got around London that I was writing about Playland, I was contacted by a few gentlemen who were active in the Soho underworld of the 1970s. They were keen to ensure the books authenticity and their own anonymity. I trust I have succeeded in both these objectives and I want to thank them for their cooperation. Thanks also to an ex member of the military, who for obvious reasons, also wishes to remain anonymous.

Nexus NI offer counselling and support to survivors of sexual abuse and victims of sexual violence including rape. I want to thank them for giving me the space over many counselling sessions, to collect my thoughts, to talk about my feelings and for helping me come to terms with what had happened; to learn how to deal with it and then, through writing, to rescue a troubled 20 year old who had been imprisoned in the past.

I am indebted to Desmond J. Doherty, Michael Mansfield QC, and those Members of the House of Commons and the House of Lords who gave so freely of their time.

The team at Mirror Books have been a joy and an inspiration to work with. Executive Editor Jo Sollis diligently navigated the book through protracted legal and editorial processes and together with Paula Scott Group Publishing Director, championed the book from the beginning and saw it through to publication.

The encouragement I have received from my brothers and my sister has been incredible, I can't thank them enough for giving me the strength to face the many difficulties I have encountered since I decided to tell my story. I am overwhelmed by the support I have received from my children. They have acknowledged and accepted my troubled past and they carry this painful knowledge with a dignity that humbles me. Every day I grow more proud of them. I have survived to see the smiles of grandchildren and I am blessed.

Finally to Dympna: for support beyond measure, understanding beyond words and love beyond belief.